D1388963

THE
BUYER'S MANUAL

THE
MERCHANDISING
HANDBOOK
FOR
ALL RETAILERS

Published by
THE
MERCHANDISING
DIVISION

NATIONAL RETAIL MERCHANTS ASSOCIATION
100 W. 31st Street, New York, N. Y. 10001

Dedicated
to the late

J. GORDON DAKINS
friend of retailing
everywhere in the world

A FEW WORDS OF INTRODUCTION

Retailing, including department store retailing, has made substantial progress in the past. The immediate future will present very real problems, but it will also offer great opportunities for development. The task of the coming generation of retail leadership (to whom this book is addressed) will be to convert these opportunities into realities.

It has been clear for some time that the emphasis within our economy must be on increased consumption. Our productive mechanism is constantly increasing its capacity through enlarged facilities and increased automation. At the same time, the ever-growing increase of our population and the resultant increase in the number of new households formed seem likely to expand our already huge domestic markets. This dramatic combination of a mounting, high level of productive effort, along with a dynamic demand for more goods by more people, will present a challenge to retailers to develop larger and larger volume of sales to absorb the products that will come tumbling from industry's assembly lines.

However, it is also clear that competition for the consumers' income has become increasingly intense. Food presently demands one-fourth of the American family's budget. The promise is that this will continue. Automobile ownership continues to increase its appeal to American families. And the demand for travel and other services is absorbing a steadily growing portion of consumer income. Retailing must compete aggressively with these appeals to consumers if it is to hold its proper place in the economy.

Moreover, within retailing itself, great changes are visible and will continue to develop, bringing with them increased competition for the department store. Discount houses are not new; only their extent and multiple locations represent new characeristics. The same is true of other agencies of retail distribution—shopping centers, highway stores, factory outlets, and low priced pipe rack stores. The variety chains are becoming junior department stores. The mail order companies continue to broaden their appeal. Stores, including department stores, that formerly sold merchandise only, augment their sales and customer traffic by offering ever more services for the consumer to buy.

In the department store field itself, there is the development of branch stores, which present new problems and increase the capital requirements of the organization. Therefore, more dollars of sales and profit are required to justify the increased investment.

The opportunity and the problems that already reveal themselves make it clear that tomorrow's retail leadership must improve its operation. There will be an increasing need for more skillful merchandising and a far greater use of the computer for accelerating the speed with which the public's preferences are judged and met. There will be a continuing need for better balance of assortments, for in-stock-keeping, for better selling, for better advertising and display, and for better product packaging, along with other means of improving retailing's sales appeal.

If tomorrow's merchants can meet this challenge, the result will be increased sales, reduced markdowns, and the larger re-

A FEW WORDS OF INTRODUCTION

tained profits that are the objective of every retail enterprise.

The department store, through its selling and its service, through its understanding of the consumer and its standing in the community, has an opportunity to create and satisfy the tremendous potential demand for the products of our factories. For those who grasp the opportunity fully, the rewards will be both substantial and gratifying.

PAUL M. MAZUR

Mr. Mazur is a banker and an economist. He is a partner of Lehman Brothers, a firm that has served as investment bankers for many of the important department store corporations of the country. Mr. Mazur is a director of Federated Department Stores.

Mr. Mazur has emphasized in his books and articles his fundamental belief in the overwhelming importance of consumption in the American economy. In 1927, at the request of the NRMA, he wrote "Principles of Organization as Applied to Modern Retailing."

A WORD ABOUT THIS EDITION

It seems only yesterday that we brought out the 1957 revision. Here it is eight years later, renewed, re-made, ever-fresh and, I trust, even more helpful. While the fundamentals of retailing remain essentially unchanged, so fast are other developments in our craft that no book professing to describe the art of merchandising can afford to get that old without risking obsolescence.

This book is written for the new buyer, for the ambitious assistant buyer, and for all would-be merchants now in the junior executive ranks. It has been warming to see how many stores have been using THE BUYER'S MANUAL in the training of their junior executives; also, how many schools and colleges have it as text or supplementary reading for their students.

The roster of authors still includes a number of familiar names, I'm happy to say, and many new ones. All have been most cooperative, each giving, as the late A. Lincoln Filene wrote of this book, "some part of himself, some hard-won understanding of his own job, to help smooth the path for those who will follow him." Every chapter has been updated and new ones added.

When the 1957 edition was being written, the growth of the discount houses and the establishment of branch stores were the latest developments. Today, the vast effect of electronic data processing and the intensified use of classification

A WORD ABOUT THIS EDITION

merchandising pervade our thinking. In retailing there always *is* something new under the sun.

I wish here to thank the present contributors for their always willing cooperation. Also, I'm ever in debt to Miss Beatrice Judelle for her quiet wisdom and professional assistance.

I see THE BUYER'S MANUAL as a torch of light in our industry. I've been honored to have it from the hand of my predecessor. I'm happy to hold it high until one day I can hand it on, still burning, still illuminating, to my successor.

WILLIAM BURSTON
Manager
Merchandising Division
NRMA

TABLE OF CONTENTS

A Few Words of Introduction
By Paul M. Mazur, Partner, Lehman Brothers, New York, N. Y.

A Word About This Edition
By William Burston, Manager, Merchandising Division, National Retail Merchants Association

TABLE OF CONTENTS

TABLE OF CONTENTS

TABLE OF CONTENTS

LIST OF EXHIBITS AND FORMS

CHAPTER 1

THE ORGANIZATION OF DISTRIBUTION

BY

MARTIN B. KOHN

Distribution is the process whereby an idea, a natural product, a manufactured article, or a combination of any of these things, is brought into the hands of its ultimate user. We all know the old story about the mighty tree that crashes to earth in an uninhabited forest. It makes no sound if there is no one around to hear.

By the same token, the value of a product is in its use. A book is not a book until it is read. A pair of shoes is not a pair of shoes until it is on the feet of the person who will wear them. And how does the pair of shoes find its way from the factory to the ultimate user? Through the process of distribution.

Retailing's Obligation. In the days of hand industry, distribution was direct from the maker to the consumer, without the assistance of the merchant. Today, retailing is the final step in a complicated process of bringing to the consumer the merchandise he wants, in the form in which he wants it, and at the time and place at which he wants it. The retailer's obligation (or function) is to search the markets of this country and the world, to select and buy salable merchandise, and to assemble and present this merchandise in a location convenient to the customer and in a manner which makes the customer want to buy it.

In any ordinary community, many widely varied types of retail stores flourish side by side, each catering to a different type of customer, or to different needs of the same customer. Each has its own niche to fill in the scheme of distribution, but all have the common problem and the common purpose of studying the customer's wants and striving to assemble and present the goods that will satisfy those wants at prices the customer will pay.

The Department Store. The modern system of distribution calls for many kinds of retail stores, according to the merchandise in which they specialize, or according to the customers they serve. Very briefly, we shall examine these various types of stores and show how they dovetail with—and compete with —the department store, which is a dominant factor in distribution, and the major object of our study.

We shall start with a basic definition. A department store is a store which seeks to provide for customers of all ages and both sexes everything they need or want in the way of wearing apparel and home furnishings, as well as many other things they want or need to make living pleasanter, healthier, easier and more interesting.

Within the framework of an overall store policy, this vast and varied collection of merchandise is offered for sale in separate departments, each of which is administered by a buyer or department manager, who is a specialist in his field. Originally, the department store was a single unit, a downtown, center-of-the-city store with all its activity emanating from one central location. Today, however, most department stores consist of a downtown store and suburban satellites located in the prime shopping areas of its metropolitan community.

In addition to its merchandise, the department store offers many services, some of which are tangible and specific and others, while equally important, are more general and harder to define. Specifically, it provides for its customers the personal service of its trained sales force; the delivery of merchandise; the privileges of credit and of returns; the opportunity to shop in person, by telephone or by mail.

In more general terms, the department store, through its advertising and displays, educates and informs its customers as to fashion trends and prevailing prices. Designed as it is to attract, accommodate and serve, it provides customers with diversion, excitement and the all-important satisfaction of being wanted.

In addition, most department stores accept important communal responsibilities and are identified with most of the progressive and philanthropic endeavors in the communities which they serve.

These, then, are the general characteristics. But every department store has its own personality, its own unique relationship with its public. On the basis of that personality, department stores compete with each other for the customer's patronage. But they also compete with many other kinds of stores.

The Exclusive Specialty Shop. Prominent among these is the specialty store. Technically, this is any store that deals with a single type of merchandise, but as the term is used among department store people, it refers most often to the "exclusive" shop, dealing in women's apparel and accessories and catering to a wealthy and fashion-minded clientele.

The strength of the exclusive specialty shop lies in its distinctive merchandise, its prestige as a fashion authority. Many customers find an enhancement of their self-esteem in dealing with such a store.

A few department stores gear their entire operation to appeal to the top income brackets and are in direct competition with these shops every inch of the way. Some, on the other hand, find it is not worth their while to seek business of this type and make no bid for it. But in general, the well-rounded department store will meet this competition by, in effect, running a specialty shop of its own—a "French Room," "Import Salon," etc.—a department that differs from the rest of the store in price lines, in atmosphere and in the type of service rendered.

Other Specialty Shops. Not all women's specialty shops cater to the wealthy. There are some in the middle and lower price ranges; some that specialize in maternity apparel alone; some that cater only to women who are exceptionally tall, or stout, or tiny. In each case, the appeal to the customer lies in the fact that here is a store that can offer her a large assortment of merchandise within the narrow range of her personal needs.

Other specialty shops with which the department store finds itself in competition include men's shops; infants' and children's shops; those devoted to millinery, or shoes, or intimate apparel; home furnishings stores and those that specialize in a single branch of home furnishings.

Some of these stores are units in a chain operation; others are independently owned. Some offer credit and delivery; some are cash-and-carry. The variety among these stores is great, but the basic appeal, as compared to that of the department store, remains the same: a wide assortment of merchandise within the narrow limits of what one particular type of customer may need, or of what customers in general may need in one small field.

Variety Stores. Directly descended from the old-time five-and-ten is the limited price variety store. Originally, these stores carried a wide assortment of items at only a few retail prices, such as five cents, 10 cents, and 25 cents. Today, their price ranges are as varied as their merchandise; they carry home furnishings and wearing apparel as well as notions and knick-knacks.

Charge account and delivery service are not usually associated with the variety store, but more frequently now one sees the offer of free delivery on purchases above a specified amount, or an invitation to inquire about credit terms.

Where the variety stores are especially strong is in the matter of making quick selection available to the customer. Their merchandise is laid out in racks or bins; shopping baskets and check-out counters are common.

The customer's obvious appreciation of the ease with which she can see and select has not gone unnoticed by department stores. Even those catering to the highest income brackets have, in many cases, introduced self-selection fixtures into certain departments to make shopping faster and easier. Many department stores use the check-out system in their basement operations.

Junior Department Stores. In the department store family, but not exactly a department store, is the fully departmentized store that carries few or none of the home furnishings lines. It may have bed sheets, curtains, and table linens, possibly even small household appliances and some occasional furniture. But the customer could never furnish her home completely in such a store.

To these stores, the name junior department store is given. It is applied to independents and to chains, and may be used for cash-and-carry stores as well as those that offer charge and delivery service. They offer real competition to department stores, but lack, of course, the all-important factor of completeness, in both price range and general assortments.

Demonstration Stores. A highly specialized type of store competes with the department store in only a few of its lines of merchandise. This is the demonstration store, run for the benefit of a single manufacturer's goods. Notable in this field are the sewing machine stores.

The demonstration store has the advantage of highly trained, highly specialized personnel and of intense specialization as to merchandise carried. Its appeal is necessarily narrow, but in that narrow field, it sets a standard of selling and customer service that is hard to match.

Supermarkets and Drug Stores. Food supermarkets and drug stores may not appear on the surface to represent important competition with department stores, yet in many parts of the country they are serious rivals.

Most supermarkets now sell cosmetics, housewares, baby needs, stationery, children's books, toys, hosiery, records, pet supplies, garden supplies, and other items. Their assortments may not be comparable to those of a department store, but they have the advantage of ample customer traffic, which they tap with effective self-service displays at strategic locations.

Drug stores also carry a great number of items commonly considered in the department store field: baby needs, hair accessories, shaving needs, cosmetics, housewares items, stationery, photographic equipment and supplies—even, in some cases, major household appliances. Convenient locations, long hours of business, and the practice in some areas of keeping open on Sunday make their competition especially rugged.

The department store's advantage over both of these competing forms of retailing lies in its prestige, its services, its new locations, and above all, its broad assortments. A customer may pick up a pair of socks for her child in the supermarket, or a toaster for her kitchen in the drug store, but if she wants to outfit her child or equip her home, she needs the department store or the appropriate specialty store.

Discount Houses. The "discount house" originally concentrated on major appliances, offering nationally advertised brands at retail prices lower than those suggested or advertised by the manufacturer, or set by him for other stores through Fair Trade contracts. Often, the discounter was a privately owned firm, operating a single store or office in an out-of-the-way location where the low rent was in keeping with its cut-price operation.

Nowadays, discount houses are present in many forms. Some are privately owned; others are multi-unit corporations whose securities are listed on the stock exchange. Most carry soft as well as hard goods, and compete with virtually every department of the department store. They are to be found in prime city and shopping center locations, as well as in outlying spots. The keynote of their operation remains, however, *mass distribution,* with minimum service and emphasis upon bargains.

In many cases, the department store meets this competition by matching the discounters' prices. Also, it plays up its fashion prestige, broad assortments, greater number of departments, dependability, and services.

Because of the department store's importance to manufacturers as a showroom for their merchandise and as an advertiser to the public, many makers seek to keep their merchandise out of the discount stores. For all that, the discounters are well supplied and are serious competition for the business of families with moderate incomes. Many of these families are willing to dispense with services in the attempt to stretch their dollars.

Franchise Stores. One or more departments in a department store or a specialty store itself may face the competition of a franchise store. Such a store outwardly presents the appearance of a chain. The "parent" organization helps select the site, designs the store and its fixtures, and supplies all or most of the merchandise. The local manager, however, is not a manager but an owner who has obligated himself to operate within the pattern established by the franchisor and to buy from the franchisor, in return for the franchise to use the firm's name. The strength of such stores varies, according to the degree to which parent company and local owner work effectively together to meet local needs.

Non-Store Retailers. The public spends several billion dollars every year on purchases from non-store "door-to-door" retailers, some of whom are important competition for the department store. Even the vending machine is a form of competition in the sale of small convenience items with stable retail prices.

The door-to-door seller is usually a high pressure salesman, with a narrow range of merchandise whose features he knows well: cosmetics, vacuum cleaners, housewares, silverware, brushes, for example. His ranks include not only this type of seller but also the party plan salesman. The latter induces a housewife to invite friends and neighbors to a party at which merchandise is demonstrated and sold.

Department stores meet this form of competition not only with their broad assortment, their known reputation for dependability, their various services, and the absence of any pressure to buy, but also by selling in the home. This last is described in a chapter of its own.

Mail Order Company. Mail order companies, long firmly entrenched with the rural population, have become increasingly important to city dwellers and suburban families. The convenience of buying at home makes a powerful appeal to the housebound mother of small children, or the working wife. Mail order catalogues of today present broader assortments, a wider range of prices, and more fashion merchandise than in the past.

Some of the major mail order companies have also established hundreds of retail stores, many of which are of a size and offer accommodations rivaling the best in the department store field. They have also set up catalogue centers in these stores or separately for those who want sales help in placing their orders, or who prefer to order by telephone.

The department store, of course, is also geared to sell by mail and telephone. This is discussed in a separate chapter.

Department stores use catalogues too, at Christmas time and at other times of the year. Essentially, however, their answer to mail order competition is the customer's opportunity to see, appraise, select from many brands, many price lines, and many styles—styles that include the new and evanescent as well as the familiar and staple.

It is interesting to note that, as the discount houses and the retail mail order stores mature, they tend to duplicate and imitate department store arrangements, displays and services. Conversely, the department store has been quick to adapt the best of the innovations offered by the discount and retail mail order stores.

Shopping Centers. With the growth of suburbs and with the increasing use of the family car for shopping, there has been a corresponding growth of suburban shopping centers. These characteristically offer excellent parking facilities, and a variety of stores. A planned regional center will usually include one or more department store branches, supermarkets, small shops, recreation facilities, and medical offices.

The phenomenal growth of these centers has provided the department stores with their greatest opportunity to meet the encroachments of competitive forms of retailing—and they have responded to the challenge with a vigor and a flexibility which have kept them as leaders in the field. They were too alive to dry up as the inner city diminished in importance. They have kept their roots in the city—but their branches grow constantly wider and stronger. Instead of depending upon the customer to come downtown to a busy area, the branch brings to an easily accessible location near her home the merchandise, the atmosphere, the services, the policies and the personality of the parent store.

The merchandise selected for sale at the branches is geared to meet the needs of the customers in the area. Frequently, the branch store is smaller than the downtown store. Hence its assortments may be less broad. Nevertheless, every branch store customer knows that the merchandise displayed in the branch is backed by the stocks and the facilities of the main store.

The Challenge. Thus we see the department store facing the competition of many other forms of retailing. Some compete in price; some in convenience. Some are competitors only with respect to a limited number of items or departments; some vie with every department of the store for the customer's patronage.

These various types of competition constitute a constant, never-ending challenge. As the tastes and needs of people change, new forms of retailing develop to serve them. Each time this happens, prophets of doom hasten to predict the imminent demise of the department store. But the department store shows little inclination to collapse. It responds to each new form of competition with vigor, with practical but also with creative forward steps. Department stores in this country today are stronger than ever financially. They provide ever-increasing services. Their volume of sales increases constantly. They remain a dominant factor in the process of distribution.

The chapters that follow are devoted to showing how the department store is organized and what methods it uses to maintain and enhance its position in the community in the face of present and future competition.

CHAPTER 2

DEPARTMENT STORE ORGANIZATION

BY

RICHARD C. BOND

Just as distribution has become more complex since the days of hand industry, so has the structure of the retail store's organization. In order to accomplish the many-sided job of running a department store, the people within that store need to be organized into groups according to function and these then placed under the leadership of executives who are specialists in those functions. Organization may be considered the executive and managerial structure by which the policies of the firm are made effective, and through which each person employed in the store is enabled to make his fullest contribution to its successful operation.

The Need for Organization. Without a sound organization structure, people cannot work effectively together. People want to know where they are going, and why. They are quick to sense whether the management knows where *it* is going, and why. Management shows whether it knows where it is going and why by the organization structure that it sets up, and the kind of organization leadership that it gives.

The right leadership in a large group of people can come only through sound organization. Businesses have grown too large for the leadership to come from one man alone. Organizational leadership must take the place of individual leadership in large corporations.

The Purpose of an Organization Chart. The function of organization is to arrange into working order all the components of the whole, each having a special function, or rela-

11

tion with respect to the whole, or in respect to each other.

The purpose of an organization chart is to show these relationships in simple, blue-print form. It is the mechanical means of showing human and functional relationships. It helps to clarify the thinking of the management on organization problems.

Frequently, organizations have been built around personalities rather than around functions. If there is to be sound organization, men must be developed to fit the job and the function to be performed, and not the reverse.

This principle was clearly brought out by Paul M. Mazur in his book, "Principles of Organization Applied to Modern Retailing." He wrote, "In the long run, the man must be suited to the job, for the job is created and imposed by the rigorous competitive struggle for sales and profits. The principle of fitting jobs to men can be applied with safety only in a most limited way."

Another important purpose of the organization chart is to enable the management to make the organization structure clear to all members of the store personnel and to prospective employees. It is the only clear and simple way of showing the relationships of people and functions within the organization.

The Form of the Organization Chart. The accompanying organization chart is only one of many forms that may be used. It shows functions and relations rather than personalities. Names of people are omitted purposely, for people may change but the relationships of the various parts remain unchanged. This is basic organizational philosophy.

The objection that is sometimes raised to organization charts is that they tend to "freeze" the organization set-up and fail to give the necessary flexibility. But the basic reason for an organization chart is that the structure and the relationships should not lightly be changed. Frequent changes within an organization will destroy both its morale and its effectiveness.

While top management can, and at times should change

the organization structure, it should do so with great care and only when the change seems to be in line with long range policies. Organization charts must be kept up to date to be valuable, and so any changes that are made in the organization structure should be made at once on the chart.

Divisions of Executives. It will be noted from the accompanying chart that the staff officers report directly to the general manager. Their functions are to act in advisory capacities to the management, but they are not authorized to issue orders to line executives. Their functions are research and advisory.

It will be noted also that the line management is divided into major divisions or pyramids. Among individual stores, there is a good deal of variation in the number of pyramids required. The organization structure originally suggested by Paul Mazur, years ago, and adopted by many stores, divided the line functions among four major executives — control, operations, merchandising, and promotion. Since that time, personnel problems have assumed such importance that a fifth division for personnel, on a par with the other four and reporting to the general manager, is fairly common.

In organizations with several branch stores, the trend is toward setting up a separate division to take over all branch management responsibilities and to answer, like the heads of the other divisions, directly to the general manager. Branches vary so much in size and type that each management has to work out its own organization. Where there is no major executive in charge, it is not unusual for branch executives to combine various functions and to be responsible, either directly or through the branch manager, to more than one division head.

Our example shows separate divisions for both personnel and branch stores. Some stores have fewer pyramids, even fewer than the original four suggested by Mr. Mazur. Merchandising and sales promotion are sometimes combined, with the latter an arm of the merchandising division. In other cases, the general manager assumes the duties of general merchan-

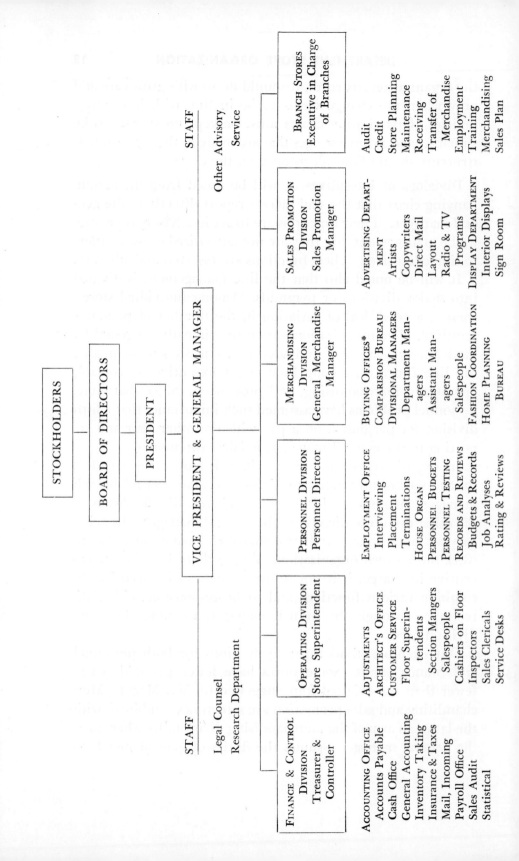

CREDIT OFFICE
Billing Customers
Cashiers in Office
Charge Accounts
Charge Author-
  ization
Credit Interviewers
Deferred Payments
CREDIT UNION
EXPENSE CONTROL
LAYAWAY OFFICE
**MERCHANDISE
  STATISTICS**

Telephone & Mail
  Orders
Register Service
DELIVERY
**ELEVATORS &
  ESCALATORS**
HOUSEKEEPING
MAIL DIVISION
MAINTENANCE
Air Conditioning
Carpenters
Electricians
Heating
Lighting
Painters
Plumbers
PACKING & PICK-UP
PRINTING
**PURCHASING DEPART-
  MENT**
RESTAURANTS
STORE PROTECTION
TRAFFIC DEPARTMENT
Order Office
Receiving
Marking
Stock Rooms
WAREHOUSE
WORKROOMS
Women's Alteration
Men's Busheling
Fur Repair
Fur Storage
Picture Framing

TRAINING
Induction & System
On the Job
WELFARE & HEALTH

**MERCHANDISE PLAN-
  NING & CONTROL**
**MERCHANDISE
  RESEARCH**
*Buying offices are un-
der jurisdiction of top
management but used
largely by the Mer-
chandising Division.

Window Displays
Exterior Displays
PUBLIC RELATIONS
News Releases
Public Fashion
  Shows
Special Events
Use of Auditorium

Advertising
Display
Special Events
. . . And any other
matters pertaining to
individual branches or
liaison with main store

Figure 1. Department Store Organization Chart

dise manager, and the divisional merchandise managers report directly to him.

Other Variations. It is a rare department store that does not have some leased or franchised departments. A leased department, either merchandise or service, is operated in the store's own name by an outside firm, which takes the financial responsibility for inventory, sales salaries, advertising, and so on. A franchised department may be run in the store's name or *as a store within a store* by the company giving the franchise. In the latter case, the outside company assists in planning and managing the department, but the store retains the financial responsibility.

In stores where leased departments are numerous, an executive may be assigned to oversee their operations and to integrate them with the store's owned departments. Such an executive is in some cases on a par with other division heads. More frequently, it is the merchandise managers, in whose divisions the departments would fall if the store ran them, who supervise the leased operations. In other cases, it may be the store manager, the controller, or store head himself.

The Use of the Organization Chart in Training. In executive induction and training, the organization chart can be extremely useful. Executives need to know what their relationships are and how they are to function together.

All new executives who are promoted from within or hired from the outside should have the benefit of an induction for executives in which they discuss their mutual problems with the operating executives with whom they will work. For example, the new buyer should have a definite schedule for interviewing the controller, the office manager, the credit manager, the publicity manager, the advertising manager, the display manager, and the personnel manager and his staff, and so on, through the major divisions of the store.

In this manner, new executives would be given a good head start on their jobs. They would know the people with whom they will work, and how they can work with them to the best advantage. They would be well drilled on the policies and procedures of the firm. For instance, the personnel director would discuss the personnel policies of the store thoroughly with the newcomer, and likewise the publicity director the publicity policies.

The organization chart is useful also in training the older executives and in clarifying misunderstandings about functions and relationships. In the hands of top management, the organization chart can be a very useful tool in the training of executives.

In the training of rank and file employees, the organization chart should be used by the training department to show relationships within the organization and how these people fit into it. It will make clear to them the lines of responsibility and it will make them much more organization-minded. Here is the opportunity to develop good organization men and women.

The Place of the Merchandising Division. The Merchandising Division, as indicated on the accompanying organization chart, is one of the five major divisions in the department store. The general merchandise manager is the chief executive of this division and reports directly to the general manager.

Under the general merchandise manager are the divisional merchandise managers, their number depending upon the size of the organization. Some small stores may operate with just one merchandise manager and no divisional merchandise managers; larger stores may have five or six.

The buyer, or department manager, comes under the divisional merchandise manager in the larger store, or directly under the general merchandise manager in smaller stores when there is only one merchandise manager.

The General Merchandise Manager. The general merchandise manager as chief of his division becomes a part of top management, reporting directly to the general manager. He participates in the formulation of major policies and assumes the responsibility for seeing that they are carried out within his own division.

His chief function is policy making and policy supervision, insofar as merchandising is concerned. He acts as chief liaison officer between the merchandising division and the other divisions of the store. Since the buying and selling of goods is really the hub around which all store activities revolve, it is evident that the general merchandise manager's position is one of very great responsibility and influence.

The Divisional Merchandise Managers. Divisional merchandise managers are in the category of middle management. Their function is to transmit the principles, policies, and procedures laid down by top management to the line management.

On the other hand, it is extremely important that the divisional merchandise managers transmit upward to top management the suggestions, ideas and grievances that originate in the organization below them.

One of the great difficulties in department stores has been to have a clear cut understanding on the part of the various merchandise managers as to their level of responsibility. If a divisional merchandise manager, for example, assumes the authority of top management in making policies, or in deviating from policies that have been laid down by top management, then confusion and difficulties arise within the organization.

Divisional merchandise managers, as part of middle management, come in direct contact with the line executives, and in this capacity they exert considerable influence. They should, above all things, have a helpful spirit toward the line executives under their supervision. They represent top management in dealing with their line executives, and represent their own subordinate executives in dealing with top management.

Department Managers, Buyers and Assistants. These executives are included in line management and receive the principles, policies, and procedures as transmitted from top management through middle management. They should execute these principles, policies and procedures as laid down by the management as faithfully as possible.

No matter how fine the philosophy of the top management may be, or how sound its policies, if the line management executives do not carry out these principles and policies at the line management level, these principles and policies will be nullified.

The rank and file employees and customers who come in contact with the line executives will judge the management by what they find in these line supervisors.

Each level of management must know its place and stay in its place. Each level of management has a definite function to perform and when it presumes to deviate from that function, difficulties arise in the organization. Each executive must know his own functions and responsibilities and adhere to them meticulously.

Organization Policies and Procedures. There should be a clear cut distinction made between policies and procedures. Without this understanding, confusion is apt to arise.

Policies are top management's long-range guiding principles of the business. They give direction and stability to the organization. Policies are the answers to problems that arise in the course of the operation of the business.

Procedures are the methods devised to carry out and make effective the policies laid down by the management. They must be flexible enough to meet new situations as they arise without violating the principles laid down in the policies.

It is highly desirable to have the policies of the firm put in writing so that there can be no misunderstanding or excuse for not knowing them. Policies that exist only in the minds of top management cannot be effective. They must be made known and explained to everyone who has any part in the execution of those policies. People must know what is expected of them before they can perform satisfactorily.

The procedures should be put in writing also, but since they need to be more flexible, they should be put in a form that can be easily changed. Systems and instructions may be put in the form of manuals or bulletins. Written instructions regarding procedures and systems are usually clearer and much more likely to be understood than oral instructions alone.

In writing policies or procedures, it is advisable to follow the organization chart, and to index the policies or procedures in the same order as the structure is on the chart. For example, the policies related to merchandising would be put under the merchandise division; the publicity policies, under the publicity division. The same applies to policies for other functions and other divisions.

Human Relations in Organization. Since every organization is made up of human beings, human relations are a chief consideration of management. Success or failure depends upon the human beings within the organization—how well they are fitted for their work, how well they are trained, and how well they perform their many duties. That is why it is so essential to have the functions, responsibilities, and relationships of every individual in the organization clearly defined.

It is vital that every executive and supervisor should understand the importance of the human factor in business. Executives can no longer think only in terms of merchandise, publicity and figures. They must come to realize that good human relations are the basis of success in all the activities of the store.

Recognize Existing Talent. It is to management's interest to make it possible for individuals with superior abilities to contribute their fullest value to the business. Good human relations will help management make maximum use of the talents and abilities it finds in the organization.

In order to find men and women who will make good organization people, the scientific tools of personnel testing are used in many stores. These tests not only enable the management to locate talent, but they also make it possible to place these people so that they may transmit their full value to the organization. Pre-promotional training should be provided for those who have superior abilities, and for those who have capacities beyond their present positions.

Morale At All Levels. It should be remembered that morale is important among executives and supervisors as well as among rank and file employees. As a matter of fact, good morale among employees is usually dependent upon good morale among executives. Human relations are important all up and down the line.

The following principles of good organization are important from the standpoint of maintaining good executive morale:

1. There must be unity of command. No one works well under more than one boss. Avoid overlapping or conflicting instructions.

2. Lines of organization should be followed in giving orders or instructions. Executives resent being by-passed.

3. Authority must accompany responsibility. A person is frustrated and confused if he is given re-responsibility without corresponding authority.

4. Each executive must have the correct "span of control." He must have enough to do to challenge his ability, but not be spread so thin that he cannot do a good job.

5. Credit for suggestions and for good work should always be given to the proper line executives.

Characteristics of a Good Organization Man or Woman. The good organization person is organization minded. He thinks of the organization first and foremost. He does not place his own personal self-interest above the organization.

He recognizes that his success is inevitably bound up with that of the organization.

The good organization man is a booster for his organization. He is always looking for the good things in the organization and in the people in it. He is on the optimistic side and never defeatist. He sees good because he looks for it.

The good organization man likes to see others get ahead and helps them on their way. He never stands in the way of the development of another individual. If he does not have a place in his own department to use all the abilities of an individual, he recommends him to another position which will enable him to grow and to develop to his full capacity.

Good organization people create job enthusiasm, because they have it themselves. People stay on their jobs if they like their work and their working conditions. People grow in their jobs if they like their jobs. In order to like their jobs, people must feel that the job is worth while and that they are important in it. It must challenge the best that is in them.

The men and women in the executive and supervisory staff have the chief responsibility for leading and molding the people in the organization. They must set the patterns and the standards.

CHAPTER 3

THE MERCHANDISING DIVISION

BY

EDWARD J. BROWN

The merchandising division, as it is organized today in the typical department store, differs tremendously from the picture retailing presented more than 80 years ago. Describing the personnel structure of the A. T. Stewart Company in that day, Laura C. Halloway (Langford) wrote:

"In the service of this uptown store about 2,200 persons were employed. The one general superintendent had nineteen assistants, each of whom was at the head of a department. Nine cashiers received and paid out money; twenty-five bookkeepers kept the record of the day; thirty ushers directed purchasers to the department they were seeking; two hundred cash boys received the money and brought back the change of the purchasers; four hundred and seventy clerks, some of whom were women, made the sales of the day; fifty porters did the heavy work, and nine hundred seamstresses were employed in the manufacturing departments. Besides these there were five hundred other persons employed about this immense store in various capacities."

No doubt, some of the jobs mentioned in Stewart's store seem rather out of place to us. It is also interesting to note that the titles of general merchandise manager, divisional merchandise manager, buyer, assistant buyer, or head of stock did not appear in this review. Apparently the merchandising division did not exist even in a store the size of Stewart's in 1870.

Origin of Merchandising Division. The foregoing description may seem like a far cry from our present merchandising establishments, but it will serve as a beginning for our discussion of the merchandising division of today. To appreciate and understand fully the place of the merchandising division in the present day department store, it is necessary to understand how and why such a division came into being.

Long before Mr. Stewart's operations were recorded, many store owners felt the need of transferring some of their responsibilities to capable assistants. When a store owner first asked one of his trusted clerks to talk to a visiting drummer and select merchandise to be purchased, he was probably creating the forerunner of the first crude merchandising division. In another description of department store organization given in 1900 by Mr. William C. Daniels of Denver, we find: "The management of a department store is vested in a number of general men. . . . They act as chiefs of staff. . . . Below them come the department heads, each a specialist and supreme in his own domain."

Early Separation. That some attention was given to the problem of separating the merchandising activities from the operating function is indicated by a description of an early set-up of the Joseph Horne Co., of Pittsburgh. At that time this store was divided into the two functions of merchandising and store operation. The merchandising division, which determined stock assortments and stock arrangement and handled the buying and selling, was headed by a major executive; the store operation division, which was responsible for the physical maintenance of the store, was headed by another. Both divisions were of equal rank, each reporting directly to the general management.

When the A. T. Stewart store organization is compared with the Joseph Horne Co.'s, it is seen that considerable change had taken place between 1870 and 1900. The general manager of the former was working through nineteen department heads, while the management of the latter was working through only two major executives.

As the development of the department store is followed, it

will be noticed that management has constantly searched for the right combination and distribution of responsibility and authority within its organization. Various functions have vied with each other from time to time for what they considered to be their rightful position in the organization. Of chief interest in this discussion is to trace these developments and note the appearance and growth of the merchandising division.

Functionalization Begins. As a store grew in size and added new lines of merchandise, the owner or founder lost some of his contacts with the markets and turned more and more of the actual buying and merchandising over to the newly appointed department heads. As a result, the owners or managers soon found themselves surrounded by a great number of department heads who were specialists and supreme in their own domains, and each of whom reported directly to the owners, acting as the general management.

Such organizations soon become unwieldy, and it became apparent that the adding of new departments only served to complicate the situation further. The unwieldiness of this departmental growth made the development of functionalization a necessity.

Growth of Incorporation. At the same time that functionalization was getting under way in the department store field, there was also a decided trend towards incorporation. Between 1900 and 1912, at least a dozen of the country's outstanding stores were incorporated. With the coming of this stronger type of organization, management naturally sought a more effective internal set-up.

Growing sales volume, changing economic conditions and keener competition made the job of buying and selling more complex and forced the subdivision of this major function into such important activities as merchandise control, sales planning and promotion, store customer service, personnel selection, store maintenance and operating records.

This period of incorporation and functionalization, soon

after the turn of the century, brought about three important developments in the department store field:

1. It succeeded in decentralizing personal responsibility and in lessening the burden resting upon general management and upon the department heads.

2. It coordinated the merchandising activities throughout the store and made the first real department store unit. Up to this time department stores had been composed largely of a series of specialty shops under individual control.

3. It introduced a period of functionalization which pushed the pendulum too far and culminated in the overspecialized condition in which department stores found themselves in 1930.

Merchandising Defined. To understand the merchandising division as it evolved out of the period of functionalization and incorporation, it is necessary to define merchandising.

There are almost as many definitions of this term as there are writers on the subject. To say that merchandising is buying and selling seems too broad in scope when thinking in terms of the modern department store. Such a definition could well include all phases of store activity, and such all-inclusiveness would be contrary to the previously stated concept of functionalization.

Although the retail store and its building equipment and fixtures, its service departments, and all of its workers, are but parts of a mechanism to aid in retail merchandising, still the merchandising division as it exists in most stores does not control all of the assisting functions. Dr. John W. Wingate* has well expressed the thinking in his definition: "Merchandising has to do with all functions having to do with bringing the goods to the point of sale, adjusting the stock

* Elements of Retail Merchandising, by John W. Wingate and Norris A. Brisco.

investments according to kinds of goods, styles, quantities and prices so as to satisfy consumer demand and make a profit."

Position in the Store. Now that the term has been defined, how well does the definition fit into actual practice? Although there may be shorter routes to follow in approaching the study of the present merchandising division, it would seem safer to become well acquainted with the changes that have taken place in store organization since the turn of the century. In order to appreciate the position held by the merchandising division and to understand clearly the functions that it performs, it is necessary first to know how it fits into the structure of the store.

During the years from 1900 to the years immediately following the first World War, most of the stronger department stores enjoyed a period of almost continuous prosperity and growth. The years following the first war found some stores in a weakened condition. However, most of them came through in good shape but determined to find and correct the weak spots that had shown up during the period between 1920 and 1923. The NRMA in 1924 appointed a committee to study the fundamentals of retail organization. Probably the outstanding contribution of this committee was the report submitted in 1927 by Paul M. Mazur. This was his book, *"Principles of Organization Applied to Modern Retailing,"* which has had a profound effect upon department store organization.

Checks and Balances. Mr. Mazur developed the Four-Functional Plan, which sets merchandising up as a separate function, along with publicity, store management, and control. There have been many variations, with anything from two to six functions, as explained in an earlier chapter. The plan, whatever the number of functions it may have, defines authority for each division, sets up each division's responsibility, and develops major executives who are not only specialists in their respective fields but who see the operation as a unit.

This creates a stable organization, and also provides a form of checks and balances through internal cooperation. The merchandising division's success is dependent upon the operation of the others, and they in turn depend upon it.

In two and three divisional set-ups, merchandising probably achieves a stronger position than it holds under plans with four or more divisions. In two-divisional plans, all buying and selling activities are grouped under merchandising, and all the other phases of store operation are in the other division. In three-divisional plans, merchandising, control, and store management make up the trio, with merchandising embracing all buying and selling activities.

Objectives of the Merchandising Division. The objectives of the merchandising division will vary according to its position within the store. Those listed below are representative regardless of store organization.

1. Accurate forecasts and estimates of what and how much will be wanted by the store's customers in kinds of goods, qualities, styles, and prices.

2. Purchases of such goods made as advantageously as possible.

3. The conservation and manipulation of capital, by limiting and distributing purchases among goods likely to sell well.

4. Effective sales promotion, including advertising, display, and salesmanship, that will induce customers to come to the store and purchase the goods made available for sale.

5. Building a permanent clientele and goodwill.

If these can be accepted as worthy objectives for the merchandising division, then the next task is to determine what functions must be carried out by the merchandising division in order to accomplish these objectives. At this point the primary concern is with those functions that are the responsibility of the merchandising division, although these objectives could not be achieved without very close cooperation with the other divisions within the store.

Functions and Responsibilities. The following functions are those generally performed by the merchandising division in an effort to achieve its objectives:

1. INTERPRET AND EXECUTE THE MERCHANDISING POLICIES OF THE COMPANY. The owner or president, the general merchandise manager, or both working together, determine the broad policies the store wishes to follow. The merchandising division must see that quality standards, price ranges, and styles conform to the established policies. Thus the merchandising manager represents the management to the buyer. Obversely, he represents the interest of his division to the management.

2. UNIFY THE EFFORTS OF ALL BUYERS. The modern department store strives to present a uniform appearance to the buying public. All buyers must work towards a uniform goal, and it is the responsibility of the merchandising division to see that their efforts are directed in this direction.

3. SENSE, INTERPRET, AND INFORM BUYERS REGARDING BUSINESS TRENDS AND MARKET CONDITIONS. It is very natural that buyers become so interested in their own operation that they fail to grasp the significance of the over-all economic picture. The merchandising division should make available and should see to it that buyers make use of accurate and current economic analysis information.

4. PROVIDE PERCEPTIVE JUDGMENT IN ADVISING THE INDIVIDUAL BUYER. Although this may be one of the most intangible activities of the merchandising division, it is of paramount importance. The general merchandise manager is far enough removed from the individual departmental operation that he can take an objective point of view regarding the individual department's operation.

5. ESTABLISH AND ADMINISTER A MERCHANDISE CONTROL SYSTEM. Modern retail organizations are thinking in terms of

both dollar and unit planning for each merchandise classification to improve the departmental operation.

6. ASSIST EACH DEPARTMENT IN PLANNING AND CARRYING OUT ITS INDIVIDUAL BUYING PLANS. This activity is a cooperative project uniting the individual buyer, divisional merchandise manager, and the general merchandise manager. The buyer should feel that he has a real part in establishing such plans and that they are *his* figures that he is trying to make. This activity also gives the merchandising division an opportunity to advise and counsel and thereby prevent costly errors.

7. PLAN SALES PROMOTIONS. With unprecedented competition, it is more important than ever that all departments throughout the store present a unified front. Sales promotion is, of course, a joint activity between the merchandising division and the sales promotion division. It is the responsibility of the merchandising division to see that all departments gear their buying to conform with the accepted sales promotion plans.

8. SUPERVISE DEPARTMENTAL ACTIVITIES OF BUYERS. There may be other divisions of the store that are also interested in the departmental activities of the buyers, but the control of the merchandising division cannot divorce itself from the buyer's activity within his department. Merchandising policies have not been thoroughly executed until the merchandise is sold.

9. ASSIST BUYERS IN LOCATING AND DEVELOPING NEW RESOURCES. The good buyer will carry most of the burden of this responsibility, but he should receive help from the merchandising division. The broader scope of the merchandising division, as compared with the individual department, gives it an advantageous position for spotting new resources.

The Divisional Merchandise Manager. These functions are only the major subdivisions of the job of the merchandising division, of which the general merchandise manager is the leader, advisor and coordinator. He is assisted by various personnel in carrying out these major activities. Divisional mer-

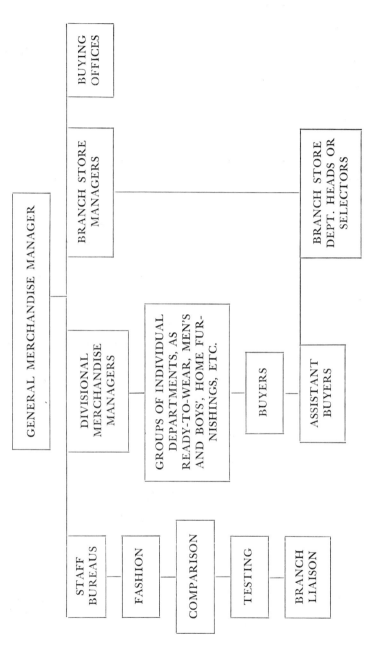

Figure 2. Organization of the Merchandising Division

chandise managers, buyers, assistant buyers, and heads of stock all carry a part of the load, along with appropriate branch store executives.

Although the responsibility for the successful operation of any individual department rests ultimately on the buyer or manager, the divisional merchandise manager must assume responsibility for the success of his division as a whole and must assume the leadership of it. His authority and responsibility must be recognized when it comes to the execution of the policies of the store, the supervision of the financial investment in merchandise, and the coordination of the various merchandising departments among themselves and with other divisions of the store.

Merchandising Staff Assistants. In order to fulfill its functions adequately, the merchandise division has certain staff assistance to gather information on which to base its decisions. In most stores these include:

1. THE COMPARISON DEPARTMENT. Its members check the store's assortments, service, and prices against those of competing stores. They note the response to advertised items in competing stores. If necessary, they purchase articles from competitors for study by the merchandising staff. Their reports give the buyer more information on local competition than he can gather solely through his own efforts.

2. FASHION COORDINATOR. The fashion staff collects information from the market, from the buyers, and from fashion analysts, as a background for working out a coordinated fashion story for the departments involved to tell. The fashion coordinator runs the fashion shows for the store and the departments. In the home furnishings division, a coordinator or decorator serves a similar function.

3. TESTING LABORATORY. Some stores maintain their own laboratories to test whether merchandise offered by vendors is as represented and is up to the quality standards of the store. Some engage outside laboratories for this service.

4. BASIC STOCK GROUP. One or more persons may be assigned to check basic stocks (about which much more will be said in later chapters) to make sure that items in consistent demand are adequately stocked at all times. In some stores, the basic stock staff merely checks and reports; in others, they do routine reordering for the buyer.

Merchandising Policies. Since one of the most important duties of the merchandise manager is to establish and maintain a consistent merchandising policy for all departments in the store with respect to buying, selling, and stock, it should be clearly understood what is meant by a policy. A policy may be said to be a definite principle or method or procedure, adopted and followed by the store in its relation with customers, employees, and the people from whom it buys. Following is a list of merchandising policies adopted by one good store:

1. THE KIND OF STORE IT IS TO BE. It is the policy of this store to cater chiefly to the great middle section of department store trade. Although this is where the emphasis shall be, we shall have customers below and above this range, and it shall be our policy to treat all customers with the utmost courtesy and consideration.

To be a store which is known for its high character in all its dealings with customer and market resources alike.

To be known as a store where customers can find the things they want. Known for fashion-rightness and for alertness to new things in the market which will appeal to our customers.

To be known as the store where a customer is sure to find executives and employees who are customer-minded and service-minded to the highest degree, and who know that good-will is even more important than sales.

To be the kind of store which does not put the dollar above and before human values. Profits are the by-product of good management and good human relations.

2. A PLACE WHERE CUSTOMERS FIND IT EASY TO SHOP. Lay out merchandise within each department so it is easy to find and easy to select, and arranged by natural classifications, and by sizes and colors within each classification.

3. QUALITIES AND VALUES. To maintain highest possible standards of quality in all sections of the store at the price ranges carried in stock. Minimum quality standards must be high enough to exclude undesirable merchandise.

Values must be as good as or better than found in any other store in the city. Values are determined by price and quality.

4. IRREGULARS AND SECONDS. Avoid carrying and advertising irregular and seconds merchandise in the upstairs store, except such items as are approved by the merchandise manager.

5. COMPLETE ASSORTMENTS. Maintain complete assortments of wanted merchandise at all times. Promotional remainders and other items of merchandise which may interfere with the maintenance of complete assortments of wanted items must be eliminated.

6. MERCHANDISING BY CLASSIFICATIONS AND PRICE RANGES. Stocks must be kept balanced by classifications and price ranges, so that maximum sales and profits may be realized.

It shall be a merchandising policy to carry stock both above and below the fastest selling price ranges. However, it is important to keep them under strict control.

7. INVESTMENT IN MERCHANDISE. It is the function of management to control the investments in merchandise, although the merchandise managers will be held responsible for such control, buyers being responsible for the buying of it.

8. PURCHASE DISCOUNTS. Merchandise managers and buyers should be diligent in obtaining the best possible purchase discounts. Buyers or department managers are expected to be good traders and secure the best terms the market has to offer or that the manufacturer offers to anyone, but we do not want them to buy terms.

9. MARKDOWNS. Mistakes in buying should be recognized and corrected quickly. Markdowns, when necessary, should be taken promptly and in a sufficient amount to move the goods quickly.

10. SLOW SELLING MERCHANDISE. Merchandise which is not selling actively should be considered as slow selling, regardless of age, and be given special attention. Merchandise must be kept moving. Seasonal merchandise must be liquidated before the end of the season for which it was purchased.

11. COMPETITION. It is the policy of the store to be competitive with other stores in prices, values, assortments and services, and to meet value as well as price competition.

12. VENDOR RELATIONS. It shall be the policy of the store to cultivate the top resources in the various markets and to work as closely with them as possible. The goodwill of such resources must be carefully guarded.

Buyers must see salesmen when coming to the store and place orders promptly for desirable, needed merchandise.

To associate the store with the best trademark lines and to give such lines special attention in publicity and selling.

All orders are to be written on the store's order form, at the time of selecting the merchandise, and approved by the merchandise manager. Delivery dates should be clearly indicated on every order and final termination date shown on the order.

Advance orders should be placed long enough in advance of the opening of the season to insure the best possible selection and early delivery of the merchandise.

Reorders should be placed as soon as the need is known. Orders may not be cancelled until after the due date on the order, unless the manufacturer indicates inability to ship on time.

Merchandise may not be returned to the manufacturer or wholesaler if it is shipped in accordance with the order, unless of inferior quality or having defects discovered at the time of receipt of the goods.

On occasion it may be deemed advisable by management

to purchase on memorandum or on consignment. When such a purchase is made, all the details of the agreement must be clearly stated on the order.

Liaison Function. In these and other ways, then, the merchandise manager fulfills his function as a liaison between top management and the buyer, and between the buyer and the other divisions of the store. He spells out policies and procedures to the buyer; he takes up an individual department's problems with other divisions of the store if necessary; he works with the buyer where an individual purchase or problem involves decisions beyond those the buyer himself is authorized to make. He is the senior partner to the buyer, not in the sense of standing over his shoulder and directing his work, but in the sense of being his adviser.

CHAPTER 4

THE BUYER AS MANAGER OF PEOPLE

BY

DAVID BLUTHENTHAL

Running a good department, attracting customers to the store, making a profit—these are basic elements in the buyer's job. Equally basic, however, is the element with which this chapter is concerned: the buyer's function as manager in his own department. To fulfill this obligation, he must accept and discharge executive responsibility for those people working under him, and he must also accept the responsibility for carrying out company policy in and out of the store.

The buyer's many-sided activities make him a vital link in management's communications network. Through his merchandise manager, company policies come down to the buyer. Through him, in turn, they are communicated to employees, customers, vendors. By the same token, *communication back to top management* from these three kinds of contact is by way of the buyer. He must be alert to notice conditions or reactions that could possibly invite a review of store policy on any point; these he should report back to top management through his merchandise manager.

The buyer does not set policies, nor does he change them. His job is to execute them faithfully and to report any developments which may suggest a change to those who make the policies.

The Importance of Communication. The most important phase of management's responsibility in any organization is communication. This is especially so in an organization as complex as the department store, with its hundreds or thousands of employees, and its many thousand daily contacts with the public.

Policies are formed and enunciated at the top. Some policies endure briefly and are withdrawn. Others remain in force from the day a store opens its doors for as long as it remains in business. Typical of the enduring kind is the almost universal department store policy of standing behind its merchandise to the extent of making refunds and adjustments if the goods fail to give satisfaction. Typical of policies that may change from time to time are those concerned with delivery, gift wrapping, and other customer services, or those concerned with pinpointing the class of customer which the store is most eager to serve.

Policies, however, are executed daily. Thus communication becomes a daily job. Whatever the store intends to stand for, each day brings new customers, new employees, new vendors, new situations, that call for an expression of policy.

Using the example of the refund policy, communication must be to every vendor on every purchase, to make sure it is clearly understood that merchandise must be exactly as represented. Communication must be to advertising and selling staffs, to make sure that they, in turn, presented the merchandise correcly to the customer. If there are misunderstandings, communicaion is also at the refund and adjustment desk. At each point along the line, the buyer is the source of information and the executive who must bring the general policy down to specifics.

Communicating Enthusiasm. The buyer has other things to communicate, in addition to company policy. One of the most important of these is his own enthusiasm—for his store, for his merchandise, for his customers. All stores have buyers, and all stores have merchandise, but the difference between those that are strong and those that are weak is usually the difference in the enthusiasm of their buyers.

Nothing is quite so contagious as enthusiasm. When the buyer shows it in the market, his resources enjoy working with him and exert themselves willingly in his behalf. When he shows it at the store, in passing the facts along to the advertising and display departments, the promotion and display people become infected with enthusiasm too, and this is reflected in the work they do for his department.

But especially when the buyer is able to communicate his enthusiasm to his salespeople are results seen. Usually the merchandise that sells first in a store or department is that merchandise which aroused enthusiasm in the buyer, who in turn transmitted his to the salespeople, and through them, to the customer.

Techniques for Communicating. There are techniques for communicating enthusiasm. One is to make notes about the merchandise on the copy of the purchase order. These should be concerned not only with descriptive details, but with selling points. Then, when the buyer is back from the market or sample room, he has his reminders of what to tell the salespeople and promotion staff about the new merchandise that is on the way.

There is also the matter of *expressing* enthusiasm. It is one thing to run down a list of selling points and another to present them with enthusiasm. Wash-and-wear is now taken for granted. But in the beginning it had to be "sold." In the early days, saying, for instance, that a garment was wash-and-wear was merely to list its qualities. Taking a sample and washing it right before the salespeople and then hanging it up where they could watch how quickly and smoothly it dried, is a way of communicating, of expressing enthusiasm.

The same thing applies to matters of store policy. If a department may give a white gift box without charge, but gift-wrapping requires sending the customer to a special station, announcement to the salespeople can be made lifelessly with similar indifferent communication to the customer, or with delight and enthusiasm over such a service, so that the store policy is accepted and similarly carried out by the salespeople.

Compare these two messages to the salespeople: "You give this white box free if they ask for it. But anything else, they

pay for, over at that station." And, "We have these good-look-
ing white gift boxes that you can offer customers free. People
who do their own gift wrapping will be happy to have them.
If anyone wants something really special by way of wrapping,
tell them about the service at that station over there. The customer can choose her papers and her ribbons, and for the little
extra money, she can get a really professional job. If you have
a minute, step over and watch the wrappers work, and you'll
see how they dress up a package."

The Problem of Getting Action. Good management begins
with the executive himself. The buyer who wants to get action out of his employees, as in the case of putting enthusiasm
into their selling, should first get his own house in order. If
he buys aimlessly, he can expect aimless, indifferent selling.
If he makes a selling plan first, and then buys to his plan, he is
working with purpose and direction. That purpose, that direction, will be felt by the salespeople, too, and they will feel that
they are selling merchandise bought especially for their customers, not articles picked up on impulse by the buyer and to
be disposed of, somehow.

Similarly, the buyer who plans in advance how to deploy his
people is bound to be more successful than the one who hands
out assignments haphazardly. Delegating work is an important
phase of the management aspect of the buyer's job, particularly in this day of branch stores, when so many buyers have the
responsibility for more than one selling location.

The Technique of Delegating. Proper delegation of responsibility involves three steps: (1) choosing the right person for
the job; (2) assigning duties and delegating authority so that
everything is completely clear; (3) following up instructions
to see that they are properly carried out.

We'll consider each in turn. It'll suffice to say that it is
never safe to assume that simply telling people to do something
is enough. If teaching, training, and follow-up are needed,
the buyer as a manager has the responsibility for doing that.
If an assignment is carried out carelessly or late, it is not

enough merely to call attention to the fault and insist that better work be done next time. The buyer may have assigned work beyond the individual's capacity, or he may not have made his instructions clear enough or detailed enough to cover all contingencies. The failure of anyone on the buyer's staff is *the buyer's* failure, just as *his* failures ultimately are the store's. It is his responsibility as a manager to analyze causes and try to prevent recurrence.

(1) **Choosing the Right Person.** Care must be taken to choose the right person for each job or assignment, whether it be counting a section of the stock or working up a departmental display. No personal prejudice or politics should be allowed to affect your judgment. In selecting persons as assistants, heads of stock, or sponsors, all personal characteristics, abilities, and work habits must be taken into consideration. So, too, must the familiar fact that a person may be highly successful in one kind of work but totally unfitted for another. Sometimes we spoil a good salesperson by making her an assistant when she lacks the qualifications for that job.

Especial care is needed in selecting those lieutenants upon whom the buyer will have to depend for help in carrying out the functions of his department. It is the mark of a smart executive, and it is also part of the preparation for a bigger job, if the buyer selects the strongest possible assistants and then trains them to take increasing responsibility.

A buyer who is afraid to have a strong person in a subordinate job, or who makes the affairs of his department a mystery to his assistants, is not only branding himself as insecure, but he is also letting himself get bogged down with details he should delegate. That is no way to prepare oneself for advancement.

(2) **Assigning the Work.** The basic principle to follow in assigning work is to make sure that the person who is given the responsibility knows exactly what is expected of him. "Get me a count of those dresses," is not as explicit as, "I'd like a count of the dresses on this rack, by size and price line. Never

mind color, style, or resource on this count. Just the number by size and price line."

The more explicit the instructions, the smaller the likelihood of error or waste motion.

When instructions are to be given for a procedure, rather than for an immediate task, it pays to take time to work out in advance exactly what is to be done and how it is to be accomplished. To make sure that everyone concerned will know what, why, how, and when each step of the job is to be done, it is worth while to make an outline of the points to be covered. If the instructions are to be given orally, the outline will serve a double purpose: It will help the buyer avoid skipping any important point, and it will be available afterward for posting in the department, where the employees concerned can consult it as often as they need to.

Even when the instructions pertain to only one or two members of the buyer's staff, if they apply to a procedure that is to become standard in the department, it is a good idea to put the essentials on paper for future reference. Until a procedure becomes a fixed habit, it is easy for people to forget or confuse instructions. A dozen or so words on paper can prevent that.

Be Clear. Good communication in assigning work also means a constant striving for clarity—clarity *in terms of the newest and least trained person concerned with the job.* This is a responsibility that requires even more watchfulness from the seasoned buyer than it does from the tyro. The more familiar a situation is to an executive, the harder it sometimes becomes to explain it in terms simple enough for the newcomer. By all means repeat your instructions. You know what you want. Your listener has heard it for the first time. Take time out to repeat. It pays.

If there is doubt about whether the instructions have been understood, ask the person concerned to repeat them in his own words. By making sure all is clear, the buyer can save himself hours of time tracking down errors that could otherwise occur.

(3) **Following Up.** There is the truism that the best executives and workers are those who need the least follow-up. But everyone needs some. Following up, however, does not mean nagging and fault-finding. It means checking on the progress of a job, to make sure that the instructions have been understood, are being carried out correctly, and are themselves correct. It is quite possible to issue instructions and procedures that do not cover every last contingency; without follow-up, this fact may not come to light until an expensive error has been made.

Follow-up also means approving what has been done correctly. The good and careful worker, being human, needs a word of encouragement if he is to continue maintaining his high level of performance. Without it, he may feel that he is not appreciated and he may become less willing to exert himself.

If there are errors or omissions to be corrected, there is no occasion for the old-fashioned "bawling out." It simply has no place in the business world today. When the faults in performance are those of an individual, that person should be taken aside and *privately* corrected. At the same time, an effort should be made to find the cause of the error: indifferent attitude, unclear instructions, inability to do the work, or whatever it may be.

Whenever the faults are fairly general, a discussion of the problem at a departmental meeting seems indicated. The discussion should be kept friendly, open, and constructive. In that atmosphere the departmental staff members may come up with suggestions for improving performance in future.

Good Human Relations. There is no inconsistency between efficiency and good human relations. On the contrary, people work better with executives who are interested, easy to understand, ready to answer questions, and who insist on jobs being done well and on time. This is true not only of those directly under the buyer's supervision, but also of those in positions more or less parallel with his and whose responsibilities overlap his—branch store executives, supervisors in sales-support-ing activities, buyers for related departments, to name a few.

The development of management skills becomes especially important when the buyer is with a store that has one or more branches. The branch staff is not under his eye every day; he may visit them at best once a week. In that case, whatever he has learned about communicating clearly and with enthusiasm must be applied with even greater care than at the main store, since his opportunities to supervise, observe, correct, and answer questions will be limited.

Branch employees pose a further problem. Often they are assigned to two or more departments, and are thus under the supervision of two or more buyers. When directions come to such employees from several executives—buyers, branch mana-ger, branch department manager—confusion has many chances to work its havoc. The buyer who has learned to communi-cate, to encourage questions and suggestions, is distinctly at an advantage in such a situation.

Vendor Relations. Good human relations are important to the buyer in his contacts with vendors, too. As a representative of his store, the buyer must do more than simply select mer-chandise. He must build confidence in his store, so that the best resources in the market will want to do business with it. No department or store, of course, can be better than its sources of supply. Its merchandise assortments, and thus its ability to fill the needs of its customers, depend upon the character of its resources.

The subject of vendor relations is dealt within greater detail in later chapters. At this point, it is sufficient to emphasize that *the resource is the store's,* not the buyer's personal contact. The relationship should be in line with company policy, as it has been spelled out to the buyer by his store's management.

Public Relations. Of course, the success of any retail store ultimately rests on the good will of the buying public. Since good public relations are important to the store, it is essential that every executive and every employee should be customer-

and service-minded. The buyer, as management's representative in his department, should set the pattern for the people working under him. Rank and file employees will be quick to follow his lead.

The Professional Viewpoint. Finally, the buyer who hopes to succeed should develop a professional viewpoint toward the management aspects of his job. This means keeping abreast of new techniques, new theories, new developments in management, as well as in merchandising. The department store organization today is a complex one, and it demands more of the buyer than simply knowing how to buy and sell; he must be a manager of people and himself, an ardent member of his store's management team.

CHAPTER 5

INTERPRETING CONSUMER DEMAND

BY

HERBERT L. SEEGAL

A retailer's basic objective is to satisfy the needs of those customers he expects to serve. A store, no matter how large, cannot be everything to everybody. A great store earns its reputation by knowing its customers, understanding thoroughly their merchandise wants, stocking the store to satisfy those wants, and providing the level of service these customers expect.

Every buyer, therefore, has an obligation to study and interpret consumer demand as it applies to his organization's aims and objectives in general and to his department's merchandise in particular. His success in this phase of his job enhances the company's prestige as well as his own department's volume and profit; his failure on this point is equally far-reaching in its effects. It is sometimes disastrous when a store, because of a change of buyer, changes the type of merchandise carried by a department without first determining whether or not this will be buying for the customer demand of the community and the store's established customer group within the community.

Eyes On The Customer. Ours is a customer-oriented economy. Its momentum is generated by the ever-expanding demand of customers for new and more goods and services. The rising purchasing power of customers keeps a steady demand for the new kinds of merchandise that pour off the production lines of industry.

The merchant's responsibility is not necessarily to understand *why* customers want certain types of merchandise. Such a study could involve him deeply in analyzing the complexities of human behavior. More to the point, the merchant should develop an attitude and strategy for interpreting what people want and how big that want is. Armed with such information, he can keep in the forefront of competition.

The true challenge and the real fascination of retailing is to trace and satisfy the shifting and expanding demands of customers. If these demands were static, buying and reordering would become relatively automatic. Demand is anything but static, and it is just as likely to be for types of merchandise *not yet available* as for articles that are in the store. The essence of skillful retailing is to establish techniques that will allow for shifts in demand and for recognition of new trends.

How People Live. Important in the study of customer demand is a study of how the store's customers live, and the ways in which they are being affected by the changing patterns of national and community life. In the past few decades, we have seen a marked increase in leisure time; an equally marked increase in the number of working wives; more travel; more home ownership; a vast migration to the suburbs, and now a return in some areas to city living.

We have seen teen-agers asserting the prerogative to spend their clothes money without parental supervision at progressively earlier ages. We have seen a great increase in the number of babies born per year, and a sharp climb in the longevity of the individual. These last two trends have given us a population with many young, many old, and a relatively small middle-aged group.

Other changes that have occurred within the past few decades, and which affect customer demand noticeably include the leveling out of income, with fewer very poor, with more in the comfortable middle class brackets; also the willingness of customers to serve themselves to a degree unheard of even a generation ago, and to dispense with many free services from stores. We have seen the car, the second home, the use of credit, and many other factors change the nature of customer demand.

Clues to Changing Trends. Recognizing the clues that signal the emergence of new demands and new trends is a vital part of the buyer's job. His sources of information are many. They begin with what he sees around him of how his customers live. They include the media of mass communication—consumer magazines and newspapers, and the broadcast media. They include trade publications, buying office reports of consumer reaction elsewhere, information from resources, a study of one's own competition, discussions with buyers of non-competing stores, discussions with other buyers in one's own store. Especially helpful are the men and women on the buyer's own staff: the salespeople who are in daily contact with customers, and their supervisors, in the main store or in its branches.

Particularly in using salespeople as an aid in analyzing consumer demand, the buyer should learn to encourage discussion at departmental meetings. Even if, for instance, he has some sound reason for not wanting to stock an item on which a salesperson has reported a request, he should encourage the salesperson to talk about it. There may just be some facet of consumer demand that the salesperson has seen and that the buyer has missed.

Similarly, the buyer should never be offended if a salesperson reports an adverse customer reaction to merchandise in stock. Learning from the people on the firing line about what is *not* acceptable is also a valuable way to appraise consumer demand.

Control Records. A primary source of information on what customers desire is, of course, the department's own experience as reflected in its sales and stock records. The theory and techniques of merchandise control are discussed in chapters of their own. Here, however, it should be emphasized that unit control records should be studied not only for the information they contain on the rates of sale of individual items, but also for *indications of trends.*

All of the thousands of categories of merchandise stocked by department stores are continuously undergoing some degree of change in demand. Skillful merchants organize their merchandising information systems so that items are grouped and their sales activity is summarized into classifications and sub-classifications. In this way, they minimize the chance of being misled by the few outstandingly strong or weak items. Instead, they study the sales of groups of homogeneous items in terms of ascending or declining trends.

In some categories of merchandise, shifts in demand are subtle and gradual and hardly recognizable without the aid of formal record-keeping systems. In the fashion-sensitive wearing apparel categories, changes are sharper and the demand is likely to be of shorter duration. Changes in fashion categories, moreover, are usually well publicized, and an informed merchant can usually tell when demand is reaching or passing its peak. Having the techniques and the knowledge to recognize a trend when it is in its infancy, or when it is about to tilt into a decline, is the mark of a good merchant. This ability is not achieved through a sixth sense; it grows out of a combination of facts, watchfulness, and trained judgment.

Launching the New. Manufacturers continue to produce new items, each designed to meet some real or imagined new customer need. The objective retailer does not pre-judge customer acceptance; he tests it by exposing the new items as candidates to his customers and then evaluating the voting record they achieve on the cash register.

It can happen that a buyer has confidence in an article, even though his customers are slow in accepting it. In such cases, he continues to stock it, but in small quantities. No one can hope to create a demand for what the public does not want, but the buyer who believes he has found a good thing can nurture the demand for it by giving it exposure until it has had the opportunity to prove itself.

Fast Sellers and Trends. A fast selling new item often heralds the emergence of a new category or classification—the spreading of demand that means a new trend. Alert merchants seek to find the common denominators of their fast sellers, and then stock in greater depth not only the items that have already demonstrated their appeal, but others that appear to have essential features in common with them.

The spread of customer demand is not necessarily limited to the category in which the fast selling new item first appeared. The feature that created the excitement in the first place may apply to other classifications and other types of merchandise. For example, the Teflon coating that has won acceptance in aluminum cookware may also be wanted in stainless steel. Or, a color that is popular in women's sportswear may spread to men's sportswear and even to articles for the home. An influence that is accepted in home furnishings, like the Oriental touch, may spread to women's at-home wear.

The key to understanding and acting upon these shifts in demand is for the buyer to think beyond the items themselves, to think in terms of classifications, categories, and ever broader groupings of merchandise. It also involves thinking beyond the merchandise alone and in terms of how the customer lives, in order to consider the possibility that a trend in favor of an item may be the foreshadowing of a trend in favor of a look, an idea, or a whole new way of life.

Customer Demand and Profit. There is more profit in selling the customer what she wants than in trying to push upon her what is less acceptable. Wanted items sell readily, whereas those that are not wanted can usually be sold, if at all, only on a price basis and at the risk of damaging the store's future chances of selling to that customer.

When an individual department achieves an outstanding sales and profit showing, the chances are that its merchandise is very much in line with consumer demand. Such departments have hit the right note in quality and price, and their merchandising should be carefully studied, so that their character, their appeals, and their price ranges can be adapted to the buyer's own department as far as possible.

Price Ranges. Price levels should be such as to meet the economic demand of the customers sought by the store. To know what prices are in line with consumer demand, the buyer should know the normal buying habits of his customers, and in what direction they are most ready to make adjustments when economic conditions, either at home or in the markets, bring about a change.

Asking the Customer. Up to this point, we have discussed the kinds of evidence the customer provides by her purchases or failure to purchase. She also gives us some indication of her preferences when she is questioned directly about them. Research experts have developed ever sharper techniques for getting a picture of consumer demand by this means.

A typical procedure is to station interviewers at the entrance to an important department, there to ask customers what they want by way of style, color, fabric, etc. Another method is to ask the departing customer if she has been able to buy the article she came in for; if so, what she bought; if not, what she had hoped to find. Still another procedure is to go to the customer in her home, either in person or by mail, and ask what she has bought or intends to buy. This last approach is quite common among consumer magazines, as a means of measuring the size and nature of the market represented by their subscribers.

The customer, however, is not always the best and least fallible witness to her own preferences. Her answers to questions are bound to be colored by what she knows or does not yet know about merchandise available. She may give an offhand answer, or give an opinion on merchandise she really has no definite plan to buy.

To the buyer, however, any survey that offers a glimpse of the way his customer's mind works is valuable. With modern research techniques, consumer surveys turn up increasingly dependable results. The buyer should familiarize himself with as many studies of consumer plans and preferences as he can. He should weigh each in the light of who made it, how it was made, and whether or not the questions were such as to yield useful data.

The results of such surveys should not be taken without qualification as directives to guide a department's buying. They become part of the mass of evidence a buyer accumulates on consumer demand before he makes his final decision as to the items he will offer his store's customer.

Meeting Customer Demand. In meeting customer demand, the buyer must assume the responsibility for offering his customer the best version of the wanted item at the price the customer is willing and able to pay. He should then present the merchandise intelligently, through displays, signs, open fixtures, and especially through well-informed salespeople. He must provide facts, both to salespeople and customers, to permit intelligent choice. Finally, the buyer and his store must assume leadership in consumer education. An informed customer demands merchandise will best meet her needs—the kind of merchandise that a good merchant most wants to sell.

CHAPTER 6

THE TECHNIQUE OF BUYING

BY

FRANCIS A. COY

As purchasing agent for his community, the buyer fills a dual role. He is both buyer and seller. He is, in fact, even more: student of the consumer, promoter, analyst of merchandise trends, and many other things. In every phase of his job but one—the crucial one of looking at a line and making his selections—he is part of a team. He has experts upon whom he can call, and senior executives to oversee his work, suggest improvements, and correct his errors before they become costly.

When he does the actual buying he is on his own. If he uses his time unwisely, if he comes to market poorly prepared, if he fumbles the ball, both sales and profits will suffer. It is important, therefore, that he should acquire methods and techniques that will safeguard him against error and that will help him to use his buying time with the greatest possible productivity. Such methods and techniques are the concern of this chapter.

Preparation for Buying. The first step in preparing to buy any merchandise is to see what can be learned about it from the store's own experience with the same or similar goods. This first step sounds almost too elementary to be mentioned, yet it is a fact that many buyers fail right at this point.

It is hard and unglamourous work to get down to facts. There is nothing romantic about stock records, or comparison reports, or cold figures. *But these are the working tools of our profession,* and we must use them to our best advantage.

In preparing to buy, it is not enough to know how much was purchased last month or last year. It is far more vital to know what happened after the merchandise was purchased. How much of it was sold in a given period? At the original price? At markdowns? How much was carried over? How much is now on hand? How much more could we have sold if we had planned differently? Were there any extraneous factors that favored or worked against the merchandise last year?

Only after these facts have been collected and studied is the buyer ready for his next step, which is to weigh the potential of the merchandise, consider its market value, judge its competitive position, and decide whether to give it more or less emphasis than in the past.

Planning for Multi-Store Operation. One of the most common mistakes made by buyers of multi-store operations today is their failure to plan separately for each branch store's needs. Whereas a downtown store may have a customer mix that demands of it to be many things to many people, branch store customers have more in common.

The spread in income in local areas is less, community and social activities within local areas cause people's desires to be similar. A strong price line in one store may be weak in another. One area may be more casual-minded than another. It is important then that a buyer make separate plans for each store.

In doing so, a buyer should never overlook the information that can be gained in discussing plans with the branch store supervisor. This is the buyer's line of communication between the customer and himself in his branch store market.

Buying Plan Forms. There are many different types of buying plan forms, but the one illustrated in Figure 3 is typical. In addition to showing details of the purchases planned on the market trip, it is important to show the current condition of the open-to-buy by months for which purchases are to be made. The information about the quantities on hand and on order should be filled in, as well as the detailed information about the proposed purchases for each month by classifications and price lines.

The proposed purchases should be carefully summarized by months of delivery, by classifications, and by price lines before the plans are submitted to the Merchandise Office. This is *the only way* to insure well-balanced purchases, essential to well-balanced stocks. Careless buying will result in unbalanced stocks, which are certain to result in lost sales and profits.

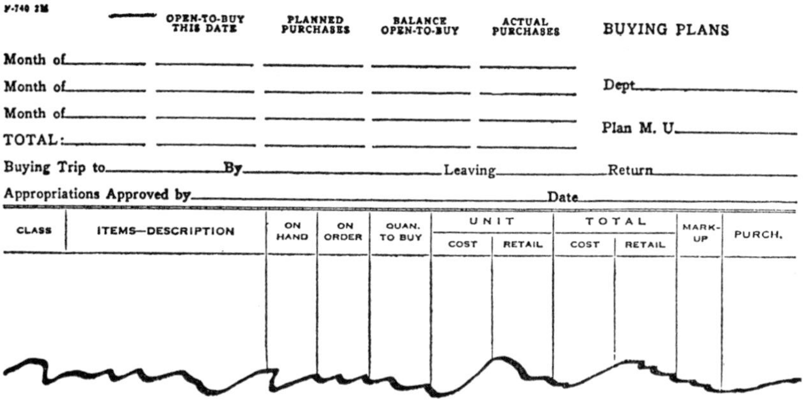

F-740 2M

BUYING PLANS

	OPEN-TO-BUY THIS DATE	PLANNED PURCHASES	BALANCE OPEN-TO-BUY	ACTUAL PURCHASES
Month of				
Month of				
Month of				
TOTAL:				

Dept.

Plan M. U.

Buying Trip to By Leaving Return

Appropriations Approved by Date

CLASS	ITEMS—DESCRIPTION	ON HAND	ON ORDER	QUAN. TO BUY	UNIT		TOTAL		MARK-UP	PURCH.
					COST	RETAIL	COST	RETAIL		

Figure 3. Buying Plan Forms

Programmed Merchandising. Some of the plans made for a department and its buying are beyond the scope of what the buyer alone can undertake. Many stores today, for example, do what is known as programmed merchandising. The store's top management executives join the buyer to develop with a key resource a plan for vastly increasing the amount of business done with that line. This may cover a special event or several events in the course of a season, or even a year. It will include every form of promotional effort—all set down in advance and timed.

In a situation of this kind, when the buyer has management on his team, ready to make commitments for him on advertising, selling space, windows, etc., his department can usually obtain maximum cooperation from the resource on all fronts.

This procedure is good for the store, the vendor, the department—and the buyer. The close relationship that develops between store and vendor creates an excellent climate in which to operate and affords the buyer a greater opportunity to turn in strong volume and profit figures. His prestige with the vendor is enhanced by the attention management gives to his department; his prestige with the store is enhanced by the results of the plan.

Where To Buy. The buyer's decision to buy at home or in the market depends a good deal upon expediency. There are definite advantages to both. In the store, the buyer has his records at his elbow and his salespeople nearby; his superiors can be consulted readily if the occasion should arise. In the market, the buyer can see the resource's complete line. He has an opportunity to meet the sales manager or president of the vendor's firm, and to learn more about the company's plans and programs than a traveling salesman may be able to tell him.

The extent to which the buyer does his buying in the store or in the market depends, naturally, upon how much time he has available for market trips and how far his store is from the major centers. But whether he does 90 per cent of his buying in the market or 90 per cent in the store, he should not turn away visiting salesmen merely because his own market trip is in prospect soon. Nor should he overlook local trade showings in his area.

One of the buyer's major responsibilities is to be informed at all times about all lines of merchandise that he may be able to use. Occasionally, the very information he plans to scour the market for may come to his doorstep by way of the traveling salesman or the regional show. And the line he declines to see at the store may just possibly contain a good new item that some other retailer in the area will buy and promote eagerly.

Buying in the Market. The average market trip lasts three to five days, except at the beginning of a season. So much work is crowded into those few days that intensive preparation is essential. A trip to market is no lark.

Preparation for a regular trip to the market should start at least one week in advance. However, the finishing touches on the buying plans may not be completed until two or three days before departure. The buying plans themselves should be completed long enough in advance for the buyer to summarize the planned purchases by classifications and price lines, and to have the plans examined and approved by the merchandise office.

The buying plan then should be used as a guide, not as a rigid governor. It is drawn up, after all, before the buyer leaves home, and it is quite possible that conditions affecting the store's buying may not come to light until the buyer is actually in the market. In such cases, the buyer should discuss the indicated changes with his merchandise manager. The plan is not intended to stifle initiative; it is meant to help, not hamper.

Working in the Market. If a store belongs to a buying office group, the buyer should use the services of that office to the fullest possible extent. (A separate chapter discusses the buying office and how it fulfills its functions.) The management of a store expects buyers to use their own judgment, but it also expects them *to get all the advice and information they can,* so that their judgment will be that much surer.

Also part of the market visit agenda for the buyer should be a tour of stores in that area, particularly those that are doing an outstanding job in the buyer's own merchandise. These store visits should be made on the first or second day of the market trip, to provide part of the background for the actual buying that is to be done. Opportunities to discuss markets, merchandise, and methods with outstanding buyers from other stores should be exploited fully.

Technique in the Sample Room. Under the heading of the technique of buying should be considered what goes on in the sample room. Most salesmen are trained to control the interview. Few buyers have been trained in this respect and so are at a disadvantage in the presence of the "master salesman." Under such circumstances, much merchandise is "sold" but little of it is "bought."

This is not as theoretical as it may seem. In every personal contact between two or more persons, regardless of occupation or position, there is a leader and a follower; one who directs the interview, and one who follows along. By controlling the interview, the buyer may have the merchandise presented in a manner suited to his own method of working.

No two salesmen present merchandise in the same manner. If the buyer tries to follow the method of presentation of all different types of salesmen, he will find himself very much confused. But if he knows what he is looking for and how he wants to go through the line, he can direct the presentation according to his own method of working.

Information From Resource. The wise buyer draws as much information from the salesman as possible, without being unduly influenced by what is said. Good salesmen pick up many worthwhile ideas as they visit various stores, and the clever buyer draws on this information to his own advantage. Statements about quantities purchased by other stores should always be taken with a large grain of salt; but the information does give the buyer the starting point for getting more information from those stores, if he wants it.

Buyers should resist the temptation to look "big" in the market by placing unduly large orders at the start of a season or on untried items. The satisfaction felt in the showroom when the order is placed cannot compensate for the distress felt later in the season when an overstock develops. The wiser course is to buy neither more nor less than the buyer honestly feels he wants. If he feels he should sample and possibly re-order later, he should not let himself be pushed into an unwisely large opening purchase.

Before Looking at Samples. Before viewing a line the buyer should take up each major classification in turn; and within each, start with the highest price lines and work down to the lowest.

One reason for starting at the top is that new and acceptable colors or details often make their first appearance in better goods. Some reflection of these desirable features should be in the lower priced merchandise, too. Vendor A may have such reflections all through his line, in which case the buyer's problem is simple. But if the lower end of the line fails to have the touches the buyer seeks, then he can buy only his better goods from Vendor A, and go to Vendors B, C, D—and maybe Z—until he finds what he wants.

Organized Selection. As the buyer goes through the line, the merchandise will probably appeal to him in one of three ways. He can divide the items into three groups.

1. "Sure-fire"

2. Doubtful

3. Undesirable or "duds"

As each classification is finished the "sure-fire" items and the "doubtful" should be put to one side for further consideration after the whole line has been seen. Obviously, the "duds", if they still appear to be "duds" should be eliminated entirely. After the preliminary selection has been completed, the buyer should go back over the items set aside for further consideration, drawing from the "doubtful" group to round out the "sure-fire" items. In some instances, where the number of "sure-fire" items seems top-heavy, the least desirable in this group may be eliminated. But by careful consideration of these two groups together, the buyer should be able to arrive at a very satisfactory selection.

After the line has been gone through in this manner, the buyer is ready to assemble his selection so that he may see how the various styles, designs and colors *balance within each classification and price line.* This process of viewing the selection as a whole is very important, and one that is commonly neglected.

Good Taste in Selection. It is not enough to organize the selection, each buyer must exercise good taste in making the selection. Good taste has been defined as "the ability to discern that which is beautiful and appropriate for the occasion." Everyone should cultivate a sense of what is beautiful, not merely to himself as an individual, but in the sense that the object conforms to the principles of art and appeals *in the long term,* to the great majority of people.

Art gives a wide latitude to originality in creating new and unique articles. Let it be violated and the object becomes grotesque and merely something different. The buyer who is aware of what to look for in the objects he buys will be quick to discern those which are beautiful and distinguish them from the grotesque, which so frequently masquerade under the name of "new".

Buyers often buy things which they say they do not like in order to be sure to have a wide enough range of colors and designs to satisfy everyone. Of course, it would be very foolish for buyers to buy only the things they like for their own use, but it is always a mistake to buy objects which are inherently ugly.

The definition of good taste also means that whatever is selected should be appropriate for the occasion for which it is intended. This may require reading and a certain amount of social contact on the part of the buyer in order to know exactly what is appropriate. The buyer of evening wear accessories cannot hope to buy correctly such items without knowing definitely what is considered appropriate by well dressed people who attend functions requiring evening clothes.

It should also be kept in mind that what is appropriate sometimes changes quickly. Buyers cannot judge what is appropriate today by the standards of yesterday.

Writing the Order. No mention has been made up to this point about writing the order. We have been discussing the selection of merchandise. Now let us turn our attention to the placing of the order.

The merchandise within each classification and price line has now been arranged in order of desirability, with the most desirable first. Then if the numbers are put down in this order, it is obvious that the most desirable numbers will always appear first on the order and the least desirable last. Later, if the buyer desires to make any change, he knows that he should increase the quantities on the first numbers and cut down on those at the end. If it is desired to cut the quantity, the end numbers may be eliminated entirely.

Using Store Order Blanks. The buyer should write his own order in his own order book. This is the only record of a transaction which may involve the store in an obligation for hundreds or thousands of dollars, and as such it must be capable of correct interpretation at any time. If the order is made out by the salesman, as frequently happens, it contains just enough information to satisfy his own firm, but definitely not what the store requires.

In the first place, it must be written so that the receiving and marking clerks in the store can readily identify the merchandise when the invoice and the goods are received. In the second place, it should be so written that it may be used in merchandise control, also summarized by classification and price line if required.

The description space on the order blank should be used for the purpose for which it was intended: i.e., to describe the merchandise in an intelligent manner; the name of the article, such as gloves, shirts, hose, dresses, or whatever it is, should be set down with one or two adjectives to describe the material and design. When colors and sizes are required, they should be given in detail in the columns usually provided for them. If there are any special features about the merchandise that may be used in training the salespeople or for publicity, these features should be written up on the order blank so that they are not forgotten or lost. If photos of the merchandise are available, the buyer should attach these to his copy.

Indicating Prices. The retail price should be placed on the store copy of the order. This helps in checking and serves as a guide in marking the merchandise when it is received, as well as enabling anyone to summarize the order by price lines.

It has been mentioned a number of times that the merchandise should be grouped by price lines. This means retail price lines in all such cases. The buyer knows in advance how much he can afford to pay for each of his regular price lines. Upper and lower limits for each retail price line are predetermined, and if the wholesale price does not fall within these limits he must either break his price line, take a lower markup, or eliminate the item entirely. Usually there is so much merchandise to be bought at the regular price lines that the buyer does not need to worry about passing up merchandise which would fall between his regular prices.

If he is buying specials for a promotion, he may want such "in-between" merchandise, but he should not buy it inadvertently through failing to check his price lines when ordering.

Indicating Markon. The buyer may not wish to calculate the initial markon on each item, but he should not fail to do so for the order as a whole. If this is not done cumulatively and the buyer does not keep track of his markon, there is likelihood of his falling short of the planned figure. The buyer can make correction either on subsequent purchases or go over those he has made and make the necessary upward adjustments.

Seasonal Orders. In placing orders for advance delivery it is wise to hold all orders until all lines have been seen. Each order should be written up, as already indicated, and summarized by classification and price line, but it should be held until all orders are summarized. The reason is obvious. You may wish to make changes after surveying the whole.

Make Summary. When all the seasonal lines have been seen for a season, a master summary of all the orders should be made, so that the stock as a whole may be balanced. This summary should show the quantity and total cost of each type of merchandise, each price line, and each color or design.

The same procedure should be followed in ordering any merchandise where there is a large number of items involved or where the investment is considerable. Learning how to summarize is perhaps one of the most valuable arts a buyer can acquire.

Care in Reordering. Reordering, too, has its techniques. If done without thought, shipping charges can take so large a bite out of markon, that profit will be greatly reduced. Therefore, especially in dealing with staples, it is important to consider the quantity, frequency, and the most economical method of transportation. Never put through a small order to a resource without first checking to see if anything else is needed from that resource, or is likely to be needed within the next few days. Consolidating small reorders and special orders saves clerical time for both store and resource, often means lower transportation costs per item, and also conserves the buyer's own time.

Remember, please, the importance of *preparedness to buy*— the necessity for having the facts about the sales and stocks in the departments before buying. Remember also that any plan is only as good as it works. After the buyer once gets the habit of making his plan on the basis of facts and summarizing his orders to see that they actually fit into his plan, he will have developed the technique of buying.

CHAPTER 7

HOW TO WORK WITH RESOURCES

BY

CHARLES G. TAYLOR

Every keen and far-sighted merchant readily agrees that profitable business over the long term can be achieved only when his suppliers and he have a feeling of mutual respect and confidence for each other and a full appreciation of the contribution made by each. He realizes that his success or failure depends upon his ability not only to choose merchandise his customers will buy but also to select profitable sources of supply. Both of these jobs are difficult. It is the purpose of this chapter to focus attention on the latter and highlight certain standards of vendor relationship which, if established, can be used in attracting and sensibly rating suppliers.

Large sums of money are spent annually on market research. Manufacturers, wholesalers, and importers are searching for outlets; retailers are searching for suppliers. Each seeks to locate, attract, select and retain the *tops* in outlet or supplier, as the case may be. Each rates the other, or should, according to its special requirements and performances. In the final analysis the relationship between supplier and outlet must be profitable to both, if it is to stand the test of time.

Problem of Satisfactory Relations. The problem of establishing and maintaining satisfactory relations between buyer and seller is of long standing. During periods of great demand retailers clamor for goods, and during periods of small demand vendors clamor for buyers. Especially during extreme periods, ethics are apt to be cynically flouted and contracts ignored. Strained relations are not uncommon even during normal times and consequently business is adversely affected.

No retail business has as yet been singled out because it had a vendor relations policy that was perfect at all times. Even more difficult to find would be a retail establishment whose personnel always would correctly interpret and apply a policy established by top management. Nevertheless, it is strongly recommended that every store put in writing its code of vendor principles and regularly publicize it to its personnel and suppliers. Each store should have its own set of principles, tailor-made to fit its own needs.

Establishing Good Vendor Relationships. The following are basic fundamentals extremely valuable in cementing good vendor relationships:

1. Establish key resources for every line of merchandise, classification and price line. Assign to each resource a definite role to play in your merchandising program, and demand that each play the role well. Limit the number of resources so that those selected will receive maximum business. Be certain that the particular resource you choose is the best available for the specified purpose. The fewer the resources, the simpler the buying, the greater the profits. Make every buying plan a resource plan.

2. Continue to purchase from resources as long as they produce profits for you, and abide by arrangements mutually agreed upon. Should their performance prove unsatisfactory, review the cause disturbing the relationship. If the product has deteriorated, advise and encourage the supplier to improve it. He will appreciate constructive criticism, and especially your loyalty. If there are other differences, make a sincere effort to settle them. If the decision to discontinue purchasing from a key resource has to be made, inform him the basis for such action and in ample time to permit him to obtain another outlet.

3. Top management, divisional merchandise managers, as well as buyers, should know personally someone of top management of every key supplier.

4. Maintain an open-door policy at all times for all re-

sources. The small supplier is entitled to the same courteous attention as his larger competitor. Provide adequate sample rooms and reception facilities for the convenience of vendors' representatives. Encourage salesmen to visit your store first. You are likely to get many "firsts" in merchandise. Retain the goodwill of all vendors and their salesmen even if you don't buy from them. They are potential customers and future suppliers.

5. Vendors offer merchandise first to those from whom they can obtain quick action. Learn to give a "Yes" or "No" answer quickly.

6. Good buying is based on a thorough knowledge of merchandise and value. Intelligent trading by buyers should be encouraged but sharp practices prohibited, such as:

    a. Copying of merchandise.

    b. Cancellation of orders before delivery is due.

    c. Taking of discounts and anticipation of bills in excess of that agreed upon.

    d. Reversing charges of telephone calls and sending telegrams collect.

    e. Charging excessively on cooperative advertising.

7. Promptly confirm in writing all commitments with vendors. All details, specifications and conditions of purchase should be clearly stated on the order.

8. Buyers and merchandisers should be good ambassadors in the wholesale markets as well as good buyers. They should make only such agreements and promises to vendors which can and will faithfully be kept, appointments not excluded.

9. Whenever possible promote to buying and merchandising positions from within the organization. This helps continuance of business with key resources. When new buyers are appointed, key resource arrangements should be reviewed thoroughly so there will be no misunderstanding later. A meeting between the new buyer and principal suppliers should be arranged.

10. If any buyer believes he has a better resource than the established key supplier of a given line, he should carefully review all facts with his superior before a change is made.

11. Respect the confidence of vendors.

12. Discourage memorandum purchasing.

13. Maintain a strict control over returns to resources. Do not permit unjust returns. All returns should be made promptly and properly packed.

14. Have all controversial subjects between vendors and store referred to executives who are skilled in handling them. Accounts payable, advertising and traffic departments occasionally create poor vendor relationships. They need censoring at times.

15. Maintain a list of vendors from whom you would like to buy, who currently are not selling you. Visit them regularly. Invite top management of these vendors to visit your store.

16. Never forget that suppliers rate their outlets, too. Fair, sincere, courteous treatment accorded them will result in material benefits to your business.

17. There must exist a sincere conviction that a continuously successful business relationship must be mutually profitable to vendor as well as retailers.

Rating Resources. There are several practical methods for rating the performance of resources to establish the relative importance of each one to the store.

1. An analysis of the customers' preference for the resource's merchandise as revealed in:

  a. Buyer's Fast Selling Book (Figure 4). This system is generally used in men's, women's and children's apparel and accessory departments. It can be employed effectively throughout the store with few departments excepted. It rates not only supplier, but item, style, color, pattern, and even size. If the store uses electronic data processing, such information comes to the buyer in report form at regular intervals. If EDP is not available,

NAME John Doe Hat Co. ADDRESS New York TERMS 7/10 EOM MFR'S NO. 102

	ORD. (BLK.) CANC. (RED) DATE	ORD. (BLK.) CANC. (RED) QUAN.	REC. (BLK.) RETD. (RED) DATE	REC. (BLK.) RETD. (RED) QUAN.	1	2	3	4	5	6	7	8	9	10	11	12	13	14	15	16	17	18	19	20	21	22	23	24	25	26	27	28	29	30	31
F184A J 4					3	3	3	3	3		3	3	3	3.	4	4		4	4	4	4	4	4		4	4	4	4	4	4					
STYLE 341			00		22	23	24 60	25	26		27	29	30	31 84	1	2		3	5	6	7 48	8	9		10	12 48	13	14	15	16					
COST $28.50			R		60						60							84							48		48								
RET. 3.95			S		6	7	15	5	6	*39	24	5	6	19	7	8	*69	29	6	5	13	7	5	*65	27	5	4	10	7	6	*59				
STYLE			OH		54	47	32	27	21	*21	57	52	46	27	20	12	*12	67	61	56	43	36	31	*31	52	47	43	81	74	68	*68				
COST																																			
RET.	Black		(24)		4	2	8	5	3		(24) 10	2	2	8	3	1		(36) 10	4	4	7	5	4		(24) 12	4	3	(12) 6	4	3					
STYLE	Navy		(18)		1	2	6		1		(12) 5	1	2	1	3	2		(18) 5	1			2	1		(12) 9			(12) 2	1	2					
COST	White		(6)			1	1		1		(6) 2			3	1	2		(12) 3			1				(6) 1			(6)							
RET.	Toast		(6)		1	1			1		(6) 3		1	1		2		(3) 2			2				1										
STYLE	Mauve		(6)			1					1		1			1		2							1			(12) 2	1	1					
COST	Brown										(6)	2		3				(12) 4	1	1	3				(6) 3	1									
RET.	Gray										(3) 2			1				(3) 3										(6)	1						
STYLE	Green										(3) 1			2																					
COST																																			
RET.																																			
STYLE																																			
COST																																			
RET.																																			

OO = On Order
R = Received
S = Sold
OH = On Hand

Circled figures show color quantities received.
*Red figures are Totals sold and on hand end of week.

Figure 4. Buyer's Fast Selling Book

then double-stub price tickets and sales checks make it possible to record activity daily, for daily, weekly, monthly, and yearly analysis.

b. Staple stock control records used to determine selling rate and stock-sales ratios. Generally preferred where stub price tickets not practicable, or where weekly or less frequent analyses prove satisfactory.

c. Regular, frequent physical examination of stock.

d. Want slips, comments of salespeople and customers.

2. The contribution of each supplier may be periodically evaluated on the basis of the following factors:

a. Confinement or non-confinement of merchandise.

b. Purchase markup. (Information taken from invoice register.)

c. Markdowns. (Record and total markdowns, by vendors.)

d. Alteration, repair, refinishing cost analysis, by vendors.

e. Customer credits, complaints and adjustments. (Bureau of Adjustments.)

f. Speed and dependability of delivery of goods. Adherence to specifications on order.

g. Cooperative advertising, demonstrators, pre-packaging.

h. Other special services.

Without complete knowledge of such factors as enumerated above, an accurate rating of resources is not possible. Illustration: One supplier's goods may show a higher markup than others but due to f.o.b. shipping points, greater markdowns, adjustments, alterations, etc., the gross profit is less favorable. The cost of advertising, selling, delivery and packaging on one supplier's merchandise may be less, due to cooperative advertising, demonstrators, pre-packaging.

The Vendor's Diary. The Vendor's Diary (Figure 5) is one of the most important instruments of periodically rating resources. It is both a past and up-to-date record of experiences. It is kept by the buyer and used by him and his superiors. It is particularly useful information to the newly appointed buyer. He is promptly and accurately posted on the background of all suppliers and enabled to give each firm the consideration to which it is entitled. Divisional merchandise manager and buyer are to examine semi-annually each vendor's records with the objective of developing with him as large and profitable a business as possible. Fullest cooperation should be extended to those vendors with best performances. Vendors with records not up to *par* should be investigated and corrective measures undertaken. Unprofitable resources should be eliminated.

Develop Key Resources. A principal or key resource list should be developed for each department. Vendors who have been regular suppliers should be on this list. For new merchandise classifications or departments, names of outstanding resources may be obtained from other buyers, cooperating stores, and resident buying offices.

Copies of principal resource lists should be kept in offices of (1) general merchandise manager, (2) divisional merchandise manager, (3) accounts payable, (4) buyer. Two easy-to-maintain forms for listing and rating of principal resources are illustrated—(Figures 6 and 7).

Stores find it advantageous to divide resources into five classes:

> *Class A*: Volume, prestige and profitable resources most important to store. These are the store's *partners* and deserve maximum consideration.

> *Class B*: Resources less important than Class "A" who produce satisfactory profits for the store.

RESOURCE DIARY

Dept. No.

Date

Resource

Merchandise   Top Grade____Medium____Low-end____

Activity (Mfr., Jobber, Importer, etc.)

Sales Office Address

Factory or Warehouse Address

Company Officers and Titles

Buyer Contacts—State peculiarities or special handling required by

    a. Sales Office

    b. Factory

Rating—Dun & Bradstreet

Ethics of Firm

Ranking in Industry

Vendor Importance to Store

Store Importance to Vendor

Record of All Arrangements (Terms, Trade Discounts, Cash Discounts, Cooperative Advertising, etc.)

Remarks (State clearly any additional information not covered above that will guide any member of our organization who may have to deal with this vendor.)

Semi-Annual Review

Date   By Whom

NOTE: It is recommended that this Resource Diary be kept in loose leaf form.

Figure 5. Vendor's Diary

PRINCIPAL RESOURCE LIST

Dept. _____

Resource - Key Contact	General Comment	Season	19 -	19 -
Design For Living M. E. Andrews, Pres.	Top quality maker - exclusive with us - nationally adv. - most cooperative - better than average markup - low markdowns Class A Terms 2/10/60X	Spring	37,007	81,116
		Fall	24,119	59,412
Hobbies - Antiques and Stamps		Total	61,126	140,528
Modern Age John Jackson, Sales Mgr.	Excellent novelty house - alert to new ideas - also sells Store A - very reliable and profitable - repairs at minimum	Spring	16,981	44,051
		Fall	19,128	38,946
Hobby - Fishing		Total	36,109	82,997

$ COST PURCHASES

Year	Dept.	Approved	Date
19 -	343,017		2/17/-
19 -	604,359		2/24/-
19 -			
19 -			

$ COST PURCHASES

Year	Dept.	Approved	Date
19 -			
19 -			
19 -			
19 -			

Figure 6. Principal Resource List

PRINCIPAL RESOURCE LIST

Left Page

No.	Manufacturer	Contact	Address	Comments

ANNUAL PURCHASES   MONTH, SEASON OR YEAR_____

Compare purchases from each supplier with total purchases of department shown on this line ---

These two sheets' which comprise Exhibit 4 are to be inserted in a loose leaf notebook opposite each other so that the right page, forms a continuation of the left. On this form is recorded the total amount purchased monthly, semi-annually or annually from each resource. The column headed "Rank" is used to indicate the #1, #2, #3, etc., resources according to their volume importance each year.

Right Page

Terms & Dating	Shipping Terms	Rank	19 -	Rank	-	Rank	19 -	Rank	19 -	Rank	19 -

DEPT._____

Amount Purchased

Figure 7. Principal Resource List

Class C: Resources whose profit record needs watching.

Class D: Resources from whom you would like to buy who currently are not selling you.

Class E: Resources with whom store has had unsatisfactory experience. Buyers are asked not to purchase from *these* manufacturers until top management approves.

Top management frequently maintains direct contact with suppliers who are on special resource lists such as:

1. One hundred key vendors most important to store because of volume of purchases.
2. Fifty prestige resources most important to store.
3. Outstanding suppliers confining merchandise to store.

Program Merchandising. With resources of such importance as these, it is possible to work out *program merchandising*. This means that the buyer, with the help of his management, estimates what his department will need by way of inventory, delivery service, promotion, and other elements, in order to increase its sales of a particular resource's merchandise by a specified amount. The possibilities are then discussed with the resource, to make sure that the necessary cooperation will be available. When each side understands the other's goals and knows what help is expected from him, substantial improvements in sales and profits can be achieved.

Margin of Advantage. Intensive competition demands exactness, experience and judgment, not only in the selection of merchandise but in resources as well. Often the margin of advantage over a competitive store is very slight—just the difference that *care in selection and support of suppliers* will make.

Good business depends on good business relationships and outstanding merchants and manufacturers know that good business relationships depend on complete and full understanding of each other's problems, possibilities and responsibilities.

CHAPTER 8

SOUND BUYING PRACTICES

BY

DAVID E. MOESER

When a buyer goes into the market, he is entrusted by his store with more than just the money for the purchases he is about to make. He is entrusted with the store's good name. Stores that have adhered to ethical buying practices enjoy respect and prestige among vendors far in excess of what would be accorded to them on the basis of volume alone. A good reputation in the market is as priceless a jewel as a good reputation among one's customers.

The buyer, who is often the only representative of his house with whom the resource has contact, has a special responsibility to protect the integrity of that house. He should recognize the ultimate advantage to his store, to himself, and to the consumer in pursuing only those practices which are based on a spirit of fair play and honesty. These are outlined in trade agreements referred to on page 86. Merchandise men and buyers should have copies and should know them. Such practices not only increase the esteem in which the house is held in the market, but they also avoid costly and wasteful controversies.

Extent of Trade Abuses. For all that, unfortunately, some buyers and sellers indulge in unfair practices with no apparent reckoning of the cost which they, as well as the consumer, must pay eventually. These unethical practices, or trade abuses as they are commonly called, have been considered so serious as to warrant the attention, not only of progressive trade associations such as the National Retail Merchants Association but also of the Chamber of Commerce of the United States, the

Federal Trade Commission and other similar bodies concerned with the promotion of the best interests of industry.

Some years ago a detailed survey of this subject was undertaken through a committee of the National Distribution Conference.

This committee stated:

"The extent of unethical trade practices in any industry is very difficult to estimate. Very few attempts to figure the cost and number of such practices have ever been made. This survey shows that they are of great variety and are indulged in sufficiently frequently to constitute a rather serious indictment and that they impose an important economic burden on American business and on the consuming public."

Importance of Eliminating Abuses. It may be imagined how beneficial the effect upon business would be if the time and money spent by parties in attempting to secure unfair advantages against one another were devoted to cooperative effort to improve trade relations, each element in industry recognizing that it can best further its own prosperity by helping to build the prosperity of the business with which it deals. A state of hostility may bring temporary advantage to one side or another, but individual gains are equalized in the course of time and all industry finally bears the burden of strife.

It has been said that we suffer from the fact that relations between buyer and seller, instead of being a firm, solid and level bridge across which merchandise can flow steadily, are in truth a sort of see-saw, with the buyer at one end and the seller at the other. When the buyer's weight pulls his end down the advantage slides to him, and vice versa.

On this same subject, we have the opinion of the late Mr. Lincoln Filene, as expressed in an address before the International Chamber of Commerce, Fourth Congress, at Stockholm:

"In all business dealing, there is a certain amount of distrust between manufacturers as a class and distributors as a class. . . . The existence of distrust between buyer and seller makes more difficult and costly the exchange of goods. Suspicion between producers and distributors arises because there exists what are known as trade abuses; that is, attempts by either a producer or a distributor to take an unfair advantage of the other.

"In every trade, one will always find a minority of business men whose business practices are regarded by the concerns with which they deal as uneconomic and unfair. . . . Unfair actions in business are essentially wasteful. They impose conditions which hinder the buyer or seller from the most economical operation of his affairs. Not only do they increase the cost of doing business, but by keeping alive suspicion between distributors and producers, they become a barrier which interferes with the easy and profitable interchange of goods."

Causes of Trade Abuses. As pointed out by the National Distribution Conference, and as substantiated by many subsequent studies, there are a great many causes of trade abuses, some originating with the buyer and others with the seller. Many of these trade abuses arise from honest misunderstanding between producers and distributors. Others are inherited from a business era which was less alive than the present one to the economic as well as the moral disadvantages of "sharp practice"; and still others are the results of attempts on the part of unscrupulous business men to secure an unfair advantage in the market at the expense of those with whom they deal.

More specific causes of these abuses are:

1. Rapid fluctuations in price or supply, resulting in speculative buying, unjust cancellations and attempts to evade contractual obligations.

2. Lack of sound business methods in purchasing and selling.

3. Sub-standard business practices and sub-standard products.

4. Discrimination based upon superior bargaining power of large organizations and groups, and

other discriminatory practices not legally or economically justifiable. The Robinson-Patman Act makes it illegal in interstate commerce to grant or demand concessions not available to all buyers on proportionately equal terms.

5. Retaliation for past injuries in an attempt to "get back" at the other fellow when market conditions are to his disadvantage.

6. Excessive demands for service, such as unjust price concessions, over-generous allowance on returned goods and abnormal credit extensions not warranted by the character of the order and contrary to sound business practice.

Effects of Trade Abuses. The effects of trade abuses are far-reaching and the cost enormous, not only in actual money but in lost time, lost energy and loss through disrupted relations. The innocent as well as the guilty suffer through unethical practices. The manufacturer must usually take a loss when reselling goods that have been returned or cancelled. The retailer who has been oversold under pressure must resort to markdowns which cut into his profits and weaken his future buying power. Delayed deliveries are a loss to the retailer by the amount of trade which his competitor may take from him. The customer pays for unethical practices in such things as substituted merchandise and wrong sizes.

Any gain which the customer reaps from the mistakes or the abuses of retailers or manufacturers is temporary or illusory, since in the final analysis the burden of these unfair trade practices and trade abuses must be borne by the consumer.

Every dispute resulting from an unethical practice means waste. Even when an attempted unethical act is finally prevented, the cost in arranging for a settlement is considerable. A market in which manufacturers, wholesalers and retailers attempt to outwit each other is an unhealthy one from the consumer's point of view, and the energy which should be devoted to constructive work, such as lessening the cost of distribution and production, is foolishly spent in destructive activities.

The Buyer's Responsibility. From the foregoing it will be seen that the buyer who would serve his house well will consider carefully the methods which he pursues in dealing with his resources. He will protect his house from the effects of mistakes of his own which may result from carelessness or disregard of lawful practices, as well as from possible deliberate abuses on the part of the seller, and will thereby establish a reputation for integrity and sound business dealing.

The Order as a Contract. It is understood, of course, that an order constitutes a contract which both parties are expected to honor. For this reason a buyer should not obligate his house for merchandise except by means of a regular merchandise purchase order authorized by the proper house official.

Many stores incorporate into their order forms, specifically or by reference, the set of basic trade provisions adopted by the National Retail Merchants Association. These were agreed to in 1947 between the NRMA Vendor Relations Committee, under the leadership of the late Irwin D. Wolf, then vice-president of Kaufmann's, Pittsburgh, and the Apparel Industries Inter-Association Committee. The provisions have been accepted by 29 industry associations. The text of these provisions appears at the end of this chapter.

Oral understandings or informal memoranda in place of formal orders, while not in themselves ethical breaches, are nevertheless unsound practice because they are usually resorted to by reason of unwillingness to face facts, and in many cases lead to unethical conduct. This applies with equal force to buyer and seller.

What Orders Should Cover. Orders should be specific as to date of delivery, terms, quantities, assortments, sizes, colors, materials, prices, and any special conditions of purchase.

A specific date of delivery is important for the reason that only when the date of delivery is definitely stated on the order is the buyer justified in cancelling if delivery is delayed beyond the time the merchandise is wanted.

The terms of purchase should also be stated fully and definitely on the order. The phrase "as had", as it relates either to costs or to cash discount or to the arrangements, should never be used.

Be specific in every case. If the order is placed personally, never fail to ask the price. It may have been reduced since your last order.

The buyer should be thoroughly familiar with the industry terms accorded in the line he is buying and should insist that his house receive discounts and dating equal to the best given to any other house buying the same line under similar conditions.

Conversely, the buyer should not accept or demand special concessions in the way of discounts or dating not economically or legally justified by the character of the order.

Specific notations on the orders as to quantities wanted, sizes, materials and color assortments will protect the buyer against substitution and, in the event that the seller attempts to substitute, will serve as an indisputable basis for returning merchandise substituted.

The same applies to any special conditions of purchase. If the seller fails in any respect to carry out his agreement with the buyer it is the specification on the order that is the deciding factor in any controversy which may arise.

Pitfalls to Avoid. After an order authorized by the buyer's house has been accepted by the seller, the buyer should make no attempt to trade on the goodwill of the seller by asking for concessions beyond those agreed to in the order—whether these be in the form of goods or service.

Overbuying is to be avoided and no buyer should allow himself to be unduly influenced in buying because of the seller's predictions of price advance or scarcity. The buyer who refuses to overbuy is protecting himself and the seller against loss and the tendency toward violation of good practice which attends an overbought condition.

Memorandum or consignment purchases should be retained by the buyer no longer than the time agreed upon with the seller, except by special permission obtained before expiration of the time originally agreed upon. As a matter of courtesy to the seller, the buyer should return the remainder of such purchases prepaid and with all necessary precautions to insure the receipt of the goods by the seller in first-class condition.

A standard arbitration clause in an order form is an excellent practice, as it minimizes the tendency of either buyer or seller to act unfairly. Such a clause is included in the NRMA's basic trade provisions, mentioned earlier.

Cancelations and Returns. Other phases of the contract are cancelations and returns—some legitimate; others not. Cancelations may be resorted to by both buyer and seller. Care should be taken to see that cancelations are made only for reasons which are generally recognized as justified.

Perhaps the more serious problem affecting the contract is the return of merchandise. Manufacturers in practically every line of industry complain of retailers abusing the return privilege, while retailers, on the other hand, claim that the manufacturers are to blame for the returns being necessary.

Reasons for Returns. Among the legitimate reasons for returns by retailers to the seller are the following:

1. Failure to deliver within the time specified on the order.

2. Substitution of styles, sizes, colors or materials.

3. Defective merchandise.

4. Unsolicited and unordered merchandise.

5. Merchandise inferior to the samples shown, on the basis of which the order was placed.

6. Merchandise received in excess of that actually ordered.

7. Merchandise which was bought as exclusive but which has also been sold to competitors.

8. Merchandise returnable by reason of special arrangements with the seller.

In all cases, the buyer should make the return promptly and notify the seller that merchandise is to be returned. This is a simple matter of courtesy to which the seller is entitled and one which will prevent needless correspondence. As it is the practice of many manufacturers to refuse a shipment if not notified in advance that merchandise is being returned, the sending of *some form of notification* (see Article No. 3, Basic Trade Provisions, page 86) will avoid possible loss to the seller through depreciation in the value of the merchandise that has been refused when first presented.

Merchandise Which Should Not Be Returned. Merchandise which has been bought in a lot should never be returned in part without permission of the manufacturer. It is a recognized principle of law that the buyer must accept or reject the whole shipment. The buyer who attempts to do otherwise not only invites controversy in which he will be the loser but also is resorting to practice which may well be considered unethical.

Although it is well known that some manufacturers accept unjustified returns because they do not wish to offend the buyer or run the risk of losing an important customer, the buyer who has a sense of fair dealing will not ask a manufacturer to take a loss for which he is not responsible.

Unfair Returns. Outstanding among the circumstances which do not represent legitimate cause for canceling orders or returning merchandise and which incur the ill-will of manufacturers if indulged in by the buyer, are:

1. Merchandise which has been delivered in full compliance with the order.

2. Merchandise which the buyer has ordered for a promotion which has not proved successful.

3. Merchandise which has been bought in excess of needs in expectation of price advances or scarcities which failed to materialize.

4. Merchandise received on orders placed with several manufacturers to protect the buyer against slow or partial deliveries, with the mental reservation that some of the orders would be canceled later. This practice is particularly objectionable because it creates an artificial demand, and the reaction which must inevitably follow over-production brings loss to the manufacturer and to the buyer as well.

5. Merchandise in stock on which the market price has declined.

6. Merchandise which has been damaged in handling after receipt by the buyer.

7. Questionable claims that merchandise is short in quantity, damaged, or not according to specification, or delayed too long in delivery to be salable.

8. Higher priced merchandise bought earlier in the season which has depreciated in value because of copying in lower priced materials by other manufacturers.

9. Merchandise purchased early in the season which has not caught the fancy of the public.

10. Merchandise returned by customers for causes not attributable to the seller.

11. Merchandise returned only because the buyer finds himself with too heavy an inventory.

Cooperation That May Be Expected. The buyer's expectation of service or cooperation from the manufacturer should be based on fair price concessions when occasions warrant, fair allowance on merchandise which has been unsatisfactory due to causes which can be attributed to the manufacturer of the article, normal discount concessions and credit extensions.

The buyer should not take advantage of any highly competitive conditions in the market to make excessive demands for service in these respects, nor should he buy so closely as to lose out on quality.

Individual buyers whose houses are affiliated with group-buying organizations should not attempt to trade unduly on the buying power of the organization and the seller's desire to be in standing with the group by demanding undue concessions. Such conduct is not only unethical but it is illegal.

Particularly in the matter of service expected from manufacturers on customers' adjustments, there is an inclination on the part of some buyers to attempt to make the manufacurer take the loss although the adjustment is a matter of policy with the buyer's house. In such cases the buyer should take the loss, but in any case where the adjustment is due clearly to defective merchandise, the buyer has a right to demand that the manufacturer take the burden of the adjustment.

Relationship Between Buyer and Seller. Between the buyer and the seller there should be a friendliness of a sort that benefits both parties. There should be understanding and consideration of mutual difficulties and problems. There should be human interest and courtesy.

Complaint is made by manufacturers that buyers are discourteous to their salesmen; they fail to keep appointments; they keep salesmen waiting an unreasonable length of time; they refuse to look at their lines; they seek personal favors in the way of entertainment and gifts. There is no doubt that these complaints are justified in many instances.

Courtesy to Seller. The seller is entitled to quite as much courtesy from the buyer as the buyer expects from the seller. A salesman's time is valuable and the buyer has no right to waste it. If the buyer finds he cannot keep an appointment, he should notify the salesman so that the latter's time may be used to advantage elsewhere. If a salesman calls without an appointment, he should be seen promptly; salesmen should not be asked to call back several times needlessly. The alert buyer who is always on the lookout for new things will not refuse to look at a new line. He will welcome the opportunity. Courtesy to the seller in all these matters will foster goodwill and will prevent waste of time and money.

Gifts from Sellers. Undoubtedly the most undesirable and uneconomic relation that exists between buyers and sellers is that brought about by commercial bribery—in other words, the acceptance of entertainment, gifts or special favors. Aside from the fact that the acceptance of favors of whatever nature is unethical, the buyer who declines to put himself *under obligation* in a personal way to his resources is in a better position to demand the best the manufacturer can furnish in values, prices, terms and legitimate service. When a manufacturer has rendered full measure in these respects, he should be made to feel that his obligation is ended.

Should any circumstances or occasion warrant the acceptance of any personal courtesy from the seller or his representative the buyer should accept it only on a reciprocal basis, so that there shall remain no obligation on either side. An expense thus incurred by the buyer should be included in his expense account and paid by the firm as an item of expense.

These facts are sufficient to indicate that unfair practices in business represent an economic waste which should be eliminated. Buyers in all lines of merchandise will do well to look into their practices and correct those which are faulty.

In the elimination of trade abuses, the buyer has a major responsibility. Without intention on his part to operate on sound business principles, it is futile for trade associations and store owners to draw up rules and regulations and enter into agreements.

To Whom the Resource Belongs. The buyer may on occasion wish to discontinue doing business with one or more key resources. He may have a better source or sources. Such changes should not be made before discussion with the merchandise manager. *A resource belongs not to a buyer but to the store,* and before a rupture of such a relationship is made—and the relationship may be one of long standing—the store's top management should be informed. Only upon their agreement should such a change be made.

Basic Trade Provisions. Mention was made earlier in the chapter of the Basic Trade Provisions adopted by the NRMA for inclusion in an order form, specifically or by reference. This last means that when the resource accepts the store's order he agrees to conform to the Basic Trade Provisions. The text of these provisions follows.

1. It is mutually agreed and understood that all the terms and conditions set forth on this Order are satisfactory unless the Seller notifies Purchaser to the contrary, before shipment is made, within 15 days from the date of this order.

2. Purchaser may not cancel this Order for any reason before date for completion of delivery; cancellation after date for completion of delivery shall be effective only upon Purchaser's written notice to Seller, but shall not be effective with respect to any shipments made by the Seller within three (3) working days after receipt of such notice.

3. No returns of merchandise shall be made except for defects therein, or for non-conformity with some material provision of this Order. Where defects are discoverable upon reasonable inspection, or where non-conformity is claimed, such returns shall be made within five (5) working days after the receipt of goods affected. The Purchaser shall send the Seller a separate written notice, setting forth the nature of the defects or non-conformity claimed, prior to or simultaneously with the return. Seller may replace such returned merchandise, provided such replacement is made within five days after the last permissible delivery date.

4. In the event of the material interruption of the business of either the Seller or Purchaser by reason of fire, war, Act of God, governmental action, or strikes which materially affect the performance of this contract, the party so affected may

cancel the order for such merchandise as has not been delivered, upon notice to the other party, notwithstanding any other provisions herein.

5. In the event that the Seller should be unable to manufacture, or determine not to manufacture, any style contained in this Order, he shall immediately notify the Purchaser to that effect and thereupon the Seller shall not be liable for nondelivery of such merchandise. Purchaser shall, however, accept delivery and pay for all other merchandise.

6. Seller shall have the right, from time to time, on any unfilled portion of this contract, to limit any credit to be extended hereunder or to require payment before delivery.

7. Any controversy or claim rising out of or relating to any of the provisions of this Order shall be settled by arbitration in accordance with the rules of the American Arbitration Association. For any purpose relating to this arbitration clause or an award rendered hereunder, the Purchaser and Seller consent to the jurisdiction of the Courts of the State in which the Seller has his principal place of business, and any legal process or paper may be served outside of such State by registered mail, or by personal service, provided that a reasonable time for appearance is allowed. Purchaser and Seller further consent that service in accordance herewith shall be sufficient to confer upon the Court jurisdiction *in personam* over the Purchaser and Seller.

8. No modification of the terms of this agreement shall be effective unless stated in writing, and no waiver by either party of any default shall be deemed a waiver of any subsequent default.

CHAPTER 9

THE IMPORTANCE OF THE CASH DISCOUNT

BY

JEROME M. NEY

Department store top management is extremely sensitive to the importance of the cash discount on purchases—so much so, that it is not at all unusual for the heads of stores to insist that any variaions from customary discounts be brought to their personal attention, and to refuse to sanction any orders at lower than prevailing rates unless they personally approve the individual transaction.

Manufacturers, on the other hand, are trained to think in terms of net costs and net selling prices. They find it hard to understand why retailers insist upon cash discounts and resist efforts to reduce them.

The buyer, in discussions with his resources, may find himself called upon to explain why the rate of discount means so much to a store. The better he understands the cash discount and its function as a *profit cushion,* the more effectively can he present his case, and the more conscientious will he be in securing all the discount to which his store is entitled.

History of Cash Discount. The whole idea of the cash discount originated, generations back, with manufacturers who allowed their customers certain discounts on condition that they paid their bills promptly. Although such discounts have been and still are referred to as cash discounts, because they are contingent upon prompt payment, they have never borne any relationship to the changing value of the use of money. They do not fluctuate with interest rates.

Originally, the rate of discount on any transaction was a

matter of haggling between buyer and seller. Gradually, the terms for each industry stabilized. They became standard. Custom established a rate like three, or five, or eight per cent for payment by the tenth of the month following billing. There are differences as to prevailing rates of discount from one industry to another, and sometimes there are exceptions from the customary rate within an industry.

The Buyer's Responsibility. The buyer should know the prevailing rate in the industry or classification he buys in. He should resist any variation from commonly accepted figures. Certainly, any reduction should be taken up with his superior before a decision is made as to whether or not to buy from the resource concerned.

The buyer's vigilance in matters of discount should extend also to special purchases, imports, and any other variations from everyday buying patterns. In some cases, he may be required to have the resource "load" the price to retain the customary discount. By loading, the retailer means raising the purchase price sufficiently to give the resource the net price that he demands, after deducting the customary discount.

For example, if a resource offers merchandise at 95 cents, net, and the customary discount in his industry is five per cent, the buyer should have the merchandise invoice at $1.00 less five per cent. If the discount is eight per cent customarily, then the invoice price will have to be $1.03¼ to yield the desired 95 cents, net.

Except in special cases, the buyer does not have to request loading. *The resource knows the prevailing rate in his own market and figures the discount into his cost when he prices his merchandise.* In allowing the retailer the industry's customary cash discount, the resource is simply giving back to the retailer the extra charge he has included in his price for that purpose. The general recognition of this fact by merchants is one reason why they feel strongly that any arbitrary action on the part of manufacturers to reduce discounts from standard levels is unfair.

Retailer's Aid. The retailer uses his cash discount as a *profit cushion*. He doesn't figure on it when he sets the selling price for his merchandise. (In the example above, the cost of the merchandise is no longer 95¢ but $1.03¼. He uses the $1.03¼ as his base cost in figuring his retail.) In the heat of competition, or under stress of lagging sales, he may set his retail prices too low to cover his costs and yield a profit. Many a store or department has reached the end of a strenuous year with only a net loss to show for its hard work and its risk in investment in merchandise.

Here is where the cash discount comes to the retailer's aid. If the year's operations show a loss of one or two per cent, *the cash discount* (which has been 2.7 per cent of total store sales for several years past) *turns that loss into a tiny profit.* That is why seasoned merchandisers insist on cash discounts.

A question that sometimes comes up is why shouldn't the buyer deduct the cash discount before working out his retail price? Suppose the item's cost is $3.00 less five per cent. Why shouldn't he declare his cost is $2.85 net, and calculate his retail on that? The answer goes back to the original reason for the cash discount: *it's an incentive to prompt payment.* If the merchant does not pay his bills on time, he forfeits the reduction. Therefore, he has to consider his cost to be the gross amount exclusive of the cash discount; he cannot assume that the discount is his until he has paid the bill and earned it.

Profit Cushion. The discount, then, is not really a reduction in cost of merchandise, but a contribution to profit that management has made by providing sufficient cash for prompt payment of its bills. It is a return on *management's capital,* almost in the same sense that rental income would be if part of the store building were leased out to other businesses.

Since the department has no capital of its own and does not manage the store's cash, it has *not of itself* earned the cash discount. The fact that many managements credit cash discount back to each department at the end of the accounting period is fine for the buyer's operating figures and possibly for his bonus—but nevertheless, that doesn't give him the right to claim the discount as part of his day to day operations, or to use anything but the gross invoice cost when he works out his retail prices.

Need for Profit Cushion. Another point that comes up frequently in discussions of cash discounts is the question of why a retailer should need a profit cushion at all. The manufacturer, working with relatively few items, can usually allocate practically every penny of cost to each one. He sometimes asks why the retailer cannot do the same and, knowing exactly what his costs are, price his merchandise to make a profit or at least break even.

The typical store or department, however, works with a multiplicity of items and has no way to allocate to each the precise cost of the buyer's time, the salesperson's time, the elevator operator's time, and so on, that should be charged to that item. The buyer may know the merchandise cost of each article in his stock, but because of the retail method used, *it is all averaged.* In pricing his stock, therefore, the buyer faces a more complicated situation than the manufacturer.

Similarly, the manufacturer, doing a regional or national business, finds it hard to realize how intensely the retailer is affected by local conditions, how easily a slight worsening of business in a particular city can upset the merchant's apple cart and wipe out his season's profits. A few days of bad weather, a slacking off of employment in the area, and the merchants in a town find themselves paring down their prices in the hope of attracting customers.

Even when business in an area is good, one merchant who has managed poorly and who has dropped his prices to stimulate sales can play havoc with the profit picture of the other merchants in town. Competing stores usually have to drop their prices, too, not only to protect their sales, but also to protect their reputations. Dealing with the ultimate consumer, the retailer knows that when there is a disparity in prices among stores, the customer tends to accuse the one with a higher price of overcharging.

Then there are the price wars that sometimes spring up between aggressive competitors, or that may be touched off by the appearance of discount houses and other cut-price sellers in a community. Even without these special situations, however, the cost of meeting ordinary competition is frequently sufficient to involve a loss for the departments concerned. In this situation, the retailer needs a cushion against the losses he takes in his daily competitive efforts—his cash discount.

How does this strictly retail problem concern the manufacturer? In this way: Retail competitive enterprise not only helps maintain the retailer's volume; *it also moves goods for the manufacturer and thus helps maintain his sales volume.*

Cash Discount Offsets Buying Errors. So far as the buyer himself is concerned, the discount serves as a valuable counterbalance to those errors in judgment that, being human, he will necessarily make. Just as a resource cannot hope to create a line which is made up exclusively of best sellers, neither can a buyer hope to select nothing but reorder numbers each season. Nor can he hope to appraise every item he buys so accurately that he can determine to the penny the price he should pay for it. His mistakes in the course of the year swell the markdown figure and reduce the operating profit of his department. *But if his department has earned adequate cash discounts,* there is a profit cushion to lessen the impact of his errors.

No matter how skilfully run, the operating profit in a department store is rarely so high that, if the cash discount were eliminated, there would be anything left at all. Small wonder that management—and the buyer—is always alert to any threat to this safety factor—the cash discount cushion.

It may not concern one business man that another operates without a profit or at an actual loss. Yet the deparment store is more than just a business. It performs a vital service for its community; it sells millions upon millions of dollars worth of manufacturers' products; it serves multitudes of customers; it provides work for the great number of employees on its staff; *it helps keep its suppliers' employees working steadily.* The department store helps the manufacturer make *his* profit.

Therefore, it is distinctly to the interest of the manufacturer that any reasonable, established trade custom which gives the retailer added security without in any way penalizing the manufacturer should not be interfered with. Cash discounts provide that security, and the buyer will find it an important part of his job to see that his store gets the percentage to which it is entitled, and also to help his market to understand why the discount is vital to retail well-being.

CHAPTER 10

COOPERATIVE ADVERTISING

BY

R. K. EINSTEIN

There are occasions in almost every department of the store when the maker of a product agrees to participate with the retailer by paying part of the cost of advertising that product in newspaper or other media. Such participation is called cooperative advertising—a subject around which a good deal of debate swirls. Every buyer should be well informed on this subject.

Within the framework of his store's general policy, the buyer will often find himself obliged to request, accept, or refuse deals involving cooperative advertising. As his store's spokesman in discussions with resources, he should be familiar with what such advertising can do for the resource and the store, and what the hazards are for each of them.

How Cooperative Advertising Works. Although cooperative advertising may occur for radio and television time, in catalogues, direct mail, or other media, it is most common in newspaper advertising. An important reason is that retailers, being huge advertisers in their local papers, earn a more advantageous rate than a manufacturer can with only occasional insertions. If the space is billed to the store, the resource's money buys more space than if he purchased the ad directly.

The resource enjoys many other advantages, too.

Not the least of these is that the product is linked to the name of a locally known and respected store. The prestige thus achieved adds impact to the resource's national advertising. Or, if the firm is new or small or only regional in distribution, the cooperative ad puts it on a level locally with bigger and more widely advertised lines.

In the preparation of the ad itself, the store's highly skilled, retail-wise advertising staff is enlisted. These are people who understand the consumer in general and the people of that community in particular, and who are equipped to do an excellent job for the product.

If the item or line is generally distributed in the trading area of the store concerned, the manufacturer's cooperative ad is seen throughout the area, thus improving his impact in all his outlets there.

Additional Aids. If the store does radio or television advertising, or in-store closed circuit television selling, or if it advertises in local foreign-language papers, neighborhood newspapers, and other media, the manufacturer can be fairly sure of a mention of his product, without further charge, in these media. His statement enclosures are more likely to be accepted than those of other manufacturers.

This is not just because cooperation begets cooperation. It is also because it makes good sense for the store to push an advertised product all the way, if it gives it any push at all, no matter who pays for the ad.

Thus when the ad for his product breaks, the resource can count on the department to be amply stocked and prepared for customer response. He can expect copies of the ad to be posted throughout the store; he can count on departmental meetings being held on his merchandise; he can count on departmental tie-in displays, and frequently on window displays as well.

Such all-out retail effort is invaluable to a manufacturer. It is something he cannot otherwise reasonably expect or exploit, no matter how much he spends independently in any advertising media.

Advantages to the Store. The store, of course, has the obvious advantage of having more dollars to spend on promotion as a result of cooperative advertising. This benefits not only the merchandise and the department concerned, but also the store itself.

With the help of resource cooperation, the store becomes a bigger user of advertising space and time; it becomes a more important customer of the local newspapers and broadcasting stations; its name gains force through more consumer impressions. If it uses catalogues, cooperative advertising contributions can help finance their production and mailing.

Meantime, the job of its advertising staff grows in size. With the money added by cooperative advertising, there are funds for more advertising, and sometimes for a larger and more skilled staff. The additional advertising itself draws more traffic, sells more goods, and encourages retail growth beyond what would be possible within the limits of the store's own funds.

Problems That Arise. Cooperative advertising is not all smooth sailing for the advertising staff. Manufacturers sometimes demand complicated billing arrangements, and add a burden of confusion, correspondence and clerical work to the problems of the advertising department as well as additional expense. In many stores, a full time person works on nothing but the complex detail work arising from cooperative advertising.

The buyer can help by reminding his resources that his store's advertising staff serves a great many departments and, through them, has to work with a great many manufacturers. He can urge them to keep their arrangements as simple and reasonable as possible, so that the advertising department can get on with its main job of creating effective ads.

The Cost to the Vendor. Most stores add a percentage to their net linage rate in determining vendor rates. There are many sound, defensible bases for this practice. A substantial percentage of the store's total advertising expense is represented by the production cost—and some of it can reasonably be passed on to vendors who participate. The store earns a sliding scale discount through its use of space, from which an individual vendor should hardly expect to profit, and which it would cost more to apportion among advertisers at the end of the year than the rebate itself. Some newspapers include engravings and revisions as part of their space rate—others do not. Some newspapers give extra discounts for multiple insertions on a single day—others do not. Some newspapers give frequency-of-insertion discounts—others do not.

Whether or not the store's participation rate is lower than national rates, it is rendering its resources a unique contribution to the reduction of their advertising expense in any given market.

Pitfalls. Buyers who are dazzled by the possibilities of cooperative advertising may sometimes find themselves buying *advertising* instead of *merchandise.* They choose the best cooperative arrangement, even if it means taking second or third best in terms of salable merchandise, or buying larger quantities than they need.

This is a mistake that has serious effects upon a department. *Advertising does only minor miracles.* If the merchandise isn't salable, the ad can't make it so, no matter who pays the bill. Whatever was gained in advertising money for poor selling items may be lost in markdown on the stock the ad couldn't move.

If burdened with too many such poorly chosen items or lines, the department finds itself in an overbought condition, unable to purchase new, good items that continually crop up. Some of these good things may have cooperative advertising arrangements every bit as attractive as those that went with the poor sellers—with the buyer in no position to take them on.

The Eager Advertiser. Another trap for the buyer who sets too much store by cooperative advertising is the not too good resource who seeks to buy his way into store on the strength of advertising cooperation. In some industries, competition at times seems to be in terms of poorly advised advertising deals, rather than in terms of the value and desirability of the resource.

Still another trap is the new and untried item, whose maker offers to share the risk of promoting it by offering an extra-liberal cooperative advertising plan. If the article proves a no-day wonder, neither the retailer nor the manufacturer has gained.

What has been frequently overlooked in the debate about cooperative advertising is the fact that in most such arrangements the store (department) must make *its* contribution. All the more is it foolish to take on a doubtful promotion. The retailer's own money goes out the same window!

There are always some new items, however, that are worth the effort. A good test is for the buyer to ask himself, *would he spend his own advertising money on the item?* If he would, then the cooperative offer simply means that he can spend more money promoting the item than he would otherwise have been able to do.

Who Cooperates? Many of the best resources in each industry are liberal in this respect, if for no other reason than that they have taken the trouble to study retail operations and they know exactly how much more their advertising money will buy when they use it in this way.

There are also, however, some excellent resources who will spend fortunes in other media, but who will have nothing to do with cooperative advertising. Usually, they consider the retailer's ad something he and he alone should pay for. They fail to see all the additional advantages the resource can buy for itself through sharing the cost of a retail ad. An individual buyer can seldom hope to bring about a change of policy in such a firm single-handed, but he should try, and so should others. Eventually, the manufacturer will realize that he is depriving himself, as well as his retail accounts, of a useful, powerful, selling tool.

If the resource has merchandise that has won acceptance among the store's customers, however, the buyer should continue to feature it, providing other considerations—markon, for example—are acceptable. Customers are not concerned over advertising arrangements. Continued consumer accept-ance, however, requires constant promotion. Today's best brand can be forgotten tomorrow—without adequate pro-motion.

Balance in Advertising. The buyer's department's advertis-ing must have *balance,* just as his inventory must; its emphasis must be placed on the most wanted and most profitable items.

It is quite possible for a buyer to let cooperative advertising distort the picture he wishes to present of his department. For example, a corset buyer may have twice as much cooperative advertising money to spend on brassieres as she has on girdles. Yet girdles may be the larger part of her business. If she can-not supply from her department's own funds enough advertis-ing money to give girdles their rightful share, she may find it wiser not to use all the money available to her for bras.

When to Stop. Or there may be a housewares buyer who has built up a profitable business in unusual items for cooking and serving food—things a little more distinctive and more expen-sive than customers can find elsewhere. If he is offered a great deal of cooperative advertising on low priced cooking utensils, he can actually harm his department by using so much of it. He will be attracting customers interested in cheap merchan-dise, and he will be trading his store down in the eyes of his quality-educated, quality-loving customers.

For reasons like these, some stores reject as much if not more cooperative advertising than they accept. There are also other reasons. There may, for instance, be occasions when an other-wise satisfactory offer must be refused because the store has had just too much advertising lately in that price line, or that classification. In such cases, the buyer should explain to the resource that there is no reflection upon the maker or the product—it is simply a matter of balancing the store's over-all advertising in terms of the face which management wishes to present to the public.

CHAPTER 11

THE BUYER AND FEDERAL TRADE REGULATIONS

BY

IRVING J. ZIPIN

The buyer in today's complex merchandising scheme must add yet another function—he must be a bit of a lawyer. To the extent of his activities in the resource markets, he must know something about the Federal laws regulating price and advertising and promotional programs and facilities; about exclusive dealings, etc. To the extent of his duties as an administrator or supervisor of a department, he must have familiarity with the labeling and related trade practice laws and regulations.

In all of this, it is important that he not assume the role of lawyer. Any questions or doubts should be checked with his company's counsel, either directly or through his superiors. In the fast moving merchandising world and the rapidly expanding field of Federal trade regulations, the buyer should keep close to his legal department. The lawyer's job is to advise and counsel. The buyer must present the problem in the first instance and at a time when advice may be given and legal liability avoided. Lawyers and management prefer preventive measures.

Retailers Beware! The law and the policies of governmental enforcement agencies are changing and are now aimed at the retailer. What may have been valid at one time may be doubtful and even "verboten" today. As we shall see, very recently the Federal Trade Commission has adopted a new or reconstructed attitude toward certain so-called discriminatory promotional and advertising allowances given to bigger retailers.

Today, as between a large retailer and a supplier, if the allowance or payment is deemed preferential, the retailer (not the supplier) is subject to possible penalties of law. Instead of *Buyer* (as the customer) *Beware!,* the new theme of government enforcement is *Buyer* (as the retailer) *Beware!*

It is, therefore, more important than ever before, that the buyer and lawyer have closer communication. It would, of course, be ideal if legal principles could be simply documented in a booklet or manual which the buyer could have at his or her elbow. It is impossible to cover all pertinent laws and regulations in this fashion and it would be dangerous and wrong to do so. Factual situations change legal solutions. A buyer should not and must not attempt to interpret the rule or law based on a particular situation for fear that he may incorrectly rule himself out of a good "deal" as well as into one. Yet, it is just as impossible to expect the buyer to be on the other end of a telephone every place he makes a purchase or arrangement. There is no ideal formula for obtaining legal advice on the spot, but there should be a procedure in every retail organization to keep the buyer aware and advised.

How to Get Legal Help. Let us suggest here some pointers on communications and hope that all or some are practiced regularly or fairly often.

1. The executive training program for the young would-be buyer should include a brief session on all phases of law relative to the buyer's job—especially Federal trade regulations. Even before this, marketing courses at school levels should include a general review of the pertinent law.

2. New and important aspects or changes in the laws and legal principles applicable to retailing and to the particular industries covered by a buyer should be reviewed constantly. This can be done by reading, by discussion and contact in the market place and by memoranda from the store's legal department and/or merchandising superiors. Discussions at staff and group buying meetings, at conventions, etc., are important. Trade press and industry releases help. In addition, it would

be helpful for the store to own a copy of "Manual of Federal Trade Regulations Affecting Retailers," published by the National Retail Merchants Association. Also, "An Antitrust Primer," by former FTC Chairman Earl W. Kintner, is particularly geared to the business man.

Beware, however, of complete reliance on industry or resource interpretations and impressions concerning applicable laws and regulations. Too often, these are wrong or slanted.

3. There should always be, I repeat, direct, personal contact between buyer and lawyer. But it would be wise first to consult with the merchandise manager.

4. In those situations where the lawyer is not readily available or full-time counsel is readily available but too costly, someone in top management should be the buyer's source of authoritative counsel. This could be the controller or someone on his staff with legal background. The internal audit procedure should be used to check compliance with various laws, trade regulations, labeling, etc.

5. Interpretations of current regulations should also be sought from the National Retail Merchants Association. When new rules or laws are passed, these are analyzed by experts at the Association. If particular angles affecting the department have not been anticipated, an inquiry to the NRMA will secure assistance.

The foregoing relates to preventive measures. No one wants the heavy hand of the law to be placed on the company or employer. As we shall see, once a cease and desist order is entered against a violator or a consent decree agreed to, activities of significance and value may be prohibited or seriously circumscribed. The old adage of "an ounce of prevention is worth a pound of cure" is especially applicable here.

The Important Laws. Let us now turn to the areas of law which concern the buyer. We shall here consider only the law of Federal trade regulations. There are also, of course, local and state laws relating to sales below cost, fair trade, price discrimination within localities, food, drug and cosmetics, trade diversion (e.g., misrepresentation as to "wholesale"), weights and measures, labeling, deceptive advertising, etc.

Three major statutes affect the marketing activities of business in interstate and foreign commerce. These are the Sherman Act, Clayton Act, as amended by the Robinson-Patman Act, and the Federal Trade Commission Act.

According to FTC Chairman Paul Rand Dixon, the purpose of the antitrust and trade regulation laws is two fold: "Thou Shalt Compete!" and "Thou Shalt Compete Fairly!" The retailer's suppliers must refrain from engaging in unreasonable restraints of competition; the retailer must be permitted access to the products of the suppliers. On the other hand, the retailer must not engage in competitive restraints so that, in turn, the consumer may realize the full measure of the goods meant to reach him. Says Mr. Dixon: "We ask only that you (the retailer) refrain from eliminating competition and that you treat the American consumer and your fellow merchant fairly. Competition . . . is good for the consumer, good for the retailer and good for the producer."

A brief summary of these laws will provide a basic orientation of this subject.

The Sherman Act prohibits agreements or combinations by or among suppliers and retailers to restrain trade by price-fixing, allocation of markets or boycotts or refusals to deal. Thus, retailers cannot agree together to such conduct, whether in trade associations or buying groups or by a substantially uniform course of conduct.

The Clayton Act essentially extends the prohibitions of the Sherman Act to specified anti-competitive practices, such as price and promotional discriminations, exclusive dealing and mergers, where these have a tendency or probability of substantially lessening competition.

The Sherman Act attacks injurious conduct and activities and the Clayton Act concerns possible and probable violations.

Of paramount importance to retailers is the Robinson-Patman Act, which amended Section 2 of the Clayton Act and which will be discussed more fully.

The Federal Trade Commission Act is a supplemental, overall law meant to pick up all practices and situations overlooked by the basic Sherman and Clayton Acts. It prohibits unfair methods of competition and unfair or deceptive acts or practices and is the basis of the new approach to enforcement against retailers of prohibitions against discriminatory advertising and promotional allowances and facilities. It is also the statute prohibiting or regulating false and deceptive advertising, comparative price advertising, labeling, etc.

Other Laws and Rules. In addition, retailers are required to know about and comply with the Wool Products Labeling Act, the Fur Products Labeling Act, the Textile Fiber Products Identification Act and the Flammable Fabrics Act. Each of the latter has rules and regulations.

There are also Trade Practice Rules covering certain types of conduct and activities which indicate the FTC's interpretation and enforcement attitude and practices. Some of these cover general misrepresentation or deception in advertising and promotional material, price representations (such as comparative price advertising), bait advertising, "close-outs," "discontinued lines," "special bargains," use of word "free," advertising of "guaranties," lotteries, commercial bribery, push money, etc.

There are also Trade Practice Rules or Guides which do not directly apply to retailing but apply to industries and products purchased and sold by retailers and hence affect the retail level since they generally cover the marketing aspects, including advertising thereof. These are advisory and not compulsory and cover a large number of industries and products ranging from aluminum sidings, anklets and art supplies to wire tacks, walnut wood, hand knitting yarn and zippers. In all, there are about 200 Trade Practice Rules applicable to retailing.

We now turn briefly to the more significant areas of law which more consistently affect the buyer's duties and activities and, therefore, with which he or his merchandise manager or general merchandise manager or, at least, "someone" ought to have some familiarity and awareness. We will only scratch the surface, for books have been written on these subjects.

Robinson-Patman. First, the Robinson-Patman Act sections: These are not too clear and still linger in areas of debate, conflict and confusion. They concern and test the conflicting roles of the supplier and the buyer of goods, sometimes at varying levels. However, on one point it has become painfully clear: The enforcement attitude of the government, aided and abetted by new and developing court cases, definitely points to increased activity against the *retailer* as the possible errant and violator.

In a recent important change in view, the FTC actually cites the fact that these sections of the law were aimed at practices of the *buyer* in the market place and that very often, big buyers are guilty of causing, inducing or even forcing preferential and discriminatory favors. This is an unrealistic and unfortunate attitude, for too often the supplier is more anxious to make the "deal" or retain the account, sometimes at any price and he alone knows whether the "deal" is equally available to others. Too often, the supplier initiates, explores or has a new item or program to be tested and sells hard. It is basic and traditional to the buyer's role to negotiate terms of a purchase and impediments to the normal fulfillment of that function are unfortunate. There are unfortunately those buyers who demand their price of doing or continuing to do business and therefore abuse their proper position. *Extreme measures employed by either or both sides are wrong and lend themselves to violations and resultant enforcement.*

Price Arrangements. The statute, as framed, seeks to require suppliers to treat competing customers on a proportionately equal basis. The supplier is not to gain unfair advantage over his fellow suppliers. As a corollary, it requires these customers (the retailers) not to induce or exact unfair advantages from suppliers over their competitors, their fellow retailers.

Thus, a supplier cannot give a buyer a preferred or discriminatory price advantage, whether in cash, allowance or other form. However, a buyer cannot induce or receive such a discriminatory price advantage, so that, if the first is proved, the second is vulnerable.

A defense may be that the price differential does not cover the same goods or was given to meet competition or results from cost savings to the supplier. However, these are often difficult of proof and require the accountant, as well as the lawyer, to help. The buyer should not attempt to determine the validity of these defenses.

Examples of price arrangements which must be reviewed in the light of these provisions are volume or quantity discounts, rebates, better credit terms, mark down allowances, special delivery terms, free goods or bonuses and price decline guaranties. Also, discriminatory promotional allowances or terms may be a form of price concession.

Obsolete, perishable or distress or discontinued goods, however, may properly warrant a price differential.

The act or conduct complained of must have the effect of injuring competition, so that if all customers are treated equally, there is no violation. Thus, the same percentage (e.g. 2%) discount on purchases will be valid, whereas percentage brackets, which are too wide, too few, and hence available to larger buyers only, are vulnerable.

In summary, retailers, alone or through buying groups, should not misuse their mass purchasing power so as to obtain favored prices or pricing arrangements from suppliers not afforded to competing retailers. If a buyer knows he is buying substantially the same quantity under the same arrangements as a competitor, *but at a better price,* he may be guilty of such knowledge as to establish a violation. Knowledge can be attributed to the buyer if he knew or should have known from all facts and conditions of the industry that he was obtaining a preference. FTC presumes that buyers know their markets and hence imposes a standard of knowledge which has to be refuted.

If the arrangements establish cost savings or the suppliers' competitors have also lowered the price, the retailer is safe in receiving the reduction.

A basic question is when does the buyer have such knowledge that he is receiving such "discriminatory" lower price so as to require him to ask the seller if a price is really lower and if the above defenses exist? Generally, in industries where prices fluctuate and there is great competition, the buyer is not compelled to raise the question. In industries with standard and published uniform prices, it is safer to ask the question, especially if the price is lower than the known established price.

Coop Advertising and Promotional Allowances. In addition to provisions aimed at pricing of goods, the law also prohibits discrimination in the granting and receiving of allowances or payments for advertising or promotional services or facilities. These may take many forms: advertising in newspapers, radio and television, catalogs, mail pieces, displays, push money, demonstrators, buyer credits in magazines, special packaging, warehousing, consignment, etc.

As above, the supplier may be guilty in giving a discrimination or preference and the buyer may be just as wrongful in *inducing or receiving one*. The defense here is that the arrangement has been made in good faith to meet competition of other suppliers. No discrimination exists if the allowance has actually been offered or clearly made available to all competing customers (retailers) on proportionately equal terms. The offering or availability must not be negative or passive, but affirmative and active; the supplier must do something clearly to make the offer known or available.

As to competing customers, the tests are that the retailers must compete in the same trading area and on the same level of distribution and the content of the terms must be something of real value to the competitor, if they cannot realistically be equal. Thus, the "mom and pop" store cannot exact nor need it be given the same terms as the large retailer, and may, for example, receive window displays instead of newspaper or radio allowances.

The rule is that the benefits offered or available must be honest, real and have practical use and significance to all competing retailers. They must not be so limited in their aspects as to effectively exclude all but a few preferred buyers. Since the payments or allowances are for some kind of service, the service must be performed by the retailer. The *quid pro quo* need not be exact, but should be reasonably and substantially equal in value. As in the case of pricing arrangements, the liability of the buyer depends on his knowledge of a preferred or discriminatory arrangement and this will require that he should have known or should have inquired.

Knowledge of a Preference. Some rules-of-thumb may be set forth as to this aspect of "knowledge" or "inquiry":

1. If a large or important buyer, the onus is greater to inquire if the terms have been offered to others.

2. If the buyer initiates the terms, there is a greater duty to inquire. A custom-made, buyer-made proposal is patently dangerous. If the supplier initiates, it will depend on the circumstances, some of which will be discussed later.

3. If the buyer receives a lot for a little, he should ask whether this is also available to other buyers.

4. If the buyer asks for or receives special deals or allowances, such as for special events, promotions, catalogs, without inquiring about their being offered to others, he is vulnerable.

5. Group buying terms, specially made, should be subject to inquiry.

6. If, on the other hand, the terms are part of a well established plan which appears reasonable on its

face or is historically or traditionally known or publicized in the particular industry, the buyer has no duty to inquire. *But, do not ask for deviations from the plan.* A plan which reasonably offers many choices which would be available to various buyers, at their option, is valid and no inquiry is required.

7. Payments or allowances measured by volume of purchases or units have been held valid.

Thus, if the supplier initiates the proposed terms, the buyer has less obligation to inquire concerning their availability on a proportionately equal basis to his competitors. If the plan is established or known in the industry for some time or if the industry itself (such as the apparel business) makes available a choice of plans or makes varying and reasonably fair and practical arrangements, it is *not* incumbent on the buyer to determine whether the plan or terms he works out is or has been offered to others, *as long as it is not unusual or unique or tailored for the particular buyer.*

Other Areas of Federal Trade Laws. The buyer must also be concerned with dealings for confinement, exclusivity and so-called full requirement contracts. Generally, a seller can select his own customer or retailer and refuse to deal with anyone he does not want as a customer. This, however, must not be part of a conspiracy, understanding or agreement *with another retailer* or vendor, nor be part of a scheme to monopolize or otherwise restrain trade. Also, a retailer can refuse to purchase from a supplier as long as the refusal is not pursuant to a combination or agreement with other retailers or vendors in this regard.

The buyer should avoid agreements with a vendor not to sell to other retailers unless retail prices are maintained, and a seller cannot require a buyer to maintain price as a condition of continued business, except where Fair Trade laws are upheld. This entire area of exclusive dealing and refusals to deal requires careful review by lawyers and depends on the special circumstances in the industry, competitive markets, etc.

With respect to fair trade agreements or resale price arrangements, the buyer should immediately check their validity within his state. Quite often, these have been declared illegal by his state's courts. There is much controversy among retailers as to the desirability and value of these arrangements.

Each fair trade arrangement must be reviewed by counsel and should contain clauses protecting the retailers from payments of penalties and inability to return merchandise and should provide for the right to sell off-price goods which are discontinued, end-of-season or damaged or in certain special sales, and the right to stop buying or to lower price if competitors fail to maintain the fair trade price.

Labeling Requirements. The foregoing treats the buyer's functions in the market place. Today, more buyers, particularly in chain operations and in large organization operating branches, have been limited to the resource markets and the purchase of merchandise. Their duties no longer encompass responsibility for a department or departments and the supervision of assistants, salesclerks and supporting personnel, or these responsibilities have been greatly limited. The buyer, whether or not he has greater or less responsibility for his department, must however be aware of and familiar with the labeling laws and the requirements of the respective statutes and regulations concerning the content of the merchandise he buys and the description on tags and labels in or on the goods. Too often, a buyer has not familiarized himself with the ingredients of merchandise, including what it is made of and how it may be washed, worn and generally serviced. Above, we have referred to the labeling laws and the Trade Practice Guides which are applicable. Generally, these regulations pertain to truthful labeling of merchandise, including description of content and service requirements on the product or the package and on invoices to customers. Also, these requirements also pertain to fair and proper descriptions and information in advertising of merchandise. They provide for certain forms of guaranty from the vendor that the products have been properly labeled, which protects the retail store, and should always be obtained. The buyer can help the control division in securing these guaranties.

"Deceptive Price" Advertising. Another area with which a buyer must be concerned is so-called deceptive retail price advertising, including price comparatives or price savings claims. The subject matter is too voluminous to attempt details but the basic rule is that there should be no deception and the products or merchandise should be fairly and honestly represented. The law protects against all representations in advertising and other promotional media so that the elements of price, quality, durability and performance are truthfully told and competition flourishes honestly and clearly. The big problem is the shaving of the truth and the half-truths. There is a difference between puffing and the hard sell and deception.

The buyer should familiarize himself with the recent "Guides Against Deceptive Pricing" but must be warned that in a specific matter, the problem should be checked with counsel, for these Guides lend themselves to interpretation which only a lawyer's training can properly handle. The buyer's responsibility is firstly to obtain, to the extent possible, the correct information from the manufacturer or vendor or to make it his job to ascertain the truth of representations of the supplier or manufacturer with regard to the content of the goods and their quality and serviceability and to use shopper reports with respect to comparative price data. Too often, suppliers mis-state the facts *and the retail store is held to account since it cannot defend* on the basis of wrong information.

The courts and the government feel that today the retailer is sufficiently sophisticated to make himself familiar with the information necessary to make honest and fair disclosures. Buyers must particularly be skeptical of pre-ticketed items and manufacturers' price lists. These are not comparative tools unless they represent realistic prices in the trading area. Finally, the buyer is the individual responsible for transmitting the correct information to the advertising department with respect to prices, quality and serviceability.

Summary. As we stated at the beginning, the buyer's task has become a weightier one. This is quite evident just from the size of the preceding material. The buyer, like all executives in retailing, must be aware of and familiar with the areas of law pertaining to his job. In addition to Federal trade requirements, there are other areas such as the Federal Wage and Hour laws, equal pay laws pertaining to men and women and, more recently, the Civil Rights legislation. Compliance with the law, whether we agree with it or not, is a first essential. The act or conduct of the buyer, no matter how innocent or how inconsequential, may involve the employer in costly legal activities involving lawyers and litigation and the time of personnel involved in these legal problems. A one-time and innocent violation may result in a consent decree or a cease and desist order which may eliminate a program or course of conduct which had been well established by the retailer and is of significant value to his operations. The retailer will be required thenceforth to exercise vigilance and surveillance so that the violation is not repeated on penalty of contempt proceedings.

In addition, the buyer who is guilty of a violation is not sheltered by the employer and may also be subject to fines, penalties and enforcement action. Both employer and employee would suffer greatly from the unfavorable publicity of any action. Finally, in the Federal Trade area, injured competitors may sue for treble damages.

Thus, it is the responsibility of the buyer to recognize any possible legal problems and questions *before he has committed himself and his employer* to a possible violation. If there are any doubts, the buyer should immediately check with his supervisor and with counsel.

It is recognized that sometimes the action in the market place is too rapid—decisions must be made too quickly—for counsel's review. Therefore, it is wise to be cautious and to arrange the terms within the areas of compliance with the law or, if practicable, to condition them upon approval of counsel.

In sum, we offer the buyer the following rule: Be alert, be aware, be informed, and in case of doubt and for the sake of being assured, be advised by counsel. In accomplishing this, do not play lawyer—only enough to recognize a legal problem and call for help.

CHAPTER 12

BALANCED ASSORTMENTS

BY

PAUL L. DOWD

Who doesn't recall how Alice, when she entered Wonderland, found herself constantly trying to adjust herself to her new environment, sampling all kinds of strange potions which caused her to hit either her head on the ceiling or her chin on her shoes? She was for a time always too large or too small, seldom just right.

In the wonderland of today's merchandising conditions, we need to know how to organize ourselves so as to be constantly adjusted to current conditions of demand and supply, to own neither too much nor too little stock, but to present balanced assortments of what customers want at all times.

Why Have Balanced Assortments? The fullest development of a department store's ability to serve its customers best and thus to achieve maximum sales and profits depends on the combined strength of all of its departments. Weakness anywhere weakens the whole. Strengthening throughout the store of all of its departments will have a remarkable effect on the total store sales and profit performance.

Increased strength by departments will come from the perfection of the day to day rightness in the assortments of each kind of merchandise.

Thus it is vital that the merchandise management of a store at the general, divisional, and buyer level clearly understand and agree upon the nature, breadth, and depth of the assortments that the store shall carry in each department. Then, methods must be established that will as nearly as possible guarantee their maintenance. These methods also provide ways to adjust the assortments to the perpetual changes in the kinds of goods wanted by the customers and provided by the markets.

Classifications and Sub-Classifications. Most good stores today break down their records in a department into major classifications and in turn set up under these major classifications, sub-classifications.

It is important therefore to review what is meant by these terms and why modern merchandising conditions make this approach necessary. It is also essential to understand how changing consumer products, new items and new customer demands make it necessary to edit and revise classifications and sub-classifications from time to time.

The word "classification" simply means a particular kind of goods. Other terms less commonly used but with the same meaning are "category" and "dissection." A sub-classification of a major classification may be described as any type of merchandise within a major classification that justifies separate significant stocking, separate significant presentation, separate significant promotional effort.

For example, a misses' sportswear department contains the major classification, misses' sweaters. Within this major classification, there are sub-classifications for each currently important fiber: mohair, all-wool, fur blend, cashmere, synthetic. In a major classification for broadloom carpets, there are sub-classifications for Acrilan tufted, nylon tufted, and all-wool woven. In a major classification for sheets, there are sub-classifications for white, striped, solid color or printed.

Changes in Sub-Classifications. Sweaters, for instance, which were once merely something to keep people warm, come in six or seven fibers today, and each of these may be treated in various ways to impart special qualities. Some of these fibers, in a given season, will be on the way up in demand; others will be on the way down, or out. When one of these no longer justifies "separate significant stocking," presentation, and promotional effort, it no longer requires a sub-classification of its own. When a fiber or specially treated fiber, previously lumped with others, gains sufficient importance to be separately watched and promoted, it requires a sub-classification all its own.

Classification Change. With today's great flood of new materials, styles, and colors, changes in the sub-classifications are constant and usually rapid. The major classifications themselves are also changing, although more slowly, in relation to the department as a whole. The buyer therefore must have some method, however simple, by which these changes can be evaluated and acted upon promptly. Only by knowing these trends specifically and currently can a buyer intelligently adjust his buying so that his or her assortments will be balanced accurately to meet the current composition of customer demand. Only by such knowledge can a buyer avoid getting caught with too much of what was wanted last year and not enough of what the customer is asking for now.

Facts About Classifications. What does a buyer need to know about each major classification in his or her department? He or she should know, at least each month, how many dollars of sales this major classification produces and how many dollars of inventory at retail is invested in this kind of merchandise. He should have this information, if possible, the first of each month; more often, in some departments like millinery and dresses, where a weekly recapitulation of sales and stock is the common requirement.

This total major classification information should be built up from similar total dollar monthly sales information previously compiled for each sub-classification and wherever possible first of month total dollar inventory of each sub-classification.

Taking the information thus obtained, a buyer will then have a knowledge of how his business is constituted by classification each month and how much money is invested in the inventory of each class at the first of each month. From this, he can see the relationship of stock investment to sales and how fast one turns compared to another. With a history of a year or two, the buyer has a means of building a set of detailed departmental plans for required stock and projected sales. Trends can also be observed from one year to another and from month to month. (See Figure 8, page 118.)

Why The Facts Are Necessary. To illustrate how vital this constant analysis is, consider the constant drastic change that has taken place in ladies' coats at the time this chapter was written. Where in most areas fur-trimmed coats were 70 per cent of the business two years earlier, there has been almost a complete reversal to untrimmed coats at 60 per cent to 70 per cent and fur trimmed to 30 per cent to 40 per cent. Perhaps, when you read this a swing back to fur-trimmed may be occurring. Thus, a buyer obviously must constantly follow these extremely significant swings in demand.

A similar situation may develop in men's shirts. There may be developing a strong demand for a new blend of Dacron and cotton and for Dacron tricot. A major manufacturer states that these two types of fabrics in shirts represent 20 per cent of of his sales where previously they were insignificant. As a result, we may radically readjust the composition of our dress shirt inventory before the season is out. Obviously, if customers want these shirts, they will want fewer of the former favorites and we must know the proportions of this demand to stock them correctly.

Units of Merchandise by Price Line. So far we have spoken of analyzing our stocks by classification in dollars. These dollar figures give us the broad proportions we need to know about the composition of our sales and the competition of our stocks.

We arrive at these dollar figures by multiplying out the number of units sold in each price line in each sub-classification and the number of units we own in stock at each price line in each sub-classification. We also must know the number of units we have on order in each price line in each sub-classification. (In some departments that lend themselves to major classifications without sub-classifications such as refrigerators,

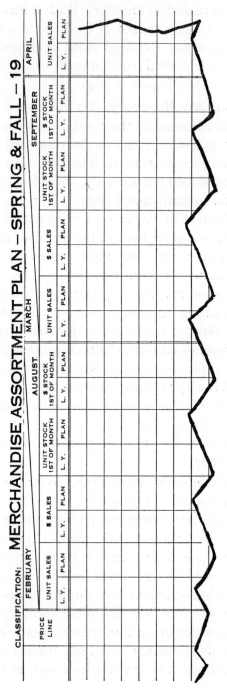

Figure 8.   Merchandise Assortment Plan

washing machines, stereo sets we would omit the prefix "sub" in stating the same thing above.)

The *unit figures by price line* are the key merchandising decision figures. It is here that one sees the balance and weight of our business as presently constituted. We then make decisions to strengthen price line assortments where we are weak. Unless a department dollar plan is built on knowledge of units it is very unlikely that the dollar plan will be valid. It may be too low and stifle progress or it may be too high and result in poor turn and poor profits. *There is only one right way to build a plan and that is in units, then extended into dollars.*

There is an additional reason for dealing in units. Suppose you're buying in a rising market. Suppose the increase amounts to 5 per cent. *If you buy by dollars you'll be buying always 5 per cent less than you should.* You may end up 5 per cent behind!

Balance in Price Lines. To have a balanced assortment in any kind of goods, we must have a balance in the price lines we offer our customers. A good rule is the three price line standard. This means that in any strong sub-classification of goods a department should offer the goods at budget, moderate, and better price lines *(good—better—best)*. For example, in men's shirts there will be budget customers who can best afford to buy shirts in the area of 3 for $10 or sometimes as low as $2.99, depending on competition. National brands at $4.00 and $4.50 currently are regarded as budget shirts. $5.95 would be a moderate or better price and $7.95 to $8.95 would be considered "best."

The balance of a stock by price lines depends on the store and the composition of its trade. Some stores have a very strong budget business, a fair business at moderate prices and a very small business at better price levels. Much can be accomplished by careful study of the price line composition.

Coordination of Assortments. The balancing of a department's assortments entails also its coordination, through the merchandise manager's direction, with other departments.

Merchandise management strives to be sure that a customer can completely outfit a child, a man or a woman in appropriate apparel and accessories at the budget level, or the moderate level, or the better level. In other words, we should have shoes, bags, gloves, hosiery, jewelry, and millinery to go with dresses, coats or suits at each level of price. These goods ideally should not only be at the right coordinated prices, but should be in colors and styles that will be appropriate worn together. This is a very challenging and continuous task but a necessary one in which all buyers must cooperate under the direction and leadership of a merchandise manager.

End of Month Comments. One of the most successful means of steadily building the strength of assortments is for buyers to analyze their units by price line and their dollar totals by classification at the end of each month. Some stores require the buyer then to record conclusions as to what was well done and what could have been done better. This analysis and writing of comments immediately helps a buyer exploit her strengths and correct her deficiencies. If conscientiously done, it also enables a buyer and merchandise manager to make a sounder, more complete assortment plan for next year based on this history. Figure 9.

Basic Assortments. There are many departments in a store which deal in staple or basic goods: notions, stationery, housewares, and many others. Here there is a tremendous premium on having in stock every staple item in the styles, colors and sizes customers expect us to have.

A buyer for such departments needs a positive method of making sure that all of these items are in stock at all times in both the main store and the branches. A recommended method is to spell out in an assortment list, basic stock list, or never-out list exactly *what quantity is to be maintained as a minimum* in each style, each size, and each color. Once spelled out, the filling of these items must be on a scheduled basis. A person must be held responsible for the maintenance of these records and the stock with regular counts, regular reorders, and regular

END OF MONTH REPORT

TO: _____ DIVISION MERCHANDISE MANAGER

      _____ PRESIDENT AND GENERAL
                               MERCHANDISE MANAGER

FROM: _____, BUYER Dept. ____ Dept. Name_____

EOM Report For _____ STORE _____

Total Department Planned Sales_____Actual Sales_____Last Year_____

Here are some guiding suggestions to refer to in writing up comments on sales and stock by classification and sub-classification.

A.   Comment on customer preference selling experience with reference to style, fabric, color, trim. How well stocked were we in those preferences?

B.   Give sales by price line wherever available; also sales by size if available.

C.   Where weak; where strong; best sellers; slow sellers.

D.   What would you do to improve next year? How was timing?

E.   Did we test early enough? What should have been tested?

F.   Did we peak stocks correctly if something should have been peaked?

G.   Did we taper off correctly if a season is ending in a classification?

H.   Did we miss any natural, profitable promotional opportunities?

An additional page is given for continuation of EOM Classification comments. A third page asks for "Overall Departmental Comments" under these specific headings: Advertising, Stock Rearrangement and Display, Adequacy of Fixtures and Merchandise Presentation; Housekeeping, Receiving and Marking; Adequacy and Quality of Personnel Coverage, Outstanding Competitive Events, Branch Stores, and Other Comments.

Figure 9. End of Month Report

reviews to see if the quantities provided in the list for the item are adequate and not sold out between counts.

Usually the lists are worked out by the buyer, reviewed carefully, and approved by the divisional merchandise manager and the general merchandise manager. These lists are totaled in dollars so that ample money is provided in the six-month stock plans. Many stores set up such assortment plans for Spring and a new set for Fall.

In the case of branches, such assortment lists spelled out in detail are the result of collaboration among the buyer, the divisional merchandise manager, the branch group department manager or the branch department manager. Usually sales-people are given supervised responsibility for counting the stocks. Then authority can be given to the branch group department manager to requisition or even place direct orders automatically to keep those stocks complete.

Conclusion. Thus in this brief treatment of this important subject we will all agree that it wouldn't do to be like Alice in Wonderland when she said, "I can't understand it myself to begin with, and being so many different sizes in a day is very confusing." Nor can we nibble a cake or a mushroom, drink out of strange little bottles, or wield a fan to adjust ourselves to the changing environment.

We must organize our records so that constant alert analysis will tell us where we are going, enabling us to adjust the proportions of the various kinds of goods we stock constantly to the ebb and flow of demand for them and to the new merchandise offerings that will never cease appearing on the scene in the fascinating, dynamic merchandising world we live in. If we do this we will achieve day to day rightness in each kind of goods we stock and our sales and profits will grow. (Figure 8, page 118.)

I would therefore urge that we—

Think and plan by classification and sub-classification.

Organize departmental records by classification and sub-classification.

Edit the records as demands change.

Use the records to obtain periodic summary information in units and dollars on hand, on order and sales by price line and in dollars for each classification.

Balance our assortments of all major kinds of goods to meet the proportionate demands of budget, moderate and better price line customers.

Work with merchandise management to coordinate assortments with those of other departments, to enable customers to purchase complete wardrobes for men, women, or children, or to furnish and decorate a home fully at good, better and best price line levels.

CHAPTER 13

PRICE LINES AND PRICE LINING

BY

FREDERIC S. HIRSCHLER

Few elements of the buyer's job call for more thoughtful judgment than the pricing of his department's merchandise. Obviously, too high a price chokes off volume, and too low a price reduces the spread between cost and retail below the danger point. Errors in either direction jeopardize profit, that necessary and important end product of the department's operation. Less glaring errors, too, endanger profit, but in more subtle ways, by making the merchandising job more difficult and complex than it has to be.

Over the years, department stores have developed certain principles that buyers can apply to the pricing of their merchandise in order to achieve maximum sales, profit, and good will. These principles are the subject matter of this chapter.

Price Lines. When we substitute a single retail price line, like $2.00 (or $1.98), in place of a variety of prices within a narrow range, like $1.95 and $1.98 and $2.00 and $2.09, we set up a price line. We present the customer with an assortment of merchandise from which to make a selection without being distracted by *inconsequential differences* in price. If the price line proves acceptable, our future buying is guided by the fact that we plan to continue to offer our customers a good assortment in that retail price.

Building stocks by price lines has been a natural development in department stores. It makes it possible to offer the customer complete assortments in a limited number of prices, rather than incomplete stocks at many prices. In this way, the store can meet the constant demand for increased variety of styles, yet keep its dollar investment within bounds.

Number of Price Lines. Successful stores know that relatively few price lines are needed in a department or classification. Where there are many, it is usually found that a few price lines provide the greatest part of the volume; that some produce a fair volume; and that some account for such small volume that they can be eliminated or carried with the smallest possible investment. By droping a poorly accepted price line, the buyer risks very little volume, but frees some of his investment in stock for use in those price lines that do get good response.

On the other hand, if there is a gap between two price lines and there is reason to believe that interesting merchandise, acceptable to the store's customers, is available at an intermediate price, it may be worth experimenting with an additional price line. *The price line picture can seldom be considered static;* testing and checking are always helpful—above and below and in between the established price lines.

As a general rule, price lines in a department or classification should be *far enough apart* so that differences in quality of merchandise offered in each are obvious to customers and salespeople. Here is a simple test: If the price tickets are removed from a few pieces of merchandise and it is hard to decide to which of two price lines each item belongs, then the chances are that those two price lines are too close together, and that one could do the work of both.

The important judge of any price line, however, is the customer. If the sales in a price line are not sufficient to permit the department to offer an adequate assortment of types, styles, and colors, it is usually better not to carry that price at all.

Price Zones. Occasionally, there are several price lines, each of which has only a small potential for the department, yet which in the aggregate represent a segment of volume that cannot safely be eliminated, or a service to the customer that should not be interfered with.

In some stores and departments, it is possible to merchandise a group of such price lines as if they were one. In such cases a price zone is substituted for price lines in merchandising, and the assortment of styles, types, sizes, and colors is worked out for the zone instead of for each individual price.

The term, "price zone," means a series of price lines (whether merchandised individually or as a group) *that appeal to one group of the store's customers.* In a given store, there are likely to be three such zones in which the bulk of the volume is realized.

The most important of these is the volume zone, which is generally the middle price range for the store, and which may represent anywhere from 50 to 75 per cent of its volume. Next in importance is the promotion zone. It is generally lower in price than the volume zone, but sometimes runs up into the prices of that zone. It accounts for 15 to 50 per cent of the store's volume, according to the character of the store.

The third zone is the prestige zone, always the highest, and including merchandise that is carried to tone up the department rather than to produce large volume. It may produce five to 25 per cent of the volume, depending on the character of the store.

A buyer's problem, then, is to study his department's clientele and analyze their demand in terms of prices. Then, within the framework of over-all store policy, he should determine the general price limits for each zone in each classification carried and plan to build adequate and attractive assortments in proper proportions within each zone.

Advantages of Price Lining. Studies have indicated that the largest volume is realized in relatively few price lines in each zone. Successful stores have found that *fewer* price lines usually mean increased volume, profit and good will. It becomes easier to keep assortments complete, inventories active, and turnover high when inventories are planned into the price lines of greatest volume importance in each price zone.

Advantages that accrue from the maintenance of well planned price lines are: increased sales, increased good will, better control of stocks, better turnover, decreased markdowns, increased markons, more effective advertising, improved displays, reduced selling cost, reduced cost of reserve space, decreased marking cost, decreased stock shortage, saving in the buyer's time, reduction in the number of vendors—and finally, increased net profit.

Price lining alone doesn't do all these things, of course, since it is only one of many elements in sound merchandising. But let's see how it operates to bring us closer to our goal of successful retailing.

Increased Sales and Good Will. A department that is not burdened with stock at prices that sell slowly can concentrate on offering a selection at those prices at which demand centers. The customer then finds a complete selection at the price she is willing to pay, rather than bits and pieces of an assortment at each of a number of prices. It is easier for her to buy, and she buys more readily.

Moreover, price lining so systematizes the assortment that the buyer finds it easier to check his stock and avoid being out of wanted items. Having wanted items always in stock, especially staples, not only builds volume, but it also builds good will. Completeness of stock in a few price lines has been proved to be more important to the customer than incomplete stocks at many prices.

Better Control of Stock. From the store's own standpoint, it is much easier to control a stock when it is decided in advance what price lines shall be carried and what importance shall be given to each. The buyer can plan his stock and his purchasing so that his most important price lines have the widest assortment, and so that the stock in his lesser price lines does not grow disproportionately large.

The stock itself can be arranged by price as well as type, making it easier for the salespeople to find what they want, and at the same time making it easier for the buyer to check the condition of his stock at any time. If, for example, he knows that he needs three lines of $5.00 shirts, a check of his

$5.00 stock will show him whether or not all three lines are present in a complete range of sizes.

Price lining usually means fewer items and larger stocks of each—an easier stock to keep track of both physically and on paper. Control records and basic stock lists are easier to maintain when the stock is planned and orderly, rather than haphazardly selected.

Turnover, Markdowns. Analysis of performance becomes easier, and with it, the correction of merchandising mistakes. The buyer can watch his turnover now by price lines within each classification and can pinpoint those elements that are slowing down his department. By decreasing his stocks of slow selling price lines, he improves his departmental turnover and cuts his markdowns; even his markdowns decrease when he spots the slow sellers and weeds them out promptly.

By the same token, in a price lined stock, it is easier for the buyer to spot fast sellers and single them out for special development—a process which has demonstrated its healthful effect on volume, turnover, and markdowns.

Savings in Selling and Stock Time. When the assortment is grouped behind relatively few price lines, the customer needs less time to reach a decision to buy; she doesn't have a price decision to make at every turn, but can concentrate on choosing from among the items offered at her price.

For the salesperson, a price lined stock is easier to learn. There are fewer prices to memorize, and the differences between grades of merchandise are easier to grasp and easier to explain to the customer.

A price-lined stock, since it consists of fewer numbers and adequate stocks of each, can be laid out systematically on the selling floor and in the forward stock. Customers can help themselves or salespeople can serve them with a minimum of waste motion. Time required per transaction is kept down, and salespeople are able to handle more transactions in a day —thus achieving a lower selling cost figure for the department.

The smaller assortment resulting from price lining also

makes for more economical use of reserve stock space. A stock which has a tremendous over-assortment is very hard to handle in reserve, since each item must be accessible. A small assortment, with a large stock of each item, can be stored systematically, using the space to greatest advantage. If it is arranged by price as well as type, articles can be more readily located by stock clerks.

Decreased Marking Cost. A department that is well price lined, with relatively few selling prices, is better able to achieve economies in marking costs than one with a multiplicity of prices. In some stores, price tags can be run off in slack time, cutting marking room costs and speeding delivery of merchandise to the floor. In other cases, it is possible to have the merchandise premarked by the vendor, or to put it on sale (as in the case of low priced binned items) without marking. The opportunities to effect savings will vary from store to store and from one department to another, but they are more likely to occur where sensible price lining prevails.

Similarly, if markdowns are necessary, there is less actual labor needed when fewer prices are used. The merchandise can be located more readily by the marker, since it is sorted according to price on the floor and in the reserve fixtures.

Decreased Stock Shortage. Experience has shown that price lined stocks have smaller shortages than those that are not price lined. This is no doubt a result of better control and of fewer opportunities for error.

When merchandise is returned by customers without price tickets, for example, it is easier to be sure of the price in a price lined stock. If there are markdowns, there is less chance for error if all the items involved are being reduced from identical original prices to identical new prices. The more complicated the job of marking, entering, and calculating, the greater the opportunity for error in recording a markdown.

Vendors and Values. A department that concentrates on fewer price lines usually finds it possible to concentrate its buying with fewer vendors as well, and to enjoy all the advantages, explained in detail in other chapters of this book, of making the store important to the resources that are important to it.

In many cases, price lining enables the buyer to buy larger quantities of individual items. In some instances, this results in a lower cost price, and a consequent improvement in his markon. In other cases, the assurance of ample volume makes it possible for the manufacturer to buy and produce more economically, and to pack more value into the product than he did before.

The buyer himself, knowing the retail price lines at which he will offer the merchandise for sale, usually shops the market for the best values at those prices. If he is working on a $5.00 price line, for example, he is better able to decide which of two items is the better value at that price than to decide whether one item at $5.25 will be more appealing than another at $4.75.

Improved Advertising and Display. Knowing which price lines have best acceptance among his customers, the buyer knows which ones to feature more heavily than others in his promotion—which ones, in effect, have natural pulling power to enhance the pulling power of his advertising and display.

In the actual execution of the advertisement, the fact that one price is featured, rather than a variety, has been found to make for greater effectiveness. Whether or not price is the featured element in the ad, the fact that there is just one price to be emphasized makes for clear-cut appeal.

Display, too, is more effective when it features certain things in order to concentrate the customer's attention. It should not be confusing—as a heterogeneous collection of merchandise at varied prices would be. The display that plays up an assortment at a single price gains in force and sales punch from concentrating on the one price.

Merchandising for Profit. When the buyer buys to specific price lines, he knows what he can afford to pay and can readily eliminate merchandise that costs more than the top figure he has set, unless there is some good reason to make an exception for it.

In highly competitive price lines, the buyer may have to content himself with whatever markon circumstances allow. To offset this situation, he may develop price lines, either for his store alone or in cooperation with others served by the same buying office, that are above or below those in which competition is keenest. Into these special price lines, he may be able to get manufacturers to build special values—workmanship, style, material, for instance. Under such conditions, these price lines may give more a liberal markon and average out the low percentage that he has had to take on some others.

The profit-conscious buyer will realize that the merchandising of a price line is not a simple slide-rule operation. There will be times when he should take more than his required percentage of markon, and times when he must take less. He cannot substitute percent-itis for good judgment in setting his cost limits for a specific price line.

Pennies and Profits. Buyers sometimes forget that pennies affect profits, and price their merchandise at traditional points, even though the customer is quite willing and able to pay a few pennies more. A case in point is the propensity of retailers to use odd-ending prices like $1.98 or $2.95 instead of even dollar amounts. The odd prices date back to the days when clerks had to send to a central cash desk for change, with the customer waiting for her few pennies to be returned. Later, the custom of odd prices continued, apparently on the assumption that $1.98 sounds cheaper than $2.00 to the customer and helps sales along.

Recent experience, however, shows that all the buyer accomplishes by adhering blindly to traditional price points is that he gives away profit unnecessarily. If the customer will pay $2.00 as cheerfully as $1.98, there is no reason to give away one per cent of sales in the form of an unappreciated customer discount. When one considers that the average department store's net profit at the end of a year is little more than two per cent of sales, it becomes obvious that the pennies and in some cases dollars are worth worrying about.

Exceptions. Price lining, it should be remembered, is a tool for better merchandising, not a strait-jacket. Changing conditions, in the store and in the market, may make revisions of the price lines in a department necessary. Testing or comparing with other stores also may indicate that changes are needed.

Special situations may arise, too, that require exceptions. Closeouts and markdowns, for example, may not fit into any one of the regular price lines of a department. Such special merchandise may require a special price—in fact, it may stand out more sharply as an exceptional offer *because of the very fact that the price is not one of the usual ones for that department.*

Another example: The department's regular merchandise sometimes can be made to move more rapidly and profitably if several identical or related articles are combined and offered together at a new unit price; they may even be packaged together by the store or the resource. Such articles may be, for instance, layette sets in infant departments; combinations of different colors and sizes in towels; men's undershirts in pairs or threes; handkerchiefs by the half-dozen; pencils by the dozen. Stores have successfully sold an increasing variety of items at multiple prices with no mention at all of a single-unit price. The advantages to the department of greater volume and higher unit sales in such cases outweigh those that accrue from rigid price lining.

Other Exceptions. There are still other places where price lining may not fit easily into the picture. Buyers for high style departments, fine furs, or fine jewelry, for instance, may want to accentuate the distinction of their merchandise by pricing each article individually, instead of setting up groups at given prices.

Operations of the bargain basement type (which are not necessarily limited to basements!) may also find that price lining is not quite for them. If a major portion of the merchandise consists of closeouts and odd lots presented as such, there are advantages in pricing each item on its merits. To the customer, small differences in price underscore the bargain appeal and challenge her skill in judging values.

From the store's point of view, there is the danger that unwise stress on lumping items into groups at a single retail price can wipe out profit. For example, suppose a buyer is in the market for $1.00 sellers. He plans to pay 60 to 65 cents for each, to yield him markons ranging from 35 to 40 per cent, but averaging 37 per cent.

If he sees some really excellent items at 70 cents and throws them into the assortment too, he is getting only 30 per cent on these sweeteners. They will drag down his average markon and, moreover, they will make the 60-cent items look decidedly inferior. He may find himself selling only the items on which he loses markon, while the ones that were supposed to restore or improve it remain on his counters.

If he believes his customers would like better merchandise, let him set up a higher price line—let's say $1.25. Here he could include the 70-cent items (if they were worth it and competition permitted) as well as 75-cent and 80-cent items, so long as in the "mix" he averaged his required 37 per cent markon.

Branch Stores. A word should be said at this point about price lining for branch stores. The price line picture for the branch may or may not differ from that of the main store. Usually, the buyer finds points of difference. Some price lines come up in importance at the branch; others that do well at the main store languish there.

Careful study of branch sales records, frequent discussions with branch personnel, and, if possible, time spent on the branch selling floor, will help the buyer to recognize the important differences in price line emphasis and to adjust his merchandising accordingly.

CHAPTER 14

THE DOLLAR MERCHANDISE PLAN

BY

C. S. THOMPSON

A departmental merchandise plan is a carefully integrated sales program backed up by sufficient stock to achieve the planned sales. The plan is worked out in detail necessary to fit into the store's over-all budget and financing; thus embracing turnover, stock-sales ratio, markdowns, planned initial markup, and purchases by months. This plan should generally cover a six-months period, and should be completed not less than 60 days before the beginning of the period.

Purpose of the Plan. The true purpose of this plan is to procure a net profit from the department at the end of the year. Past experience has shown that careful planning results in higher net profits. The careful plan necessitates considerable thought and research into past successes, which are to be repeated and improved upon; and discloses past failures which are to be avoided as one would a plague. For that reason the past season's actual figures are an indispensable part of the plan. They should be considered as an index or guide and not as a goal.

The initiator of the plan is the department manager or buyer. He generally sets down on a six-months plan sheet last year's figures for the coming season. Then, with the divisional merchandise manager, the entire program is gone over in detail. The controller makes available the detailed actual figures of the previous year's operations. Also, comparative store operations are seriously considered. Such reports are available from the Harvard Graduate School of Business Administration, the Federal Reserve Banks, the Controllers' Congress of the NRMA, and other sources. Local conditions and immediate economic prospects are then considered. The departmental competitive situation and its comparative position of dominance are determined.

Sales. The immediate trend of the departmental volume is the best single index. That is to say, if a department is exceeding regularly each month its previous year's figures by 10 per cent, it is relatively safe to forecast a 10 per cent increase for the ensuing six months, all other local conditions being constant.

In the accompanying illustration (Figure 10) the last year's sales figures are inserted on line A-1. Having decided that a 10 per cent increase for this season over last year's operation is reasonable to expect according to present trends and future probabilities, this forecast is then entered on line A-2.

Line A-3 is left blank until the actual period. Then the situation is reviewed on a weekly basis and such changes are made as may become necessary. Line A-4 is the place to insert the *actual* sales figure at the end of each month. This makes the review much easier as the period goes along.

Stocks. After the sales volume figure by months has been determined, the stock figure is the next consideration. A rule of thumb working with stock plans is: "High stocks bring low sales, high markdowns, low turnover, and high stock shrinkage." To avoid the retailer's disease, "last-year-itis," last year's sales and stock figures should be used as a guide, not a gospel.

The factors to consider in estimating the stock needed at the beginning of each month are:

1. Staple or basic assortment stock requirements.

2. Promotional merchandise needed to produce the planned volume for the month.

3. What type of department it is to be, and what price lines are to be intensified.

		Department_____					No. __X__	

THE DOLLAR MERCHANDISE PLAN

			Plan. This Yr.	Actual Last Yr.
	GROSS MARGIN $			
SIX MONTHS	%		32.3	30.1
MERCHANDISE PLAN	Cash Discount to Pur. %		2.0	1.9
	Charges to Cost of Mdse. %		1.0	1.0
~~Spring~~	Allowable Mark Downs %		˙5.2	6.9
Fall Season 19·	Shortage Reserve %		1.5	2.0

SEASON TURNOVER			~~FEB.~~	~~MAR.~~	~~APR.~~	~~MAY~~	~~JUNE~~	~~JULY~~	~~TOTAL~~
Last Yr.		1.5							
Plan This Yr.		2.0	AUG.	SEPT.	OCT.	NOV.	DEC.	JAN.	

A1		Last Year	5,000	9,000	11,000	8,000	12,000	5,000	50,000
A2	SALES	Plan	5,500	9,900	12,100	8,800	13,200	5,500	55,000
A3		Adjusted Plan							
A4		Actual							
B1	RETAIL	Last Year	21,000	31,000	35,000	35,000	45,000	35,000	33,000
B2	STOCK 1st	Plan	22,000	27,500	33,000	27,500	33,000	25,000	22,000
B3	OF MONTH	Adjusted Plan							
B4		Actual							
C1		Last Year Mdse.	300	500	180	255	800	795	2930
C2		Disc.	50	90	110	80	120	50	500
C3	PLANNED	Plan Allow. Mdse.	200	400	200	200	700	600	2300
C4·	ALLOWABLE	Disc.	55	100	120	90	130	55	550
C5	MARKDOWNS	Actual Month Mdse.							
C6		Disc.							
C7		Actual Agg. Mdse.							
C8		Disc.							
D1		Last Year	15,000	13,000	11,000	18,000	2,000	---	59,000
D2	RETAIL	Plan	11,000	15,400	6,600	14,300	5,200	2,500	55,000
D3	PURCHASES	Adjusted Plan							
D4		Actual							
E1	INITIAL	Last Year	40	40	40	40	40	40	40
E2	MARKUP %	Plan	40	40	40	40	40·	40	40
E3	ON	Actual (Month)							
E4	PURCHASES	Actual (Agg.)							

·Represents Stock **End** of **Month**

Mdse. Mgr. _____   _____ Buyer

·Controller Office   _____ Div. Mgr.

Remarks:

NOTE: Stocks are "first of the month" figures. The plan does
not show February 1 stock although this figure is included in
the average stock calculations.

Where not specifically stated for "last year," the figures are
for the current season.

Figure 10. Six Month Plan

4. Relationship between stock and sales to permit complete assortments with maximum turnover. In order to achieve desirable turnover, however, the stock must not be allowed to get so low that basic or staple items cannot be maintained in proper depth.

For purposes of illustration, it will be assumed that the turnover for this hypothetical department is four turns a year, and that that is considered satisfactory. We are further taking for granted that equal turns for the Fall and Spring season are acceptable and desirable. Therefore, if a two-time turnover for the Fall six months can be achieved, it will be a satisfactory accomplishment.

Correcting Past Errors. In reviewing the preceding Fall season's operations, line B-1 is considered first to see what the actual figures were for the beginning stock of each month. Thus, it is observed that only one and one-half stock turns were achieved for that period, or an average stock of $33,000 as against a desired average of $25,000. This average stock figure of $33,000 was divided as follows:

August 1st ...... $21,000   December 1st ... $45,000
September 1st ...   31,000   January 1st   35,000
October 1st   35,000   February 1st   30,000
November 1st ...   35,000

This was manifestly a most unsatisfactory operation. The stock on hand for December 1st was $45,000, and the total sales for December and January combined were only $17,000. It was mathematically impossible to get the February 1st stock down to a point that would give the full number of stock turns, and in order to get it down to the $30,000 that actually was reached, it was necessary to cease buying almost entirely—a form of retail suicide.

Notice that only $2,000 was purchased in December, and

nothing was purchased in January. The net result of such a method of operation must have been that sales volume was lost in December, January, and throughout the first part of the following Spring season's operations, due to the fact that the stocks must have been unbalanced, the assortments starved, reorders ignored, and sizes and colors broken. The constant flow of new, wanted merchandise, which is the life blood of a good retail operation, was not only interrupted but completely curtailed.

The entries on line D-1 show the retail purchases for each month of the preceding year as against the actual sales. Although markdowns and stock shortages are not considered here, obviously the department was far overbought continually.

Stock-Sales Ratios. Some store prefer to work on the stock-sales ratio basis for purposes of arriving at stock figures rather than the turnover basis. Although this system is not included in Figure 11, it is included in others shown.

The stock-sales ratio is easily arrived at, by dividing the stock at the beginning of the month by the sales volume figure for that month. The turnover figure is somewhat more difficult to obtain because an average stock figure must first be determined, and then the total sales are divided by the average stock figure. However, the difference in computation is not so great as to preclude the use of either one or both.

Monthly variations show up more markedly in the stock-sales ratio than in turnover, because of the fractional turnover achieved each month as against the larger decimal variation seen on the stock-sales ratio figure. Many stores use both systems and it is wise for a buyer to understand each one.

Now, having arrived at the point where we have all the necessary information on last year's sales, stocks and purchases, and having determined our desired sales plan for this season, it is comparatively easy to complete the plan for this season's operation. Obviously, the plan must avoid the errors and pitfalls of the preceding year.

MERCHANDISE BUDGET

PERIOD FROM Aug. 1, 19__ TO Jan. 31 19__   DEPT. NO. 11

KIND OF GOODS___ Silks, Velvets and Synthetics

	AUG.	SEPT.	OCT.	NOV.	DEC.	JAN.	CURRENT SIX MONTHS TOTAL
SALES							
2 YEARS AGO							
1 YEAR AGO							
PLANNED							
ADJUSTED PLAN							
ACTUAL SALES							
TO DATE LAST YEAR							
TO DATE PLANNED							
TO DATE ADJUSTED PLAN							
TO DATE ACTUAL SALES							
RETAIL STOCK E. O. M.							
LAST YEAR							
PLANNED							
ADJUSTED PLAN							
ADJUSTED PLAN							
ACTUAL STOCK							
OVER OR UNDER PLAN							
STOCK SALES RATIO							
LAST YEAR							
PLANNED							
ACTUAL							
RETAIL PURCHASES							
LAST YEAR							
LAST YEAR % TO TOTAL							
PLANNED % TO TOTAL							
PLANNED							
ADJUSTED PLAN							
ADJUSTED PLAN							
ACTUAL RETAIL PURCHASES MO.							
" " " TO-DATE							
COST PURCHASES							
LAST YEAR							
PLANNED COST INV. BEG.							
ADJUSTED PLAN							
ADJUSTED PLAN							
ACTUAL COST PURCHASES .MO.							
" " " TO-DATE							
OPEN TO BUY							
MARK UP							
LAST YEAR % TO DATE							
PLANNED % TO DATE							
ACTUAL % TO DATE							
MARK DOWNS							
PLANNED MONTH							
ACTUAL MONTH							
LAST YR. % OF SALES MO.							
PLANNED % OF SALES MO.							
ACTUAL M. D. % OF SALES MO.							
ACTUAL M.D.% OF SALES TO-DATE							
GROSS MDSE. MARGIN							
LAST YEAR TO DATE %							
PLANNED % TO DATE							
ACTUAL Gross Margin % To Date							

UNFILLED ORDERS AND MERCHANDISE INVOICES NOT INCLUDED IN YOUR LAST MONTHS BOOK INVENTORY MUST BE DEDUCTED FROM THE AMOUNT "OPEN TO BUY" OR ADDED TO THE AMOUNT "OVER BOUGHT"

Figure 11. Merchandise Budget

In the case of the department used here as an example, care must be taken not to overbuy early in the season, and it must be certain that some open-to-buy will be retained for the end of the season. The stock must be correctly peaked to coincide with peak planned sales, and the department must end up with an inventory consistent with both a two-time turnover for the Fall season based on the planned sales increase, and a well rounded assortment inventory to begin the Spring season. The buyer and merchandise manager must arrive at an average stock figure of $27,500, or one-half the planned volume of $55,000.

The largest volume months are September, October and December, and the stock figures for these months will be set in keeping with their sales volume. The stock figures are then set down for the first of each month on line B-2, as follows:

August 1st	$22,000	December 1st ...	$33,000
September 1st ...	27,500	January 1st	25,000
October 1st	33,000	February 1st	22,000
November 1st ...	27,500		

Notice that this season's stock plan does not call for any such tremendous peaks as were found the previous year. Also observe that the ending stock is planned lower than the year previous.

Planned Purchases. The stock figures having been determined and set down on line B-2, the planned purchases at retail are next determined. During the month of August, for example, $5,500 is expected in sales, and it is also planned to increase the stock to $27,500 on September 1st, which is an increase of $5,500, or a total change of $11,000 upwards. Thus, by adding the sales plan and stock increase together, we have $11,000 as the planned purchases for the month of August. The same procedure is followed for each successive month, and these figures are inserted on line D-2.

In the preceding year little new merchandise could be bought in December and none in January. On this plan, the department is open to buy at all times, and still ends the season with a $5,000 sales increase and inventory decrease of $8,000.

This will make for a profitable operation, and not merely a lot of wasted exercise. Note that markdowns are not figured back into allowable retail purchase plan. They are kept as a cushion and automatically become available as taken and thus decrease the inventory and increase the open-to-buy.

Initial Markon. Next is the all important matter of initial markon or markup (interchangeable terms) per cent on purchases. No buyer or merchandise manager can give too much attention to it. No purchase is profitable or successful unless it can stand the planned markon per cent that was intelligently arrived at for the department at the beginning of the season.

Likewise, a markon percentage figure is not intelligent unless it allows the department to be competitive with other stores and does not unreasonably increase customer resistance or unnecessarily increase markdowns or the cost of selling the merchandise, or slow up the turnover.

Markon is the real test of a good buyer. It is no trick, nor does it reflect great credit on anyone, to buy and sell merchandise at a low, unprofitable markon. The buyer who generally is successful for his firm, and for himself, is the one who can buy and sell his merchandise is such a manner that it will carry a reasonably high markon, and a reasonably low markdown.

A proper markon percentage is one that can cover the operating expenses of the department, allow for freight into the store, provide a margin for such markdowns as may be necessary and unavoidable, and leave a reasonable net profit for the store. It should not be so high as to result in high markdowns and slow turnover of stock. It is much better to have a somewhat lower initial markon per cent, considerably lower markdowns, better turnover of stock, and an increase in sales and net profit. It is only the very foolish buyer who looks only at volume and disregards his markon and markdown percentages.

Automatic Markon. Markon should not be considered automatic, nor the relation of cost to retail inviolate on each item. Very often several articles bought at exactly the same cost will carry three or more different retails. Such factors determine the retail price as: competition, quality, availability, how advantageously it was bought, and countless other variants.

It is ridiculous to follow blindly a mathematical figure. For example, simply because it has been determined that the departmental markon is to be 40 per cent, that does not mean that every item costing $6 must be sold at $10. Perhaps one will bring $12 just as easily; or perhaps it will sell slowly at $10, but will sell very rapidly and in much greater quantity at $9, and thus, by its volume, justify the price reduction. If a straight 40 per cent markon is taken, what item is going to make up for the lower markon on promotions or leaders? What is going to take up the cost of freight or other transportation of goods from the resource to the store?

Markon requires intelligent appraisal of each item as an individual problem, with the departmental average as an overall consideration. Thus we have thought over all the problems affecting our markon percentage, and in the case of this particular department, it has been determined that it is to be 40 per cent and so we place this figure on line E-2. This is the same figure that was achieved the previous year, but by the increased sales volume, increased stock turnover, and lower ending stock as well as lower markdowns, it is planned to make a higher net profit this year.

Markdowns. The markdown problem is next discussed, and in order to see where heavy markdowns occurred the previous year, the actual figures are inserted on lines C-1 and C-2. On line C-1 are merchandise markdowns taken for various errors or failures that occurred, and on line C-2 are the discount markdowns attributed to store policy as a result of allowances to fellow-workers, clergymen, etc. These are unavoidable, and run almost always constant percentagewise. To determine a reasonable allowable markdown percentage, figures of other comparable stores are needed. These can be obtained from such sources as the Harvard Graduate School of Business Administration, the Controllers' Congress of the NRMA, and other sources.

Markdowns are the adjustments which all buyers have to make in selling prices. A separate chapter discusses how to analyze causes and minimize losses on this score.

Recognizing the dangers inherent in this situation, the errors of last year which resulted in a markdown per cent of 6.9 are studied and 5.2 per cent is planned for this year. These dollar amounts are entered on lines C-3 and C-4. Line C-2 ran 1.0 per cent last year on discount markdowns, and so 1.0 per cent of this year's planned sales are entered on line C-4. By better buying and better control of stocks it is planned to reduce merchandise markdowns from last year's high figures shown on line C-1; and, therefore, on line C-3 only 4.2 per cent is entered, or a reduction of $630, or 1.7 per cent. This should help to improve the department's net profit.

Putting Completed Plan into Operation. After the buyer and divisional merchandise manager have finished the plan sheet, it is gone over by the general merchandise manager and controller. If the plan has been intelligently worked out, and ties in with the general over-all financial plans of the store as a whole, it is approved and becomes operational. If changes are to be made, a discussion among all parties takes place and adjustments are made. Copies of the plan in its final form are then given to each of the interested parties.

Although the plan has been carefully and intelligently thought out and set down on paper, the most important phase is yet to come. That is, it must be made to work. The plan must be kept elastic in operation. Lines A-3, B-3 and D-3 allow for adjusted plans of sales, stock at beginning of month, and retail purchases for each month. The entire picture is reviewed on a weekly basis and as adjustments become needed, either upwards or downwards, the necessary changes are made.

Sales are the real determining factor. As they increase or

decrease from the plan, so must the stock and open to buy be changed to keep the operation in line. If the sales are much higher than have been planned, it follows, as night follows the day, that the stock figure must be increased to keep the staple and needed assortments always on hand.

If the sales decrease, and thus the stock is creeping upwards, we must strive to get the stock figure lower. However, it must be emphasized that in such a predicament merely closing the order book is not a panacea. It is better to dig in and clean the stock, and by intensifying the selling effort, to get back into line. The assortments must not be allowed to become broken, and reorders on fast selling items must be continued, even in the face of an overbought condition. To do otherwise is to invite even greater disaster.

Weekly Merchandise Report. In order to make the needed adjustments and see that the plan is working, it is necessary for the buyer and divisional merchandise manager to have weekly reports on the progress of the department. The buyer must have information as to his sales to date for the month and for the period; his stock figure for this year as against last year; his purchases, current open to buy, initial markon per cent, markdowns in dollars and in percentages for the month and the season to date.

All of these figures are shown for the current year and the preceding year on the report. It also shows the plan; where changes have already been made, it shows the adjusted plan. The outstanding orders, both for immediate and future delivery, are shown so that the open to buy becomes evident with respect to the future. Figure 12 shows these figures all on one form and following in logical sequence.

With these reports, it is easy to follow the plan and make any necessary adjustments quickly. Failure to make this review on a weekly basis is to invite trouble by reacting too slowly to danger signals as they occur.

It must be kept in mind that these reports are tools that the buyer can use in order to achieve a successful operation.

WEEKLY MERCHANDISE REPORT AS OF _____

_____ SELLING DAYS THIS MONTH

DEPT. NO.	SALES SEASON TO DATE — THIS YEAR (1)	TO FIRST OF MONTH — LAST YEAR (2)	% CHANGE (3)	SALES THIS MONTH — LAST YEAR (4)	ORIG. PLAN (5)	ADJUSTED PLANNED SALES THIS MONTH (6)	ACTUAL SALES MONTH TO DATE — THIS YEAR (7)	LAST YEAR (8)	ESTIMATED SALES BAL. OF MONTH 6-7 EXCEPT END OF MONTH (9)	PLANNED STOCK END OF MONTH (10)	ADJUSTED PLANNED STOCK END OF MONTH (11)	(12)	OUTSTANDING ORDERS BEYOND NEXT QUARTER (13)	STOCK & INVOICES LAST YEAR (14)
Branch A														
Branch B														
Women's Hosiery A-B-M														

_____ SELLING DAYS PASSED

STOCK & INVOICES TODAY (15)	OUTSTANDING ORDERS THIS MO. DELIVERY (16)	OPEN TO BUY RETAIL 9-11 MINUS 15-16 (17)	ADJUSTED PLANNED PURCHASES BALANCE OF QUARTER (18)	ORDERS FUTURE DELIVERY — BALANCE OF QUARTER (19)	NEXT QUARTER (20)	OPEN TO BUY BALANCE OF QUARTER 18-19 +OR-17 (21)	MDSE. RECEIVED AND CHARGED MONTH TO-DATE (22)	INITIAL MARK UP % — MONTH TO DATE ACTUAL (23)	SEASON TO DATE AT BEGINNING OF MONTH — ACTUAL (24)	PLAN (25)	SEASON TO DATE AT BEGINNING OF MONTH $ (26)	MARK DOWNS % (27)	MONTH TO DATE $ (28)

DATE _____

Figure 12. Weekly Merchandise Reports

Each smart buyer must learn to use these tools even as a carpenter learns to use hammer and saw in order to ply his trade.

Other Forms. Although most stores follow a procedure that is in general very similar to the one described, the forms used vary in some respects. Among those shown in this book is one that includes cost figures for the previous year's purchases and sales, one that includes spaces for Controllers' Congress figures, and one that provides for branch stores. (See Figures 13 and 14.)

Branch Store Planning. Most stores that have branches include the branch figures in their main store plans, thus creating a master plan on which the needs and performance of all the stores are set forth. In developing the plan figures for the branches, buyers and merchandise managers should consult the personnel at the branch for an accurate appraisal of stock needs and sales potential.

Individual open-to-buy figures for branches are not necessarily figured. The main store usually has the responsibility for all the stock, under whichever roof it happens to be. The buyer must be careful, then, to remember branch needs when purchasing, and to allocate to each branch its share of the departmental open to buy.

The weekly merchandise report should, of course, include branch store figures as well as those of the main store, so that the buyer has the total picture before him.

Buyers and merchandise managers, as well as management, have a stake in the success of branch stores. One of the best ways to insure that success is to make realistic merchandise plans for branch needs and to recognize their sales potentials.

Foreign Purchases. In view of the increasingly large number of stores interested in foreign operations, a word should be added about the necessity of taking into consideration the special problems of imports in connection with the merchandise plan.

Most importing is done on a long range basis, and may in-

MERCHANDISE PLAN

Initial Markup............................

Mark Downs............................

Stock Turns............................

Cash Discount............................ ....SEASON..

....DEPT. No............................

4007

	1	2	3	4	5	6	7	TOTALS
	8	9	10	11	12	13	14	
ES								
LAST YEAR								
PLAN								
RESULT								
AIL STOCK 1st Mo. LAST YEAR								
PLAN								
RESULT								
T STOCK 1st Mo. LAST YEAR								
PLAN								
RESULT								
AIL PURCH. LAST YEAR								
LAN								
RESULT								
T PURCH. LAST YEAR								
LAN								
RESULT								
RK DOWNS LAST YEAR								
LAN								
RESULT								
ARK DOWNS LAST YEAR								
LAN								
RESULT								
M.U. ON PURCH. LAST YEAR								
THIS YEAR								
MAINTAINED M.U. LAST YEAR								
THIS YEAR								
GROSS MARGIN LAST YEAR								
THIS YEAR								
TNOVER LAST YEAR								
LAN								
RESULT								
NED L.Y. COUNT								
T.Y.								
NSACTIONS L.Y.								
T.Y.								
SALE L.Y.								
T.Y.								
LING % L.Y.								
T.Y.								

Figure 13. Merchandise Plan

		LAST YEAR	PLAN	AGE OF MERCHANDISE	LAST YEAR $	LAST YEAR %	PLAN $	PLAN %
Initial Markup	%			FASHION 1-3 MOS.				
Markdowns	%			FASHION 4-7 MOS.				
Shrinkage	%							
Workroom Cost	%			FASHION OVER 7 MOS.				
Gross Margin	%			NON-FASHION 1-7 MOS.				
Discount on Cost Purchases	%			NON-FASHION 8-13 MOS.				
Gross Margin Plus Discount	%							
Turnover				NON-FASHION OVER 13 MOS.				

SPRING, 19___		FEB.	MAR.	APR.	MAY	JUNE	JULY	TOTAL SEASON	AUG.
FALL, 19___		AUG.	SEPT.	OCT.	NOV.	DEC.	JAN.		FEB.

SALES

BOJ	LAST YR.									
	PLAN									
	REVISION									
	ACTUAL									
FOJ	LAST YR.									
	PLAN									
	REVISION									
	ACTUAL									
MOJ	LAST YR.									
	PLAN									
	REVISION									
	ACTUAL									
POJ	LAST YR.									
	PLAN									
	REVISION									
	ACTUAL									

RETAIL STOCKS 1st OF MONTH INCL. INVOICES

BOJ	LAST YR.							*		
	PLAN							*		
	REVISION							*		
	ACTUAL							*		
FOJ	LAST YR.							*		
	PLAN							*		
	REVISION							*		
	ACTUAL							*		
MOJ	LAST YR.							*		
	PLAN							*		
	REVISION							*		
	ACTUAL							*		
POJ	LAST YR.							*		
	PLAN							*		
	REVISION							*		
	ACTUAL							*		

TOTAL SALES	LAST YR.									
	PLAN									
	REVISION									
	ACTUAL									

TOTAL STOCK	LAST YEAR									
	YARDSTICK									
	PLAN									
	REVISION									
	ACTUAL									

3 MONTHS STOCK-SALES RATIO	YARDSTICK									
	PLAN									

PLANNED RECEIPTS	PLAN									
	REVISION									
	ACTUAL									

MERCHANDISE MARKDOWNS	LAST YR.									
	ACTUAL									

Figure 14. Branch Store Plans

volve extended delivery periods. First of the month stocks must be flexible enough to allow for the receipt of large quantities of merchandise. Usually imports are brought in to be sold over a period of several months, and care must be taken that the plan is flexible enough to allow for this.

Delivery dates on imports are not as easy to pin down as those on domestic purchases, and may bring on stock problems that the buyer and merchandise manager will have to work out together. Many stores show outstanding import orders separately on their weekly merchandise reports, so that they can see the exact status of their foreign commitments.

Pricing of imports, incidentally, is a real challenge to the merchandising talent of the buyer. There is no room for catch-all automatic markon here. The buyer should be conscious of getting the best price possible in line with the merchandise's customer appeal, and he will frequently find his imports the source of valuable extra markon.

What Plans Cannot Do. Plans and results can never be exact. They can at best only encourage a complete analysis of past operations, and a determination to avoid last year's errors and to repeat, intensify, and augment last year's successes. Of paramount importance is their educational value and their tendency to develop a thinking rather than an emotional approach to a problem.

The work of planning a merchandise operation is a continuous process—it is unceasing. Adjustments are made continually as needed. These adjustments are then available as a guide to the following year's plan, and the circle is then completed.

CHAPTER 15

THE THEORY OF MERCHANDISE CONTROL

BY

EDWIN L. HARLING

The purpose of this chapter and the one immediately following it is to outline the principles and to illustrate the procedures for determining and maintaining ideal merchandise assortments in any department.

Ideal assortments are those which, consistent with the established objectives and policies of a particular store, will produce maximum sales and profits. To accomplish this, an assortment must be maintained, consisting of current, wanted merchandise in proper price lines, colors, styles, etc., for meeting customer demand.

Customer demand changes almost daily. Ideal assortments must therefore also change. When a department is first stocked, the assortment may be well balanced and complete. A short time after selling from this stock, the assortment has changed and it becomes necessary to make another evaluation in order to ascertain the stock position and determine what specific merchandise should be brought into the inventory. The basic problem of the merchant is to replace the items he has sold with others currently in demand by the customer.

Definition of Merchandise Control. Merchandise control is a tool designed to implement the maintenance of ideal assortments. It is a system of recording and reporting quantities on hand and on order of individual items, and their respective rates of sale. There are several kinds and forms of merchandise control, depending upon the needs of individual stores and departments, but the purposes in all instances are the same—to assist in:

1. Making assortment and *unit* sales plans
2. Planning purchases by price lines within classifications
3. Ordering merchandise
4. Selecting items for sales promotions
5. Liquidating slow-moving items

Stock controls cost money. But the true cost of operating without scientific merchandise control may well be more than the expense attributable to unit control on the operating statement. The buyer should understand the true cost of stock controls or the lack of them in relation to the results his department achieves.

Classifications and Merchandise Control. In all but the very smallest of stores, to plan in terms of departmental totals is to use too much generalization for accuracy. The department is usually so large an entity that its total figures tend to conceal both outstanding performances as well as weaknesses in individual kinds of merchandise carried.

Therefore, an important step is to break each department down into several "natural" classifications, each an important, separate, distinct category of merchandise. For example, a men's furnishings department could consist of the following classifications: dress shirts, pajamas and nightwear, underwear, hosiery, neckwear, gloves, handkerchiefs, jewelry, gifts, robes and housecoats.

Classifications change, and so does the emphasis within classifications. It is a part of the buyer's responsibility to keep his department's classification lists current and in proper agreement with customer buying habits.

The ultimate development of the classification concept is the budgeting of sales and stocks by classification and, in turn, translating these budgeted figures into open-to-buy information by classification. Figure 15 shows how this can be done. Each classification has a block of lines across the width of the form, and each month, or other accounting period, has a group of five columns down the form.

In the form illustrated, we show this year's actual figures on the first line for each classification; next, this year's planned figures; next, the actual for each of the two previous years; finally, the current year's orders. The columns are: stocks (in-

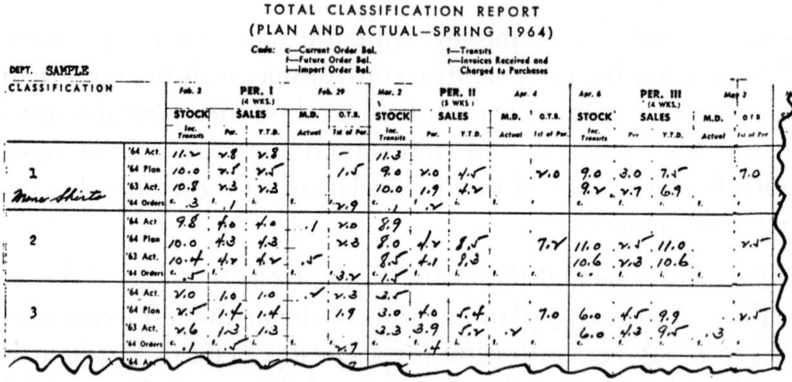

TOTAL CLASSIFICATION REPORT
(PLAN AND ACTUAL—SPRING 1964)

Code: c—Current Order Bal. f—Future Order Bal. i—Import Order Bal. t—Transits r—Invoices Received and Charged to Purchases

DEPT. SAMPLE

CLASSIFICATION		PER. I (4 WKS.) Feb. 3 STOCK Inc. Transits	SALES Per.	SALES Y.T.D.	M.D. Actual	Feb. 29 O.T.B. 1st of Per.	PER. II (5 WKS.) Mar. 2 STOCK Inc. Transits	SALES Per.	SALES Y.T.D.	M.D. Actual	Apr. 4 O.T.B. 1st of Per.	PER. III (4 WKS.) Apr. 6 STOCK Inc. Transits	SALES Per.	SALES Y.T.D.	M.D. Actual	May 2 O.T.B. 1st of Per.
1 Mens Shirts	'64 Act.	11.2	2.8	2.8		—	11.3									
	'64 Plan	10.0	2.5	2.5		1.5	9.0	2.0	4.5		2.0	9.0	3.0	7.5		7.0
	'63 Act.	10.8	2.3	2.3			10.0	1.9	4.2			9.2	2.7	6.9		
	'64 Orders	c. .3	.1			2.9	c. .1	.2								
2	'64 Act	9.8	4.0	4.0	.1	2.0	8.9									
	'64 Plan	10.0	4.3	4.3		2.3	8.0	4.2	8.5		7.2	11.0	2.5	11.0		2.5
	'63 Act.	10.4	4.2	4.2	.5		8.5	4.1	8.3			10.6	2.3	10.6		
	'64 Orders	c. .5				3.2	c. 1.5									
3	'64 Act.	2.0	1.0	1.0	.4	2.3	2.5									
	'64 Plan	2.5	1.4	1.4		1.9	3.0	4.0	5.4		7.0	6.0	4.5	9.9		2.5
	'63 Act.	2.6	1.3	1.3			2.3	3.9	5.2	.2		6.0	4.3	9.5	.3	
	'64 Orders	c. .1	.5			2.7	c.	.4								

Figure 15. Classification Report

cluding those in transit) ; sales for the period and the year to date; actual markdowns taken; and the calculated open-to-buy.

Classification controls have a definite and worthwhile function in controlling the assortment of items within each basic type or classification of merchandise. To accomplish this function, classification data should be built up from item data, rather than broken down from department dollar statistics. Only in this way are the component elements of the classifications subjected to the kind of study that permits mature decisions on the adding or dropping of items from an assortment. In order to obtain the unit data, we use unit controls.

Model Stock: First Step in Merchandise Control. The first step in setting up a workable merchandise control system is to list the items which make up the assortment. These usually include staple items, fashion items, novelty items, and prestige items.

Considerable thought and care are called for in the setting up of these lists. In setting up basic or staple item lists, minimum quantities may be as much a part of the list as the description of the items themselves. In some instances, the number of brands or lines to be carried in each price line, and the number of price lines also, must be specified. The objective is to make sure that all wanted types of merchandise are included, with quantities and breadth of assortment balanced against current customer demand.

Items should be described in the same detail as specified by customers. For example, shortly after information was published to the effect that white and yellow raincoats were safest because of best visibility in murky weather, color became the deciding factor in the customer's selection of raincoats. For that item, then, color would be specified first on our lists, with style and other factors following.

In some lines, brand names are the important element, and should be listed first. In other lines, fabric or some other variable may be the determining factor. The importance of style varies with the merchandise.

Reviewing Model Stocks. At the start of each season, it is advisable that a model stock be reworked to see what additional items need to be added, to identify items to be eliminate from current assortments, and particularly to round out basic stocks to make sure that the range and quantities of items are in keeping with demand.

This work necessitates a careful analysis and review of the unit control records. Through them, the buyer can study and analyze the flow of merchandise with respect to specific items and take whatever action is appropriate to develop those in good demand or prune away those that do not have sufficient sales potential in that store and department.

Using the Merchandise Control System. A merchandise control system yields facts and figures, but these are useless in themselves unless they serve to trigger action by the buyer. It is the buyer or department manager who actually controls the stock; therefore the system of records covering that stock should be designed for the buyer's use. It should provide him with the statistical data needed to make decisions with minimum effort but maximum use of his talents.

The buyer, by the same token, must assume responsibility for having an operable stock control system. It is his duty to collaborate with the personnel responsible for his unit records; to influence proper standards in maintenance of the system; and to work with unit control clericals in a climate of mutual understanding and respect for the principles of good stock control.

If the store uses electronic data processing for unit control purposes, the work itself may be performed at some point, either in or out of the store, remote from the buyer's desk. This does not in any way lessen the importance to the buyer of giving intelligent cooperation to those in charge of the activity. The more accurately the computer experts understand his department's needs, the better can they adapt the input and output of information to those needs.

Types of Merchandise Control. Basically, there are two major types of merchandise control, namely perpetual and rotated. There are also several auxiliary types, such as the partial visual, best seller control, and slow selling or problem merchandise control. And there is also the want slip system or its equivalent for alerting the buyer to items called for but not in stock.

Perpetual Controls. The perpetual system of merchandise control derives information as to the quantity of an item on hand by subtracting individual sales from stock. It involves the use of stub price tickets, analysis of sales checks, or the use of tallies.

Perpetual controls are recommended for departments in which items are subject to abrupt changes in fashion, calling

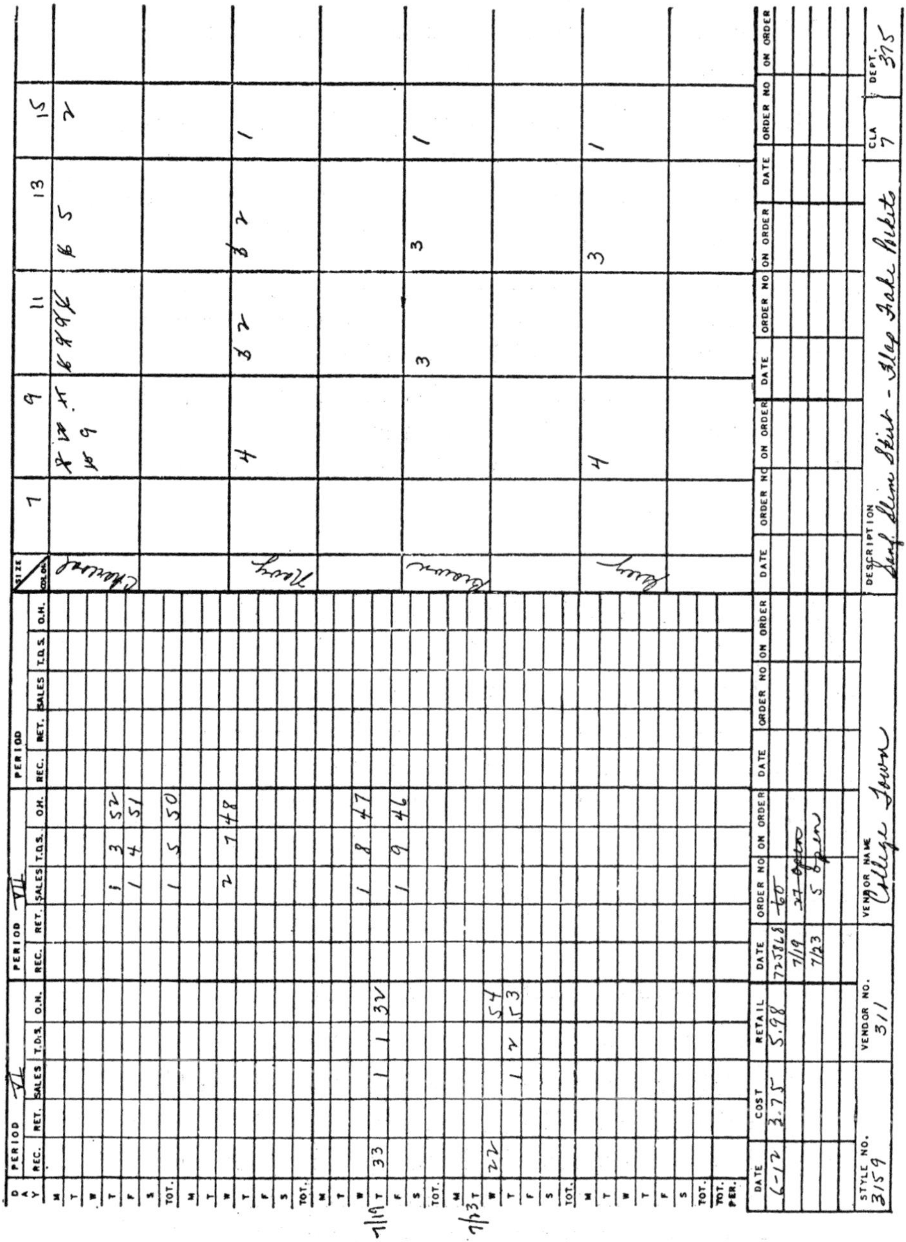

Figure 16. Style Activity Record

for fast reordering and liquidation. They are also used for items with high unit value.

The well-rounded perpetual unit control system includes all four of these basic elements:

1. Style activity record: History of the item from the first order, showing receipts and sales to date. Figure 16 illustrates such a form; other versions are shown and explained in the chapter following.

2. Daily report of item activity: A listing of all items sold the previous day; items on which there was activity; items which should be reordered or replaced in stock. The fashion buyer can take prompt action from this report, without going through all the detail of the records. Figure 17 is an example.

MFG. NO.	MANUFACTURER	STYLE NO.	CLASS	RETAIL	COLOR	SIZE	NO. SOLD TODAY	CUMULATIVE UNITS SOLD	CUMULATIVE UNITS RECEIVED	ON ORDER
301	College Town	3159	7	98	Charcoal	9	1			
						11	1			
						13	1			
				Navy	11	1				
						13	1			

DAILY SALES AND STOCK REPORT — DATE 7-19 19___ — DEPT. 375

Figure 17. Daily Report of Item Activity

3. Weekly report of unit sales and unit stocks by price lines within classifications—in effect a price line open-to-buy. It shows up lack of balance in the assortment and permits prompt action. It is also used as summary background data in determining reorder, promotion, or liquidation action

PRICE LINE OPEN-TO-BUY FROM *Aug.* TO *Oct.* YEAR CLASS 7 DEPT. 375

PRICE LINE	PER	STOCK BEG. PLAN	L.Y.	PLAN	SALES 1	ACT. WEEKLY 2	3	4	5	ACT.	PER. VII O.H.	O.O.	O.T.B	PER. VIII O.H.	O.O.	O.T.B	PER. IX O.H.	O.O.	O.T.B
	VII	300	316	150	27	18	9			1									
	VIII	450	920	975						2	123	33							
5.98	IX	700	811	900						3									
										4									
										5									
										1									
										2									
										3									
										4									
										5									
	VII									4									
	VIII									2									
10.98	IX									3									
										4									
										5									
										1									
										2									
										3									
										4									
										5									
	VII									1									
	VIII									2									
12.98	IX									3									
										4									
										5									
										1									
										2									
										3									
										4									
										5									
	VII									1									
	VIII									2									
14.98	IX									3									
										4									
										5									
Total	VII									1									
	VIII									2									
	IX									3									

Figure 18. Price Line Open-to-Buy

for individual items. It helps plan purchases by price lines and classification and reveals trends in sales by price lines. The divisional merchandise manager can use it as a guide in evaluating the buyer's performance. Figure 18 is an example. Each price line in the classification has three lines across the page, one for each accounting period or month. Columns provide space for planned opening stock in units; last year's actual and this year's planned monthly sales; weekly and monthly sales this year. The triple column set-up at the right is for calculating the open-to-buy, in units, after entering stock on hand and on order each week.

4. Monthly sales and stock plan and report. This is similar to the weekly report, but compares the sales of the past four weeks with the commitment.

These unit plans should be so organized that they can be summarized into quarterly or seasonal dollar plans, since the purpose of this entire procedure is to enable the buyer to develop the seasonal plans from the unit or assortment point of view.

In perpetual control systems, it is considered desirable that a procedure be instituted which will provide open-to-buy information in units by price line and classification for the current month and for the two months in advance. Plans so made must be flexible.

Controls are not to be restrictive, but should serve to direct the planning and purchasing in order to provide proper assortments in relation to demand.

Rotated Merchandise Control. The rotated or staggered system of merchandise control schedules the physical stock counts on a rotated or staggered basis. Sales figures are derived by subtracting each stock count in turn from the total of the previous one plus any merchandise received. Such controls are for merchandise which is largely of a staple or semi-staple nature.

There are two major elements in the rotated system: the basic record and the seasonal item report.

The basis record should have the following features: Sales history of the item for the previous year by quarters; number of weeks coverage to be provided for each item; indicators as to seasonal peaking or tapering of stocks; sufficient details to enable assistants or clericals to prepare the reorders.

Figure 19 is an example of such a form. It shows stock counted every two weeks, with minimum pack of four units

ROTATED UNIT CONTROL					1	2	3	4	5	6	7	8	9	10	11	12	13		1	2
STYLE NO.	DESCRIPTION	MIN. PACK / AVR. DEL.	COST / RETAIL	SEA. IND. / COUNT DATE	2/8	2/22	3/8	3/22	4/6	4/20	5/6	5/19	6/2	6/14	6/29	7/12	7/27	6 MO. SALES		
			28.50	O.H.	23	23	22	22	20	20	20	19	20	20	17	18	18	T.Y.		
		4		ORD.														8		
			3.95	REC.														L.Y.		
Dart	15 — 36	1 wk.		SALES	0	1	0	2	0	0	1	-1	0	3	-1	0	3	11		
				O.H.	29	38	25	12	9	22	22	21	22	17	12	12	11	T.Y.		
		4		ORD.														19		
				REC.														L.Y.		
	15½ — 30			SALES	-9	13	13	3	-13	0	1	-1	5	5	0	1	1	44		
				O.H.														T.Y.		
				ORD.																
				REC.														L.Y.		
				SALES																

Figure 19. Rotated Unit Control

and delivery in one week. Stock is entered at each count and sales (or negative figures for returns) are calculated and entered. There is space for entering orders and receipts and, at the end of each six-month period, total sales compared to last year's total.

The procedure is simple. Certain portions of the stock are scheduled for counting on certain days, the frequency depending on the needs of the department, the rate of stock turn desired, and the practice of resources as to shipping. Counts are made preferably by salespeople or heads of stock responsible for the particular classifications or lines. The actual exercise of counting the stock yields the salespeople certain intangible values, such as intimate knowledge of the stock and the feeling of participation in the proper reordering and maintaining of assortments.

Coverage Formula. There is a simple formula for arriving at quantities to be ordered, based on the interval between scheduled stock counts, plus the delivery period (time between placing of order and time when merchandise will be delivered and placed on sale), plus the safety factor of an extra week or two for unforeseen delays. Add up all these weeks, multiply them by the expected weekly sales of the item, and subtract the amount in stock. The result is the amount to be reordered.

The formula is predicated upon prompt action, with reorders placed on the day the count is made, if possible, to prevent out-of-stock conditions later on.

Merchandise listed on the basic record should be in logical sequence, following the direction of customer inquiry, just as merchandise in the selling department itself should be arranged. By listing items according to customer demand, the summaries that are drawn off make it easier for the buyer to do item planning and control on the basis of the customer's wants.

Although the basic record form, Figure 19, summarizes results for each season, it is also helpful to have a seasonal item report, showing sales and stocks by classification and price line, month by month, over an entire season. This provides the buyer with a detailed recapitulation of item sales by classification, which can be used in reviewing the department's assortment condition. It also gives him a summary dollar report of sales by classification. For smaller details, such as size, color, etc., he would refer back to his basic record.

Partial Visual Merchandise Control. Some automatic reorder systems can be based on the storage space, each fixture being so designed as to contain a supply of merchandise sufficient to cover the reorder interval. Then, a glance shows how much should be reordered.

Many stores ignore forward stock quantities in their unit

control records, basing their systems on the receipt and withdrawal information from stockrooms or warehouse stocks.

Forward stocks are then controlled by a visual method. The fixtures are laid out with specific places for specific items, and the most casual inspection will show what needs replenishing. Wherever possible, the designated forward stock areas should house standard quantities in proportion to selling rate—a standard number of days' supply.

Not only does such a method minimize record keeping, but it improves the appearance of the department and makes for greater efficiency in selling. Thoughtfully planned arrangements of the stock can encourage customer self selection and, by placing related items near one another, encourage second-item sales.

Weekly Stock Reviews. The buyer and assistant should make regularly scheduled reviews of the sales and stock summary reports, and at the same time plan for buying, sales promotion, and liquidation of slow sellers.

Under an effective system of unit control, the stock control clerical can relieve the buyer of routine reordering. The buyer must first provide information as to the number of weeks' supply to be carried, and indications of expected upward and downward trends, as in the case of seasonal variations.

It is usually better to indicate the number of weeks' supply to be provided rather than to set minimum and maximum stock quantities. Minimum and maximum figures tend to become fixed, and not flexible enough to reflect changes in the rate of sale; a system of figures that must be computed at each reorder period encourages attention to changing patterns of demand.

Other Uses of Merchandise Control. With good merchandise control and frequent physical review of stock on hand in comparison with rates of sale, the buyer can quickly spot best sellers as well as merchandise in excess of current requirements. The buyer can can single out for attention both his old-age merchandise and any relatively fresh stock that is moving

Lost ... a Sale!

Because we were out of:

_____

_____

_____

Remember:

- A sale lost is money lost in commission.

- We don't know you're out of something 'til you tell us.

- Don't wait . . . tell us now before you lose another sale.

Name	Dept.	Sales No.	Date

- If no sales were lost, please so indicate by checking here . . . ☐

9481-43

7①4113R   The Baltimore Business Forms Co., Atlanta, Ga.   BUY-38

Figure 20. Want Slip

slowly—including fashion items, for instance, which are found unwanted within a matter of days after arrival.

The information about problem merchandise, whether it is accumulated from unit control records, inspection of the stock, or both, should be consolidated for the buyer's study, so that he can work out ways of moving it with minimum markdown costs and minimum disruption of the basic assortment operation.

Want Slip System. Up to this point, we have considered items actually in the stock and their rate of sale. An important additional element of control is the conscientious reporting of customer calls for merchandise which the department did not have on hand.

Figure 20 shows a want slip form that can be filled out by each salesperson each day. The information, compiled into weekly summaries, points up customer preference trends and also reveals basic stock weaknesses and new volume potential areas. The buyer who recognizes the value of this information will encourage his salespeople to report customer wants conscientiously and correctly. Like every other part of this unit control system, wants slips help him achieve profitable volume.

Summing Up. Succintly stated, the purpose of merchandise control is to maximize sales, minimize stocks, provide more of items that are currently wanted, and to eliminate undesirable merchandise. Therefore proper merchandise control leads to proper actions that will increase the average sales check, and ultimately will provide more profit for the department.

CHAPTER 16

MATHEMATICS OF MERCHANDISE CONTROL

BY

JEROLD S. MEYER

The value and use of merchandise control systems having been discussed in the previous chapter, let us consider the step-by-step procedures involved.

The mathematical procedure used is exactly the same as in dollar control. The only reason units are used instead of dollars is the ease of keeping track of sales, and of merchandise on hand and on order. It is easier, for example, to use a record that shows 50 handbags at $7.50 in stock, 24 on order, and 14 sold last week, than it is to say we have $375 of $7.50 handbags in stock, $180 at retail on order, and that we sold $105 last week. Should anyone wish to do so, retail dollars can be substituted for units in the examples that follow and the results will be the same as if units had been used.

Methods of Obtaining Sales Records. There are two general ways by which we can find out how many of an item were sold in any given period. One way is by *stock count,* and the other is by sales recording.

The stock count method requires a good deal of clerical work and is preferred over the sales recording method only when the total number of work hours used in providing the information in this manner is less than the work hours used in providing this same information by sales recording.

In obtaining sales by stock count, the stock on hand at the beginning of the period is physically counted and written down, as, for example:

78 units

To this is *added* all merchandise arrivals during the period:

a.	From vendors	24
b.	Transfers from other stores or departments	10
c.	Returns from customers	2
d.	Markdowns from higher price ranges	10
	Total	124

From this total is *subtracted* all merchandise known to be removed by operations other than sales, and the stock on hand at the end of the period:

a.	Returns to vendors	12
b.	Transfers out of the department	6
c.	Markdowns out of this price range	8
d.	Stock on hand at end of period	80
	Total	106

The difference equals sales or merchandise otherwise removed from the department without having been recorded: 18

If the customer and vendor returns, department transfers, and markdowns are so small that they do not seriously affect the sales and stock figures they can be disregarded.

Sales Recording. When obtaining sales by sales recording, there are three main ways of doing so:

First, by removing all or part of a stub or tag when the merchandise is sold, then sorting and adding, or tallying these stubs or tags in order to arrive at the total of units sold.

Second, by hand writing or tallying each item as it is sold. This can be done on a tablet handy to the salesbook, on a tally card stored in the salesbook cover, on the cash register tape, on the cash register receipts, or in any of a number of other ways. The totals must be accumulated by some sort of tallying daily, weekly, or at the end of the selling period.

Third, by electronic machines which record each sale made, accumulate totals, and render a report of the accumulated number of sales at the end of the selling period.

Methods of Obtaining Stock on Hand. There are two ways in which to obtain stock on hand: first, by *stock count,* and second, by *perpetual inventory.*

The first is sometimes literally a piece by piece count, or it is sometimes done by a glance at the stock and a guess as to how much there is. Stock that is in the warehouse or stock room in original cartons can be counted without handling each piece. Sometimes, where the amount of forward stock is inconsequential, the count of this stock is omitted and only the reserve and warehouse stocks are counted.

Obtaining the stock on hand by perpetual inventory is done by writing down the previous stock on hand, as, for example:

78 units

To this is *added* all merchandise arrivals during the period:

a.	From vendors	24
b.	Transfers from other departments or stores	10
c.	Returns from customers	2
d.	Markdowns from higher price ranges	10
	Total	124

From this total is *subtracted* merchandise known to have been removed from stock:

a.	Sales to customers	18
b.	Returns to vendors	12
c.	Transfers out of the department	6
d.	Markdowns out of this price range	8
	Total	44

The difference equals stock that should be on hand in the department:

80

Methods of Obtaining Stock on Order. There are two ways to obtain the stock on order: first, by a *tabulation of outstanding orders;* and second, by keeping a *perpetual inventory of outstanding orders.*

The tabulation of outstanding orders is the simplest way of obtaining the number of units on order. Each order is inspected and the unfilled orders or portions of orders tallied or written down and totaled.

In unit control systems, it is important to separate the outstanding orders into various delivery dates: immediate, next month, and future, or other similar divisions. This separation is important when we come to figuring open-to-buy.

The perpetual inventory of outstanding orders is accomplished by writing down the previous total of outstanding orders at the beginning of the period, as, for example:

	108	
To this, we *add* new orders placed during the period:	264	
Total		372

From this total, we *subtract* the sum of the following:

a. Vendors' orders cancelled by us or by the vendor	80	
b. Merchandise received	100	
Total		180

The difference equals the total of outstanding orders at the end of the period: 192

Definition of Open-to-Buy. The open-to-buy is the amount of merchandise that should be received into stock during the buying period. The buying period is either days, weeks, or months, but in no case should it be less than the sum of the reorder period (number of days between stock reviews) and the delivery period (number of days expected to elapse between placing of order and the day the merchandise is available for sale in the department.)

The formula for open-to-buy begins with the amount of stock planned to be on hand at the end of the buying period. This figure is the sum of:

a.	The basic stock of the item	16
b.	A cushion to allow for sales spurts and delays in delivery. (Suggestions for setting this amount are given later.)	24
c.	A specified number of weeks' supply for selling until the next shipment arrives in stock	76
	Total planned ending stock	116

To the planned ending stock we *add* the following:

d.	Sales planned to be made during the buying period	60
e.	Merchandise to be returned to vendor	0
f.	Merchandise to be transferred to other stores or departments	0
g.	Merchandise expected to be marked down out of this price range	8
	Total to be provided for the period	184

From this total we *subtract* the sum of:

a.	What is on hand at the beginning of the period	62
b.	Merchandise on order that is expected to arrive during this period	72
c.	Merchandise that is expected to be transferred from other departments or other stores	0
d.	Merchandise that is expected to be marked down into this price range during the period	15

continued on next page

e. Merchandise that is expected to be returned from customers during the period   <u>5</u>

The total of these items equals the total that is already provided: <u>154</u>

Subtracting the total already provided, from the total to be provided, we get the open-to-buy for the period: 30

If the amount of merchandise already provided is greater (suppose it is 274 instead of 154) than the amount to be provided (184), then the difference between the two is a red figure of 90, which means that we are overbought 90 for the period.

If any of the items in the above formula are so small that they are of little consequence, they can be omitted from the calculation.

Abbreviated Formula. An abbreviated formula for open-to-buy which includes only the very important elements is the one most often used. *Add:*

a. Planned ending stock   116
b. Planned sales for the period   <u>60</u>
    Total   176

From this, *subtract:*

a. Stock on hand, beginning of period   62
b. Merchandise on order, beginning of period   <u>72</u>
    Total   <u>134</u>

Open-to-buy for the period: 42

This abbreviated formula will be the one used in the illustrations, examples, and forms that follow. It is important to understand the detailed formula so that merchandise returns to vendors, or transfers, or customer returns, or markdowns, or markups, can be taken into consideration if any of these becomes an important sized figure.

Open-to-Buy by Classifications. While the open-to-buy formula is generally used for the entire department, it is increasingly used also for classifications. It is also used for price ranges and items when figuring out how much to buy.

In determining which of these segments to use in figuring open-to-buy, we should ask, "What information do we wish to obtain?" We could figure the open-to-buy in units for a total men's furnishing department, but the figure would not be very helpful. When we break the department down into classifications and figure the open-to-buy for each price range within each classification, we get useful figures.

A true classification is a grouping of merchandise in which the items in the group are reasonably substitutable for each other to the customer.

The number of classifications is becoming more or less standardized as a result of the NRMA's work in classification analysis by departments, but the store itself is the final judge of precisely what should be the number of classifications, depending upon the degree of detailed information desired.

Item Control. In this type of control we refer to an item that is of sufficient importance to the stock that (1) it should always be in stock and (2) there is no other item readily substitutable to the customer. An example of one such item would be a black ready-tied bow tie at $1.00. Such an item should be controlled separately.

Merchandise Control for a Single Item. The first record of value to have is a sales record by months which extends back for at least two years. Such a record is shown on Form #1, Figure 21. A glance at this record shows the annual and monthly unit sales, and whether the item is on the ascendency, static, or in decline. This information is important to know when we attempt to forecast or estimate the future potential sales of an item.

The source of our sales entry for the month on Form #1 is Form #2, Figure 22. On Form #2 we start off with 48 units

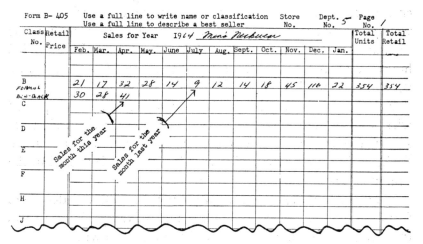

Figure 21. Form 1. Merchandise Control for Single Item

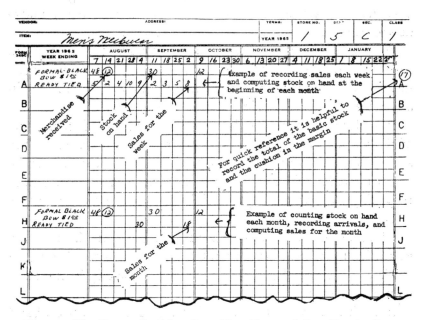

Figure 22. Form 2. Merchandise Control for Single Item

on hand (in the upper square) at the beginning of the week ending on Saturday, August 7. The sales recorded in the squares on the lower line (5, 2, 4, etc.) represent sales made during the weeks ending August 7, 14, 21, etc. The circled figure 12 represents a shipment of 12 received from the manufacturer during August.

By adding to the 12 received during the five-week period what was on hand at the beginning (48) and subtracting the sales made during the five weeks (30) we arrive at 30 on hand at the end of the five-week period. This figure is posted in the upper square as shown.

The sales for the next four-week period (18) are deducted from the stock on hand at the beginning of the period (30) and the new stock on hand (12) is written in, as shown.

Correcting the Control Count. This procedure continues throughout the season. At least twice a year, it is important to take a physical inventory to correct the on-hand figure, as it does not remain accurate—due to customer returns, markdowns, carelessness, and other unrecorded causes.

For convenience in figuring open-to-buy, it is helpful to record the total of the basic stock and cushion in a permanent location on the form. You will note the figure 17 recorded in a circle at the extreme right.

In order to obtain weekly sales to record on this form, one of the two methods previously described must be used: either a weekly stock count, or sales recording. If a weekly stock count is too laborious and no method has been set up for sales recording, we can still get useful information by a monthly stock count.

The manner of keeping a monthly sales record by taking a monthly stock count is illustrated also on Form #2 on line "H". In this case the calculation is made exactly in the same manner as before.

In both illustrations we find that we have 12 units on hand October 9th. The question now arises, "Should we reorder and if so how much?" To answer this question we apply the open-to-buy formula. We first determine how far ahead we should buy. The formula for this is: the buying period is the sum of the reorder period and the delivery period.

The Reorder Period. Let's assume that we review the stock of this item once each month; the reorder period is then four weeks. We know from past experience that it is readily re-orderable. In fact, it is locally made and so is delivered the day following receipt of re-order. But we must allow for possible delays: failure to get the order promptly counter-signed, delay in the mail, congestion in the receiving and marking room. Hence, instead of one day's allowance for delivery, we allow a week. The extra days are our "cushion."

It may be that the vendor is out of town, and that it takes longer for our order to reach him and for the merchandise, in turn, to reach us. Our experience tells us how much time to allow for the individual item and vendor. Whatever that period is, we add still another period (a week, a month, or even more, as in deliveries of china) as a cushion for unforeseen delays, and *the sum of the two is our delivery period,* inclusive of cushion.

To return to our example: The review period is four weeks, and the delivery period is one week; hence, five weeks is our buying period. Now let us apply the abbreviated open-to-buy formula: *Add*:

Planned ending stock	17	
Planned sales for five weeks	45	
Total		62
Minus:		
Stock on hand, beginning of period	12	
Stock on order, beginning of period	0	
Total		12
Equals open-to-buy for period		50

If the item is packed in dozens or half-dozens, we order four dozen and show that 48 have been ordered by recording that figure next to the 12 for stock on hand on the upper line. When the shipment arrives, the figure is circled to show that the order has been filled.

Merchandise Control by Manufacturers' Lines. Because of ease and convenience in counting stock and reviewing the items to be ordered, it is often desirable to arrange all of the items purchased from one vendor on one form, Form #2. The top heading is adapted for this purpose. Each item is assigned to one line on the form and as many pages are used as may be necessary.

Style Number Control: Sizes and Colors. On Form #3 we show how to keep a style number control in ready-to-wear, (Figure 23). On August 6 we received 20 coats style #8175, from Excelsior Garment Company. (We have assigned them vendor number 135.) Cost is $51.75; retail, $89.95. When these 20 coats are received the entry is made "8/6—20," as shown under "Received". Also a tally mark is made in the color and size chart for each coat received.

On August 25, 11 more coats of the same style number arrive and the notation "8/25—11" is made as shown, and each coat is tallied in the color and size chart.

As each coat is sold, the stub is detached and used for the purpose of making two tally marks on Form #3. The first stroke is a tally mark in the 1st, 2nd, 3rd, 4th, or 5th week of the month in which the coat was sold, as shown. The second tally stroke is a cross through one of the tally marks in the color and size chart to indicate which particular size and color was sold.

At any time this record will show how many coats were received and when; how many coats were sold and when; in what sizes and colors the coats are selling; and what is presently in stock to be sold by size and color.

Handling a Customer Return. If a coat is returned from a customer a tally is made two times in red: first, a red stroke is made through one of the tally marks in the weekly sales chart

VENDOR NAME *Excelsior Garment*
Cost 51 ⁷⁵ Ret 89 ⁹⁵

VENDOR NUMBER *135*

Style #8175		AUG	SEPT	OCT	NOV	DEC
RECEIVED	1		////			
8/6 - 20	2	//				
8/25 - //	3	///				
	4	/				
	5					

	8	10	12	14	16	18
Black	X /	XXX	X ///	///	X /	
Blue		//	//	//		
Red		/	/	X /		
Tan	X	X /	//	/	X	

Merchandise received is listed twice -
first, date and total quantity received,
like 8/6 - 20 (as shown above)
size and color chart as above

Merchandise sold is tallied twice -
first, in the week of the month in
which it is sold as in the upper chart,
(note two tally marks in the second
week of August)
second, in the size and color chart (note
one size 8 in tan)

Reorders are tallied in green in the size
and color chart and then tallied over
in black when received. This will show
the outstanding reorders at all times.

Customer returns are tallied in red in the
size and color chart.

Returns to vendor are crossed thru in red
instead of black.

Figure 23. Form 3. Style Number Control

to show that one of the sales has been returned, and another tally is made in the color and size chart to show the arrival of another coat via customer return.

If it is decided to reorder the coat, a green tally is made in the color and size chart for each coat ordered. This shows the coats that are on order at all times. When the coat arrives in stock, a black mark is made over the green mark. This shows that the coat is no longer on order but in stock.

In a department where the volume of units is so large that the information cannot conveniently be recorded on Form #3 (three styles to a page), Form #4 can be used (two styles to a page). There are 28 spaces to record sales. These may be used either for daily or weekly sales as needs dictate. Note that the same data has been illustrated on Form #4 as was shown on Form #3. (See Figure 24.)

Selection Controls. Here we will describe the procedure for controlling a selection of items in a price range. This would apply to some apparel and many accessory and home furnishings classifications.

In ready-to-wear, we review the open-to-buy position weekly. Slower turning classifications are reviewed monthly. Men's four-in-hand ties at $1, for instance, represent such a classification. In this type of control, we group together all of the items reasonably substitutable for each other from which the customer will make her choice when making a purchase.

Because a market trip or a review of manufacturers' lines by the buyer is necessary before reordering in this type of merchandise, we use a different form on which to record stock, sales, and on order. Usually the stock fill-in will be accomplished by a number of orders from different manufacturers, rather than by sitting down at the desk and reordering a style number already in stock, as was done when reordering the black bow tie at $1.

There are three kinds of Selection Control items. One group comprises items that do not come in sizes: jewelry, handbags,

Form 93

Date	Quan.	Color	8	10	12	14	16	18	Vend. Euclair	No. 135
8/6	20	Black	X1	XXX	X111	111	X1		Style 6175	Cl.
6/25	11	Blue		11	11	11			Cost 51 75	Ret. 89 75
		Red		1	1	X1			Reord.	O.O.
		Tan	X	X1	11	1	X			

Bgt - Mink Collar

Date	Quan.	Color							Vend.	No.
									Style	Cl.
									Cost	Ret.
									Reord.	O.O.

Date	1st ½	2nd ½	Total

Date	1st ½	2nd ½	Total

Figure 24. Form 4. Style Number Control

pillows, lamps, etc. These would be *Style Selection Control* items.

A second group would include dresses, gloves, coats, etc.,— items that come in simple personal sizes as well as in various styles. These would be *Simple Size Selection Control* items.

A third group, of which shoes, slippers, and men's shirts are good examples, would be examples of *Complex Size Selection Control* items, because in each size there are sub-sizes to consider. In shoes, for example, we have lengths and width; in men's shirts, we have neck sizes and sleeve lengths.

Style Selection Controls. Form #5, Figure 25, illustrates a form which can be used for Style Selection control classifications. The mathematical computations for this are identical

Men's Neckwear

UNIT PURCHASE PLAN		TOTAL RETAIL DOLLARS SALES PLAN	DEPT	YEAR	EXACT DATE STOCK ON HAND IS TAKEN	ACTUAL UNITS ON HAND NOW 3	UNITS ON HAND AT BEGIN	CLASS
FEB 1- to APRIL 30			5	1963	1/15			1E
FORM B254 REV 6-1-1948								

RETAIL PRICE RANGE	TOTAL RETAIL DOLLARS SALES PLAN	UNIT SALES PLAN			TOTAL UNIT SALES	PLAN END STOCK UNITS 2	EST. SALS FROM NOW TO EON. OF PERIOD 4	UNITS ON ORDER 6	UNITS TO BUY FOR PERIOD 7	LIST PURCHASES HERE AS MADE	O.T.B
		FEB	MAR	APR							
FOUR-IN-HAND TIES AT $1 (100)	LAST YEAR	181	216	221	618		280	200		Grand Neckwear 240-391	
	PLAN	200	225	250	675	300	80	144	631	Esquire 120-271	
	ACT.	190									

For quick reference it is helpful to record the total of the basic stock, since the cushion in the margin. Since the planned ending stock (300) exceeds the basic stock plus cushion (100) by 200 it indicated that we are bought 200 into the second quarter in our planning.

This shows that as of January 15 the open-to-buy for the balance of January and February, March and April is 631 units.

As each order is placed the amount is written in this column and the balance recorded at the extreme right. To be accurate this still open-to-buy. This shows 271 still open-to-buy. To be accurate this figure should be reduced by the amount the actual sales to date was under the plan. In this case it is 10 so that the accurate open-to-buy is 271 minus 10 or 261. If the sales exceed the plan the amount of the excess should be added to the open-to-buy.

Figure 25. Form 5. Style Selection Control

with those used in item control. In our example, we make an open-to-buy for three months for men's four-in-hand neckties. It is January 15, and we wish to find out how many ties we need to order for February, March, and April business.

First, we record last year's sales for the three months in the indicated spaces: 181, 216, 221. If desired, we can make room for two years' previous sales by drawing a diagonal line through the square and writing above the line our year-before-last sales (as was done on Form #1).

Next, we plan the monthly sales for each of the three months and write down these figures: 200, 225, and 250. Adding these together, we write the total (675) in the column indicated (Column 1).

Now, we plan what we think our ending stock should be on the last day of the period (April 30). We conclude that we want the stock to be 300 ties, which is 200 above our basic stock plus cushion. We write 300 in Column 2. This will give us 200 ties to sell in May and thereafter, without cutting in to our basic-stock-plus-cushion of 100 ties. We have circled this figure (100) in the left margin for handy reference.

Since we are doing this on January 15, we must project the stock on hand to the beginning of the new period (Feb. 1). We count our stock and find 280 on hand, writing it in the proper space (Column 3). We estimate we will sell 80 ties from January 15 to February 1; so we write 80 in the proper space (Column 4).

We note the calculation formula printed for convenience in the upper left hand corner of the form: $3 - 4 = 5$. We therefore subtract 80 (Column 4) from 280 (Column 3) and get 200 ties which we estimate will be on hand on February 1. We write this in Column 5.

We then write in Column 6 what is already on order for delivery between January 15 and April 30. This figure is 144.

The open-to-buy formula is printed in the upper left hand corner of this form so we can easily follow it: Planned Sales (Column 1) plus Ending Stock (Column 2) minus the sum of

On Hand (Column 5) and On Order (Column 6) equals Open-to-buy (Column 7). That is: 675 plus 300, minus the sum of 200 and 144, equals 631, the open-to-buy for the period.

As we place orders they can be recorded in the space at the right and the amount of each order deducted from the open-to-buy remaining. This will give us a correct open-to-buy figure at all times during the period until we make out a revised calculation or until it is time to make out the open-to-buy for the following three months on a new sheet.

Author's Note: The foregoing will give the reader the rudiments of the mathematics of unit control. For more detail and an explanation of Size Selection Control, which has not been covered in this article, consult Jerold S. Meyer's and Edwin L. Harling's, "Merchandise Control and Budgeting," also published by the NRMA.

CHAPTER 17

MERCHANDISING BY CLASSIFICATION[1]

BY

FRANK BURNSIDE

Precision management of inventory, which is a primary concern of the buyer, has its foundation in merchandising by classification. Classification merchandising began as a buyer's tool, with simple, do-it-yourself methods. Today, in many stores, it is as much a merchandise management tool as a buyer's device and the methods used are highly sophisticated and accurate. Whatever the equipment and procedures in his own store may be, the buyer should be acquainted with those of the past, present, and possible future, so that he will know the virtues and shortcomings of each and will be able to use this approach to improve his department's volume and profits.

A classification has been defined as a segment of customer demand. It is a special kind of segment, however, made up of homogeneous items, reasonably substitutable for one another in the customer's eyes. "Bathing suits," thus can constitute a classification; all suits, allowing for price and size differences, fill the same customer need. "Pins," in a notion department, cannot be a classification if hair pins, clothes pins, safety pins, and hat pins are all lumped together; one type cannot substitute for another in filling a customer need.

Earliest Steps Toward Controls. A fair case could be made for the proposition that the establishment of departments in

---

[1] For many of the ideas in this chapter I'm very deeply indebted to the thinking of The Keystone Group, a voluntary association of independent stores for figure exchange purposes, of which our store is a member. Under the leadership of Lloyd Jones Co., New York, the Group in the last 16 years has developed the concept of customer-oriented merchandising by classification which I describe in this chapter and which our store with others in the Group has been using with excellent fiscal results.

stores was in itself a merchandise control device by which the early entrepreneur hoped to apportion his purchases and inventory investment in relation to his customers' wants and needs. Many of our great stores had their beginnings in a period when both the available assortment and the quantity of merchandise were limited—particular in contrast to present-day variety and abundance.

In the early days of department stores and departmentalized specialty stores, eight or 10 departmental groupings were adequate. As the assortment and quantity of production increased, stores added new departments and broke large ones down into smaller units for better merchandising supervision and consequent increase in volume and profits.

Early stores frequently designated departments by letters of the alphabet. In time, when the number exceeded 26, a two-digit department numbering system became standard, to be succeeded still later by the three-digit system now in general use for the more than 100 merchandise department accounts commonly found in department stores.

As markets and stores and departments were expanding and the flow of merchandise was increasing, retail owner-managers hired assistants, or buyers, for departments or groups of departments. The present organization chart evolved, with divisions or groups of departments headed by divisional managers and staffed with buyer specialists, frequently with assistants of their own for each department, and sometimes even for important classifications within a large department.

This development in store organization took place because *the number of merchandising decisions required to be made increases in direct proportion to the increase in the assortment and quantity of merchandise produced.*

Ways to Control Stocks. As the available variety of merchandise grew, resourceful buyer-merchandisers devised various control techniques to apply within their own departments in order to help them make more intelligently the increasing number of decisions required of them. It soon became clear that different types of control techniques were needed for different parts of the merchandise assortment. Thus various forms of control developed: classification or dissection control, basic or staple and model stock controls, unit controls. These systems are discussed in detail in other chapters of this manual.

Managements generally encouraged these developments, but only rarely was there any effort to institute one standardized, centrally administered system or technique of merchandise control over the entire store. Within the past decade, however, store managements have become increasingly concerned with developing standardized merchandise planning and control techniques. This may be due in part to the vastly accelerated increase in assortments, even in departments historically considered basic; in part to a radically declining trend in turnover rates; and in part to some shocking results of surveys of customer walkout rates.

Early Forms of Classification Merchandising. Since classification controls originated with buyers in their efforts to break departments down into smaller pieces, the earliest concept of the classification was that of a sort of sub-department. There would be a limit of 10 or 12 such breakdowns per department, because of the practical problems involved in tabulating sales on some sort of tally board maintained by the cashier or the individual selling personnel.

The buyer or his clerical accumulated and posted these sales records from tally boards to a subsidiary merchandise record. To this, purchases or other additions to stock were also posted. Thus was achieved a rudimentary running dollar value of inventory, sales, and purchases, by classification or sub-department.

Advantages of the Method. The method served a useful purpose, although it was far from accurate. Markdowns and returns to stock were ignored, and errors crept into the tabulations. At the end of a fiscal period, there could be discrepancies of five to 20 per cent in reconciling these classification records with the official departmental records. Yet the system helped in the planning and merchandising process, particularly in large volume departments where the inventory was composed of a wide assortment of relatively low ticket items.

As an example, a men's furnishings department could be conveniently broken down into classifications such as shirts, underwear, pajamas, neckwear, sweaters, socks, gloves, jewelry, robes, and "miscellaneous." The catch-all classification would be used for items not sufficiently important to justify individual classifications of their own—handkerchiefs, belts, suspenders, gifts, etc.

This early type of dollar classification control had the advantage of simplicity and flexibility. It could be started with one or two classifications at a time, and gradually expanded. To set it up, a buyer needed a starting inventory at retail for each classification, plus an identification code or number to be marked on the price tickets.

The procedure was simple, too: Arrange to post sales and purchases, at retail, on a regular schedule. Add purchases and subtract sales to compute stock on hand daily, weekly, or monthly, as seemed necessary for that merchandise. Watch the movement of inventory in the classification and earmark part of the departmental open-to-buy more precisely in accordance with actual needs than would be otherwise possible. Avoid choking off purchases in a "live" classification because of sluggish performance elsewhere in the department.

New classifications could be introduced or old ones split up almost at will, so that items that became seasonally or fashionably active could be treated as special classifications. The purpose of all this, it should be remembered, was to pinpoint the sales and inventory conditions in each small section of the department and thus achieve the improved volume and profits that come with improved merchandising.

Disadvantages. The system had its shortcomings. As we saw earlier, the percentage of error accumulating in the control can be large enough to impair the method's usefulness for planning purposes. Further, with no standardized definition of the merchandise content of the classifications used, comparisons among stores or with the same store's figures for earlier years, or between main store and branch, were of little value.

Most important, however, is the fundamental consideration that such classification controls gave only dollar figures, not merchandise figures. In retail stores, we do not sell dollars; we sell merchandise, and that is what a system should control.

The classification reports would have told a buyer, for instance, that he needed more dollars worth of pajamas or shirts in the men's furnishings department—but not which price lines, colors, or sizes, or styles were moving and which were gathering dust. For that vital information, the buyer had to go to his unit controls or take a physical inventory.

A dollar merchandise classificaion control alone may actually be misleading. It may indicate a well balanced relationship between stock and sales—*dollar-wise*—at a time when there are out-of-stock conditions in key sizes, colors, or items. Identifying and correcting such conditions may require changes in stock balance, and may also step up volume and profits. These last are our merchandising goals, and if dollar classification alone does not lead us toward them, then we must supplement the system with other appropriate control techniques.

Middle Management Tool. Because the advantages far outweighed the disadvantages, many larger stores developed the technique of classification controls to an extraordinary degree of refinement. Buyers learned the usefulness of breaking their jobs into more easily manageable segments. As these buyers advanced to positions as divisional managers or attained general management level, it became plain that classification merchandising control was even more effective as a tool for supervision and control purposes at these higher levels of responsibility than it was on the firing line of department management.

Classification merchandising became recognized as what it most importantly is: An opportunity to gain the advantages of further departmentalization, further fractionalization, without incurring the disadvantages of the Chinese Walls that invisibly separate departments in many stores, and without the increase in expense usually associated with the fiscal establishment of new departments. In figure exchange among stores, moreover, classification sales figures began to be recognized as a more accurate yardstick for merchandising performance than departmental figures.

Introduction of Refinements. As higher levels of merchandising and general management became interested in classification merchandising, stores sought methods and tools for achieving more precise figures. Cash registers with as many as 20 totalizers for classifications, or with printer keys for indexing up to 99 classifications per department came into wider use, conquering the bottleneck and the inaccuracies of recording sales data on tally boards.

Accumulation and posting of records and reports were centralized, first on distribution accounting machines and more recently on punched card tabulating equipment and more sophisticated EDP machines, capable of producing daily stock balance reports or open-to-buy figures for 99 classifications in each of 100 or more departments.

Refinements were introduced for more effective use of the figures. Markdowns, sales returns, stock transfers, and other exceptions were taken into account. With these improvements, however, the method lost some of the flexibility it had when it was run by and for the buyer alone.

Refining the Definition. Gradually, there evolved a new and more precise definition of the classification. The elements of substitutability, mentioned in the opening paragraphs of this chapter, was clearly explained by Jerold S. Meyer, in 1956, in his "Dollar and Unit Merchandise Planning and Budgeting," an NRMA publication. It was recognized that breaking up a department into classifications means breaking it up, in Meyer's words, "into elements of customer demand so the buyer can measure each demand and buy to it."

Many stores, large and small, have constructed systems of merchandise classification control on this principle. The reports these systems generate, weekly or even daily, greatly facilitate the buyer's planning and decision-making. At the same time, they also provide divisional and general merchandise management with a convenient and precise tool for reviewing departmental operations, inventory status, and performance.

The buyer enjoys certain definite advantages when this is the case. Now his superiors are looking at his performance classification by classification; the one that prospers is not being penalized for the faults of the one that is lagging. His errors or ill luck in one classification are not starving the stocks of others that can continue to nourish the department's volume and profits. When his department was considered as a whole, however, the buyer who was overbought in some areas might not have been able to salvage enough open-to-buy to keep the healthy classifications going.

Planning by Classification. With "customer demand" classification controls to provide data on both historical and current trends in consumer demand, the buyer can construct a realistic and far more accurate forecast of future demand than with only the lumped figures on a total department basis. This means that the very heart of the buyer's job, planning and predicting sales, is done in terms of readily understandable and clearly defined segments of customer demand. He works up his forecast and his estimate of needs for each classification, and for price ranges and units within each one, to guide his market efforts. His dollar classification totals are combined to provide the projection that his store needs for control and financial purposes.

Required stock, in terms of dollars, is determined by various methods. Usually an "allowance period" of a specified number of weeks' supply is assigned to each classification based on the desired turnover and the lead time needed. For example, if a men's underwear classification is working on a turnover of about 4.5, it could have a 12 weeks' supply in stock, and it could need an additional four weeks' supply to cover commitments or merchandise on order. The allowance period required stock would then be 16 weeks' projected sales. For slower moving classifications, like upholstered furniture, for instance, the turnover might be 1.5 and the lead time quite long, yielding a 40 weeks allowance period.

Planning Open-to-Buy. Projected sales for the weeks ahead may be planned by the buyer on the basis of previous experience, or developed by a computer that has been programmed to forecast the weekly planned sales by classification. Relating the planned sales figures to the allowance period for that classification shows how much stock is required to produce the expected sales. From the required stock figure, subtractions are made for current stock and open commitments. The result is the "merchandise position" or the dollar "open-to-buy." (See form 26, page 189.)

More sophisticated statistical methods and programs for making these computations are available. Those who are interested will find much help in Robert G. Brown's "Statistical Forecasting for Inventory Control," McGraw-Hill, 1959.

Classification vs. Department. Recent developments in electronic data processing, particularly in the areas of optical scanning and pre-punched price tickets, have spurred a renewed interest in the possible Utopia of a completely automated store-wide system of unit merchandise control as part of an integrated EDP system. This raises the question of the possible obsolescence of the classification control system.

Quite to the contrary, a strong case can be made for further and standardized uniform development of the classification technique. This is because the homogeneity of departmental merchandise content is steadily diminishing—a development which, in turn, makes traditional departmental merchandising statistics progressively less valid indicators than they were in the past.

Reflective study of any store's layout compels the conclusion that merchandise departments have been created and designed to meet situations or conditions no longer related to the way

FOWLER, DICK AND WALKER, WILKES-BARRE, PA.

MERCHANDISE POSITION
CLASSIFICATION REPORT

DEPT. NO. 651   DEPT. NAME CHINA GLASSWARE   DATE JANUARY 2 1965   WEEK NO 49 PAGE 1

CLASS / COMMENTS	ALL PER	BASIC STOCK	WEEK THIS YEAR	PLAN	OVER UNDER C/R	WEEK LAST YEAR	Y.T.D	Y.T.D LAST YEAR	MARKDOWNS Y.T.D	MARKDOWNS Y.T.D LAST YEAR	STOCK ON HAND C/R	ON ORDER FOR THIS PERIOD	REQUIRED STOCK	OPEN TO BUY C/R
02 OPEN STOCK C S 2.00	52		349	13		330	13	3409	3859	832	195	3952	5	4028	69-
03 2.01 TO 5.00	52		10-	37	47-	37	1085	2169	3	109	2718	21	2149	590
04 OPEN STOCK 5.00 UP	52		33	19	14	19	6592	5908	132	134	11742	330	6441	5631
07 OPEN EARTHEN TO 1.00	52		43	4	39	4	1011	1138	126	9	408		1305	897-
08 EARTHEN 1.01 TO 2.00	52		92	43	49	43	6031	2085	357	1192	1045		2224	1179-
09 EARTHENWARE 2.01 UP	52		3	12	9-	12	3236	3318	216	167	3536	100	3609	27
11 CHINA SET UP TO 2.00	26		125	173	48-	173	7233	6325	1299	1467	2621		2524	97
12 CHINA 2.01 TO 5.00	26		395	175	220	175	8221	6967	735	758	5145	1680	4443	2382
13 CHINA SETS 5.01 UP	26		5		5		60	82			60-			60-
14 EARTHENWARE TO 1.00	26		208	73	135	73	10004	9100	919	1496	3926	298	5536	1312-
15 EARTH SET 1.01 2.00	26						355	90	165		236			236
16 EARTHWARE SET 2.01	26							16			143			143
21 CORNING PYREX WARE	16		107	73	33	73	10997	8486	107	126	3773	29-	2165	1579
22 OTHER DOMESTIC WARE	20		16	67	51-	67	2660	3633	80	245	2292		1440	852
23 IMPORTED COOK SERVE	20		1	17	16-	17	646	617	9	78	62-		256	318-
31 DOMESTIC	16		6	26	20-	26	1460	2084	32	77	335		353	18-
32 IMPORTED	20		42	76	34-	76	3522	3322	590	607	1422	220	774	868
41 GLASSES TO .50	16		329	237	92	237	9022	5477	186	112	2941	1	1438	1504
42 GLASSES .51 TO 1.00	16		34	58	24-	58	1568	2176	291	693	944		441	503
43 GLASSES 1.00 TO 2.00	16		7	53	46-	53	799	1904	59	211	622	56	766	88-
44 GLASSES 2.00 UP	20		7	17	10-	17	1698	1305	90	140	2658	871	488	3041
45 GLASSES BOXED 5.00	16		115	25	90	25	3134	2862	205	160	3906	105	539	3472
46 GLASS BOXED 5.00 UP	16		42	66	24-	66	1217	1776	152	216	716		403	313
47 JUICE BEV SETS ETC	20		59	8	52	8	3391	3167	135	131	1972	40	956	1056
51 MILK COLOR DOMESTIC	24		137	117	20	117	10598	8141	415	217	2529	1756	2250	2035
52 OTHER DOMESTIC GLASS	18		134	49	85	49	6300	5724	165	125	3583	509	1273	2819
53 IMPORTED GLASSWARE	24		40	15	26	15	4295	3596	256	391	962	410	1564	192-
61 PLASTIC TABLEWARE	16		32	14	19	14	939	3563	115	587	208	1	1036	827-
86 CLEAN POLISH AGENTS	06						169	92			9		4	5
91 PROMOTIONAL TO 1.00	16		6	31	25-	31	1830	1776	49	112	118-		195	313-
92 OTHER PORMOTIONAL	16		10	40	30-	40	106	474	36	36	15		239	224-
95 REPAIRS AND SERVICE														-
99 POSTAGE			2	3	1-	3	2407	625	109		247-			247-
				1541		1541		101857		9791		6374		21409
			2363	824			113995		7865		63872		48837	

Figure 26. Classification Report

customers want to buy. Stores have been adapting to these changing needs by introducing boutiques, outposts, and shops, and by setting up assortments in branch store departments that are quite different from those in the parent store departments, as the situation warrants.

Moreover, the merchandise content of departments is less constant than in the past. Key resources go in for new items and lines, which some buyers take on without regard to where the merchandise logically belongs. Strong buyers search out new items that other departments of the stores should carry. Sometimes there is space to be utilized, or a department that needs supporting volume.

Crossing Departmental Lines. This present situation suggests that classification lines must in time cross department lines, so that merchandise can be sold wherever the customer prefers to find it in the store. If we consider the department as a wall, and the classification as one of its bricks, we can see at once that it is easier to change the shape of the wall, brick by brick, than to try to alter the wall as a whole.

The decisions involved are not for the buyer to make, of course. But when management makes the decisions and the buyer must live under them, he is better able to understand and cooperate if he recognizes that a classification is a segment of customer demand. This element is fundamental; department assortment content is not. To maintain department lines at the cost of adulterating the content of a classification is to obscure the facts needed to point the way to maximum volume and profit.

A Look Ahead. There is now developing among merchants a school of thought which holds that the merchandise operating records of a store should be carried through the gross margin line, and perhaps even to the net profit, for specifically defined and standardized classifications, rather than departments.

With standardized classifications, merchandise control and even merchandising itself will become scientific. Classifications may eventually be universally standardized, coded and numbered for purposes of electronic data processing. Producers and distributors, as well as retailers, will have meaningful, precise, and valid statistical measures to guide their inventory control and sales promotion. Preticketing by manufacturers will become practical and economic. Merchandise control, which is today in a period of fairly confused transition, will become a specialized branch of modern mathematics.

What This Means to the Buyer. Merchandising by classification is a tool for the buyer to use, in terms of the policies of his own management and the portion of the assortment for which he is responsible. In some stores, precise reports of sales activity and stock balance by classification may come to his desk periodically from a central merchandise control or data processing group. In others, there may be no such centrally produced data by classifications.

The astute buyer does not have to wait for data processing to come to him. He can define the centers of customer demand in his area of responsibility, classify his assortment in this pattern, and collect sales activity figures by these classifications. He must then balance his stock as accurately as he can in accordance with the trends of sales activity projected for these classifications.

While it is very difficult to isolate precisely either the costs involved or the results produced by classification techniques, broad experience indicates that the cost of locally produced tally-board classification sales data is nominal. Its expected results are impressive: a reduction of about 10 per cent in average cost inventory investment, a reduction of about one-quarter of one per cent in markdowns, an increase of several per cent in sales volume. All of these should add up to a 20 to 25 per cent increase in net profit.

Centrally produced weekly classification merchandise position reports of the sophisticated sort described earlier will cost about one-fifth of one per cent of sales. If the buyer's management makes such data available to him, the expected reduction in average cost inventory investment will be 20 per cent; the reduction in markdowns, at least one-half of one per cent; the increase in sales, five to 10 per cent. The net profit increase will approach 50 per cent. When coupled with appropriate complementary unit and basic stock controls, effectively administered, these improvements may be doubled or tripled over a three- to five-year period.

The Buyer's Opportunity. The concept of classification merchandise control as a mechanism for the orderly breaking down of the centers of customer demand into specifically defined segments, to which manageable portions of the inventory can be related, spells challenge and opportunity for today's buyer-merchandiser. Whether his store provides him with the most modern tools or leaves him to his own devices, classification merchandising offers him invaluable guideposts to a more successful and profitable operation.

CHAPTER 18

FASHION MERCHANDISING[1]

BY

ALFRED H. DANIELS

The merchandising of a fashion department is one of the most challenging assignments that can be given to a buyer. To handle it successfully, he needs no mysterious sixth sense, but he does need certain backgrounds and skills that he can acquire. He must have an understanding of fashion, of course; he must be conscientious in the use of unit controls, unflagging in his alertness to change in customer preference or market offerings, eager to study and apply new developments in merchandise presentation. These attributes are the unmysterious ingredients of what is sometimes called "fashion flair."

In the discussion that follows, it is assumed that the reader has already mastered the various aspects of merchandising covered in other chapters of this book. This chapter is concerned only with their application to those departments handling feminine apparel and accessories—the fashion departments of the store.

Understanding Fashion. Fashion itself has been defined as *a conception of what is currently appropriate*—in simpler terms, a conception of what the customers of a particular store and department want to wear.

The broad, main trends of fashion usually move slowly. *Specific* manifestations of fashions do change quickly, however.

[1]. For a fuller discussion of fashion retailing, the reader is referred to Mr. Daniels' classic article, "Fashion Merchandising," in the Harvard Business Review, May 1951. Despite such changes in the department store as the development of boutiques and the establishment of branches, the article remains fundamental in the education of a fashion buyer.

An example of a main trend is the growing importance, year after year, of sportswear, a reflection of our relaxed and casual way of living. Within that main trend, there have been such passing manifestations as a demand for bulky sweaters, for tight slacks, for lean looks or layered looks, or for particular colors or textures.

Within a general fashion trend, individuals who seek distinction will try to be different through their use of a new color, or fabric, or line, or other detail. As soon as their individual touch becomes commonplace, the pace-setters are off once more on some new variation of their own. Other persons emulate—and there we go again!

The distinguished group cannot bring about a fundamental change in fashion. In its efforts to be different within the general fashion trend, the distinguished group helps to speed the introduction of new styles within the main trend.

Fashion Is Not Price. Students of marketing used to talk about fashion as something that began at the top price levels and gradually worked its way downward—and out. In the past, fashions did tend to begin with the very wealthy and sift down the rungs of the social and economic ladder. Today, however, almost everyone wants the same thing at the same time. Television, the movies, the theatre, the press, all spread the word rapidly, and customers respond at all price levels.

In general, women buy fashion to look pretty and glamorous, to be "in," or to belong. Some women like to lead; most, however, are followers. If the department's clientele consists primarily of leaders, the buyer must present a stream of new, high styled ideas at all times; numbers that fail to click must be quickly weeded out. In most departments, the bulk of the volume will be on accepted styles, with a small percentage of new or "prophetic" fashions to lend prestige.

The ratio of new to accepted fashions that a department should offer is a matter of careful judgment, based upon unremitting study of that department's customers. The buyer must pace himself according to the degree of fashion independence his customers show. He can no more afford to outrun them in the race for novelty than he can afford to let them outrun him.

Sources of Information. The buyer's first source of information is, of course, the customer herself. The more he knows about her way of life, the occasions for which she dresses, and especially the leaders that she follows, the more accurately can he forecast her demands. To his own first hand observations, he can add those of other executives in the store: his merchandise manager, the buyers for related departments, the store's fashion coordinator. Salespeople and branch personnel can also contribute.

The nerve center in this study of the customer is the unit control card. The buyer should be constantly studying these cards, analyzing them, summarizing them. If the actual merchandise is available during this process, it is often possible to recognize *a common characteristic* among several strong sellers and thus to spot the first indications of an incoming change. A neckline, a texture, a skirt type, may stand out when a department's 10 or 20 best sellers are placed together on a rack, and may offer an early clue to what is beginning to take hold and should be more strongly represented in future purchases.

In addition to what the buyer learns within the store, he has information available from fashion publications, trade publications, and the reports of the fashion consultants and the buying office employed by his store. These sources will give him the general picture, which he will then translate in terms of his department and his store.

Resource Relations. Especially important are the department's major resources. Resources that are currently strong in any part of the fashion field are strong because their batting averages in anticipating customer preferences are high. If they are also strong with the department's own customers, then they are doubly valuable as sources of fashion information.

Aside from the know-how and fashion genius that successful

resources offer, many of them nowadays maintain elaborate records of sales. From these records, they can see the national and regional trends and local variations; they can compare an individual store's performance with that of other stores of similar type. Thus they can highlight not only trends, but also strengths and weaknesses in the buyer's handling of their lines.

Other chapters of this book have stressed the value of making the store an important customer to its valued resources. For a dependable customer, a resource will exert itself to make deliveries on time—a vital point in fashion merchandising. Late and erratic deliveries are a two-way disaster: no merchandise when it is wanted, too much when the demand is over.

While concentration of resources is desirable in all goods, including fashion, it remains particularly important to have open to buy, and an open mind, for all sources in the fashion business. That new young designer may be tomorrow's genius. So, too, even the most sophisticated of resources cannot completely interpret the demand of all of your customers all of the time.

Thus, a fashion buyer needs a base of major resources—a base she challenges from time to time—*and* an attitude that is constantly curious and flexible to all fashion offerings and developments.

Projecting Sales and Stocks. Planning sales and stocks for a fashion department is done with the same tools as those used in other departments: the six-months' merchandise plan, classification data, and an open-to-buy broken down as finely as the records will permit.

There is this difference, however: The mathematics alone are not a sufficient guide. Fashion trends sometimes work for or against a classification to such an extent that last year's figures become a futile yardstick. If suits, for instance, have attracted little interest for several seasons but are at last showing signs of a comeback, then they may need a more liberal budget than past experience alone would seem to warrant. On the other hand, if jumpers, let us say, appear to have passed the peak of their popularity, then the budget for them should be cut back in spite of good past sales.

As a season progresses, errors in anticipating the effects of fashion trends may show up, and this will necessitate a change of plans. If a buyer sees that he has nipped off a fashion too soon, it doesn't matter that the rest of his department is doing well without it; he must build up the neglected item or classification or run the risk of having customers go to other stores. Similarly, if he has overestimated the growth rate of an incoming fashion, he must clear his stocks quickly, while a modest markdown can still do the trick.

In fashion departments, more than in others, hesitation is fraught with danger. The fashion buyer must be bold to plunge in when he sees an opportunity developing. He must be equally courageous about admitting his error and backing out when he sees that he has misjudged the strength of a trend. There is a premium on quick action in fashion merchandising—provided that action is based on facts and sound observation.

Timing. Timing is an important phase of all merchandising, but in fashion it is especially crucial. Fortunately it is not as mysterious as some would make it.

Although it is important to keep abreast of market openings, offerings, and deliveries, proper timing is determined by the customer, *not* the market. The customer always decides what, and when. Happily her past history and pattern give plenty of clues as to the future.

Thus, we have learned that thoughtfulness about predictables can be more helpful in decisions about timing than so-called intuition. Throw out the ouija board—and buy yourself instead a good five year book or diary!

In fashion departments, timing also means speed. Styles change quickly, and seasonal demand changes. Even more important is the highly competitive nature of the fashion business. If a buyer is late in recognizing and acting upon evidence of demand, some competing buyer in another store may be quicker to move—and to get the sales, the prestige, and the profits.

Promotions. Fashion departments can use a wide variety of promotions, and the buyer's task is to strike a balance among them in accordance with store policy and customer response. The department's own past experience is a guide to what may logically be expected to succeed in the future. So is the experience of other comparable stores. The fashion buyer cannot afford to cut himself off from a good idea simply because someone else thought of it first. Neither can he afford to turn his back on innovation.

If an idea appears sound, in spite of the fact that it has so far excited no great interest, to promote it is to gamble a bit—which is all right, if one recognizes the gamble for what it is.

The fashion buyer has many types of promotion among which to choose: special values, typically in assortments; item promotions; idea promotions; department promotions aimed at making the store a headquarters for a particular age or type; brand name promotions—fiber, fabric, or finished product. Also tie-ins with consumer magazines on themes or on individual styles, and tie-ins with local events, from fund-raising drives to football games.

The precise balance to be struck among these and other types of promotion is a matter of knowing one's customers and the appeals to which they respond most readily.

The Sales Staff. Selling personnel—trained, enthusiastic, patient, helpful, interested—can contribute more to the success of a fashion department than any other single factor. The late Hector Escobosa, one of the great fashion merchants of our time, urged stores to "pamper, love, and cultivate" salespeople, so that they can do a significant job of projecting fashion in the fitting room or over the counter.

Training the selling staff goes beyond teaching them the sales points and explaining the fashion appeal of the department's own merchandise. They also need briefing on the overall fashion picture, so that they know what goes with what. This may mean working with buyers of related departments and staging a fashion show now and then for the combined staffs, so that the salespeople can see how a properly accessorized outfit looks, or just what the new kinds of foundation garments can do for the lines of a dress. The time a buyer spends working with and training his staff is time well invested indeed.

As others have pointed out elsewhere in this book, finding time to work with the selling staff is not always easy, particularly if branch stores are involved. The resourceful fashion buyer will use every facility available to him—meetings, bulletins, shows—to get the needed information and stimulation to his people.

Basics. Every department, fashion or otherwise, has its share of basics that should be in stock in good assortment throughout the year or some specified part of it. But fashion buyers, in their eagerness to introduce the new, or in their concern for a classification that is moving slowly, often neglect to reorder their basics promptly. This is especially so where there are branches and the buyer has to divide his time among many stocks and many selling floors.

There are store systems for the control and automatic reorder of basics, and there are helps to be had from resources in this area. But somehow, no system or outside help ever does the job quite so effectively as when the buyer himself is dedicated to the idea that he will not be out of stock of items that enjoy steady demand.

Basics mean day-to-day sales, minimum markdowns, maximum profit. Few departments can afford to ignore their contribution—least of all fashion departments, which pay heavily in markdowns for mistakes in judgment, late deliveries, or unseasonable weather.

The Boutique. The little shop of exquisite fashion treasures is no longer found solely in the very chic stores. In fashion departments at almost every price level today, the boutique technique is used to highlight items of special charm. Some of these shops assemble items that would normally be sold in several departments; others simply highlight a trend, a look, or anything a bit special within a single department.

Boutiques that cross department lines bring together in one spot goods as the customer likes to buy them, rather than as markets or departments sell them. They may be run by buyers who roam the markets for different and unusual goods, or they may be fed merchandise by the buyers of several departments, each of whom has a special open-to-buy for certain classifications in the shop.

In either case, the buyer's responsibility is to understand thoroughly the look or taste level the boutique exemplifies, to buy for that look, and to make very sure that the salespeople who serve in the boutique know its merchandise and its customers.

Salespeople in the boutique get much closer to the customer than in ordinary departmental selling. They sell her a complete outfit rather than one component of it. They get her reactions all down the line, and can transmit these to the buyer for his guidance. This is especially useful in high style boutiques where the merchandise is rarely reordered, but replaced constantly with new items. A good salesperson's report on a preference for a color, or texture, or length can be an early and meaningful sign of a trend to watch.

Merchandise Presentation. Enormous strides have been made by department stores in displaying soft goods so as to permit the strongest possible impressions upon the customers. The development of open-selling fixtures has not only given the customer quick access to the merchandise, but it has also made it possible for the merchandise to tell its own story at a glance.

The essential thing for the buyer to have uppermost in mind is the question of what fashion message he wishes to convey to customers. If he wants to make them aware of bright colors, he should keep his neutrals and darks to a minimum in the exposed stock. If he wants them to see that they can mix the colors of sportswear separates effectively, he should arrange the stock on his double-tiered racks to show that this is possible. For instance, if he has gold jackets above, he may put forest green slacks below in one size grouping, or red skirts in another size grouping. If he wants to emphasize matching, he will, of course, put greens under greens, and blues under blues, and so on.

The garments the buyer selects to place on manikins, or to show on hangers at the ends of racks, should be chosen for their ability to sum up the fashion features that are currently important—color, texture, neckline, or whatever they may be. Wherever he shows basics, like staple shirtwaists, he should show also a few and more daring variations, to appeal to the customer's fashion appetite.

Management provides the buyer with certain display facilities within his department. It is up to him to pour energy and ingenuity into his use of them, so that they do their share in telling the fashion story.

The Department's Face. The face a department turns to its public is important everywhere, but especially in a fashion department. Clean fitting rooms, clean counters, immaculate displays, and a well groomed selling staff are every bit as important as the merchandise and the promotion. The cleanliness or lack of it that a department exhibits volumes about the buyer.

A daily inspection of the fitting rooms by buyer or assistant can help to keep standards of neatness high. Even on a flying visit to a branch, a quick glance into the fitting rooms should be on the buyer's agenda. A careful word of praise or kindly criticism can encourage salespeople to be personally neat and smart looking. The habit of checking displays for neatness and cleanliness should become second nature with the buyer.

If the buyer's standards are high, her whole department's standards, in main store and in branches, will be high, and her department will turn a clean and shining—and fashionable— face to its customers.

No good fashion business has ever been built without some degree of personalization with the customer. The more personal, the greater the business. No one needs to be told that one needs to be tidy in a personal relationship!

CHAPTER 19

FASHION PROMOTION AND COORDINATION

BY

RUSSEL D. CARPENTER, JR.

In any department of the modern store, the buyer has the problem of coordinating his own merchandising and promotional efforts with those of other buyers in his division, to the end that all related departments should present a clearly told, consistently merchandised fashion story. The pace of fashion, however, is so much faster in women's apparel and accessories departments that the techniques for fashion coordination and promotion are more highly developed here than—so far—in many other areas. Fashion department methods repay study by any buyer, whatever department he may be associated with.

Fashion Can Be Learned. You will find in the fashion field many people with so little true knowledge of fashion that they cover up their lack with double talk. If you really know fashion, you will not need such defenses and you will not have to lean on the well-worn clichés in speech or in thinking.

Fashion is not a strange whim of someone's imagination, nor is it anything elusive, intangible, or even awe-inspiring. To know fashion is not a privilege reserved for a chosen few. Almost anyone with respect for the subject, deep interest in it, and willingness to study may become expert in fashion promotion or coordination.

The necessary knowledge and skills, however, cannot be acquired in a short time. Just as a good lawyer, or doctor, or scientist has to devote many years of study, research, and practical application of what he has learned to the task of making himself an expert, so in fashion, many years are needed. One cannot really know fashion unless he has devoted a substantial amount of time to watching fashion's slow, elegant evolution, and has also learned to accept its occasional revolutions.

Good taste, too, is essential to an understanding of fashion. Some people seem to be born with that quality, but if you feel that you were not, count on the fact that *exposure to good fashion over a period of time will develop that taste and give you the knowledge and authority you need.*

The Goal of Fashion Coordination. The goal of fashion promotion and coordination is simple and universal: to project the personality of your store to the public. The manner in which this is done varies from store to store, according to the clientele and location of the establishment. In all cases, however, the problem falls into two parts.

First, top management must decide on the fashion direction in which the store shall head.

Second, everyone in the organization must be conscious of this fashion direction.

Our concern here is with the second element of the problem. In order to illustrate how that problem can be handled, we shall describe here the procedures followed by one of the finest chains of fashion stores in the country. Its pattern can be adapted to any store in any part of the country and at any price level, and it is quite possible that your own store is now doing some or all of the things mentioned in the discussion that follows.

The Fashion Coordinator. The fashion director and/or coordinator in any retail organization should be selected with the same care as that given to selecting a president or vice president. His or her position is just as important, since the store's fashion image is in the hands of this executive.

In the store whose procedure we are about to describe, the arrangement is rather unorthodox, but worth your study. *The president and merchandising vice president are the actual fashion promoters and coordinators.* Naturally, such an arrangement is not true of or even possible in every organization, but the heads of this store feel that this phase of their business is the most important part of it. They have excellent figure men, advertising staff, merchandise managers, buyers, etc., but the fashion direction and coordination over a period of many years have come from the top. As a result, every person in the organization feels the importance of fashion and respects it.

Now for some of the actual and practical ways of promoting and coordinating fashion.

Apparel Buying: First Day. Buyers of all departments at every price level are brought together on their first day in the market at one large meeting. They are briefed by the store's top fashion experts on what to look for in the market. Then each buyer speaks for her own department. The objective is *not to try to repeat last season's best sellers always,* but to study the customer's acceptance of a new fashion that was covered only lightly last season and that could be among the coming season's best sellers.

For example, only a few smooth fabrics may have been presented last season against a preponderance of deep mohair fabrics. If the customers gave immediate acceptance to the smoother fabrics, that fact should influence your new season's buying. If you, last season, purchased bright pinks in greater depth than pale pinks, but customers headed in the pale pink direction, this fact should influence your color decision.

This is the sort of information that each buyer should contribute to a conference just before market work begins, both to clarify his own thinking and to contribute to that of other buyers. In addition to the experience of his own department, the buyer can learn much from the high fashion departments of his own store. *Their successes of the season before can usually be counted upon to influence the following season's lower price levels.*

Apparel Buying: Mid-Period. In the middle of the buying period, an open forum is held and early trends are discussed. If you participate in such a forum, bring to it the trends that you found at your top resources in every market you cover. For example, if you have seen skirts with a softer, fuller look and jackets with slightly shorter lengths, or if you find reds with a blue cast looking newer than reds with a yellow cast, these are the points to bring up.

Such an airing of opinions and impressions prevents any one buyer from going off in a direction different from that followed by the others, and perhaps being the only one to buy tight skirts, yellow reds, and jackets in the wrong lengths. A forum like this does not take away from the buyer's individuality in selection and taste, but it does *provide a guide to the general look that management expects to present throughout the store.*

Apparel Buying: Last Day. At the last day in the market, buyers meet and report highlights of what they have bought for each department. A more detailed report from every department is written out later and submitted to the fashion coordinator, so that one overall fashion report can be made for the entire organization.

Afterward, back at the store, meetings will be held and a forecast for the season will be presented, illustrated by a fashion show (to be discussed later). At these meetings, the store's fashion report will be distributed.

Millinery and Accessory Buying. For some strange reason, the millinery and accessory markets are ready only after the apparel orders have been placed. Buyers for these lines, therefore, must be thoroughly briefed on the important fashion trends in apparel that their own purchases will complement for that season. A millinery buyer can always select beautiful hats, but she has a much better chance of a good season's operation *if she can concentrate on hats in types that will be worn with the apparel already chosen for her store.*

In the same way, if the accessory buyer knows that, for example, necklines have dropped, she will realize that multistrand necklaces may be important. If necklines go high, pins and earrings may be stressed. Sleeve lengths will certainly influence the glove buyer's choice.

As soon as the millinery and accessory buyers reach the market, therefore, a meeting is held with the fashion promoter and coordinator. A complete outline of the silhouettes, important colors, and fabrics is presented to these buyers by top fashion experts. Planned local and national advertising and windows for the apparel already bought should be discussed.

Relating Accessories to Apparel. Before any buying is done by the millinery and accessory buyers, appointments are made for them to review the best of the apparel lines in each category. This is not because the apparel designers accessorize their collections well; only a very few of those at the top do the job properly. But an accessory buyer's eye will note fashion trends and colors in an apparel collection, and will profit by the experience in her own purchases.

At the end of the buying period, a comprehensive report should be made by all departments, so that at any presentation of fashion—meetings, shows, advertising—each apparel buyer will know how to accessorize her own purchases. This exchange of information among the buyers helps the accessory department, and also helps the apparel departments and everyone in the store to project a *complete, coordinated look* to the salespeople and the customer.

European Influence. European collections are shown after initial American purchases have been made. It is nevertheless extremely important to study cables and other reports after each Paris collection, since the Paris showings can influence the activity on the domestic scene greatly. For example, the store may have touched only lightly on navy, but if this color is strong in Paris, that fact will affect the reorders still to be placed.

Because the evolution of high fashion is universal, you will always find in your own early purchases a reflection of the new Paris look. If you have already bought the well sponsored ideas in depth, so much the better; if you haven't, you can slowly guide your reorders and later purchases in the right direction.

Often accessories will have a completely new look at the Paris showings. Cables and advance sketches can be sent to domestic manufacturers for immediate work, and advertising can be prepared in advance.

Meetings and fashion advertising can be prepared from early Paris cables and reports. Go through your stocks or outstanding orders at the first authentic word from Paris and find examples among your own selections of ideas that have received sponsorship abroad. Then your windows, your ads, and your fashion shows can stress the point that cables from Paris authenticate the fashions you are promoting.

Buying in Europe. If you are sent to Paris, work with your top manufacturers, not only on plans for immediate copies, but also on a long range plan. Discuss the trends and colors you particularly want to project in your store for the next season.

After you have finished the Paris purchases, make up a complete report on the important look of each great designer. Sketches of the best of the silhouettes of each house should accompany this report. Later, this information will be distributed to your entire staff. In that way, you will bring back from Paris not just the merchandise you selected, but also a *recapitulation of the showings for the benefit of those who remained at home.*

European Fashions: Using Judgment. You do not have to accept a fashion simply because Paris presents it. For example, when Paris houses showed skirts above the knees, some high fashion stores thought this length vulgar and refused to buy or show such short skirts to their own elegant customers at home.

Likewise, you will often find that you must take a lot of fashion reporting with a grain of salt. Many fashion writers are inclined to report only the extremes and the far-out changes. *The subtle evolutions,* which are really the important fashions, tend to be overlooked in the emphasis upon the newer and more exciting variations. In your own Paris report, you will often reject extreme fashions and stress instead those that your store will eventually accept and promote.

Store Level. After fashion influences have been evaluated and initial purchases have been made, there is much to be done by way of promotion and coordination at store level. The organization whose procedures we are using as an illustration believes it so important to give the fashion story to everyone that there is a night fashion show for all employees early in the season. This is called the store's Fashion Forecast.

The president and vice-president of the store direct the show's preparation. Merchandise managers and buyers vie with each other to present their most outstanding fashions. Actually, *as much and more attention goes into the preparation of this show as is given to any public fashion show.* This is right and proper, because everyone—salespeople, fitters, stock people—comes away with a thorough knowledge of all the important fashion trends, not only from her own department, but from every department in the sore.

After a presentation of this kind, a jewelry salesgirl can say with authority that a necklace of a certain type is needed for the new necklines, or whatever the case may be. A shoe salesman can say with assurance that a particular heel height is perfect with the new suit look. The display staff will know how to accessorize their windows correctly.

The influence of such a showing is infinite. This store, however, does not count on everyone to carry home a clear picture from a fashion show alone. Instead, *a written report is prepared and illustrated and distributed after the meeting.* Thus every employee who is in any way concerned with fashion merchandise has a personal copy of the store's overall fashion projection to review and study.

Staff Meetings. *Every week after that, a morning storewide meeting is held and attended by the entire staff.* Salespeople are especially helped, because they come away feeling that they now have knowledge and authority superior to those of the customers. The fashion knowledge that fitters gain, too, not only helps them in their fitting but can also help confirm a sale. Such a state of affairs is far more desirable than when the people who are supposed to guide the customer are less up-to-date on fashion information than she is.

Daily department meetings are held also, and all new items are presented, along with their salient selling points and the reasons why they were purchased.

When the imports arrive, another storewide meeting is held, and the entire staff again is made aware of the latest fashion influences. It is at this time that the written report on Paris is distributed.

Advertising and Windows. Once a month, an all-day session is held to plan the next month's advertising and windows. A committee sits in consultation: the president or vice president, store managers, fashion director, advertising manager, and display manager. During the day, each merchandise manager and his buyers present their planned items for advertising. Naturally, the ones with the best presentation and coverage get the best space. And naturally, too, there is keen competition among the buyers to present the most desirable merchandise.

The committee procedure also allows top management and everyone else concerned to know what fashion ideas and items will be presented to the public. *Advertising and display can be controlled so that every department's presentation reflects the store "look."*

One result of this approach to promotion is that apparel buyers work with millinery and accessory buyers in preparing their presentation to the committee. Thus, even at that early stage of planning the advertising, there is already a well coordinated overall look.

Application to Your Own Job. Each store has its own procedures, and these procedures may bear much or little resemblance in detail to those just outlined. But whatever the system followed in your own store for coordinating fashion merchandising and promotion, it should be clear that no buyer can sit on the "tight little island" of her own department and ignore all the others.

Neither can a fashion coordinator or director be successful simply by studying, reading, and observing fashion in the outside world. She must also learn a great deal from her merchandise managers and buyers and, in turn, see that they head in the direction of the overall store fashion personality.

On your own, as a buyer, you have to learn the art of give and take so far as fashion information is concerned. Whatever your store's procedures may be, you yourself must learn to analyze what you see in the market and to draw off the generalizations you want to pass along to your merchandise manager, to the fashion coordinator of your store, and other buyers. At the same time, you will want to develop skill in applying the information about other markets that is passed along to you from other buyers or from the fashion coordinator.

Above all, you should form the habit of keeping your own salespeople informed about fashion as it affects your own department's merchandise and whatever other merchandise goes with it. However much or little is done for your people at store level, their *day-to-day coaching* remains an important responsibility for you to handle.

Summary. Good fashion coordination then, means a constant evaluation and exchange of information among members of the fashion merchandising staff. It means comparing notes and working in the same general direction before, during, and after market work, and doing the same thing again with regard to the Paris openings. It means presenting the fashion picture, as the store sees it, to the entire staff, and *through them,* to the store's customers. There is no place in fashion coordination for the buyer or department that wants to go it alone. Cooperation every step of the way is the vital ingredient for success.

CHAPTER 20

IN-THE-HOME SELLING

BY

HOWARD M. BINGHAM

Today in the home furnishings business, any department store that does not do some selling in the home is not getting the maximum business possible. With the growth of our communities and with increasing traffic congestion in the center of the city, people are increasingly reluctant to make the necessary effort to come downtown when they can find reasonable selection in the neighborhood. Furthermore, your competitors are already going into the home and making sales that at one time you might have had. Therefore, whether or not you like the increased selling cost resulting (and it does cost some more to sell in the home) you are faced with that necessity if you want to maintain your position in the community.

Of course there has always been in-the-home selling in the home furnishings field. Interior decorators have been doing it successfully for years. In fact, few good decorators would think of planning a job without seeing the home and what else is in it. But in recent years department stores and specialty stores have been making increasing use of this technique. Such items as draperies, slipcovers, reupholstering, and carpets lend themselves ideally to this type of operation; other departments, such as electrical appliances, television and even furniture are experimenting too with ways to make this method successful.

While this approach to selling is still in the formative stages, at least as far as department stores go, there are a few fundamentals that experience has taught should be observed if this venture is to be successful.

Adequate Supervision. First, and most important, you must have adequate supervision of your selling force. If you have four or more people selling outside, a full-time supervisor is indicated. Without this close supervision, you are courting failure and disappointment. Salesmen are just like you and me. Unless we have a boss looking over our shoulders and checking on our efforts we sometimes get careless and do less than our best. An outside job presents temptations to take it easy, if no one takes the time to ask, "What did you do today?"

See that a full day's work is scheduled for each outside man each day. The supervisor should keep an accurate and detailed account of just what each man is supposed to do on his day out. This must be scheduled *in advance* and if the salesman cannot supply sufficient leads himself, these leads must be furnished by the supervisor.

Call Review. A review of the salesman's calls by the supervisor at regular intervals is a must. This review can take place the day after the calls are made or on a weekly basis. But a detailed report of each outside call is the only way to insure proper follow-up.

The supervisor should sit down with each salesman individually and go over his prospect cards one by one. On each call, this question must be answered: "Did you close the sale?" Wherever the answer is "No," an inquiry into the reasons is essential. Perhaps the salesman did not use the right approach; perhaps he was too aggressive; perhaps he was not aggressive enough; perhaps he did not use good judgment in the merchandise he showed the customer; perhaps his competition had cut prices.

A careful inquiry into the true reasons for failure to close will bring out points of value to the supervisor, to the salesman, and to the department. In this way, the supervisor can help the salesman strengthen his approach and advise him on ways to improve.

A useful tool for the supervisor in his reviews is a continuing and current production record of each of his outside salesmen. A cumulative record of the sales totals by salesmen is a necessary instrument for keeping your sales force producing at a high rate. By setting a minimum production goal for each man and comparing each man's production with the department average, you let your men know what is expected of them and how close they are coming to achieving their goals.

Advance Training. A thorough advance training of the outside men is very important. This training should include a complete study of the merchandise and its proper uses as well as the techniques of measuring and estimating where these services are required.

The actual technique of presentation in the home is somewhat different from presentation in the store and these differences should be carefully analyzed and worked into a training course. In the decorative home furnishings departments, a good knowledge of color and pattern co-ordination and a knowledge of the basic rules of decoration, are very important. The salesman should be trained quickly to observe what the customer has already in her home and to choose only those samples which will enhance the appearance of those articles the customer intends to keep.

A good first impression is important and the salesman must be trained on proper approach and proper conduct while in the customer's home. A careful screening of your prospective salesmen is important to provide against getting an overly aggressive type that will damage your store's reputation.

Selecting the Staff. The supervisor of your outside men must be selected with the greatest care. This man should be a successful salesman with a good personality and a potential for leadership. Picking the top salesman in your department may not always be wise; often these top salesmen have stepped on too many toes amongst their co-workers in reaching the top.

Your sales manager must have, or must develop, the complete confidence of your selling force and have a personality which will enable him to lead without irritating and to set and maintain a high standard of performance. He should have an understanding of human nature and a genuine liking for people, as well as enthusiasm and a belief in himself and in your store. He may also need training. Training in the technique of prospect systems and the proper follow-up can be given him; his personality and leadership qualifications are the important things to look for when you are hiring.

The results you get from outside selling depend largely on a strong sales force. Good salesmen who can sell on the outside are not easy to find. Some of your older men may be excellent on the outside. Others may be total failures. You may have to start from scratch and train your own sales force. But don't try outside selling without a well trained, high-producing group of salesmen. If you do, it will be money wasted. An untrained salesman can cause you a lot of trouble.

Sample Control. You must keep your samples current and your sample kits complete if your men are to do the best job and avoid complaints. This is particularly true in departments like draperies and carpets. Without a formal system of checking, you may find your drapery salesmen selling patterns you no longer stock or which are out of print. In carpets, a poor sample checkout system will mean much unnecessary additional expense replacing lost items.

The sample kits should be made up by the sales manager in consultation with the buyer. They should be checked regularly for completeness of selection and to weed out dropped patterns. Your supervisor must be constantly on the lookout to see that a salesman's samples are up to date and fresh looking and also that he is showing a full range instead of just a favorite one or two. The checking of the salesman's sample kits is an important duty of your sales manager.

Problems to Anticipate. The above fundamentals offer a good basis for starting your in-the-home selling venture. There you must have a good answer ready for the customer who calls up and wants your in-the-home service but also wants to see the sale merchandise you advertised last night.

Furthermore, the superimposing of a large purchase of off-price merchandise on a stock which is already heavy enough to insure adequate quantities poses a financial problem which many departments may not be able to answer successfully. You may find it will be necessary to limit your specially priced promotions to considerably fewer than has been your custom in the past.

Inside Work on Outside Calls. If you use the system where your men work in the store as well as outside, the question of who takes care of their calls in the store while they are outside may cause some trouble. In some cases, the team operation has proved successful. Men work in pairs and one of the pair is in the store while the other is outside. The inside man takes care of the other fellow's customers and the other chap reciprocates when it is his day on the floor.

Another solution can be worked out with the sales manager taking care of the personal calls of the men who are out that day. Other methods can, of course, be worked out, depending on the store and the personnel.

If you have a group of salesmen who work full time out of the store, the problem of serving their orders requires study and thought. This is particularly true in departments like draperies and floor coverings where a workroom operation is involved. If a man spends all his working time outside the store, you must make some provision to have his paper work taken care of and a follow-up instituted to see that his jobs are processed through your organization efficiently and according to the promise date.

You will also need someone who can become familiar with the various jobs so that he can answer customers who call in to inquire about the progress of their work. Ordinarily, under the traditional department system, the salesman handles his own inquiries and follow-up. If he is outside full time, the department must assume this responsibility.

Paying the Men. A sixth problem involves the method and the amount you pay your outside salesmen. Generally speaking, you have to pay them more than floor salesmen.

In a commission department, you may have to raise your commission for outside selling and then the problem arises as to how to determine whether a man actually closed the sales on the outside or on the inside. If you pay a straight salary, you may find it advisable to go to a commission for the outside work and this further complicates things in trying to decide where they closed their business. If you have a crew who work entirely on the outside, you may run into difficulties with your floor salesmen because of the different rates you pay.

The solution to this problem must be worked out with your personnel department but it is a problem that each store will have to face.

Leads. Obtaining sufficient leads for outside calls is a problem in some departments and some stores. A box inserted in each ad, outlining the home-selling service, is effective in many cases. Cross reference of customers between two or more departments is also used with success.

Some stores give a P.M. to service men who turn in names of customers who they think may be in need of a new appliance or a new carpet, etc. A tie-up with rental agencies or real estate companies has been used by many stores. There are many ways of obtaining leads and each department should work out those best suited to its merchandise and circumstances.

The foregoing fundamentals and problems are usually basic in any outside selling venture. There are others you will undoubtedly run into as you expand this service. One thing you as a department manager must remember: no program such as this can be left to run by itself. You must show a personal interest and give it enough of your personal attention to assure its success.

CHAPTER 21

SUCCESSFUL CHRISTMAS MERCHANDISING

BY

WILLIAM BURSTON

Successful merchandising in the department store, as earlier chapters have shown, is largely the result of careful planning. Especially is this true of the months of November and December, for these two months, the Christmas selling period, contribute one-fourth of the year's volume. Their merchandise is too important to be based on inadequate planning or upon superficial or unrealistic plans.

Getting the Facts. Good planning starts with figures—last year's figures. If they are not available in convenient form, then the first step in planning is to go back to last year's records and dig up the facts.

To avoid such burdensome chores, and at the same time to make sure that they have a sound basis for Christmas planning each year, some stores require each buyer to keep what is literally a diary—a daily record of Christmas season impressions, of notes, of mistakes that crept in this year but should be avoided next time.

In addition to those kept by buyers for their individual departments, the merchandise managers keep their own and thus have a double check when planning time rolls around.

In some stores, the Christmas diary is a report filled out immediately after Christmas by the buyer. Appended to this chapter is the form used at J. L. Brandeis & Sons, Omaha, Nebraska.

A glance at the questions it asks will show that it leaves very little unrecorded that may prove useful to guide next year's plans. It asks the buyer to report not only on merchandise but also on how the advertising and service departments performed in behalf of his department. The buyer, making his report in the month of January, puts his ideas and suggestions on paper while they are still fresh in his mind. Human memory being what it is, many of these points will have become hazy or forgotten by planning time next fall without benefit of the record. In fact, best results are obtained when buyers and merchandise managers *in their own best interest* make notes as the ideas occur and then transcribe them during the week between Christmas and New Year's. The same arrangements should be made for the department managers in the branches.

Planning Begins. Christmas merchandise planning actually begins in June, when sales and merchandising plans for the fall season as a whole are being drawn up. By August, stores are ready to get down to detailed plans. At this point, figures for the department as a whole are no longer adequate; they have to be broken down into classifications and even items for the next steps in the plan.

If the buyer's store maintains classification control throughout the year, it is a simple matter to extract the figures he needs: his November and December sales for each classification individually.

Some stores have found that it pays handsomely to take a physical inventory of their big Christmas departments about November 15, and then to take a second such inventory after Christmas. Both inventories, of course, are taken by classification.

From the November 15 beginning stock, the purchases after that date, and the post-Christmas inventory, it is a simple matter to determine what the sales were in each classification during the period. Then, whether or not he has this assistance throughout the year, the buyer has at least classification information to guide him in planning his next year's Christmas operations.

With last year's classification figures as a guide and last year's Christmas diary as a source of suggestions and ideas, the buyer is ready to ask himself a critical, two-part question: (1) Where did I do well, and so wish to do even better? (2) Where did I do badly, and so wish to do well?

Yardsticks for Planning. In the course of planning, buyer and merchandise manager will apply this two-sided yardstick first to every classification in the department, and then to items within the classifications, systematically and realistically. Their planning will also consider any changes in conditions since last Christmas: improvements that will make it possible to set this year's sights higher than last year's; unfavorable conditions that must be allowed for this year; any elements of sheer good luck that contributed to last year's fine showing but cannot be expected to occur again this year.

The wise planner looks even further for information. From his own records, he can tell only what he has accomplished in each classification but not what he could have accomplished. At this point, if he can compare figures with stores like his own, through his buying office or a figure-exchange group to which his store belongs, he can get a much clearer picture.

For example, a department may seem to be going great guns, yet when it compares its figures with other stores on classification percentage to total department volume, it finds itself running behind the others in one or more classifications. Thus, if the buyer knows where his department is deficient, he knows where to search for increased volume opportunities. That's the great value of figure exchange.

Basic Items. There are two kinds of items for Christmas, and the buyer has to consider both in his plans. One is the basic, the daily bread-and-butter seller. The other is the "item," the extra volume maker that sometimes pops up seemingly by accident and provides a windfall for the department.

Cliché or not, Christmas continues to be an opportunity to sell *basics;* if they sell well the year around, they usually sell better at Christmas. Hence it is vital that they be carefully and practically planned for.

Some stores take care of their basics by making it a rule that single orders to cover their entire needs during the Christmas period be placed with resources during the first or second weeks of November, with arrangement for staggered shipping dates.

Others use a rule of thumb method, and increase the basic stock by an extra three or four weeks' supply early in the Christmas season. This is over and above what would be needed for the normal November-December rate of sale.

Availability of Basics. In every classification of every department, there are some basics that show an enormous leap in sales during the Christmas period. For these items, heavy advance stock can represent a very considerable investment. In such cases, it is sometimes possible to arrange with the resource to "back" the store with stock—to require no firm commitment from the store, that is, yet to carry sufficient stock so that immediate fill-ins can be made as needed.

Whether the store does advance purchasing or the manufacturer arranges advance availability of the basic stock, neither is running a very great risk. The item is basic and will remain in demand after Christmas. If the expected boost in sales doesn't materialize in December, the worst that can happen to either store or resource is that there will be an extra three or four weeks' supply of a good item to be worked off in the month or two following.

Finding and Testing "Items." So much for basic stocks. Now for the "item," the accidental piece of good fortune that came along last year and that doesn't seem possible of duplication this year. Yet it made a substantial bulge in sales last year and we'd like to top it. Big volume makes for bigger volume!

Of course, it is always possible to land another windfall, to run across another close-out, to find another good seller by accident. But if last year's volume is to be met, the buyer can't wait for an accident. He begins in August to comb the market for likely replacements. If he should fail to uncover the equal of last year's volume maker, he doesn't give up. He begins to test less sure-fire items to see if there is a possibility that they may make the grade.

Testing is done early—perhaps in September for toys, or October for sweaters, for example. It is one of the soundest devices in merchandising, since it involves minimum risk but may lead to a winner.

If the item proves to be only so-so when tested, the buyer knows he must try another item. If the test indicates a good potential, he takes the plunge and orders early and in substantial quantity—unless he is fortunate enough to be dealing with a resource who is willing and able to back him with stock for fast fill-ins.

Layaways. If any of the department's merchandise lends itself to layaway promotion, September is the time to begin your campaign. The customer who pays for the goods on instalments in advance of accepting delivery needs an early start, in order to have the item paid for by Christmas. Along with early promotion, remember to review layaway procedures with the selling staff, so that transactions will be handled smoothly.

Business Gifts. Business firms that give gifts to customers at Christmas usually plan their buying quite early. If the department has merchandise suitable for this purpose, the appropriate items should be brought to the attention of prospects among nearby factories and service organizations, or to the attention of the special executive within the store, if there is one, who is charged with soliciting this business.

Services from Vendors. In many departments, it is possible for vendors to render extra services at Christmas that add to the salability of their merchandise, save money for the store, or do both. Gift wraps or sleeves on packaged goods are one such extra. Pre-ticketing merchandise with prices (if the store management approves) is another service that saves time at the store and quickly gets the goods on sale in the department, by-passing possible bottlenecks in the marking room.

Such extra services should be investigated early and arranged for well ahead of the Christmas season.

"Christmas" Departments. *Every department of the store should regard itself as a "Christmas" department.* Some are obviously so, like toys. If only because of the larger crowds in the store at this season of the year, *every* department is capable of greater than normal sales. *All* are Christmas departments; all should put themselves in readiness to tap the vast amount of traffic Christmas generates; all should canvass their assortments for items with strong gift appeal and make sure that these are highlighted. There is hardly a department of the store for which December is not the biggest month of the year.

Personal Shopping. If one's store offers personal shopping service or other special facilities to assist the Christmas shopper, it is important for each department to call its best items to the attention of the bureau handling this assignment. Suitable items should be listed, along with complete details as to sizes and colors, etc., and, above all, their selling points.

The Sales Staff. The buyer must remember that, with the store open longer hours during the Christmas season, his department has many more temporary and part-time people than usual. If he is to do the best possible job in his department, he must make the time to see that these newcomers get instruction from him or his assistant in the selling points of the merchandise and in suggestions to offer to customers.

With varied shifts, branches, and possibly some very green help, this is no easy assignment. Yet it must be done, or the department will not reap the benefit of all the work and planning that has gone before.

Departmental Arrangement. By now, the buyer has the framework for his Christmas plan. He knows the facts and is ready to act upon them. But there are still a few other details to be attended to.

One of these is departmental arrangement. It is not at all unusual for whole departments to be shifted from one spot to another at Christmas, giving the more desirable locations to those with greater volume potentials at this period. Nor is it unusual for a department to be given one or more outposts on other floors to handle some of its extra Christmas volume.

A rough layout of the department, on paper and prepared well in advance, will make it easier when the day for the actual rearranging comes around. In preparing the layout, the buyer should look with a cold eye upon any classification that is not capable of carrying its weight at this time of year. It is wisdom to contract the space of such classifications drastically, in order to make more room for the ones that will be more productive.

Especially important at this season when customer traffic is at its heaviest, is the matter of *making good use of counter ends.* In many departments, activity is at the center of the counter, and the ends are dead spots. Those same ends can be made highly productive if the buyer will take a tip from the supermarket and place "hot" items at these locations. *The items do not necessarily have to tie in with the classification to which the counter belongs.* The important thing is that the item should be so hot that it pays to put a special clerk behind it.

Boutiques. When planning the layout of his department, the buyer should keep in mind that it is a rare department that does not have some boutique merchandise at Christmas. He should set aside a table, or a counter, or an alcove, for presenting this merchandise and setting it off from the rest of the department.

The boutique may offer merchandise a little better in quality, a little newer or more individual, than the department's regular assortment. Or it may simply present related items chosen from regular stock and assembled at the one spot for shopping convenience. In some departments, the boutique approach can be applied to just some particularly attractive gift items with nothing more in common than their appeal to the shopper who is looking for ideas.

If there are items in stock that gain from being lifted out

and highlighted in this way—and what department does not have such items?—then the boutique possibilities should not be overlooked.

Reorders. Think twice about reordering merchandise, other than basics, at the height of the Christmas selling period. Is there a quantity of merchandise in the house that can adequately *substitute for the item you want to reorder?* What "bulges" do you have that can be made to move with mass display? Unless an item is either a staple or something whose sales are phenomenal, don't reorder it in December without first checking to see that the last lot isn't lying around somewhere. Go less by the figures on merchandise control at this time of year than by what your own eyes tell you. You don't want to buy markdowns!

If the store has branches, this is a time of year to keep in particularly close touch with them in order to know how the merchandise is moving. Stocks can be kept alive and well-rounded often by switching goods from one location to another, in addition to making substitutions of the kind outlined above. Visual inspection of the stock, by the buyer or his lieutenants, is important at the branches as well as at the main store, before reordering. Otherwise, the buyer may reorder what he does not actually need.

Markdowns: One final suggestion: Take markdowns during Christmas, not after. Some stores have a deadline before which buyers must systematically examine their merchandise and take their reductions. That deadline is usually Friday or Saturday of the week before Christmas. In a department like toys, however, the buyer doesn't wait that long; he takes his markdowns throughout the Christmas season as needed.

Christmas is also the last opportunity to move out some of a department's *prior stock*. It's smart to take reductions necessary to move it so that the department comes out clean at the end.

J. L. BRANDEIS'
DEPARTMENTAL
CHRISTMAS DIARY

NOVEMBER 15 TO DECEMBER 31, 19—

The value of this questionnaire is self evident. Please complete it while the Christmas selling season is still fresh in your mind. It is imperative that the completed form be returned to this office no later than *January 23, 19—*.

*   *   *   *   *   *

1. ADVERTISING—Good Fair Bad (Circle one) If "fair" or "bad," explain how they could have been improved. Be specific.

_____

_____

_____

2. Were events properly timed? (Give instances, if not) _____

_____

3. Were your ads in proper position in the newspaper? (Specify) _____

_____

4. Cuts were— Fair Good Poor (Circle one)
5. Were these original or old Art? (Circle one) Original Old
6. Were ads proper size? (Specify, if not:) _____

7. Would you prefer fewer large ads, or more small ones? Large Small (Circle one)
8. Did you see proofs in ample time for correction? _____

*   *   *   *   *   *

1. DISPLAYS—Did you get enough window space? _____
2. Were your windows properly trimmed? _____
3. What suggestions would you make for improvements? _____

_____

4. Department Displays. What suggestions would you make for improvement of these? _____

_____

_____

_____

*   *   *   *   *   *

1. SALESPEOPLE—Did you have enough salespeople? _____
2. Were your salespeople properly trained? (If not, specify) _____
3. Do you have in *your* files the names of Christmas extras for next year's follow-up? _____
4. Will you take on a few Xmas extras earlier next year to insure a more effective selling force at the Xmas "peak"? _____

5. What suggestions would you make for improvement in this area? _____
_____
_____

*   *   *   *   *   *

1. STOCK PEOPLE—Comments and suggestions _____
_____
_____
_____

*   *   *   *   *   *

1. RECEIVING ROOM SERVICE— Good   Fair   Bad   (Circle one)
2. Did the "do not mark" technique help you? _____
3. Did any selling confusion result? _____
4. Was your other merchandise marked quickly and properly? (Specify)_____
_____
5. Did you have lost shipments? _____
6. Are you satisfied with _____ as a shipment forwarder? _____
7. Could you get merchandise to the floor quickly? _____
_____
8. What suggestions would you make for improvement of Receiving Room
    service? _____
_____
_____
_____

*   *   *   *   *   *

1. SIGNS—Comments and Suggestions: _____
_____
_____

*   *   *   *   *   *

1. MERCHANDISE—What three classifications produced the most volume?
    1. Bought _____ Sold _____ Est. Purch. Next Year _____
    2. Bought _____ Sold _____ Est. Purch. Next Year _____
    3. Bought _____ Sold _____ Est. Purch. Next Year _____
2. List your three best *single items* in each classification:
    1. _____
    2. _____
    3. _____
3. Which ones do you think will be good next year (or an adaptation thereof)?
_____
_____
_____
4. Which items were flops? _____
5. What classifications increased in sales production over last year? _____
6. What classifications decreased in sales production over last year? _____
_____

7. What "fringe" or "sleeper" items could be exploited next year in volume?
_____

8. What type of merchandise sold best in what spots? (Specify) _____
_____

9. Please attach to this report your Xmas floor plan of departmental re-arrangements.

10. What changes would you make in next year's re-arrangement? _____
_____
_____

11. Attach list of "outposts" you had this Xmas with exact record of dollar volume, also items used.

12. Attach list of "bargain square" items you had: by days, by items, by $ volume _____
_____
_____

13. Did you do any cooperative advertising? List: _____
_____
_____

14. Did it pay off? (Specify): _____
_____

15. What approach should we take next year as to price lines, prices, brand-selling during the Xmas promotion season? _____
_____

16. Did you sell more or less branded goods? _____

17. Did your unit sale increase or decrease? _____ List devices you used to raise unit sale _____
_____

18. What was your experience with imports? _____
_____
_____

19. How would you advertise them next year? _____

20. Christmas Catalogue items:
    1. Best items: 1_____
                 2_____
                 3_____
                 4_____
                 5_____
    2. Worst items: 1_____
                 2_____
                 3_____
                 4_____
                 5_____
    3. Why were the "worst items" worst? _____
_____
_____

21. General comments for improvements of the catalogue: _____

_____

_____

_____

*   *   *   *   *   *   *

SERVICES—Please give your comments or suggestions on the following:
1. Elevators: _____

_____

2. Delivery—Packing: _____

_____

3. Breakage of Packages delivered: _____

_____

4. Christmas Boxes: _____

_____

5. Gift Wrap and Wrappers: _____

_____

6. Porter and Maintenance Service: _____

_____

7. Bargain Square Space allocation: _____

_____

8. Further General or Specific Comment or Suggestions: _____

_____

CHAPTER 22

BASEMENT MERCHANDISING

BY

J. FRED CAESAR, JR.

The basement, or downstairs, or budget store, as it is variously called, is a store in itself, managed by its own merchandising staff, employing its own more aggressive promotional techniques, and generally carrying merchandise different in quality from that offered upstairs. The customers are sometimes quite different from but sometimes very similar to those who patronize the upstairs store, but the basic services are much the same, and the basement shares with upstairs departments the prestige of the store name and the responsibility of living up to the store's image and its standards.

Value is the outstanding appeal of downstairs merchandise. Customers come to the basement to save money. Fixtures therefore are generally less elaborate than upstairs; departments are less spacious; salespeople are fewer in proportion to the number of customers. The basement store thus operates on a lower expense ratio and a lower markup than the upstairs departments.

Types of Basement Stores. There is a great variety of merchandising philosophies in today's downstairs operations. The day of the real bargain counter types has all but passed out of existence, although a very few stores still cling to this idea. Many good stores operate their basements on strong basic assortments, with strong emphasis on day-to-day fashion rightness, augmented by special purchases of closeouts and some irregulars and seconds. The appearance of downstairs stores has improved and, especially in branches, they look like good, medium priced stores.

Where the merchandise standards of the basement are high, the lower prices are achieved through a lower original markup, cooperative large purchases, promotion of own brands, and opportune special buys. The basement customer knows values and will buy merchandise of good grade if it is priced right.

In basement stores of this higher type, where first-grade merchandise predominates, and where the sales force is alert, intelligent, and well trained, it is possible to have a fairly high average sales check, even without such big-ticket items as major electrical appliances or furniture.

Service in the Basement Store. In their constant search for new methods of low-cost merchandising, basement stores were an early proving ground for self-selection fixtures, self-service, check-out, and other low-cost selling techniques. Efforts to restrict other services, however, have not worked out well. Where the basement store does not deliver bulky packages or extend charge account privileges to qualified customers, the basement shopper transfers her patronage to more favorably located stores. Management has found that it must probe carefully before permitting wide deviations in service within the store, particularly in the downstairs store.

Lines Carried. Although some basement stores carry almost every line of merchandise represented in the upstairs departments, it is rarely possible to handle bulky items like living room or bedroom furniture. As there is only one selling floor, or at most, two, the basement usually restricts itself to items which do not require much space. Nevertheless, some articles that represent a considerable expenditure on the consumer's part, such as fur coats, can be handled successfully.

The backbone of most basements is ready-to-wear. Dresses and coats can be promoted consistently, to produce a large volume of profitable business at a somewhat shorter markup than prevails upstairs, and with a quick turnover. Men's furnishings, children's and infants' wear, piece goods, domestics, curtains, lamps, housewares, and smaller pieces of furniture also do well in basements.

Basement Stores in Branches. More and more managements are including basement or budget stores in the rapid branch development now under way. Their presence in the branches makes it possible for a store to achieve its full potential volume in a community and to meet, aggressively, all levels of competition encountered.

The basement in the branch may take the form of a downstairs store on the lower floors of the building. Or it may be in a building of its own, adjacent to the main building. In some cases, the basement is free-standing and is set up where there is no other branch of the upstairs store.

Occasionally, these free-standing basements add to their roster of departments one or more of those carried only in the upstairs part of the parent store. This is usually a device to meet important price competition in the area, and the upstairs deparments chosen for the purpose are those which enhance the drawing power of the branch with respect to that segment of the public whose business is its target. An example would be a record department, to draw young people, or a hardware section, added to attract home owners, even though the basement in the parent store carries neither records nor hardware.

The Basement's Contribution. The basement's contribution to the store is by no means small. In typical stores, its sales represent from 15 to 25 per cent of total sales, depending upon the amount of space that is available and the aggressiveness with which the basement takes advantage of its merchandising opportunities.

The store's operating figures benefit in other ways from the activities of the basement. Downstairs stores, when well operated, achieve higher rates of turnover than the upstairs departments. Their profit showing is usually good, because of the lower expense ratios that prevail. Working in a smaller area, the basement usually has higher sales per square foot; it does less institutional advertising and has less institutional activity of all kinds; it usually gets greater productivity from the sales staff; it keeps a tight control on expenses. The lower the operating costs, the more aggressive can the basement's merchandising effort become, and the more favorable is the effect on the total store operating ratios.

In any type of store, the basement must be aggressive to maintain its fair share of the low-price volume. In particularly high grade stores, the basement can do much to bring traffic through the main floor, and thus expose customers to better merchandise. Its ultimate aim should be that, as its customers progress and their incomes increase, they will become customers of the upstairs departments. Similarly, it can hold the patronage of upstairs customers who, for one reason or another, seek merchandise in lower price ranges than those carried in the regular departments.

Flexibility Is Essential. Basement merchandise is essentially promotional. If a department is to take full advantage of its opportunities for buying and selling exceptional values, it requires more freedom with respect to deviations from planned figures than would ordinarily be given an upstairs department.

Since, in volume merchandising, he who hesitates is lost, the basement usually has complete buying independence of the upstairs store, in order to avoid the delays attendant upon explaining each exception to someone remote from the operation.

Basement layout, too, must be flexible. Departments are frequently moved, expanded, or condensed, according to their immediate needs. An opportune buy of women's coats, for example, may require not only a special dispensation with respect to budget, but also a substantial increase in floor space. Later, the very same coat department may have to crowd itself into smaller space than ever to make room for some other department's event.

Flexibility in Pricing. Pennies are vital in the operation of basement stores. Flexibility in pricing is therefore essential, not only to adopt prices lines that the competition may be using, but also to arrive at higher acceptable selling prices on promotional items.

With the low markup percentages which prevail in basement departments, it is often wiser to run a special price line than to throw away valuable initial markup. A difference of even two per cent in the average prices of a department may be the difference between profit and loss. If a certain item, for example, should bring $2.10 to provide adequate markup, and if it is a good value at that price, it is a mistake for the basement merchandiser to offer it at $1.98 simply because that happens to be the nearest regular price line.

Similarly, if job lot merchandise is bought, the buyer should not be afraid to "merchandise" it—to sort it into, let us say, $1.49, $1.69, and $1.79 sellers, instead of retailing everything at $1.69.

Overlapping. Overlapping of price lines between downstairs and upstairs stores is inevitable. To a reasonable degree, an aggressive store management will foster such overlaps. The upstairs store, however, is usually restricted to certain price points below which the buyers may not go, in order to assure that the standard of quality and the desired store image will be maintained.

The downstairs store merchandiser should be free to go up in price, so long as the new and higher price line can be adequately stocked and can afford a profit. The buyer who moves up to a new higher price level, however, should make sure that he will be able to maintain an adequate representation in that price level for customer satisfaction. Too many buyers raise their price levels without considering their responsibility to the store for good price line assortments.

This does not apply, however, to special purchases of a one-time nature. In such cases, the price line consideration is secondary to the merchandiser's judgment of how the customer will accept the items.

Promotion. Like the upstairs store, the basement must strike a balance between basement-wide events and departmental promotions. Traffic-producing merchandise events like Dollar Days, Mill-end Sales, Sample Sales, for example, have long been stand-bys of basement promotion.

The importance of many familiar basement-wide events, however, is decreasing in some areas as customers and their needs change. The young population fills its needs in a different manner from the ways of their parents and grandparents. It goes without saying, also, that basement-wide events must be eliminated if there are not sufficient legitimate bargains available so that all major departments participate aggressively.

There is an increasing need for replacing basement-wide events with well timed, stronger departmental efforts on specific classifications. Departmental promotions can be worked out in cooperation with resources, in order to have the right goods available at the right time and at a volume-getting price. This calls for good planning, strong buyer-resource relationships, and the participation of the merchandise manager.

Advertising. Wherever possible, the basement should have its own advertising office. Its problems are different from those of the upstairs store, and the methods and media which are effective for one may prove useless to the other. Copy must be factual and forceful, without the subtle appeals appropriate for upstairs departments. In larger communities, basement advertising can use newspapers that the upstairs departments would not.

The advertising cost to dollar volume is usually higer in the downstairs store. With the squeeze on profits because of this and other rising operating costs, this segment of expense must be strongly controlled. Built-in success is essential in every downstairs store ad.

Upstairs departments are able to use many other media to attract customers: windows, direct mail, fashion extravaganzas, teas, breakfasts, trunk shows, etc. Downstairs stores use only one importantly—the newspaper. Newspaper ads, then, must be well thought out and carefully reviewed to assure continued profitable results. No basement merchandiser can rule out other media, but rather must search for new methods to offset the sometimes declining pull of newspapers. Above all, he must be certain it is possible for the customer to get what she wants in his department every day in an assortment of prices and values, and at a reasonable standard of quality.

Fashion presentation is vital to a modern downstairs store. Its customer is increasingly well informed and wants to look fashionable at budget prices. Thus a well planned and executed program of fashion advertising is important. This must be intermingled with price presentations of fashion.

It is also important that good interior display be developed, to present fashion to the customers who are shopping in the store. It is no secret that attractive displays sell merchandise—profitably!

Statistical Aids. An important element in the success or failure of basement operations is the use of statistical analysis as a guide in buying and merchandising. The same thoughtful planning that is given to the budgets and promotional plans for the upstairs departments (and is described in other chapters of this book) is also given to basement planning. Basement operations put a premium on flexibility and the ability to adjust stock and sales plans to accommodate opportune buys, but nevertheless, good merchandising requires good guide lines. The basement merchandiser must constantly satisfy himself that his basic actions are sound.

Some merchandise controls are necessary if a basement department is to learn from experience. One of the simplest systems to use is the periodic stock count, described in another chapter under "rotated unit control." This will give a quick indication of what is selling and what is not—particularly important where merchandise is bought in assortments or where several styles have been sampled.

The operation of merchandise control records can often be simplified by the use of rough sketches in place of descriptions. Articles that cannot easily be described or that do not have style numbers can often be sketched directly on the control forms, to make stock-taking easier and more accurate.

The more successful ready-to-wear operations use unit control systems which develops sales and stock information from stubs. Larger basements with multiple outlets are experimenting with computer-type stubs, in order to provide stock and sales information more rapidly.

Many large basements also maintain classification records, to keep the buyer up to the minute on sales trends and stock position in downtown and branch locations. These systems are not yet for all basements, however, as they are expensive and can increase cost without sufficient contribution to gross profit. Simple and elaborate procedures in classification merchandising are described in detail in a chapter elsewhere in this book.

Application of Merchandise Control. Regardless of the method of merchandise control used—visual, rotating counts, stub counts, or computer systems—the information is valuable only in proportion to its use. A buyer must review stock conditions with sufficient regularity to assure proper assortments as to price lines, colors, sizes, types, and merchandise on order.

At least weekly, the buyer should review stock conditions and take steps to move slow sellers, thus freeing open-to-buy for new, quick-selling merchandise. Staple stock lists should be studied and updated constantly to establish a base for proper assortments. Want slips should be reviewed daily for indications of trends and opportunities to promote. If the buyer can develop rapport with the salespeople, the want slips and never-out reports will become invaluable aids to improving performance.

All of these records—unit control, staple stock, and want slip—have real value when the buyer plans his market trips. They help him to project his needs accurately and serve as the basis for commitments, for dates of delivery, and for promotional needs.

Watching Competition. The basement buyer should also keep a watchful eye on his competitors. His customers are essentially value shoppers, and he may be sure that they are seldom ignorant of what other stores offer. He too, should know what other stores offer and apply that knowledge, along with his own store's experience, in building better selections and planning more effective promotions. Careful timing of events can make his store a leader, not a follower, of its competition.

Watching competition does not necessarily mean constant price cutting. The successful basement merchandiser must not miss the chance to get his full markon, if the value is good and if the price does not place him in an unfavorable competitive position.

The Basement Buyer. The basement buyer must contantly provide something new for his customers to keep their interest and patronage, and should plan always to promote some item that will produce extra volume. To that end, it is to his advantage to maintain close and friendly relationships with his resources, so that he can draw upon them for suggestions, guidance, and cooperation. In his dealings with them, particularly if he buys a great deal of close-out or distress merchandise, he should exercise tact and diplomacy to avoid giving the impression that he is a "chiseler."

It is vital that the buyer develop an expertness in *value, quality, specifications, and workmanship.* Such knowledge materially increases his advantages in negotiations when he is called on to make quick decisions on purchases, as so often happens, and this in turn helps volume and profits.

Above all, the basement buyer must be an opportunist, alert to see his chance and quick to take it. He should be in the market as often as the size of his department will permit, particularly if he merchandises fashion goods, to keep in touch with market conditions and trends.

He should manage his stocks so that he is always able to take advantage of buying opportunities. He buys closer to the actual selling period than the upstairs departments do, and he must be especially careful to adjust planned figures quickly to any fluctuation in sales or market trends. If the market falls, he must take quick markdowns, offsetting them with special purchases at better than average markon to the new retail levels of the merchandise. Only by keeping always in a position to take advantage of market opportunities will he hold his volume and make a profit.

The Basement in the Branch. With the development of branch stores, the job of the basement buyer has become more complex. Many of the regular basic stocks can be ordered and shipped separately for each store, taking into account variations in demand and in competition at each location. In the case of job lots or other purchases where the retailing has to be done after the goods have been received, the usual arrangement is to have the entire shipment go to the main store or warehouse for retailing, marking, and transfer to the various locations.

Like the buyers for upstairs departments, the basement buyer usually has department managers to assist him at the branches, each manager covering one or more departments. By learning to work with the department managers, and with the branch basement manager, the buyer can get valuable help in the management of basic stocks, in spotting slow sellers, in keeping in touch with the competitive situation, and in reacting to fluctuations in customer demand.

In the branch as in the main store, the basement brings additional volume at materially lower direct costs of operation. Major strides have been made in profit results of branches as a result of the basement's lower buying costs, publicity costs, and other direct expenses. Further, as more and more distribution of buying and similar costs is made, a real advantage accrues to the downtown or main unit in lowering the overall costs of doing business.

Training the Staff. In many well run stores, management considers the development of people on a par with other responsibilities. This is especially important with rapid branch expansion and the growing need for trained executives in multi-store organizations. Good training gives a store a distinct advantage in getting new units to move quickly up to planned volume and profit figures.

Like any other buyer, the basement buyer has a serious responsibility in the training of his staff. If he wants to get the enthusiastic cooperation of his salespeople, he must try to convey to them some of his own enthusiasm for the merchandise. He should neglect no opportunity to give them merchandise information, style news, pointers on salesmanship, and some idea of his plans for the department.

The buyer who is burdened by too much detail does not have enough time to perform this function well, or to scout the market adequately. Therefore, it is especially important to develop good assistants. The effort a buyer spends in training his right-hand man or men brings direct dividends in the form of increased time for other phases of his work.

The Future of the Basement Store. The rapid growth of all types of retailing has placed a strain on traditional department stores. Certainly their basements have had to come to grips with new problems and new forms of competition. There has been much indecision, much experimenting, much research, to find the right solutions.

There is surely no one right way for all basements to go, nor is there one right basement philosophy. This much is sure, however: The basement merchandiser who can meet the challenge of the future will be really aggressive—in merchandising his assortments, in seeking good resource relations, in seeking newness, in making sound plans and executing them, in using every means to learn more about the customer and her needs, in training an better organization.

The basement store, through branches, must be able to get to the budget buying public just as its prime competitors are getting there. It may well be that some long held beliefs will have to be changed and some methods and systems will have to be altered in order to help basement merchandisers meet their problems. With flexibility on the part of management, the basement will continue to make its important contribution to total store volume and profits.

CHAPTER 23

MERCHANDISING ASSORTMENTS AND ITEMS

BY

HAROLD B. WESS

The merchandising of a store or department involves the mastery of two distinctly different techniques. One is assortment merchandising, or the assembling of stocks whose kinds, prices, colors, and other features reflect the needs and interests of the customer and the store's position in its community. The other is item merchandising, or the ability to make the most of a particular article that has shown exceptional potential for the short or long term.

Assortment Merchandising

Before a store can make available the merchandise that will best fill the needs and wants of its customers, it must first have a proper understanding of the customers it hopes to serve. Next, it must plan its assortment in terms of this understanding. If it follows these two steps, then even the small store can compete successfully in its chosen concentration of assortments.

Limitations to Consider. No store can be all things to all men. Within the framework of the limitations management sets up, the buyer plans his assortments. These limitations may develop from the physical size of the store, its financial condition, and the degree of risk management is willing to assume in terms of losses due to markdowns and slow moving inventory. Competitive conditions must be considered, along with the nature of the community and of the place the store wishes to occupy in that community.

Management establishes the framework, but the buyer also

takes time to study the community, its social and cultural levels, and the competitive position of the store. With this background, he proceeds to plan his assortments.

Why Assortment Planning. A store or department without a correctly conceived assortment plan is like a ship without a rudder. In effect, in making its assortment plan, the department is placing merchandise orders for Jane, Mary, and Tom Customer, so that they can find what they want when they come in to buy. Otherwise, the department will have a little of this and a little of that, and its sales will reflect its lack of character.

In assortment planning, the store and the department must decide *where to place greatest emphasis* as to scope, price range, specific price lines, number of price lines, type variation, number of styles, number of sizes, and number of colors. There must also be a decision as to what to de-emphasize. Just as no store can carry every product offered by the market, so no store can emphasize every merchandise category available to it. The decisions, of course, will be made in terms of the limitations we have just discussed.

Such decisions must not be left to chance. In order to make sure that the desired character is maintained throughout the store, wise managements spell out their decisions in writing for the guidance of buyers. Only in that way can they be sure of seizing dominance in areas where the competition is weak, and playing classifications up or down in terms of their importance to the customers or the store's opportunity.

Price Line Range. Knowing the kind of store management wishes to have, and the economic, social, cultural and taste level of the customers we are to serve, it should be relatively easy to decide how low and how high to plan our price lines. This decision must be made not only for specific items but for the specific customer.

Too frequently, the high-low price line decision is different in various departments of the store; the store's customer then can buy in one department but not in others. There may be good reasons for exceptions, but *the price line range should by and large fit the store's customers throughout the store.*

How Many Price Lines? How many price lines should be stocked? It would be unrealistic to make a hard and fast rule. There are, however, some common sense principles that we can use to guide us. They are:

1. *Competitive price lines*: These are fairly common and accepted as pivotal competitive price lines or price points.

2. *Built-in price lines*: These are developed by a single store in cooperation with a manufacturer, or developed by cooperating stores or buying offices for their clients. They fall between competitive price lines and yield a higher markup because of special values built into the item, such as better workmanship, better material, or superior style.

3. *Price Zones*: Here a group of price lines is actually merchandised as if it were a single price line. Such price zones are sometimes utilized when the risk of carrying a full assortment at each price line is too great because of the limited potential volume and the hazards of mark downs.

Basically, it is better not to carry a price line at all if the customer will not find in that price line an adequate assortment of types, styles, sizes and colors. The decision must not be left to chance but must be planned and planned carefully—first at the store level, and then in the department.

Types. Should a furniture store or department store carry exclusively borax, semi-borax, period, or modern furniture? Should it, on the other hand, carry some of each type of furniture and if so, in what proportion to the total stock? Should a men's clothing store or a men's clothing department carry exclusively conservative, sportswear or youthful clothing? Should it carry all these types and if so, in what proportion?

Such decisions in assortment planning must be made across the board, with the probable exception of strictly staple merchandise. Each store must decide for itself what type or types of merchandise it will carry, in terms of the niche it wants to occupy in the community. If the store is a large one, it must make certain that, just as in the *price line* decision, so in the *type* decision the store's customer can buy what she wants throughout the store and not in only one department. Each buyer must run his operation in line with the store's overall character.

Styles, Sizes and Colors. How many styles should the department offer its customers at a given price? This of course will differ with the kind of item. The decision must be made from two points of view: the customer's, as to how many styles give her a wide enough choice at the price she wants to pay, and the store's, based on the dominance it wishes to give a price line. The department will naturally offer a larger number of styles at a price line it considers dominant than in one it does not consider dominant or wishes to de-emphasize.

If a customer finds an item at a price she can afford to pay and finds a style at that price acceptable to her, but cannot find her size or her desired color, the store will usually lose that sale. In some cases, the determining factor as to whether a customer will purchase an item of apparel will be size first, color next, and price last.

A buyer should know from his department's records the size range that its customers will require. In some stores, larger sizes will dominate while in others the reverse will be true. Instead of guessing what proportion to buy in each size for each style, a store should offer the customer an acceptable choice of sizes in each style. Judgment will dictate the size assortment needed to satisfy a dominant assortment of styles at a dominant price. Conversely, experience and judgment will dictate the assortment to offer in a particular size.

The important point is that size assortment must not be left to chance. With experience, the correct size assortment can be pre-determined and insurance provided so that the store's actual and potential customer will find her size in her style and at her price.

While color assortments are not as easily and accurately predictable, it is possible and indeed indispensable to plan them carefully. Although color is usually an element of fashion, there is a much greater consistency in the way certain colors sell season after season. A proper assortment plan, therefore, must provide for such color consistency. Whether a price line or style or a type will be planned for a complete color coverage will again depend as to whether that price line, style or type is intended to be dominant or not. Here judgment, store personality, and the other factors mentioned earlier in this chapter will play a deciding part.

Assortment merchandising must be made to happen through careful planning and must not be left to chance. There is no substitute for intuition and judgment in merchandising.

Item Merchandising

Item merchandising is a technique and process of discovering items within the assortment that have great potential for short-run or long-run exploitation. Good assortments will produce good exploitable items. The specific techniques for making the most of *new* items have a chapter of their own.

Short-Run Winners. It may be an oversimplification to state that a department to be successful should be able to give the customer what she wants and when she wants it, but it is nevertheless true. A properly prepared assortment plan tries to anticipate, from previous experience, from what the market has available, from trade journals, and from various forms of customer research, what the store's actual and potential customers may want. *The real test comes when these assortments are placed before the customers in the store.*

For example, ten styles of a certain priced dress may be

placed on the racks on a busy morning with a range of sizes and colors for each style. Within a few hours, it will be found that one or two of these styles have been bought by customers to the extent of as many as six out of the twelve available in the one style, while other styles exposed to the same customers may show few sales or none.

This is a signal of great significance. The customers have voted. These are the winners. The speed with which these winners are spotted and reordered will make the difference in the store's share of the dress market in its community.

Usually styles in apparel departments and fads and novelties in other departments are of short duration. We may call such items "short-runners." If a store is even a day or two late in discovering these winners, it will unnecessarily lose that much volume.

Play the Winners. A store that fails to take advantage of the customers' votes for the winners in its assortments will not be able to sell them something just as good. Playing the winners at full markup is more profitable—in fact, it is a most profitable part of the store's business. Good merchants have been able to pyramid their reorders, expand sizes and colors, and play the winners to secure added sales and added profits.

Since these winners have a relatively short life, it is important to taper off the reorders when sales begin to lag and reduce the stock with a minimum of mark-downs. Knowing how to get the maximum potential sales out of such items with a minimum of mark-downs is part of the art of good merchandising. This must necessarily involve trial and error, the courage to be willing to make mistakes and accept the consequences, and the ability to learn from these mistakes.

If a buyer spots a short-run winner in a competitor's store, or through his store's buying office, or other sources, he must lose no time nor lack the courage to make the most of such a discovery. Courage and speed are of the essence in merchandising such items. Those who keep the unit control records, salespeople, and others as well as buyers should be conditioned to watch for such items. That conditioning comes from many areas: good training programs, leadership from the top, and an active interest by the buyer in the development and aggressive exploitation of these items.

Reordering Winners. The size of the reorder upon the discovery of such an item will depend on whether the discovery was made soon enough, whether it is at the beginning or near the end of the season for the item, whether a modification of the item and a change in color may make it a best seller the following season, how many were sold per day, how many may sell with adequate promotion, etc.

A buyer who is alert, courageous, and well organized to make the most of such a winner, of such best sellers, enhances his store's reputation in the community for alertness, leadership and having what is new and desirable. Actually, by honoring the customers' vote, the store enables the customer to honor it in the most significant way—by purchases.

Long-Run Winners. In a well-planned assortment, there are so-called perennials. Unlike the summer roses which are of a short-run nature, although beautiful and desirable while they last, there are items in a good assortment that have a repeat business potential over many seasons and many years. Properly merchandised, they can produce plus volume and plus profit and further tie the customer to the store.

Such items can be easily spotted. Their selling record over a long period proves that they have a repeat potential. They are usually items that are used widely and are of a replacement nature.

If such an item is recognized as a winner for the long pull, it must receive special attention. In the first place, it should be improved in quality and workmanship; plus value should be built into it. If size, color and other attributes are factors, the range of assortments should be broadened. Special plans should be made for internal display and promotions, and the item should be repeatedly advertised in a recognizable format for consumer identification. Such items not only belong to the store that builds and promotes them, but they become a source of repetitive profitable volume.

Merchandising assortments and items is both an art and a science. Success can be achieved only through meticulous planning and constant follow-up and control. Those stores which develop techniques for successful assortment and item merchandising will be well repaid for the thought, organization, and implementation they invest.

CHAPTER 24

THE BUYER AND INVENTORY SHORTAGES

BY

W. EARL MILLER

One of the most serious problems with which the buyer must cope today is inventory shortages and their control. Many other executives of the store share with the buyer a responsibility for keeping shortages within bounds; many employees other than those on the buyer's own staff can be guilty of carelessness, or laxity, or the downright dishonesty that causes shortages. *Yet the problem in most organizations remains essentially the buyer's.* He is the person responsible for the inventory, and it is his competence that is in question when shortages are high. Moreover, it is the gross margin of his department that suffers—and gross margin is one of the important yardsticks by which management judges his performance.

Extent of the Problem. In the typical department store, inventory shortages are likely to run to somewhat more than one per cent of sales. The 1963 figure, the highest over a 10-year period, was 1.39 per cent of sales. The shortage figure varies from store to store, depending on the nature of its operation, the amount and kind of traffic it enjoys, the extent to which it uses open selling, and especially the size and number of branch or sister store operations involved.

In a store of modest size with no branches, the entire inventory is under the buyer's eye, and so are the people who handle it. His personal vigilance can be a major element in minimizing the errors and indifference out of which shortages can develop.

When a store is large and acquires branches, however, no

one person's hands and eyes are sufficient. The buyer's problem then becomes one of leadership, example, supervision—of investigating possible causes of discrepancies in his department's figures and then teaching and preaching ways to eliminate these faults. Some of the causes of shortages may arise from the work of persons not under his direct supervision. In such cases, his ability to secure the cooperation of the executives who supervise those persons becomes important.

Many-Pronged Attack. The problem of inventory shortages is not one that can be solved with a simple, pat answer. What is needed is a many-pronged attack, not only upon the causes of actual loss of merchandise through theft and mishandling, but also upon the careless paper work that can create discrepancies between book and physical inventory figures. Such discrepancies sometimes minimize and sometimes exaggerate whatever the actual merchandise shortage happens to be.

Without sound facts, neither the buyer nor his management can hope to measure shortages nor track down their causes. A first step, then, toward improving the shortage picture is to make sure that *all records are as accurate as human hands can make them.* Only in that way will the records become valuable in pinpointing the sources of actual merchandise loss through shoplifting, or theft, or breakage, or whatever it happens to be.

Keeping the Records Straight. The most modern marvels of electronic data processing share one shortcoming with quill pen methods: They cannot produce accurate results unless the figures fed into them are accurate to begin with. If a department has received 11 or 13 pieces and reports 12, the record will show that 12 should be in stock. If it transfers three to a branch and the report shows four, the record will show four. If a customer buys and pays for two, the sales slip and the record will show that two were sold, even if the customer got one or three by mistake.

It is important, then, that everyone who makes any entries concerning the department's merchandise should be trained to count and re-count the actual items and to check the count against the actual entry. When the buyer decides to mark 10 handbags down from $15 to $12.50 each, for instance, he or an assistant should count to make sure there are actually 10 to be marked down; check to see that they are all presently marked at $15; check to see that the new price is correctly stated on the tags; check to see that the markdown form has been filled out properly.

Similarly, if the buyer transfers 10 dresses at $22.50 each from the main store to a branch, some one at the main store should check the count, the price tickets, and the transfer form, and sign to that effect. Someone at the branch should check the merchandise in in exactly the same way—count the pieces, look at the price tickets, and then compare with the transfer form or write up a receiving sheet, according to the requirements of store system. *And sign to that effect.* A discrepancy between the two counts may mean carelessness at either end or theft in transit. Insistence upon comparing the figures and checking out discrepancies will serve to discourage both carelessness and dishonesty.

Sources of Paper Errors. Common sources of errors in re-receipts and shipments of merchandise include:

1. Failure to count the number of pieces received from or returned to vendors, or transferred from one store or branch to another.

2. Failure to check the actual count against the figure entered on the form covering the receipt or transfer of merchandise.

3. Failure to check the prices marked on the merchandise against the prices marked on the form covering the movement of that merchandise.

4. Failure to check the department or classification number on the form against the merchandise itself.

5. Failure to make an entry covering movement of merchandise or changes in price.

Some errors of this type can originate with people not directly under the buyer's supervision. The marking room, for instance, could conceivably put the wrong price tickets on merchandise; the receiving room could grow careless and assume without checking that a package marked "Contents: 12 boxes" actually contains 12. The buyer is in no position to give instructions to receiving or marking employees, but he or an assistant can check or test-check his invoices against the stock coming into his department and report discrepancies to the appropriate supervisor.

Also to be watched are the prices and extensions on invoices and chargebacks to vendors that pass through the buyer's hands. A look at the invoice register at intervals, too, is another way to spot errors. If any entries show extremely high or low markons, an incorrect retail price may have found its way into the record.

Small Items, Too. Small errors are as important as those involving large amounts. More so, perhaps, because they tend to be shrugged off—and repeated. If, for example, one or two pieces of merchandise have become soiled or damaged and the buyer marks them down on the spot, it is easy to forget to enter the markdown. Or if a garment has been lent to the display or advertising department without making a record of the loan, it is easy to lose sight of the article permanently. And if the record was made, was its return noted?

Departments that sell merchandise by the yard face several special hazards of their own: careless measuring, failure to record end-of-bolt allowances, failure to take a markdown when a strip is cut from which to provide samples to customers. Some stores, to save record-keeping, permit the buyer to take a blanket markdown once a month for such contingencies. An occasional check should be made to be sure that this allowance is correct.

Where workroom activity is involved, in addition to the sale of yardage, as in draperies or wall-to-wall carpeting, shortages can occur if there is carelessness or dishonesty in measuring and charging for the materials used. The buyer should check the figures occasionally; if there is an abnormal number of small yardages, he has reason to look further. Also important is a test-check of the calculations on charges and work sheets; it may turn up errors, honest or otherwise, in billing. *Test-check, test-check,* all the time.

Errors On the Selling Floor. Salespeople who are unfamiliar with a department's merchandise or who are dishonest can make mistakes that increase the shortage figure. For example, if bedsheets are priced singly but packed in pairs, a new or confused clerk can charge for one but hand over two. Or small, non-marked items can slip into the wrong bins, and be sold at the wrong prices. To keep such errors to a minimum, constant training and reminder are needed.

Errors creep in, too, when price tickets become detached from the merchandise and when goods are returned without tickets. Carelessness in making out new price tickets can be kept to a minimum by insisting that *no ticket be attached without prior check by the buyer* or some other designated person who knows the merchandise.

If a selling department has more than its share of lost price tickets, the marking department should be asked to help. In a classic case, a basement shoe department handled odd lots and closeouts and frequently had shoes at various prices offered for sale on the same tables. The shoes of each pair were linked by cord, and from that cord the price ticket was suspended. The system was excellent, but the cord was not. Pairs broke apart, price tickets got lost, and salespeople took wild guesses at the prices of the reassembled pairs. As soon as the marking department found a cord strong enough to survive the yanking of basement shoppers, the department's shortage figure dropped appreciably.

Merchandising's Contribution. In general, the buyer will find that the better he merchandises his stock, the lower his shortages will be. If his department is well price-lined, for instance, there will be fewer and more familiar prices to work with. Careless errors in marking or in making entries will then stand out like the proverbial sore thumb. People will question

$1.88, let us say, if it turns up on the merchandise or in the records of a department that normally has no price between $1.50 and $2.00.

With good merchandising, too, the stock is well selected and moves quickly. It will not be on hand long enough to run much risk of pilferage, lost price tickets, damage, etc.

Outright Theft. If a buyer has reason to believe that his department is suffering from pilferage by employees, shoplifting by customers, or a combination of the two, he should certainly seek help from his store's protection department. Often the trained eye of a protection executive can spot weaknesses that a buyer would not notice. For instance, a department may be laid out so that it provides a secluded aisle that is all too convenient for shoplifters. Or its self-selection fixtures may bring small, colorful items within easy reach of young children, trailing their mothers through a suburban branch. These and other hazards are familiar to protection experts, who can generally suggest ways to cut down on a department's attraction for amateur and professional thieves without lessening its appeal to customers. It is important to train all of your people to report immediately any evidence or suspicion of theft.

Inventory Taking. Shortages and overages normally show up only when a physical inventory is taken and compared with the book figure. It is important to the buyer that such inventories be taken with the greatest possible degree of accuracy, so that he will get a true picture of how carefully his stock has been controlled.

Instructions for taking the inventory are usually provided by the controller's office, but it is up to the buyer to see that the instructions are carried out to the letter, under his eye or under that of a qualified subordinate. It is always a great temptation to inventory-takers, particularly after hours of counting, to assume without checking that all boxes on the top shelf of a stockroom are full, or that every box that rattles in a certain way contains exactly what the checker thinks it does. The wise buyer, by making himself much in evidence while the counting is in progress, can reduce the temptation to take short-cuts. By emphasizing to his staff, also, that he wants an accurate count, he can encourage a conscientious job.

Department Housekeeping. Both by example and supervision, the buyer can develop in his department a respect for the merchandise that will go far to keep his shortages to a minimum. The buyer who prides himself on an outstanding housekeeping job is far less likely to suffer large inventory shortages than the sloppy or disorganized housekeeper.

Merchandise that is wadded up instead of being neatly folded deteriorates quickly; dresses that are allowed to stay on the floor if they slip from their hangers lose salability; carelessly stacked articles are readily subject to breakage; articles in neglected open selling fixtures generally end up in the wrong compartments. A scrambled stock is an invitation to the shoplifter, whereas a tidy one is a warning that anything displaced will be promptly noticed. It pays to develop neat habits in the department's staff.

Branch Inventories. With multiple store operation, inventory shortage problems become much more serious and much harder to control. If the organization maintains separate inventory figures for each branch, then the manager at each location has a direct and specific responsibility, along with the buyer, for shortages. Where the pooled inventory concept is in effect, obviously the branch manager cannot be held directly accountable for shortages. Nevertheless, he has an obligation to correct situations which tend to create shortages as well as to work with the buyer to keep the records accurate. He has a joint and very real responsibility along with the buyer, even though he cannot be held directly accountable.

The buyer should do his share to educate the branch executives with whom he works as to the necessity for vigilance with respect to shortages. He should make sure that they understand systems and procedures thoroughly, and should discuss any lapses concerning his department's merchandise in the spirit of arming the branch against future errors. If the branch personnel report an error on the part of the buyer or of people directly under his supervision, he should accept the correction gracefully, acknowledging the interest and alertness that this demonstrates.

Setting the Pattern. In his relations with his own staff, with branch personnel, or with members of the sales-supporting divisions of the store, the buyer should set a pattern of cooperation, of willingness to learn, and of readiness to accept suggestions and corrections. Opportunities to tour such departments as accounting, receiving, or marking, to see how merchandise and records are handled, should be taken up eagerly and, if possible, should be made available to assistants and branch department managers. Rules make more sense and loopholes are easier to close, when the people who must follow those rules understand what they are all about.

But no matter how many other people or departments or branches are concerned with the merchandise and the records, the buyer must recognize that shortages are *his* problem and *his* responsibility. They reflect upon his ability and his fitness for the trust reposed in him by the store, and he cannot afford to let them get out of hand. Constant vigilance, constant follow-up and constant test-checking are his best safeguards.

CHAPTER 25

MARKDOWNS

BY

SIDNEY L. SOLOMON

A markdown is a reduction from the original or previous retail price of a unit of merchandise. Properly used, markdowns are an effective tool of retail merchandising to dispose of merchandise which is unsalable at its present selling price and thereby to keep stocks constantly liquid; to assist in the promotion of sales; and to meet competition.

Importance of Understanding Markdowns. A reduction in the unit price of an item results in a reduction in the total retail intake, which in turn means a *lower profit*. Obviously, any factor which directly affects profits is of major concern. Properly taken, markdowns are an effective means of adjusting stocks to external conditions—the market, the customer and competition.

The subject of markdowns becomes of greater importance as merchandise markets change more rapidly and become more dynamic. The appearance in the market of better quality, new styles, new materials, improved designs and new products can quickly lower the consumer acceptability of merchandise in stock. Sharp markdowns become necessary for the store that does not move fast enough to keep its stock in shape, i.e., for the store that fails to make early, effective use of markdowns.

During periods of constant price fluctuations, markdowns become a major factor in the profit picture. Price breaks in the market can be sharp and sudden; then the selling price of stocks on hand must be reduced to the new market level, or even lower, to make them quickly salable. During such a period, proper and reasonable markdown control is the most important factor in showing a satisfactory profit.

Markdown Causes. The following classification of markdown causes has appeared in earlier editions of THE BUYER'S MANUAL, and is based upon the Markdown Manual published by the Merchandising Division of the National Retail Merchants Association. By classifying and analyzing markdowns as to their causes, the buyer can distinguish between those that are avoidable and those that are not. A study of the avoidable markdowns will point the way towards improved merchandising operation.

PROMOTIONAL PURCHASE REMAINDERS. Markdowns taken on remainders from job lot merchandise and merchandise purchased for special sales. This classification is set up so that the losses on special purchases will be identified as such and not confused with those resulting from broken assortments of regular stock. The latter would come under the classification of "Broken Assortments and Remnants."

FABRICS OR QUALITY. Markdowns taken on regularly bought merchandise because it is made of a fabric not readily accepted by the consumer, or is of a quality below the standards of the store's clientele.

STYLE OR PATTERN. Markdowns taken on regularly bought merchandise because of undesirable style or pattern.

COLOR. Markdowns taken on regularly bought merchandise because of undesirable colors. This includes colors which are undesirable because of poor dyeing, as well as accumulations of unwanted colors resulting from unbalanced proportional buying.

SIZES. Markdowns taken on regularly bought merchandise because of accumulation of sizes, due to either unbalanced proportional buying or receipt of merchandise that is sized contrary to order.

QUANTITIES. Markdowns taken to speed up the sale of regularly bought merchandise purchased in too large a quantity to sell quickly at the original price; markdowns on articles which have become shopworn as a result of having been purchased in too great a quantity; markdowns taken because a department is overstocked relative to its potential sales volume; and markdowns taken on stocks which are out of balance by merchandise classification, in order to limit investment in total inventory.

SPECIAL SALES FROM STOCK. (1) *Special Sales.* Markdowns on regularly bought merchandise which is taken from stock and offered at a lower retail price than usual for special sale purposes.

(2) *Multiple Sales.* Markdowns on regularly bought merchandise when the quantity price is less per unit than the price of each single unit, i.e., 35¢ ea. or 3/$1.00.

BROKEN ASSORTMENTS AND REMNANTS. Markdowns taken on small remnants and odds and ends of regularly bought merchandise, offered at a reduction, to close out the line.

Markdowns taken on regularly bought merchandise which has become *shopworn, soiled or damaged.* This does not include merchandise which may have become shopworn or soiled mainly because too great a quantity was originally purchased. (See "Quantities.")

Markdowns taken on regularly bought merchandise used as window pieces or to create style prestige; known as *style or model pieces.*

PRICE ADJUSTMENTS. This includes markdowns taken on regularly bought merchandise *to meet competitors' prices;* on regularly bought merchandise when a falling market necessitates lowering prices *to a lower cost level;* and on regularly bought merchandise because it is desirable to eliminate and *consolidate price lines.*

ALLOWANCE TO CUSTOMERS. Markdowns taken on regularly bought merchandise because of allowances made to customers on adjustment claims. This includes only cases where the merchandise is actually at fault. *Policy adjustments,* where the merchandise is not at fault but the allowance is made in order to retain the goodwill of the customer, are an operating expense item and not classified as markdowns.

Summary of Causes. Numerous studies show that special sales from stock, excess quantities resulting from overbuying, and broken and unbalanced assortments are the major causes of markdowns; but that *price adjustments* become an important cause during an inflationary readjustment period. *Timing* is also an important factor. If goods are received too early or too late, excessive markdowns will result.

Control and Use of Markdowns. An analysis of the numerous causes of markdowns reveals that effective markdown control involves nearly all the phases of buying, selling and stockkeeping. If every retailer offered the right merchandise, at the right time, at the right price, in the right quantity, sizes and colors, and did an aggressive selling job and an efficient stockkeeping job, his markdowns would be practically eliminated. For the purposes of this chapter, the discussion will be confined to a few of the major factors which are the basic areas of error and neglect.

BUYING OBJECTIVES. Alertness to customer demand involves an analysis of buying habits and trends, and requires a study of want slips, waiting on customers, talking to salespeople and making use of all available records.

Careful analysis to determine and forecast what is fashion right requires searching for fashion information in trade and consumer publications, advertisements, in other stores, among manufacturers, fashion leaders, stylists, etc.

Selection of top resources who can be counted upon to have quality right, style right and price right goods.

Planned balancing of stocks involves careful estimates of future sales, heavy stock condition often being caused by planning sales too high; seasonal dollar inventory and turnover, based on past experience, comparative figures, business condition forecasts, etc.; effective dollar and unit stock controls to help know what, when, and how much to buy—inexpensive, flexible unit stock control systems that provide the needed information quickly and accurately; careful study of unit sales and stock records for proper price line, style, color and size assortments; and flexibility to changing conditions.

Careful experimentation with new items, styles and fashions; and reorder alertness and developments of systems for quick reordering.

Full *realization of the problems of promotional goods*—the necessity for greater alertness, flexibility, aggressiveness and speed; ability to fit remainders into regular stock.

Making certain that *merchandise received is the merchandise bought* and is in salable condition.

Analysis of past mistakes and their causes.

Continuous *study* of changing *economic conditions*.

Analysis of slow selling—season letter identification; budget and plan for disposal; monthly stock report on current situation; and review for necessary action.

SELLING AND STOCKKEEPING OBJECTIVES. The dramatic displays of merchandise to keep it from becoming slow selling; a continuously trained selling staff with the necessary merchandise information, trained to keep older merchandise in forward stock and to show it; timely and effective advertising to keep merchandise moving; neat and logical stock arrangement to simplify customer buying; careful handling of merchandise to avoid damage; proper protection to keep stock clean and unsoiled; use of incentives for salesclerks, such as P.M.'s and spiffs; and elimination of unnecessary returns, by better selling.

Planned Markdowns. Recognizing that the above objectives are a goal which cannot always be fully attained, many stores have carefully analyzed and planned their markdowns. As a result, they have made considerable progress in their reduction of markdowns, and above all in their better use.

For a number of reasons, budgeted or planned markdowns have their proponents. It is pointed out that since markdowns reduce the stock, then reductions as well as sales must be taken into account in planning purchases to maintain a desired stock figure; and that planning markdowns insures that they will be taken promptly and at the most advantageous time rather than hit-and-miss.

Also, that planning markdowns in advance calls attention to this factor as a source of loss and activates greater corrective action. It tends to curb excesses in the case of buyers who get panicky if sales are far below plan, or where a new buyer is tempted to slash his predecessor's merchandise. Furthermore, it recognizes the use of markdowns as a valuable tool in retail merchandising.

On the other hand, there are many merchandise men who oppose budgeting markdowns on the grounds that it may cause buyers to postpone necessary markdowns; or because of a provision having been made for them, it may result in unnecessary markdowns being taken. The objections, however, appear to arise from a feeling that a planned figure is a fixed figure. Once it is recognized that planned figures must be adjusted from time to time in the light of changing and unforeseen conditions, these objections to a plan lose their force.

How to Plan. In planning markdowns, it is necessary to consider these points:

Season markdown percentage. The style risk, as in fashion goods; physical deterioration of merchandise in stock; price decline outlook; comparative statistics, as reflected in such reports as those of the Controllers' Congress of the NRMA as a guide; analysis of slow selling stock that must be cleared; store policy in regard to special sales from stock, initial mark-up, meeting competition, customer returns; previous figures and causes; and planned improvements in buying, selling and stockkeeping.

Monthly distribution. Peak selling periods; end of season; clearance sales; special events; and past experience.

In using the plan, actual markdowns should be matched against planned markdowns and deviations analyzed. An amount lower than plan might indicate a failure to take a sufficient or quick enough markdown. Conscientiously used, these figures are a guide to locating trouble spots, delays in needed action, markdown causes, etc. Careful review and follow-up is a key factor in the control, effective use and reduction of markdowns.

Timing of Markdowns. Timing is important because the more accurate it is, the less is the amount of markdown needed to sell the merchandise and the greater is the gross margin realized on the transaction.

Markdowns should be taken when selling activity first indicates customer resistance by a slow-up in sales; during the selling season of the item, when there is still a sufficient consumer demand to move the merchandise quickly at a minimum price reduction; after regular item review to ascertain markdown needs; when external conditions and judgment indicate that consumer acceptance of goods in stock will be diminished by the appearance of a new style, new product, or a lower price, etc.—above all, a realistic attitude.

Most merchants favor the policy of taking markdowns on an individual item basis as soon as the need arises, on the ground that the longer the item stays in stock the less it will eventually be worth. There are many proponents, however, of monthly and semi-annual clearance sales. The latter point out that the accumulation of a large amount of slow selling merchandise enables the store to stage an important clearance event; that clearance events attract bargain hunters and customers who may not shop regularly at the store; and that clearance events eliminate the display of successively marked-down merchandise during the selling season.

While reliance upon the semi-annual clearance alone may have some foundation for acceptance by the exclusive specialty store, the generally accepted and effective practice appears to be a combination of individual markdowns, monthly reviews and semi-annual clearance, usually in January and July.

This general practice enables a buyer constantly to shift merchandise from higher to lower price lines while there is still a good demand for the merchandise at the lower price lines. In other words, it enables him to buy from his own stock.

Furthermore, the quick disposal of his own stock in a declining market enables a buyer to be open-to-buy and promote closeouts and other manufacturers' mistakes.

Leftover seasonal goods of a staple nature often raise the question of a markdown versus a carry-over to the start of the next selling season. If cheap storage space is available it may be more profitable to store the goods, but storage ties up money, involves storage cost, is time consuming and may result in breakage or damage. Furthermore, a new design or style may make the so-called "staple" obsolete.

Amount of a Markdown. The amount of a needed reduction is closely tied to the time when reduction is taken. However, assuming that the time factor is constant, the ability to determine the price at which the item can quickly be cleared is one of the major factors in the control of markdowns.

The markdown should be large enough to make the merchandise interesting to a group of people not attracted to it at the original price; probably to the next lower price zone or income group, where a new level of demand is activated.

Obviously, the ideal markdown is just large enough to move the goods. If it is too small it is generally ineffective, and will merely cause a delay in the sale of the goods and lead to a series of successive markdowns which in total will add up to more than an early sharp markdown. On the other hand, too large a markdown unnecessarily reduces the gross margin and profit. Only seasoned judgment based upon all available facts can give a correct answer.

Automatic Markdowns. Some stores have had experience with automatic markdown arrangements in limited sections of the store. Price tags indicate the date when each item is put into stock and a markdown schedule is prepared in advance. Items that are still on hand at the end of a certain period are reduced by the predetermined percentage. This reduction is supposed to be large enough to dispose of the merchandise promptly. If the goods are not sold within an additional predetermined period they are again reduced by the predetermined percentage. After a number of these *automatic* reductions, the goods are reduced to "zero" and given to charity.

The purpose of these plans is to insure that markdowns are taken on time and that the reduction in price is adequate to sell the merchandise quickly. In actual operation, however, automatic markdown plans appear to be impractical for regular merchandise because of their inflexibility. Since they are based upon predetermined rates of sale and reductions, they are not always adapted to conditions that develop while the merchandise is in stock.

Markdown Records. Records are important in the control of markdowns because they can be made to provide a classified summary of reductions by departments, merchandise classifications, and manufacturers, as well as causes. Furthermore, accurate records are essential in stores operating under the retail method of inventory, in order that the book figures of stock on hand will agree with the actual retail stock inventory.

Markdowns must be accepted as a necessary evil in modern retail merchandise operations, but at the same time they can be used as an effective instrument in improving the tempo of a store's merchandising activities. By the very nature of retailing, merchandise will at times become soiled and damaged; obsolescence is inevitable in a dynamic industrial age; and human error will always prevail in the selection of styles, colors and sizes in correct quantities and assortments; furthermore, the plans of competition and the steps that must be taken to meet them are unpredictable. The skill that an individual store can develop in the use of markdowns, however, can have an important effect in attracting new customers, in added sales, in improving the store's competitive standing in the community, and in achieving the ultimate goal of net profit.

With competition continuously becoming keener and operating costs relatively higher, an improvement in gross margin and an adequate net profit can only be attained by more alert merchandising methods. The latter objective can be realized by a full understanding of markdown causes, and by the effective use and control of markdowns.

CHAPTER 26

TURNOVER

BY

MAX ROBB

Of course, I have always believed that turnover is a consequence of selling and is therefore something less to concern oneself about than the all important job of selling. I don't want to belabor the point, but I must say that if you sell what you buy quickly and are prepared to re-order, turnover will take care of itself.

Nevertheless, it is important to know the techniques of improving turnover in addition to the, for me, cardinal technique of selling and selling fast. Hence this chapter.

Turnover measures the velocity with which merchandise passes through the merchant's hands into those of his customers; it is the number of times in a given period that a stock of goods is sold by the retailer and replaced with fresh merchandise.

Good turnover, or a healthy flow of goods into and out of a department, is a result of good management. Although it is conceivable that certain types of poor operation may temporarily yield a good turnover, it is practically impossible for a consistently good operation to fail to yield a consistently good turnover. Hence the turnover rate is a vital yardstick in measuring a store's or a department's performance.

Calculating Turnover Rate. To arrive at the number of stock turns obtained in a given period, one divides the net sales for that period by the average stock for the period. Both figures should be retail, or both should be cost.

In the department store field, turnover is generally calculated on a yearly basis, using retail figures. Under the retail inventory method of accounting, the department store usually has a monthly inventory figure available from its books without the necessity of taking physical inventory. To get the average inventory for a department, the store adds the beginning, ending, and 11 intermediate monthly inventory figures, and then divides by 13. The resulting figure is then divided into the sales figures for the total year.

To illustrate this explanation in order to make it clear:

Sales		Book Inventory	
January	$ 55,000	$ 75,000	January 1
February	50,000	100,000	January 31
March	65,000	115,000	February 28
April	67,000	120,000	March 31
May	60,000	105,000	April 30
June	55,000	95,000	May 31
July	50,000	75,000	June 30
August	55,000	100,000	July 31
September	65,000	120,000	August 31
October	67,000	127,000	September 30
November	70,000	129,000	October 31
December	85,000	131,000	November 30
	$744,000	75,000	December 31
		$1,367,000	

Now divide the total $1,367,000 by 13 to find the average stock, i.e., $1,367,000 divided by 13 equals $105,154. This is the average inventory for the year. Next divide the annual sales of $744,000 by the average inventory of $105,154 to find the number of times the stock has turned, i.e., $744,000 divided by $105,154 equals 7.08. This is the rate of stock turnover, or the number of times the goods have turned in one year's selling period.

Exactly the same method can be used in calculating a monthly turnover figure, if that is wanted. The inventory figures for the beginning and end of that month are averaged, and the resulting figure is divided into the sales for the month. Some stores compute weekly inventory figures, and where these are available they can be averaged to get a more accurate average stock figure for monthly or annual computations.

Yardsticks. The actual number of stock turns which constitute a satisfactory turnover varies with the type of merchandise and its price. Generally speaking, lower price ranges turn more rapidly than higher; wearing apparel and accessories turn more rapidly than home furnishings.

Typical figures for various departments are compiled each year and published by the Controllers' Congress of the NRMA in its annual "Departmental Merchandising and Operating Results of Departmentized Stores." In a given year, this report may show millinery departments with eight or 10 turns or better; women's dresses with five to seven turns; men's departments with two to four; floor coverings with not much more than two turns.

In using the figures for departments like his own as a guide, the buyer should realize that any average or typical figure takes into consideration both poor and superlative jobs in arriving at a representative figure. There are always many who do far better than the published typical figures. The buyer who strives constantly to better his performance will usually find himself in that elite company.

What Good Turnover Accomplishes. The constant flow of new goods into a department—the fruit of healthy turnover—is a powerful stimulant to sales. It creates enthusiasm and energy in salespeople; it pleases customers and enhances the store's prestige; it creates more traffic within the store; it makes for a sound profit.

The very foundation of the American economy is the eagerness of people for something new, something better. The department whose stocks move out briskly and steadily in the form of sales is always open to buy when something new and fresh becomes available. It is always in a position to offer the customer attractive new stock; its selling is not slowed down by the boredom salespeople feel when they have only the same stale old merchandise to show.

Turnover and Profits. Generally speaking, high turnover stocks are high profit stocks, and those with low turnover are likely to be high markdown stocks. There is a very intimate relationship between turnover and depreciation of stocks. The value of a piece of department store merchandise is something like fish—it begins to spoil the very moment it is hooked with a price tag.

The less time goods spend in stock, the less chance they have to become soiled or broken in handling, to lose their fashion appeal, to need markdowns. And the less the store will have to invest in inventory, for obviously it costs less for management to finance a stock that moves out completely in 60 days than to finance one that takes a whole year for the same process.

Fast turnover produces other economies, too. Fast turning stocks take less stockroom space in relation to the sales they produce, and need less handling in the brief time they are under the store's roof than those that move sluggishly. The cost to the store for insurance is lower if the stock is light and fast moving.

Even the possibilities for pilferage are reduced, for when the stock moves in and out quickly, discrepancies are promptly noticed and checked.

Items that are individually wrapped or packaged move out while their wrappings are still fresh and crisp; there is no need to mark down good merchandise because the packages have become soiled and shabby in stock.

In short, dozens of little profit leaks are automatically plugged up when a department turns its stock briskly.

Dangers of High Turnover. It is, of course, quite possible to operate with so exaggerated a concern for high turnover that other aspects of the merchandising job are poorly handled and the whole operation suffers.

In the desire to show a good turnover, stocks may be kept

so small that assortments are incomplete and sales are lost. Worse still, customers who find a store repeatedly out of staple merchandise may lose confidence in its ability to supply their needs. Or, in operating on too small a stock, the department may deprive itself of the fresh, new items it needs to keep its assortments interesting to the customer. And this, too, has a way of discouraging people from coming back again.

No matter how anxious a buyer may be to keep his stocks small and his turnover high, he should remember that the problem is his, and not the customer's. So far as she is concerned, she wants certain staples and attractive new merchandise. No desire for high turnover should prevent a buyer from buying in sufficient quantities those things which are in good demand among his customers. If he lets that happen, he will soon find his sales going down faster than his stock.

Correcting Poor Turnover. Poor turnover figures are often caused by buying some merchandise that does not sell readily. In an effort to correct the error, buyers sometimes choke off buying for a while, hoping to reduce their stocks sharply and thus restore good turnover. In so doing, however, they create a second and worse error.

When buying is stopped in a department, the desirable merchandise continues to sell. Presently, very little of the wanted items remain; all that is left is the slow-moving, unattractive stuff that got the stock out of line in the first place. With an assortment made up now largely of items that are of little interest to its customers, the department's sales really suffer.

The sensible way to correct poor turnover in a department is to get down to the details of its operation, and see which particular items or classifications are slowing it down. Sometimes all that is needed is to get the items on display in order to start them moving; in other cases, they may need to be marked down. But while the buyer wrestles with the problem items to get them out of his stock, he still has to keep replenishing his fast-moving staples and bringing in new items. In that way, he keeps his department interesting to the customer and his sales high while he gradually brings his stock into a healthier condition.

Tools for Improving Turnover. A department sometimes does a splendid job on turnover, yet has many weak spots that need correction. When these are located and remedied, even greater sales and turnover result.

One of the most important steps in improving turnover, then, whether a department has good, poor, or average over-all stock turn, is to study the performance of each classification within that department. If the sales and turnover figures for the various classifications can be compared with those of other stores, or even with the same store's previous year's figures, weak and strong spots will show up.

The finer the breakdown the buyer can make, by classification, by price line, by item, the more thorough the job he can do in bringing to light the strengths and weaknesses of his department. For example, there was a men's hat department that did more than half its volume in its lowest price lines, yet devoted three-quarters of its stock to its two higher price lines. The weaker price lines were getting more than their share of stock, while the strong one was being starved and was not allowed to realize its full sales potential. Looking at the over-all picture for his department, the buyer thought he was doing well; when he saw the detailed figures, he knew how to do better.

Shorter Time Periods. Similarly, the buyer will find it easier to locate and correct errors in planning if he analyzes his inventory in terms of weeks' supply rather than months' supply. He may find, for example, that he consistently keeps a two months' supply of an item on hand, thus obtaining at best a six-time turnover per year. If it is practical to operate on a six or seven weeks' supply, however, his turnover moves into the seven-time and eight-time category for that item.

Good turnover is not just a matter of paring the stocks of slow sellers; it is also a matter of getting adequate inventory behind the numbers that are capable of producing even more sales than they are already yielding. On this point, unit control systems are of great help, for, properly operated and used, they facilitate the reordering of wanted items and help the department maintain its stock of salable goods. They also reflect changes in the rate of sale, indicating that upward or downward revisions of the stock are needed. Other chapters of this book discuss merchandise control in some detail; here, it is sufficient to mention that sound unit control keeps stocks down and turnover and sales up.

More Tools for Turnover. Turnover may be increased by eliminating useless price lining. As is pointed out in the chapter devoted to that subject, departments can have too many price lines. The merchant who is determined to eliminate those prices that have no sound reason for their retention, and who is equally determined to push to the limit the price lines that produce profitable volume, will automatically be working for good turnover. The test of a good price line is the speed at which it moves goods and the consumer satisfaction that it gives.

Another important step in securing good, sound turnover is to make good use of the six-months merchandise plan. This subject, too, is discussed in detail elsewhere in this book, but it should be emphasized here that there must always be elasticity of operation in the merchandise plan. Failure to meet the planned figures can happen, and an overbought condition can result—but this must not prevent the buyer from keeping a constant flow of wanted goods coming into his department.

Importance of Better Timing. Better turnover can be secured by the better timing of merchandise. Buying peaks throughout the year must be considered most carefully for each type of merchandise within a department. In many lines, the fashion element is of extreme importance, and the finest possible timing is needed. A frequent error is to peak the stocks too early. In such a case, the buyer gives himself a double handicap: he has slowed his turnover, and he has bought so early that he may not have the open-to-buy for any new and exciting merchandise that comes along later.

Timing the Peaks. In order to plan for peaks and valleys in demand within the framework of the desired turnover, each month's opening inventory should be planned in the light of the expected sales for however many months are needed to complete one full stock turn. For the sake of example, if four turns a year are wanted, each month's opening inventory should equal the planned sales for three months—that month, and the two that follow.

As an illustration, assume planned monthly sales of:

$30,000 for January

40,000 for February

80,000 for March

60,000 for April

60,000 for May

60,000 for June

30,000 for July

50,000 for August

90,000 for September

and so on.

The January 1 opening inventory will be $150,000, or the sum of expected January-February-March sales. The February 1 opening inventory will be $180,000, or the sum of February-March-April sales. Skipping to June, the opening inventory will be the June-July-August sales total, or $140,000. Whichever three-months period one chooses, the opening inventory is planned to yield one full turn, or a rate of four turns a year.

In actual practice, sales generally fall above or below the planned mark. To make adjustments as the year progresses, simply subtract a month's actual sales from the inventory at the opening of that month. Then add the planned sales for the third subsequent month to get the new opening inventory.

To illustrate:

$150,000 — January 1 inventory
Less   33,000 — January sales, actual
$117,000
Add   60,000 — April sales, planned
$177,000 — February 1 inventory
Less   38,000 — February sales, actual
$139,000
Add   60,000 — May sales, planned
$199,000 — March 1 inventory

When to Stop Buying. An analysis of the stocks of many buyers shows that knowing when to quit buying frequently presents as much of a problem as knowing when to buy. There is never a backlog of consumer demand for seasonal goods after their peak selling period or season has passed.

In this connection, it is important to insist upon the proper completion date for an order. Delivery made after the peak selling period can only result in wasted money and markdowns. Yesterday's missed sales cannot be regained tomorrow.

Buying for Better Turnover. Since no buyer is smart enough to determine the salability of every item he buys, smart buyers usually follow the plan of testing merchandise. They buy early in reasonable quantities and then watch carefully the sales movements of the various types, colors, etc., in order to see which ones should be reordered, and how heavily.

Other things being equal, timing and turnover are helped if the buyer can purchase from a nearby source rather than from one whose merchandise must travel a long, slow, and expensive route to the store. Speedier transportation from factory to store, provided it can be secured at reasonable cost, gives many advantages to the buyer. It permits him to carry lower inventories than when he has to allow for a considerable time in transit, and thus it helps his turnover.

A buying practice that prevents many buyers from securing good turnover is "scatteration" buying—buying in dribbles from too many resources. It is a practice that usually results in an accumulation of slow selling goods that have to be marked down. It is also a practice that deprives the buyer of the feeling that his resource is his partner. No manufacturer is interested in doing business with a buyer who uses his line merely as a fill-in. It is up to the buyer to make his account important enough to the resource. Good resources always give coopera-tion to good accounts; they cannot cooperate with weakness.

"Showpiece Buying." Finally, better turnover can be achieved by eliminating much of the showpiece buying of style or prestige items. It is one thing to buy minimum quan-tities of items for test purposes, or because there is a small but dependable demand for them. It is quite another to buy items beyond the normal price range of the department simply for show or because the buyer has merely a wild hope that they will sell. Before making such purchases, it is a good idea for the buyer to be sure that these will not tie up so much of his budget that they keep him from being open-to-buy other items that are wanted by most of his customers.

In every small detail of his operation, as well as in the broad outlines of his planning, the alert buyer will find ways to root out items that slow his stock turn and to strengthen those that build it up.

CHAPTER 27

MERCHANDISING THE NEW ITEM

BY

SAMUEL EINSTEIN

The new item is the life blood of merchandising. The greater the flow of new items into a store the more successful is that store. That must be a continuing process and the more alert the organization to the stimulation of new items the surer is that store's progress. After all, every article in a store at one time or another came in as a new item.

Merchandising new items has in a large measure contributed to the nation's high standard of living. The greater the social and scientific progress, the greater is the flow of new merchandise. It is a vast reservoir for the stimulation of additional business.

Actually the department store has probably done more in the way of merchandising new items than any other form of retailing. The more enterprising and resourceful the department store buyer, the greater the representation of new items in that department.

What Is a New Item? When we speak of new items, we do not refer to lines of merchandise that are new simply because, subtly or markedly, they change with the seasons. Each year's stock of apparel, shoes, hosiery, etc., differs from what was carried last year or last season, but essentially each item is a replacement for one previously carried.

The same is true of practically every market supplying goods, hard as well as soft lines. Items that have simply been re-styled are not new items in the sense that we discuss them here.

When we speak of new items, we have in mind those that are new because *they introduce certain new and different characteristics that are not yet present in merchandise of similar type.* For instance, they may be longer-lasting, more readily washable, quicker drying; they may introduce time-saving or labor-saving features; they may incorporate improved textures, finishes, and construction.

New items generally are adaptations, improvements and substitutes for articles already in use in one form or another. For example, consider the successive changes in shaving implements: from the straight razor to the safety razor, and now to the wide assortment of electric razors.

Often the newness of an item is in the material of which it is made. To mention just a few examples: Fiberglas, plastics, foam rubber. So it is in almost every area of merchandise.

Sources of New Items. The production and flow of new items is continuous, and offerings of them are made through regular trade channels—manufacturers, importers, distributors, buying offices, market bulletins, news reporting agencies, salesmen, and specialized buying services.

Sometimes the buyer himself is the source of a new item. A buyer who is aware of some unfilled want on the part of his customers may scour the markets for a suitable item. Not finding it, he may work with a resource to create it. He thus pools his knowledge of what the store's customers want with the manufacturer's creative and mechanical skills in order to fill a gap in his store's assortments.

Creative or not, it is important that the buyer be open-minded, discerning, courageous, in searching out the new item, buying it, and creating the broadest possible demand for it.

Evaluating New Items. The market for new items is extensive; the problem lies in skillful evaluation, selection, testing, and sales promotion. Great enthusiasm generally accompanies the presentation and offering of new items by their producers. At the same time, the buyer is aware that his department flourishes when it has a flow of new items; that if he passes up a good item, a competing store may take it up.

Not every new item is going to be a success, however, and not every successful new item is right for every store and department. Here are some questions a buyer can ask himself in determining whether or not the item is for him:

1. Does the article fit in with the character of the store and the department?

2. Is it attractively priced? An article may be well worth the money the store would have to charge for it, but is that price attractive to the store's own customers?

3. Does it offer sufficient markon to produce a profit? If not, the effort to launch it may be love's labor lost.

4. Is it likely to become a volume item? If not, does it have prestige value?

5. Is it a conversation piece and does it bring interest to the department?

6. Will it perform satisfactorily? Perhaps it has been, or can be, laboratory tested. If it is mechanical or electrical, it must qualify for approval by recognized authorities or agencies.

7. Has it been wear-tested or use-tested? Have you tried it yourself to be sure that it will do the things it should, and as represented?

8. Has it been sold elsewhere? With what results and by what methods?

9. What might its effect be on similar items in stock?

How Much to Buy. When an item has impressed itself as having good sales potentials and is in keeping with the store's merchandising standards, the really difficult conclusion to reach is the quantity to purchase. Determination of quantity to purchase is, of course, tied to a number of considerations: the broadness of the appeal; whether or not every household or person is a prospect; whether it is of interest only to specialized groups because of its limited use.

The scope of the promotional program has a decided bearing on the quantity to buy, as well as the kind of cooperation the vendor will offer. Vendors' aids may be: live demonstration in the store; cooperation in newspaper advertising and other promotional media; support of the store's promotional effort with stock for quick delivery on short notice. Will he exchange colors and sizes? Such vendor supports and others available have a decided bearing on the extent of promotional effort and stock to be invested in the new item.

Are You First? If the new item has already been introduced by other stores, the buyer has the advantage of being able to check on their experience—the quantities they purchased, the promotional efforts they exerted, the success they met with. These stores may be located in other cities, but if their clientele is similar to that of the buyer's own store, their experience becomes a valuable guide. It is not unusual for a maker to present a new item, with examples of exactly how it was promoted, by whom, and with what results, in other cities.

The untried item, which the store is the very first to purchase, poses a more difficult problem. In such cases, the buyer has no other guide except his own knowledge of his customers and his own judgment of the item.

When the buyer is first to try out the item, the vendor is usually willing to cooperate very closely on returns, exchanges, and promotional support. He may give more liberal advertising help to the first store that tries out his item than to those who follow; he may work out displays for windows or department use; he may supply a demonstrator or an expert salesperson.

Through such cooperation, the manufacturer shares with the store the risk of launching a brand new item. Once it has demonstrated its salability in that store, he has a success story to tell to other stores—but the buyer who was first with a good item has the success!

Extent of Promotion. The buyer's eagerness to find and develop a strong new item should not lead him to promote it beyond its potential. Some estimate must first be made of how broad the consumer interest may be. The broader the interest, the greater the promotional effort the item can justify; the narrower its field, the more conservatively the item will have to be promoted.

In promoting a new item, the buyer should not rely simply on what his advertising can do. There are many avenues within the store for stimulating and proving the sales potential of a good new item.

For instance, his salespeople, whether or not they work in the section where the new item is to be offered, should know about it, and about its selling points. They should be asked to mention it to customers—as a suggestion sale if the geography of the department permits, or simply as a suggestion that there is a new and interesting item to be seen at another counter.

For an all-out selling effort, a new item may be included to good advantages as a suggested sale on the telephone order board. Where a new item is of a nature suited to storewide selling with displays in many departments, spectacular results can be attained through a sales contest with suitable prizes to leading salespersons.

Not to be overlooked are package inserts in the buyer's own department, if not throughout the store. Statement inserts, if the buyer can secure them, are often extremely effective for a new item, as there is usually an opportunity to illustrate and describe it, and to incorporate an order blank as well.

The departmental display, naturally, will be as dramatic as the buyer knows how to make it. If his item is new and exciting, moreover, he has good reason to seek aisle tables on the main floor and window space. To be first with something new and good enhances not only the department's prestige, but the store's also.

Watching Developments. Some new items take hold and continue to sell over a long period. Others fizzle. Still others skyrocket and drop off as startlingly as they rose in sales.

The wise buyer, however strong his faith in a new item, will keep close tab on it from day to day, to see how sales respond to the effort he is exerting in its behalf. If it shows signs of being a good item, he will make sure that his reorders are placed promptly, so that stock will be equal to the expanding demand.

On very new items that do not yet have wide distribution, he may run into the problem of a manufacturer who promises to maintain stock, but then opens new retail accounts and does not maintain a sufficient back-up stock to supply all effectively. Close contact with the resource will tell the buyer how things stand, and whether or not he can continue on a policy of small fill-in orders. It can be both expensive and disheartening to nurture a new item to the point where a large promotion can be staged effectively, only to find that stock is not readily available.

All these things the buyer must watch, with his finger constantly on the pulse of the new item's sales, stock and orders.

Important as it is to find and select new items, the job of developing those that prove themselves, or unloading those that do not, is equally vital.

The new item of today may be the staple of tomorrow. The thought will bear repetition, that practically every item now in a store's stock was at one time or another a new item.

CHAPTER 28

MERCHANDISING TO A PROFIT

BY

MOREY SOSTRIN

Making a profit starts with a state of mind. There must be the determination to make that profit, and a plan to overcome any obstacles to that objective.

It is rare, indeed, that a department's performance can not be improved by objective analysis. Often this involves changing our thinking. This doesn't mean discarding the sound things we've done in the past, but seeing what can be accomplished by a change in philosophy or a fresh viewpoint and different methods.

In order to do a good job of merchandising to a profit, a buyer has to take theory and translate it into practical performance. Knowledge of methods, procedures and rules has to be balanced with judgment.

Why Customers Buy. Customers come to a store for merchandise. By and large, most stores can buy goods at about the same price. The reason people buy at one store in preference to another is that they have confidence and trust in it; they find good assortments attractively presented at the right price, and are served by friendly, interested personnel. Adequate assortments in the various classifications are thus a principal key to attracting customers.

Quite frequently, when a department encounters difficulty in making sales increases or achieving a profit, the buyer says his advertising is inadequate or poor, there are not enough window displays, fixtures need rearranging or replacement.

Usually the answer lies within the department's assortments: it simply doesn't have enough of the items customers want.

It's human to blame external forces over which we do not have complete control; it's human to become defensive rather than objective in seeking for real reasons that curtail our sales. But the buyer who wants to make a good profit showing will first look to his assortments—the staples, the best sellers, the new fashions, and the constant flow of fresh new goods to maintain the interest of both customers and salespeople.

Pricing For Profit. Buyers need courage to make a profit when raising prices becomes necessary. The talk about competition preventing increased prices is only partly true. Many departments have exclusive distribution of certain lines in their communities, and thus have an opportunity for improved markon. Obviously, we do not propose taking identical items or price-fixed goods and marking them higher than our competitors do.

There are many items on which a few extra pennies will not hamper the sale of goods. The automatic marking procedure of many buyers—the pre-marking of invoices without the buyer looking at the goods—tends to freeze markon to a pre-determined figure.

Buyers should spend enough time in the receiving room properly appraising goods in terms of *what prices they will bring*. They should also examine the merchandise in their departments rather than rely on stock figures or unit control records exclusively. They must develop a "feel for merchandise" that tells them almost instinctively what items and styles will sell at a profit.

Cost and Retail. Learning to work with merchandise, giving each style individual consideration, both in the market and in the store, improves profit. While the cost may be identical for each of several different items, some may be readily salable at higher prices than others. The buyer should train himself to ask, *"What price can this item bring?"* rather than to say,

"This item cost $22.50 a dozen, and therefore its retail automatically becomes $2.95."

There is another face to this medal. When the buyer is in the market, seeking $2.95 items, for example, there is no reason to limit himself to items that cost $22.50 a dozen. There may be attractive items at wholesale prices below that point that will be readily salable at $2.95 retail. *No good item should be disqualified simply because it falls into a wholesale price below that which the buyer automatically associates with the retail price line.*

Psychological Pricing. Merchants for many years believed that prices like $2.95 and $2.98 were psychologically more appealing to the customer than even prices like $3.00. Tests have proved that this is not necessarily so. Moreover, in communities where a sales tax is in effect, a $2.95 price may become $3.01 when the sales tax is added, or some other such psychologically "wrong" price. Experimentation may show that a department has been giving pennies or nickels of profit away on each sale in the mistaken belief that an odd price is more attractive to customers. The test is worth making.

Buying for Profit. There will be occasions when special purchases can provide opportunities for better than average markon. Examination of the merchandise can show that even though a special lot has been bought at one price, it is good merchandising sense to separate it into groups and price each according to what the public will readily pay. Not infrequently, part of such a purchase may fit into regular stocks at regular price and thus contribute extra markon. A good test of what items can bring is to check with the heads of stock or the salespeople. Ask them what they think an item should retail for, without, of course, telling them the cost. You may find your own contemplated retail much too conservative!

One of the draw-backs to building maximum volume at a profit is trying to operate a department with rigid ideas about the percentage of markon. Not to buy goods below a certain predetermined markon may mean that merchandise of possibly substantial volume possibilities will be rejected, thus causing a dollar gross margin loss that will not be offset by the results of strict adherence to an inflexible markon standard. Judgment and balance are essential to a sound operation; a one-sided approach can actually bring about long-term harm to a business.

Too frequently, particularly when difficulty is encountered in making sales increases, buyers think that adopting a low markon policy, in itself, will correct the sales problem. Actually, a low markon department is rarely a successful one. When we permit a low markon policy, we are generally disillusioned by the results. The sound approach is having what people want in adequate assortments at reasonable markon. This is a more effective policy.

Cash Discounts. Cash discounts are very important to the profits of a department or a store—in fact, they often exceed the total net profit of a store. Occasionally, a manufacturer faced with increased costs attempts to reduce or eliminate cash discount. Cooperative as we try to be in other respects, this is one area where we must resist the reduction.

Even on special purchases at reduced prices, we should insist on the usual cash discount. Sound manufacturers agree with this view and accept it as the normal way of doing business with department stores because it fits their pattern of thinking, and it works.

In another chapter, the whole subject of cash discounts is discussed thoroughly. Buyers should familiarize themselves with the cash discount's important effect on profit, so that they know why it is worth fighting for, should the occasion arise.

Resources and Profit. There are leaders in each industry who grew big because they were better than their competitors in offering quality, fashion and value. Since a department can't buy from everyone, it should concentrate its business with good sources, become important to them, and receive their cooperation and help.

It just makes good sense to a manufacturer to do well by

those departments with which he does well. Strong resources help build sales and profits for a department. It never pays to go flitting from one resource to another for temporary gain.

Analysis of gross margins by principal manufacturers can lead to a real boost in profit. Some manufacturers have the knack of producing goods that sell in real volume at prices that permit a good initial markon. These are the resources whose good will the buyer should cultivate. What helps cement the relation is the understanding that the store will be loyal to them if their offerings are competitive.

Buyers interested in improving profit learn how to work well with their resources.

Competition and Profit. Competition as a bar to adequate profit is a factor, of course, but often its effect is exaggerated. Many buyers worry about what other stores are doing, to the point that their own business suffers.

Certainly we should be aware of what others are doing, but not to the point of being distracted by them and imitating their efforts. Let's mind our own business.

We can't be all things to all people. The best stores rely upon their own distinctions and their own appeal for what is logically their own market.

This is not to suggest disregarding competition on identical items, but we do feel that price alone is not the only factor that moves people to buy.

Advertising. The largest single item of expense, next to payroll, is advertising. Probably there is more waste and extravagance here than in any other item. There are stores that spend two percent of sales, and others that spend five or six percent. Usually *the high advertising cost stores make little net profit.* It is rare, indeed, that a poor department or store advertises itself into a good one. Not infrequently, the cost of advertising runs to 20, or 30, or 50 percent or even more of the direct sales of the advertised items.

Of course, a lot of people in buying or merchandising positions fancy themselves advertising experts. Surely the ad that didn't pull could have been written better by the buyer than the copywriter. Rarely does it occur to us that the high advertising costs include lack of confidence in a store or a department because of inadequate assortments, poor presentation of merchandise, and poor service.

The amount of advertising space to be used should depend *on the story we have to tell* and not on a preconceived notion that a half page or a page ad is necessary to sell a certain amount of merchandise.

Promoting for Profit. In our promotions, we should present a balanced picture to result in a profit. Fashion advertising exclusively, or too frequent cut price, low markon or clearance sales may be an unbalanced program for many departments. For a proper promotion diet, some of each kind of emphasis *at the right time and in the right proportion* is necessary for healthy growth.

While special market opportunities offer certain goods at prices that enable us to sell them for less than we may have previously, still, in desirable merchandise, this is the exception and not the rule. It's easy to get enthusiastic about off-price sales, special purchases and clearances but, actually, such offerings are a relatively small part of our total business.

The kind of business people take for granted, yet the kind that is most profitable, is *the day-to-day business on regular goods at regular prices.*

We have to dig out the merits of this merchandise. Good buyers learn to do this and to transmit to others their own enthusiasm.

Usually, there is far more desirability to new, regular priced merchandise than there is to off-price sale goods. We can sell much more regular goods from our advertising if we really dramatize it—give it at least the same attention we do our sale goods.

Building a Balanced Business. Retailing is primarily a selling business. Knowledge of markets is important, of course. Unit controls and the various tools for analysis of stocks and sales have their place if they're properly used and interpreted. Securing the wholehearted cooperation of our organization, delegating responsibility to create a sense of participation and helping do a training job are vital to a buyer who wants to do a good job. But all these things will fall short of achieving a profitable operation if we don't build a balanced business and get adequate sales.

A good approach for doing a balanced business and getting increased sales is to make an objective analysis. Some suggestions follow.

One, analyze your department with the eyes of a thoroughly qualified new buyer coming in to take over; check each classification for its possibilities, not for what it has done before.

Two, list the proper quantity of stock to carry in each classification by adding the items to be carried in the sizes and colors necessary, rather than only on the basis of what was in stock last year.

Three, have a list of staple items which should always be in stock regardless of the size of the department's inventory. A customer who wants the brand of toothpaste we are out of won't be any less dissatisfied because we have too many other toothpastes on hand.

Four, do something each month in the way of merchandise preparation that will be additional to what was done last year. If we only do the things we've always done, without strengthening, without substituting for worn out events, our business is not likely to grow.

Five, items make business. After staple stocks are established, after we decide the variety and assortments, materials and colors and sizes necessary to carry in less staple and in novelty goods, then we should pick out an item in each important classification and see if we can make it five or ten times as big in volume as we have heretofore.

We have to spotlight the items in our minds first. *We need enough imagination and vision and courage to see the possibilities and then do something to get the most out of them.*

Many buyers, of course, are item-conscious and do a splendid job. They're the people whose business is good—rain or shine, good weather or bad. These people make their own business conditions.

Six, of major importance in merchandising to a profit is to learn and believe in the lesson of "concentrated merchandising." This means centering our efforts on fewer styles but having enough quantity—enough to have a real range of colors and sizes in those styles we do stock. If we follow through on this, we have the nearest thing to insurance that our day-to-day business will be immeasurably improved.

To illustrate what experience shows exists in many departments: A typical department carries a retail stock of $25,000 to do an annual $100,000 volume. This is a stock turnover of four times a year, which seems to compare favorably with similar departments in other stores. *The reason it compares favorably is that many stores share with it a weakness in operation.*

This is the weakness. The store has a $25,000 retail stock. In it is a huge number of styles and colors, and the attempt is made to have them in proper sizes. *Because so many styles are carried* and *so few of the staples are outstanding,* it becomes impossible to have enough of the outstanding styles to dramatize, to push, to sell in large quantities.

Many buyers have had the experience of going to the market, making purchases, getting them in the store, and *then when they want to advertise to stimulate business,* find they just don't have enough of any one thing in a full color and size range to justify running the ad! When that happens, the buyer realizes that in spite of having been to market and having made sizeable commitments, he isn't actually prepared to obtain the fullest sales possibilities out of certain items.

Seventh, and finally, keep new goods rolling in all the time. There is no substitute for the stimulus that new goods give a business. Check the sales of a department after a buyer has been to market and the new goods start to roll in. Business usually is best during the period when new goods keep coming in. Then, when it's all in and enough has been sold so that the size and color range is broken, business starts to slip and usually keeps slipping until another market trip and the resultant receipt of newly bought goods.

We should reorder between trips; we should let our buying office keep sending us new goods, and we should be sufficiently close to our resources to have them constantly feed us the new items as they are developed.

Looking to the Future. It is practically impossible to list everything a buyer needs to know to merchandise at a profit. The nature of retailing is such that each new day brings a challenge. Unpredictable situations frequently arise. The best equipment to deal with new problems is a good fund of common sense.

The ability to get along well with people, to enlist the harmonious cooperation of others, is a fundamental need. A buyer who wants to grow in position and responsibility gladly assumes the obligation to build and train people. Most successful people, at some time early in their careers, were given a helping hand by someone who noticed ability and encouraged it by training, inspiration and example. These real trainers and leaders, by building people good enough to take their jobs, usually move into better positions themselves.

CHAPTER 29

THE BUYER AND THE
COST OF DISTRIBUTION

BY

JOHN I. GOTLINGER

For many years now, spokesmen for manufacturing industries have been stating that consumer prices could only be reduced by cutting "distribution costs." The buyer, as retailing's representative in his markets, should have a background on this subject. He should also understand some of the new trends in retail accounting, so that he will be in a position to use the information his store provides, and to use it in such a way that profitable volume will result.

Manufacturers' Accounting Methods. Because of extensive cost accounting systems, the manufacturer can pinpoint costs for each item he produces. This enables him to apply new methods, new machines, or research to cases where his costs are excessive. It has enabled him also to reduce production costs to the most efficient levels.

Having the facts about costs, manufacturers compute their "markon" so that a fixed percentage of profit is added to total manufacturing costs. Retailers do not have as thorough-going a knowledge of their costs per item. Instead they work on the basis of "averages" and attempt, by varying the markon percentage, to obtain a gross margin sufficient to cover their expenses and yield a profit.

If the manufacturer were to apply to the cost of his raw materials alone a percentage factor which would cover all of his manufacturing expenses and yield a fair profit, that percentage would be very much larger than that which the retailer uses.

It is essential that we use like statements or reports to compare. Therefore, should it be necessary for you to make a comparison with a manufacturing statement, reduce the retail markon percentage by your expense percentage, 36.5% minus 34.5% equals 2%. The result will be comparable with a manufacturer's profit per cent, and, as will be quite apparent, the retailer's profit is much lower than the manufacturer's, as is annually revealed in published NRMA reports.

Distribution Costs. The accepted method of *retail* accounting includes in the cost of sales the merchandise cost, its inward transportation, and associated factors such as markdowns, shrinkage, and workroom expense, but does not add in all the costs a manufacturer would. Store operating statements, like those described in detail in another chapter, have, as a result led many persons to decry the "high cost of retail distribution".

Distribution costs, to be understood, must first be defined. They include all of the costs incurred in getting a finished product from the manufacturer to the consumer.

Rather than say that "distribution costs" can be reduced or that they should be reduced as such, it is better to say that *retailers must establish records which will enable them to determine the true costs of distribution of specific items of merchandise.* The retailer must be able to identify *the value that he adds to merchandise* before he can make decisions.

Values Added. The function of the retailer in terms of classical economics is to add "place utility" to consumer merchandise—to bring it from one location to a second location where the customer can see it, feel it, hear it, smell it—buy it. The retailer also provides "time utility," which means having the goods when the customer wants it.

It is therefore perfectly in order *to charge to cost of merchandise buying expense as well as receiving, marking, warehousing, delivery, merchandise management, and other associated expenses necessary to place the merchandise on the store counter ready for sale.* This is adding value to the manufacturer's product; it is all "cost of merchandise".

As the late Carlos B. Clark, then controller of the J. L. Hudson Company in Detroit, pointed out, there was a time when manufacturers, wholesalers, and jobbers of this country had thousands of traveling men constantly on the road, bringing to the store complete lines of samples from which the store owner, sitting in the comfort of his own office and with no further expense to himself, could select.

Today, the function of the manufacturer's traveling man has largely been absorbed by the retailer, whose buyers now go to the manufacturers' offices and plants in all the market places of the world and at considerable expense to the store.

When the traveling men came to the store, their costs were *an expense to the manufacturer* and were included in the invoiced price of the merchandise. *Thus they became part of the retailer's merchandise costs.*

Although the circumstances have changed, retailers have not altered their accounting and reporting systems to reflect these facts. The retailer classifies his buying costs as expenses; these are added to the first cost of the manufactured product. *The markon in all these years has changed but little.* What's happening is that the increased costs come out of the retailer's original margin.

Attempts to Correct Situation. In Figure 27 is illustrated a total store statement of operations designed to parallel that generally used by manufacturing industries. The form has been adopted by the Controllers' Congress of NRMA. It evolved over the years from one first proposed in 1935 by Mr. Clark.

The chief difference between this form and the traditional retail statement lies in the treatment of those expense items which may properly be considered *cost of merchandise* rather than *operating expenses.* It is intended to minimize the possibility of a wrong impression on the part of consumers and the public concerning the operating results of retailing.

By placing under the cost of merchandise sold all the items that make up what is sometimes called the "counter cost" of merchandise, *we have a statement more comparable with the manufacturer's.* It avoids giving the impression that the retailer is working on a large gross margin, when in reality his margin and his earnings are generally less than those of the manufacturer.

How This Affects the Buyer. These concepts may seem far removed from the buyer's day-to-day responsibilities. Actually, the reasoning behind the developments outlined above has led to the introduction of a tool for buyers, supplied by the controllers of some stores.

This new tool is called an "Item or Purchase Order Profit Worksheet". If the buyer's own store does not yet provide it, the buyer can apply its principles and, using whatever information is available to him, strive for more profitable operation in his department. A sample of a typical worksheet is shown below.

ITEM PROFIT WORKSHEET

Department_____

Purchase Order #_____   Vendor_____

Unit Cost $_____   Unit Retail $_____

	$	%
Initial Markon	_____	_____
Markdowns at Cost	_____	_____
Workroom, Shrinkage, Discounts	_____	_____
Gross Margin	_____	_____
Advertising	_____	_____
Delivery	_____	_____
Warehousing	_____	_____
Selling Salaries	_____	_____
Other Direct Expenses	_____	_____
Operating Profit Expenses	_____	_____
Overhead	_____	_____
Net Profit Per Unit	_____	_____
Total Profit For Purchase	_____	_____

Item Work Sheet. The item work sheet has elements of both fact and budget in it. The buyer himself creates a cost statement for specific merchandise at the time the purchase is made or contemplated, and puts himself in a position to determine with a fair degree of accuracy the profitability of a proposed purchase.

This is the method: The buyer estimates the sales of merchandise on the specific order, taking into consideration probable markdowns, based on experience. Knowing the cost and retail price of the merchandise and using the known levels of other margin factors, such as workroom expenses, purchase discounts, and shrinkage, he makes an estimate of his gross margin on that purchase.

Some stores furnish the buyer with a chart for working out these figures quickly. Without that help, the buyer goes back to his departmental operating statement (discussed in detail in another chapter) for a guide.

Now the buyer turns to other direct department operating costs, such as buying, receiving and marking, selling and clerical costs. These are consistent enough for him to apply an average percentage figure to each purchase.

Advertising, however, is an item which is within his discretion to control, and therefore it is readily predictable in relation to a specific purchase. The buyer considers the probable cost of advertising, taking into account any cooperative advertising allowance that may apply to the merchandise.

Delivery and warehousing costs, if they apply to the specific merchandise, may also be estimated. If an outside delivery service is used, for instance, charges are usually on a unit basis, depending on the physical volume and weight of the merchandise handled.

With a schedule of such unit costs by merchandise classification for his department, and with some idea of the proportion of send to take transactions for the merchandise concerned, he can make a rough estimate of these costs, too.

Pattern of Costs. What the buyer is actually doing, when he runs through a calculation of this sort, is establishing a pattern of costs for individual kinds of merchandise, based on past experience with repetitive elements of expense as they pertain to that merchandise.

Once the pattern of costs is known for a specific item, it acts more or less as a floor below which the selling price cannot go if the department is to return a profit. It also helps the buyer to remain conscious of costs, and to become better able to evaluate any service that manufacturers may perform for him.

For example, if a manufacturer of major appliances makes delivery directly to the customer's home, the retailer still has all the elements of distribution costs concerned with selling, promotion and display. And if, in return for his service, the manufacturer increases the invoice price to the retailer and insists on a narrower retail markon, the buyer should be able to evaluate this change in terms of actual costs and actual savings—and to protest it intelligently if he finds that he is being asked to give up more than a fair share of markon in payment for that service.

Is It Profitable? With item information of the type described, the buyer is able to determine in advance those items that are likely to make the greatest profit contribution to his department, and from these he can select the ones that he will highlight. Conversely, the same method will show him plainly if his promotion is centered on unprofitable items—a frequent happening when a department sets out to meet competition without considering costs.

Thus, with as much help as his store can give him, the buyer can use averages and known costs to estimate in advance the profitability of a projected purchase of merchandise. Although this will not produce precise results, it will give him a working guide at the time when he needs it, when he is making plans and decisions for the future.

For the final results, after the decisions have been made and acted upon, the buyer will, of course, turn to his departmental operating statement. It will give him insight into the final results of the sum of all his plans and purchases.

TOTAL STORE STATEMENT OF OPERATIONS

For Fiscal Year Ending January 31, 19——

Gross Sales		$10,546,000	
Less Returns and Allowances		1,546,000	
Net Sales			$9,000,000
Merchandise Costs:			
Inventory—Beginning of Period		$ 900,000	
Purchases	$6,500,000		
Less Cash Discounts Earned	325,000	$6,175,000	
Workrooms		75,000	
		$7,150,000	
Inventory—End of Period		1,210,000	$5,940,000
Gross Merchandise Margin			$3,060,000
Merchandise Procurement Costs:			
Real Estate Costs—Whse. & Service Bldgs.		$ 150,000	
Furniture, Fixtures & Equipment Costs— Warehouse & Service Bldgs.		50,000	
Accounts Payable		25,000	
Receiving		35,000	
Checking & Marking		50,000	
Transfer Hauling		10,000	
Maintenance of Stock		75,000	
Merchandise Management		100,000	
Buying		300,000	
Domestic & Foreign Buying Offices		35,000	
			$ 830,000
Gross Operating Spread			$2,230,000
Operating Costs			1,710,000
Operating Profit or Loss			$ 520,000
Other Income and Deductions			10,000*
Net Profit or Loss			$ 510,000
Provisions for Federal Income Taxes			200,000
Net Profit or Loss after Taxes			$ 310,000

* Deductions exceed Other Income.

Figure 27

Merchandise Management Accounting. The principles dis-cussed here can be applied to specific buying situations. The buyer pre-figures a purchase's expected profitability by deducting from the offered gross profit the directly attributable costs which that product would create. This procedure, known as *merchandise management accounting,* is of inestimable value to departments whose merchandise is the target of competition. Here is a concrete example:

The store is offered a carload of refrigerators for a 19 per cent markon. The percentage is low, but you check to see if the *dollars of profit* may justify the purchase. At $229 retail, the 19 per cent markon yields $43.51 in gross profit.

You consult the Item Profit Worksheet on page 293. Will the purchase require advertising? Yes, $3\frac{1}{2}$ per cent, or $8.02. Delivery? Yes, $12. (or 5.3 per cent). Warehousing? Yes, 2 per cent, or $4.58. Selling Salaries? Yes, 4.5 per cent, or $10.31. Overhead (or direct)? Yes, 7 per cent, or $16.03. Total $50.94.

Obviously, you will lose money if you accept. You must therefore see what you can do to eliminate some of the expense or you must insist on a higher markon to cover you.

Cooperation and Costs. *The cost of distribution is a joint cost of the manufacturer and the retailer,* and it takes the cooperation of both to achieve improvement. Among steps that have been taken to date in individual lines of merchandise are such things as pre-marking, pooled stocks, direct deliveries to customers, packaging for delivery to the customer, cooperative advertising, displays, machine record reordering of staples, demonstrators, and checkers sent by resources to help count retail stocks and estimate reorder needs on staples.

Above and beyond the help a buyer may get from his resources, he should by all means utilize the information that is available within his own company. Directly or through his merchandise manager, he should consult his store's controller on marginal purchases, and on sources of figures to guide his decisions. The buyer who uses these services will best be able to continue as an efficient distributor, making a profit in an economy sensitive to costs.

CHAPTER 30

HOW TO STRENGTHEN A WEAK DEPARTMENT

BY

MYRON S. SILBERT

Opportunities to improve and strengthen a department abound. Let us, in this chapter, list some of the things a buyer can do to raise the volume and profit of his department.

Improving the Basic or Staple Stock Operation. A good place to start is with staple or basic items which the department plans to run in stock for several months or more. A staple item is by definition one which the customer expects to find on hand in good assortment throughout the year or a specific part of it. These may be fashion items or articles as devoid of fashion interest as needles and straight pins. To qualify as basics or staples, they need only the element of *continuing, consistent demand.*

There are several good systems for keeping staples in stock, some of which are explained in this book's chapters on unit control. No system works of itself, however. The essential is conscientious follow-through—and this is the buyer's responsibility. Whether or not his merchandise manager follows that desirable practice of periodically collecting and reviewing basic stock records, the buyer on his own should develop the habit of studying his staple stock records critically at intervals, seeking correctible flaws in this operation and doing everything in his power to avoid an out-of-stock condition.

Expanding Staple Lines. The opportunity is always open to the buyer to expand his staple sections until they are as broad as those of his biggest competitors. One of the most helpful methods is to obtain the list or lists of items carried as staples by other stores and seek potential additions there. These lists are more helpful if they have notes indicating the rate of sale of each item.

One way to secure such lists is through the store's buying office, or from one or two of the larger stores served by that office.

Making the Most of Best Sellers. Playing up best selling items is a good companion method to go along with building staple stocks. The staple operation builds solid, everyday business; the best sellers capitalize on current trends and help develop traffic. The two together provide a well-rounded program.

To find best sellers promptly, the buyer should not only look at his unit control records, but should also encourage every salesperson to report whatever items, or colors, or types are selling briskly. Every time the buyer walks out on the selling floor or visits a branch department, he should ask, "What's selling?" If he shows consistent interest, the replies will be specific and helpful. Replies like "Everything, more or less," are useless.

One helpful tool in stimulating the department to find best sellers is to designate a certain place in the department where a sample of each best seller is to be hung up for the attention of the buyer, with a note attached stating how many were sold and how many remain in stock. One store developed intense interest in best sellers by designating that these samples be hung up at four o'clock in the afternoon each day.

Buying office bulletins, especially if they mention which stores are selling the item, can often put the buyer on the track of a potential best seller. So can visits to other stores that are friendly and that serve more or less the same class of trade.

Many successful buyers keep in close touch with three or four others in friendly stores, and maintain a constant exchange of information on items and colors that are moving well. Knowing one another's operations, such buyers can evaluate one another's experience with an item more accurately than if the suggested new item is recommended by an unfamiliar source.

How to Make the Most of A Best Seller. Here are some questions the buyer should ask himself to make sure he is doing all he can to improve the sale of a best seller:

1. Have I reordered enough so that there will be a steady flow of this item coming, without loading up too much?

2. Is the department display as "selling" as I can make it, with the proper sign to tell the story of this item?

3. Can I get a window for the item, with a sign that tells the story?

4. Can I get an advertisement, with copy that brings out those features that make the item sell?

5. What else can I do to make my store headquarters for this item and establish in the customer's mind that we have it and know most about it?

Number Merchandising. Another step in further developing the best selling principle is to pick out the best style number in which to do concentrated merchandising. Certain style numbers each season have the magical potential for selling by the hundreds and even thousands. Each buyer should know, not only his own department's best style numbers, but also those of other stores—friendly or competitive. They may have some that he has missed.

One step that will help in number promotion is to give each of the outstanding numbers a name and develop a distinctive promotional story for it—the "Butterfly Dress," for example, or the "Beach Club Bag," for example.

Number merchandising was done in the past mostly for garments, but it can be done even more effectively in shoes, hosiery, gloves, handbags, jewelry—in any department that wants to make the most of outstanding numbers of the season.

Brand Merchandising. Within each department, several brand names, nationally advertised or otherwise, are generally represented. It is important to study these constantly for possible fluctuations in popularity among the store's customers.

If a brand appears to be in the ascendancy, whether because of improved styling, better values, more effective advertising, or other reasons, it is to the department's interest to increase emphasis upon that brand. To do this, consider broader assortments, more conspicuous display within the department, more mention in advertisements, more mention in windows, more mention from salespeople. Whatever treatment is effective for best sellers and strong numbers can be applied equally well to good and growing brands.

Repeat Items. One of the best sources of real strength for a department is repeat business on an item or idea which it has established. In any department or section, there are outstanding items for which customers come back again and again.

The best way to build these semi-permanent ideas or sections is to select those items which have sold well and which seem to indicate an incoming trend. If there is an outstanding number, highlight it and set up a permanent display for it. If there is a theme to be found for a section, use signs and displays to highlight it—as in the case of junior foundations, tall girls' lingerie, or gadget bars, for example.

Display. The first step is that the buyer should make up his mind that he is going to improve his department's display. This will immediately take it out of the class of the poor-housekeeping, poor-appearance departments.

The next step is to try to bring out in display the story of the leading best selling items in the department. It is amazing how much a department can improve, as time goes on, on this one objective. Effective, attractive ways can be developed for bringing out the story of the department's best items. That each item should have a sign telling its story briefly but with selling points goes without saying.

In working out these signs, use can be made of the ideas

presented in outstanding advertisements of stores in other cities. A department may not have the advertising money with which to run as many advertisements as other stores, but it can use their ideas around which to build its own displays and signs.

Another display technique is getting out into plain sight as much of the assortment as possible. One of the largest stores in America has spent a great many years on this technique. Samples of each item, in every classification, are systematically priced, described, and displayed so that the customer can see at a glance what the store carries. This principle of assortment display is one of which every department should make continuing study.

A Complete Program for the Department. So far, we have considered individual steps that can be taken to strengthen various operations in the department. The final goal of all this is a complete, strong department. To organize the work toward arriving at this goal, the department should be divided into sections, so that the most important sections are worked on first but ultimately all are covered.

An important department is built up by having each section right. For some sections, the procedure that is most necessary is the "staple" procedure. For other sections, the most important operation is to follow through on "best sellers." Assume that every section can be improved, that there is a way to do each section better, that the possibilities of a department are unlimited so long as creative thought is given to improving each section.

The buyer should take the attitude that *every* section has room for substantial improvement and that the total capacity for any one department, when operating at its maximum, is as great as the entire volume of a large store devoted *exclusively* to this merchandise. This is the way some very famous departments have been built.

Review Fundamentals. A buyer should never feel that he can afford to stop learning the fundamentals of his business.

Other chapters of this book discuss some of them in detail, and these chapters should be reviewed from time to time—those on balanced assortments, on new items, on price lining, on promotional planning, for example. A weak department is sometimes weak because the buyer in charge has not learned or has forgotten some of the basic lessons in merchandising. Strong buyers, along with merchandise managers and heads of stores, are constantly interested in comparing their own methods with those of others.

Learning from Competition. Important help is to be gained, also, from one's competition. Shopping competitors is, of course, standard practice for any department. The job, however, should not be done mechanically, nor should one's observations be confined to merchandise and prices alone. Without actually copying what the competitor is doing, it is often possible to compare his methods with your own and find a clue to future improvement.

Other forms of retailing should be studied—not just department and specialty stores. There is much to be learned from chain stores and mail order houses on completeness of basic assortments. These types of retailing, also supermarkets and discounters, are usually experts on assortment displays, on ways to make shopping faster and easier for the customer. What they do is not necessarily right for the department store, but constant study of their strengths and weaknesses may spark ideas for the improvement of your own department.

Branch Stores. Precisely the same approach that has been outlined here is taken in strengthening a branch store department. *But particular stress should be placed on the need to work out a plan for keeping basic or staple items in stock.* Out-of-stocks in branch stores are a recurring source of volume loss, and to correct the situation is to create immediately an opportunity for important volume gains.

One other method to use—whose value again will be reflected in volume gains—is alerting, teaching, educating the department managers in the branches to spot *selling trends.* This goes both for fashion and for staple merchandise.

If there is constant watchfulness of what is selling, if what is selling is reordered and kept continually in stock, if what is selling is then given additional display and possible advertising in order to increase its sale further, and if these selling items are at the same time drawn to the attention of the salespeople for suggestion to customers, these selling items cannot but be stimulated to substantially higher volume.

If the methods cited here are consciously kept in mind and periodically reviewed, it can be safely predicted that a branch department, weak or strong, can be developed into a stronger and more profitable one.

CHAPTER 31

WORKING WITH THE BRANCH STORE

BY

ARTHUR J. O'BRIEN

This chapter is concerned with the special demands made upon the buyer in stores with branches or in multi-store operations. It undertakes to explain the most common types of branch store organization, the conditions encountered when buying for each, and the steps the buyer should take to insure the best possible operation.

It should be explained at the outset that there is no prevailing pattern of operation with respect to branch stores. As each department store adjusts to the needs of its expanding branch activities, its organization plan changes. The number, size, and location of the branches affect the pattern, and it is not at all unusual to find a store, as it adds branches, changing from one set of procedures to a second and a third—and then possibly back to an earlier one.

When a field is as new as branch store operation still is to many department and specialty stores, a certain amount of trial and error is to be expected. This, the buyer must be prepared for. A flexibility and a willingness to go along cheerfully when management tries out new procedures are essential.

Common Types of Organization. The three most common types of branch organization are brood hen and chick, autonomous unit, and centralized administration.

The brood-hen-and-chick concept applies when branches are few, small in relation to the main store, and geographically close to it. The downtown store is the hen; the branches are the chicks.

The autonomous unit idea applies when branches are many, large, and at considerable distance from the main store. Each branch is relatively independent of the parent store and may even have a buying staff of its own. In the extreme form, management simply uses its well-known name to give an entirely new store a good start in its community.

The centralized administration concept relieves the buyer of departmental floor responsibilities at the main store as well as at the branches. The main store is thus treated, from the buyer's viewpoint, as one more branch.

Within these three main categories, there are many variations. The brood-hen-and-chick idea may apply to organizations with far-flung branches. The autonomous unit and centralized administration concepts may be applied where branches are few and close to the main store.

The organization plan is management's decision; living under the one chosen by management is the buyer's problem. His responsibilities are different in each of them.

The Brood Hen Concept. In such a set-up, the buyer makes his headquarters at the parent store. He keeps in close touch with the branches, visiting them regularly to bring merchandise information to the salespeople, to check on stocks and displays, to announce and prepare for forthcoming promotions, and to get from the branch personnel their observations of customer reactions.

There is usually little or no ordering by the branch in this set-up. Requests for merchandise are made to the parent store and filled from stock or through reorders, at the buyer's discretion. Merchandise comes directly to the main store from resources, with few exceptions, to be received, marked, and transferred as needed to the branches.

Transfers to and from branches are common. Merchandise is shifted from main store to branch, or from one branch to another, or back to the main store. Customer orders taken at the branches may be filled and delivered by the main store. Clearances, returns to vendors, and items that sell slowly or not at all at the branch are called back to the main store.

Autonomous Unit. Where the branch is completely autonomous, it has its own buyers, each of whom functions only with respect to the one location to which he is assigned. More commonly, what is called an autonomous unit is only relatively so. The branch may have its own individual inventory figures and its own unit control records (although the controls themselves may be maintained at the parent store.) The branch may take a good deal of responsibility for filling in and actually reordering staples; it may have facilities for receiving and marking much of its merchandise. The buyer at the main store, however, is in charge, and it is he who does the merchandising.

Usually, the branch has a department manager (or selector, or sales manager, depending upon the title preferred by the organization) to supervise the sales personnel and take over the responsibility for carrying out the buyer's plans as to stock, sales, display, promotional activities, and for supplying merchandise information to salespeople. A department manager of this type may "buy" for his branch from the main store's stock those items he thinks best suited to his location. In some stores, he is permitted to request items not carried at the main store, or to resist those he considers unsuited to his particular branch.

The buyer has much more executive-type help than in the hen-and-chick branch, but his responsibilities are essentially the same. He visits each branch regularly, reviews its stocks, brings merchandise information, discusses customer preferences, future plans, stock arrangements, and any problems that may come up.

Centralized Administration. Under central administration, the buyer's departmental floor responsibilities at all locations, including the main store, are delegated. He concentrates on buying, managing the inventory at each store, and sales promotion. His responsibilities are: to make efficient use of the company's working capital; to produce adequate gross margin dollars; to procure desirable merchandise for each store; to distribute that merchandise to the stores; to plan sales promotion for each; to furnish merchandise information.

In such a set-up, the buyer may be physically as well as figuratively removed from the selling floor. Attempts to place him in a location apart from the store, however, such as an administration or service building, have not prospered; stores that have tried such arrangements (and these are few) have abandoned them.

With centralized administration, the buyer is in close touch with his unit controls, with incoming merchandise, with the advertising staff, with his merchandise manager, and with the vice-president in charge of branches. The one person he is not in close touch with, however, is the customer. He needs, therefore, to use every means at his disposal to study indications of what the customer prefers, so that he can give each branch merchandise individuality.

The Problem of Individuality. Typically, where there are branches, there are differences in tastes and timing, and these must be reflected in the assortment and in its presentation. The buyer may find, for example, that the downtown store draws business women and suburban matrons with grown-up children; that the branches on the streets of well established suburban villages draw the topmost income brackets to which the store caters; that the ones in new suburban shopping centers draw young women with small children and with a strong preference for bargains, casual clothes, and last-minute buying. Each location must be merchandised in keeping with the character of its clientele.

This is true even in cases where, superficially, it may seem that one branch of an organization is much like another. A prime example is offered by a high-priced specialty store whose customers are women of great wealth and sophistication. Aside from some slight concession to climate, these women want pretty much the same thing in one city as in another—the newest and most exciting clothes that money can buy. But even in this organization, there are differences from one location to another, not so much in merchandise, as in emphasis.

A city customer may have less use for slacks, say, than one who patronizes a suburban branch; the suburbanite may buy the same kinds of clothes as her city sister, but she will have fewer occasions for evening dresses. The evening wear that she buys may be on a par with what is offered downtown, but the suburban branch will carry lighter stocks of it. In children's wear, the shoe may be on the other foot, with broader assortments and larger volume in the suburbs.

Keeping in Touch. Whatever the form of organization or the degree of differences among the branches, it should be obvious that a major problem for the buyer is keeping in touch with the branch departments. Good communication becomes the lifeblood of his job. It thus becomes important to get full value from any contact with branch personnel, and with the staff at the main store, too.

The less time the buyer himself has to spend on the selling floor, the more he must lean upon the salespeople and department managers to tell him what is wanted but not available in the stock, and what customers think about the merchandise already on the floor. To some extent, this can be done on paper, through want slips, merchandise requisitions, and memos.

It is important to be completely familiar with every means of inter-store communication available to the buyer. If messengers go back and forth regularly, it pays to know their schedules so that an urgent message will go out promptly. There may be teletype, special telephone facilities, and even short-wave radio at the buyer's disposal. If any facility is available only during a limited period of the day, the buyer should lose no time learning the schedule that applies to him.

Personal Contact. The flow of information from the branches will be steadier and more complete if the buyer uses every contact with the selling staff and the branch supervisors to let them know that he values their opinons and observations.

If this means that he may on occasion have to listen politely to discussions of the obvious, it may also mean that every now and then he will get an invaluable insight into customer preferences. This is information he does not want to choke off.

For example, customers may ask for one color, or fabric type, or heel height, and accept another as second best because the department did not have what they wanted. The unit control records can be misleading in such cases, indicating a "demand" for the color, or fabric, or heel that was bought unenthusiastically. Only someone on the selling floor can notice and report the eagerness or reluctance with which the merchandise was bought. And these are important straws in the wind for the buyer.

Visiting the Branch. Where distance and the number of branches make it possible, store organizations require that the buyer visit each branch personally every week. If he can arrange for a before-opening visit at least once a month, he can use the occasion to speak directly to the salespeople and fire them with some of his own enthusiasm for the merchandise. On any visit, however, he should brief the department head on present and incoming stock, so that that person will be able to pass the word along.

Also part of the branch visit routine is the matter of checking the stock for completeness, arrangement, appearance. For many buyers, a glance at the merchandise itself is an invaluable insight into the story behind whatever the unit controls alone may show.

For example, a style or color may be moving slowly at one branch and briskly at another. Lack of appeal to the first branch's clientele may be the reason for its lagging sales—or it may be poor lighting, poor position, poor display. Such physical factors can hold back sales quite as effectively as would the lack of merchandise information among the salespeople.

When it comes to stock arrangement, the buyer is generally more expert than his branch personnel, if only for the reason that he has both more experience and more highly specialized experience. If there is a correction or improvement to make, it is wise to take time to explain the thinking behind it to the department manager, so that he will be equipped to come up, perhaps, with something even better of his own another time.

Two-Way Communication. The buyer's branch visit is an opportunity for two-way communication. He brings with him information, advice, and enthusiasm. He should take back a clearer picture of what the branch needs. Observation of customers on the floor is one source of information for him. Chats with salespeople and discussions with the department manager are another.

The less frequently the buyer visits a branch, the more important it is for him to make his visit a source of profit and pleasurable excitement for the store staff. Corrections and criticisms should be made, of course, but in a friendly spirit and with a sincere desire to help the branch staff avoid future errors. Opportunities to praise should be sought. Information and enthusiasm should be passed along. Suggestions should be encouraged.

In these ways, the lines of communication from the people on the branch selling front to the buyer can be kept open and working throughout the year. And, conversely, the buyer's instructions and advice, by whatever means he uses to get them to the branch, will get a warmer reception there. No system of communication is so good that it can't be made better by establishing an attitude of friendliness and mutual help.

Common Buyer Failings. In their dealings with branches, buyers fall into certain errors rather frequently. Here are some of them, as a check-list against which the buyer should be on guard.

1. *Failure to recognize individual differences among branches.* In general, customers at suburban branches buy closer to the time of need than do customers at the downtown store. They may be younger, with less money to spend on clothes than customers downtown. They may react differently to styles, colors, price lines. The buyer, however, should not

accept clichés in studying the branch customer. Communities differ and communities change. One cannot rule out the more mature, the more formal, the more affluent customer at any branch simply because so many branches in suburban areas attract the young, the informal, and the budget-conscious. Constant study and constant testing are needed.

2. *Failure to maintain complete stocks at branches.* When the branch stocks are sketchy, customers and salespeople alike become discouraged. People don't always want to wait for the article to be delivered from the main store if the branch doesn't have it. The buyer's responsibility is to check, check, check.

3. *Failure to refresh stocks frequently.* Customers tend to drop in at suburban branches far more often than customers visit the downtown store. Wherever this pattern holds true, it is up to the buyer to keep the branch supplied with a steady stream of new merchandise. The customer should never be allowed to feel that the stock is dull and stale, and offers nothing different from what she saw and passed up last time.

4. *Failure to watch basics.* In some store organizations, systems are set up to reorder basics at the branches and at the main store. Systems, however, are seldom perfect. The buyer who leaves everything to the system is in no position to spot and correct errors either in the system or in the way the branch is using it. Active, demonstrated interest is the key to success here.

5. *Failure to back advertising with adequate inventory.* This can happen in a large department, and it can happen even more easily in a thinly stocked branch department. If the ad will say that the item is at the branch, the buyer should check and double check to make sure that it is actually on hand when the ad breaks.

6. *Slowness in calling back poor sellers.* Branch stores do not always clear their own markdowns. If slow sellers are supposed to be drawn back to the main store for clearance, this should be done promptly. The smaller the branch and the thinner its stocks, the more vital it becomes to weed out slow

numbers and replace them with lively sellers without delay.

7. *Failure to analyze causes of markdowns.* The markdown pattern, or the pattern of fast and slow sellers, is likely to vary from one selling location to another. The wise buyer analyzes causes of markdowns, branch by branch, and main store versus branches, to seek clues for improved future merchandising.

8. *Failure to use unit controls.* Not all buyers make the fullest possible use of their unit controls. In some organizations, the controls are operated by machine for the buyer, under the direction of an executive familiar with electronic data processing. Such a situation does not absolve the buyer of responsibility for planning and using the system. The better the understanding between buyer and EDP expert, the more useful the reports will be. Without a willingness to put work into unit control and take information out of it, a buyer can scarcely hope to keep on top of a branch store merchandising information.

9. *Failure to relate wants to controls.* Unit controls show what merchandise is moving, and at what rates. They do not show what merchandise could be sold, if it were in the stock. For this information, the buyer must turn to want slips and other forms of request from the branch, as well as comments and observation from the branch personnel. The unit controls, for example, may show that half a dozen dresses in a new higher price line failed to move at the branch; they may not reveal that customers did not balk at the price but were repelled by the meagerness of the assortment, or were looking for different sizes, styles, colors. The buyer needs to look at both faces of the coin.

In fashion merchandise, unit controls are used not only to show what should be reordered, but also to provide indication of trends. In searching out trends, either incoming or declining, the buyer should analyze the situation in each branch individually, as well as for the over-all picture. In that way, he can maximize the branch's accuracy in meeting demand and thus its volume.

10. *Failure to utilize space effectively.* Most branches are on the small side, physically, as compared with the parent store, and each branch department has a problem in making do with the space available to it. The buyer's constant concern with how the space for his department is being used is a necessary ingredient of successful operation.

11. *Failure to inform branch salespeople.* No one has an easy answer to the problem of how to reach all the salespeople in all the branches with the merchandise information they need, with the inspiration they should have. The buyer has many avenues open to him in reaching the branch staff, and he should use all: his own visits; information relayed through the branch department manager; information brought to the branch by vendor salesmen; *opportunities to bring branch personnel to the main store for special meetings;* films, demonstrations, and exhibits that can be sent to the branches; opportunities to wear-test new kinds of merchandise; others.

12. *Failure to consider the branch department head.* In many branches, the branch department manager oversees two or more departments and answers to as many buyers. Such a situation easily leads to conflicting demands upon his time. Each buyer, therefore, should show a degree of consideration, so that the branch executive can organize his time and take care of the requests from every buyer with whom he works. If it is possible to consolidate several telephone calls into one, that saves the branch department manager's time; if a request can be labeled as less urgent than others, that tells the branch personnel which job to handle first. The more considerate each buyer is, the more readily can the branch department manager do right by each of the departments he manages.

Buyers-to-Be. Finally, a word about an executive who is not yet a buyer but may become one in time: the branch department manager. So important is this post today in the training of future buyers that some stores prefer not to assign a trainee to a buying job until there has first been a stint at a branch.

In his dealings with the branch department manager, then,

the buyer will often find himself working with a person who has already shown evidence of talent for buying. If the branch department manager comes to the main store to select items from the stock there, it is worth the buyer's while to discuss the selections and the thinking behind them—certainly never to give grudging approval or an arbitrary negative.

Time taken to educate the branch department manager is a satisfying investment in two ways. First, it contributes to the making of a future buyer. Second, it develops a better qualified lieutenant for the buyer at the branch. And no buyer with branches to supervise ever has too many or too well qualified lieutenants to help him do the job he'd like to do.

CHAPTER 32

THE BUYER'S RESPONSIBILITY
FOR BETTER SELLING

BY

J. H. CALVERT

The *function* of the retail store is to place in the hands of the consumer what the consumer needs; the *business* of the retail store is to buy and sell at a profit. The buyer, therefore, in fulfilling his job has a dual role: he must not only find and purchase the right merchandise for the customers of the store, his customers, but, he must also, to a large degree, assume the responsibility for selling the goods which he has purchased.

No one is more familiar than the buyer with the merits of the merchandise that has been bought; no one is closer to the selling force than the buyer, the department head. If the buyer can transmit to each of the salespeople the merchandise information that caused the purchase to be made originally, and to show the salespeople why the purchase was made, a long step will have been taken to insure that the merchandise is sold. Since profitable sales are the standard on which a buyer's performance is judged, the buyer's self-interest is certainly strongly served by dynamic and enthusiastic sales management.

Scope of Sales Management. Many factors make up the sales management part of the buyer's job. Essentially, these fall into two categories; that of *teaching and training* and that of the *effective use of sales management aids* in the administration of the department. Both are day to day activities; there is a constant, never-ending need for help to a selling force. Better selling does not just happen; it comes about because the department buyer demands it and understands that only through better selling can *he* excel.

Most salespeople receive, in the typical store, certain basic training in the store's training department before they are ever sent to the selling floor. This training is, however, principally concerned with store systems (how to write the various types of sales checks, etc.) procedures and policies. It is not essentially concerned with merchandise, nor, because of its necessarily general nature, can it be concerned with selling techniques in individual merchandise classifications. Such information and training can best be, and generally is, supplied at the departmental level.

Merchandise Training. This type of training therefore becomes the buyer's responsibility. It is a continuing one, for old and experienced salespeople require training in new merchandise, new values, new colors, new uses, to the same extent as do new salespeople. The buyer, with the intimate knowledge that he has received at the time of the original purchase, can provide this information most effectively. The salespeople can be told why the goods were bought, what *motivated* the buyer; they can be shown the selling *features* of the goods so that, in turn, this can be passed on to the customers.

The importance of merchandise training becomes ever greater with the unending flow of new man-made materials, new treatments of familiar materials, and new products. The consumer can rarely tell, simply by examining a piece of merchandise, what virtues or weaknesses to expect from it. Customers, frequently confused by the multitude and variety of new products, welcome authoritative information from the salesperson and buy more readily where it is offered than where ignorance and uncertainty prevail.

Assistance from Vendors. The alert buyer will also make use of his resources in developing better selling among his salespeople. Most vendors today make available to retailers information for salespeople's education; many have traveling representatives who meet regularly in the department with the selling force. Well trained vendor salesmen are usually only too glad to tell the story of their own product to the salespeople who are to pass this on to the ultimate consumer. The buyer who uses these training facilities to the utmost will be more thoroughly rewarded by a better selling force.

Handling Merchandise. One of the important lessons that must be taught to salespeople to make them most effective is to handle merchandise with care and respect at the point of sale. A $1.99 pair of earrings, handled properly, will seem like a much greater value; a $5.99 slip shown with pride and interest will appear to take on enhanced quality in the customer's mind.

All merchandise should have the respect of those selling it; if this respect is well taught and properly justified, it will result in stock being kept so that it is more appealing to the customer, and it will minimize soilage and breakage, which are great thieves of profit. Pride in the merchandise handled is quickly transferred to the customer, reducing sales resistance almost automatically.

Courtesy. No greater lesson can be passed on to a department's personnel than the necessity for simple courtesy to all who come to buy or look. Customers are quick to notice the salesperson who treats them as guests at home; they are equally quick to feel slighted if they are not received with the attitude which they feel they deserve.

Customers will seek out the department where they are made to feel welcome (and especially when they are called by their name), where the buyer and the salespeople are known to make that extra effort to please. Customers will remember the department in which they are not just waited on, but waited on with attention to the "little things" that make a store either impersonal or very personal indeed.

The buyer, in his sales training, will insist on courtesy from his salespeople and will expect his sales force to be courteous among themselves as he, himself, will be courteous in all his relations with them. Courtesy is contagious; the buyer will find it easy to obtain if he, himself, is most careful to use a full measure.

Many stores adopt specific programs to encourage courtesy to their customers. These may involve rewards to salespeople for good reports on "shoppings" by outside organizations or special recognition for compliments by customers. But however effective such programs are, the buyer's own personal insistence on a superior level of courtesy in his department, and his constant emphasis on it in all departmental transactions will do more than anything else to instill this important work habit in every associate in his department.

Interest and Enthusiasm. Of all responsibilities of the buyer to insure an outstanding sales organization, certainly one of the greatest is the arousing of enthusiasm and the creation of interest among his salespeople.

Enthusiasm is the logical accompaniment of interest; if the department personnel are interested in their work, it is largely because someone has *made* them interested, made them see the excitement of the merchandise they are handling and the sales they are making. And if their interest has been aroused, their enthusiasm will follow, and that enthusiasm will make the customer want the merchandise.

Of course, enthusiasm and interest are not limited to merchandise: customers are equally sensitive to employee reactions to their store, to its personnel, to its position in the community and to its character. There is little that will more effectively place a customer in a mood to buy than the enthusiasm of a salesperson for the store, and for its merchandise.

This enthusiasm is a result of thoughtful indoctrination and consistent explanation by the department manager of store policies, both as to merchandise and as to customer relations. Many store managements with excellent store policies find it difficult to communicate these policies to the selling floor; the buyer is peculiarly equipped because of his close relationship with his selling force to communicate store policy. The importance of building enthusiasm for the store and the policies for which it stands, will be many times reflected in a better selling job if the buyer effectively harnesses this intangible. Enthusiasm is "Faith in Action." Faith in the merchandise. Faith in the store. Faith in oneself.

Understanding People. No one can do an effective training and teaching job unless he has successfully won the confidence and respect of the individuals with whom he is associated. Understanding people, their problems, their own peculiar mannerisms, will make possible the development of loyalty and devotion to the store and to the department.

The buyer must never forget he is working with human beings. No two people are alike; the same teaching will not necessarily bring the same result from two different people. But in general, the rules of obtaining maximum productivity from all people are essentially the same: people will produce if they feel that they have from their superior understanding, sympathy and help when it is needed. People appreciate praise when it is deserved just as they understand criticism when the need is indicated.

Aids to Effective Sales Management. Aside from the direct teaching and training of salespeople, there are a number of techniques that the buyer makes use of in order to insure effective selling and better selling within his department.

Some of these augment and assist in his training activities; some insure better organization of his own efforts; others provide information to be used in his buying activities. They have in common, however, the fact that they relate to the selling force, either in giving them information for the customer's benefit or receiving from them information that will make the buyer a more effective purchasing agent for his customers, and, in turn, make his staff's selling capacity greater.

Meetings With Salespeople. Regularly scheduled meetings with the sales organization are extremely important. These meetings must be carefully planned with a sound objective for each subject discussed. The active participation of the selling force is important in these sessions for, in itself, participation builds interest and makes results easier to obtain. Obviously, too, the meetings must be conducted in a friendly, helpful manner: a stern "school-marmish" attitude will tend to destroy the very benefits these get-togethers can have.

The subject matter can cover a wide range: new merchandise, particularly active items; refresher statements of policy and procedure; anything that should be stressed relative to the department and merchandise. But the meetings must be interesting and, above all, the material must be enthusiastically presented.

It is not always easy for the buyer to schedule meetings so as to reach all his salespeople regularly, particularly where there are many part-time employees and where there are branches. But when a buyer realizes the advantage of personal contact with his people, and of the opportunity for friendly give and take of information, he makes every effort to hold his meetings and make them fruitful.

Good Housekeeping and Displays. A buyer who desires *better selling* should teach the importance of good housekeeping, i.e., good stockkeeping. In this matter, the buyer's responsibility is clearly and sharply defined.

Shelves, cabinets and drawers must be arranged for easy and quick accessibility; stock should be arranged (and this is so basic) according to color, size and price line; show-cases and interior displays must reflect a true picture of stocks that cannot be seen—the countless items that are hidden in warehouses, stock rooms, or in the drawers of the department. It is useless to buy unless the customer will be shown what is in stock. People are not psychic; they cannot see into drawers or behind walls.

Allied items should be kept close at hand. Salespeople should be told *why* things are arranged in a certain way; why it is helpful to everyone in the department to adhere to a logical and planned set-up; why it is essential promptly to return stock to its proper place. If they know and understand the reason, they will be motivated to give full cooperation. And that means *better selling*.

Advertised Merchandise. A great deal of money is spent every day in the year to bring certain merchandise to the attention of the public. Better selling means that the salespeople should be kept familiar with what is being advertised.

If a buyer wishes, this responsibility may be delegated to an assistant or to the sponsor in the department. But the sales staff must know; they must be told if they are to do that *better selling job*. It is obviously important to display the advertisement prominently in the department, where everyone may see it; and the advertised items should be shown in a conspicuous place.

It cannot be stressed too strongly that the people who sell the advertised goods must be told of the merits of the goods. They will be asked questions; they have a right to expect information so they can answer these questions intelligently. The buyer knows, or should know the answers, and he should make certain that his sales staff knows, too.

Trading Up. Patient teaching by the buyer will enable a salesperson to point out the relative qualities of merchandise that may resemble something else but actually has many points of difference, making it worth more than the other. The value, in any transaction, must be apparent; in the customer's eyes, the item itself must equal in value the money left behind in the store's cash register. Otherwise, there will be a dissatisfied customer, even though a purchase is made.

With the proper stockkeeping, it should be easy for a salesperson to move quickly from one price line to another, as one senses the customer's ability or willingness to pay. With many people, price is secondary. Quality should be stressed, and the old rule of displaying the best merchandise first still holds its place in the *better selling* picture today.

Multiple Sales and Suggestion Selling. These are two important factors which go hand-in-hand, in a sense. It is so easy to point out the many advantages of suggesting other items in addition to the one requested—perhaps something that is allied or a companion item to the one sold; perhaps some piece of merchandise that is a special in the department.

The way merchandise is shown in fixtures and in displays can often suggest the second item to the customer, but a pleasant verbal reminder from the salesperson is a helpful and often appreciated clincher.

Suggesting second items is valuable beyond the consideration that it means increased departmental sales and increased compensation for the salesperson. The added interest flatters most customers (which is desirable, if not overdone) and the salesperson has the great satisfaction of having done just a little bit more than was expected.

In many instances, it is actually not to a customer's advantage to let her purchase only one of an article. For example, selling two, three or more pairs of hosiery of the same color is economical and practical, yet many women customers fail to take into consideration this possibility for effecting a saving until it is explained to them. To do this is a way of winning confidence and building personal trade.

Personal Trade Files. There is no more pertinent means at a salesperson's disposal for increasing earnings than by building personal trade. There are other names for this personal following, but the value is there regardless of what term may be used.

Every customer who comes into a store or a department, and asks for a certain individual by name, to take care of her requirements, may be termed a personal customer, and that customer's name is one that may be placed in a file for follow-up on many occasions. A "P.T." file—"P.T." meaning personal trade—can be a veritable treasure chest.

The buyer should encourage each member of his sales staff to start and keep up a file of this kind. It is important to note on index cards any pertinent information regarding a customer's size, color preference, etc. Sometimes the names and ages of the children in a family may be included. Often notes as to what has been sold will prove helpful in the future. It is a buyer's responsibility to educate his associates in this respect; he can materially help them to serve their customers better, which, in turn, again means helping themselves, their buyer, and their store.

These customers should be called regularly with information about special items that may be going on sale, or about good values of interest, or new merchandise that the salesperson's personal contact indicates may be sold to the individual or family. Customers appreciate this and will respond by building the department's volume.

"Follow-through" is important too—very important. The buyer should tell the salespeople of the way this "P.T." file can greatly increase their sales, if properly handled. The splendid results obtained by those who have made use of this system have proven, over and over, that it is well worth the time and effort.

Best Seller Information. Alert salespeople can provide the buyer with one of his most important volume building tools: immediate knowledge of what is selling best in the department whether it be an item, a color, a size, or a shape. Armed with this information, the buyer can quickly reorder wanted items, or adjust orders to take recognition of new trends in his customers' preferences.

The buyer must continually work with his selling force so that everything that is a best seller is brought to his attention. This is important not only for buying information, but also so that dramatic displays can be made and prominent positions may be given to those items the customers desire most. No greater responsibility rests with the buyer than to assure adequate communication of the development of fast selling merchandise from his sales organization to himself.

Customer Wants. Here again, a buyer has a manifold obligation—to the customer, the salesperson, the store, and himself. Unless a buyer has the needed and wanted merchandise in stock, fashion or staple, the business will go elsewhere. If that happens, there will be a great many unhappy people in the department.

In order to know what things are being asked for, that are not in stock, it is essential to have the full cooperation of the sales staff. They must be taken into the buyer's confidence and made to feel that the buyer depends upon them for this information.

The bigger the department a buyer manages, and the more branches he serves, the less time he has to be on the floor himself and in contact with customers. The salespeople must then become his eyes and ears, reporting to him personally or on a printed form any calls they have not been able to fill—either for items temporarily out of stock or for items never carried. They can also report best sellers which are moving rapidly and may need to be watched more closely and reordered more promptly than the buyer anticipated. Astute buyers welcome this information as the means of saving sales, reducing returns and increasing profits.

Encouraging People to Help. The salespeople must never be given the impression that a buyer, in any way, resents having matters of this kind brought to his attention or that he considers it an affront to his efficiency or dignity. Where buyers took such an attitude, the "want slips" from salespeople ceased—and it wasn't good for anybody, especially for the buyer.

To adopt such a negative position would be like sealing up oil wells capable of gushing forth millions of barrels of valuable fluid. A well-functioning "Customer Request" system is a well of valuable merchandising information that will bring needed and asked-for goods into a department, and from there into the customers' homes to serve a useful purpose. This means satisfaction to customers, added earnings to salespeople, and increased profits to the business—not to mention compensation to the buyer, as well.

The importance of follow-through on this information

should be pointed out. It is worse than useless to accumulate a mass of data, representing effort and interest on the part of the salespeople, and then do nothing with it. It would be far better to get no information at all than to receive good information and not make it productive and effective.

Knowledge of Competition. No greater aid to sales management can be found than the knowledge of what the department's competition is doing: what they have in stock; what they are advertising; what their prices are on comparable merchandise; and what the customer response is. Comparative shoppers are available in most larger stores to assist in this, but interested salespeople can supply much information both to the buyer and themselves.

The buyer of any department should be in a position to answer questions which may be put to him by customers or salespeople as to the relative merits of lines carried by competition. No department can possibly carry every line that is manufactured, but as Benjamin Franklin once said, "Knowledge is power." That is what we have in mind when we say that *better selling* means shopping competition, never "knocking" competition. Derogatory remarks about any competitive product do not constitute salesmanship, much less *better selling*.

While on the subject of competition, let me add one more thought. In recent years competition has greatly intensified. This has been due to the abandonment of suggested retail price maintenance, the advent of the discount house, the stronger competition of mail order houses, the changing character of some of the variety stores, etc.

The uncontrolled selling of low markon items severely reduces the gross margin. For all that, intelligent direction of salespeople properly informed of this profit problem and how to handle it, can result in considerable improvement in overall departmental gross margin.

Better Selling Responsibility. Thus it is apparent that a very major part of the buyer's responsibility rests in the sales management of the department. He must train his sales organization; he must learn in turn from them.

This two-way street of information is the buyer's greatest opportunity to increase the sales and the profits of his operation. Without understanding, without free communication between the buyer as procurer of merchandise and the salespeople as the final contact with the customer, the department is a dead, uninteresting entity. But with the aids and techniques outlined above, the buyer can make that same department come alive with interest, enthusiasm and service.

Better buying makes a good buyer possible; better selling insures his success.

CHAPTER 33

THE PERSONNEL DIVISION'S RESPONSIBILITY FOR BETTER SELLING

BY

ROY S. LEIGHTON

The personnel division shares with the buyer the responsibility for achieving better selling in his department. With a sound understanding of the objectives and the methods used by his store's personnel division, the buyer is able to make the most of the help that is offered him from this source. He is also in a position to know how to do his part in making personnel's contribution of maximum effectiveness in his department.

The Personnel Program. The responsibility of the personnel division for better selling lies in the development of a personnel program in which policies fundamental to good human relationships are integrated with good leadership practice. Every complete personnel program should include consideration of the following points—the numerical sequence does not indicate order of importance:

1. Fair compensation which recognizes the value of the work of the salesperson, rates for comparable work in the organization, current rates in the community, and cost of living needs.

2. Job security for good job performance.

3. Safeguards to health through good working conditions, health service, paid vacations, etc.

4. Opportunity for self-improvement through training in job duties and the best methods of per-

formance, through advancement when ability has been demonstrated, through praise when it is merited and correction when it is needed.

5. Pleasant working relationships with associates and department supervisors which establish a sense of partnership in and responsibility for department problems and achievements.

6. Economic security through paid sick leave, pension plans, etc.

7. Periodic evaluation of performance by supervisors with the guidance of the personnel executive to determine how the job is being done, where improvement is needed, if compensation is fair and if there would be consideration for promotion, or transfer.

Departments Within the Personnel Division. We are all familiar with the customary break-down of personnel functions into employment, training and welfare. The executive in charge of each of these departments needs specialized technical training gained through study and experience, and beyond that a developed insight into the nature of human beings. He realizes that his is a service department but with responsibility for personnel relations throughout the whole organization.

Attracting Good Applicants. To attract good applicants it is essential for a store to have a reputation in the community as a "good place to work." The source of this publicity is the present and former staff members of the organization. Their judgment, based on actual experience, is influenced by good department leadership, fairness of pay, opportunity for learning, recognition for work well done, good working conditions and surroundings, fair treatment and advancement, liberal policies on vacations, staff discount, sick leave, etc.

There are stores that place considerable emphasis on the considerations just listed but destroy much of the goodwill they have thereby developed when employment is terminated.

Instead of telling the salesperson that her performance is not up to store standards, showing her ways and giving her time to show improvement, she is dismissed perhaps with pay in lieu of notice, perhaps without even that.

Pay does not compensate for the humiliation of instant dismissal. To save her own face she must explain to fellow-workers, family, and friends how unfairly she has been treated. As a result, the people in her sphere of influence outside the store have less goodwill toward the store. At the same time her former store associates have a feeling of less security on the job.

Unless a salesperson is being dismissed for cause, it is in the best interests of the store and the staff member to tell her when work is not up to store standards, show her how she can improve, and give her the opportunity to do so. If she has not made satisfactory progress within the specified period, she should be advised and assisted to look for another job.

In that way she is given an opportunity to leave with her reputation unimpaired. There is a better chance that she will feel kindly toward the store, continue to be one of its customers, and not injure the store's reputation with potential customers and with other likely candidates for employment.

Selection of Salespeople. The employment department is responsible for the selection of salespeople who are interested in selling and giving courteous service to the customer, who are acceptable to the customer from the point of view of manners and appearance, and who have real aptitude for making sales.

Unfortunately, there is no magic pattern for making the right selection. We must depend upon an interested interviewer who, through observation, training and experience, has learned the requirements of the various selling departments and has a real understanding of human nature. In a department where technical background is a prerequisite, the assistance of the buyer in deciding the suitability of the applicant is usually helpful and should be sought.

When the applicant is hired, the conditions of employment such as wages, quotas, commissions, hours of work, dress regulations, special job demands such as heavy lifting, overtime requirements, etc., should be carefully defined. Overselling a job or its opportunities makes the new salesperson lose confidence in the integrity of management when some of the promised conditions fail to materialize and may result in her leaving.

Introductory Training. During initial training in the training department, the new salesperson is taught basic subjects which are applicable to all selling departments. These include:

1. Store policies and procedures which she must know and observe.

2. Store standards such as good grooming and dressing in good taste for business. Standards for businesslike conduct in relation to customers and associates.

3. Good selling techniques such as learning and using the customer's name and prompt and pleasant recognition of the customer.

4. Learning how to handle salescheck and cash register transactions.

5. Definition of responsibilities for care, arrangement and maintenance of forward stock.

6. Information regarding benefits of employment such as paid vacations and sick leave, etc., store organization and their place in it, store tour, and store directory.

Introduction to the Selling Department and Initial Job Training. If the new salesperson is to be properly received in her department, introduced to her buyer and other members of the staff, taught the specialized department systems and procedures, and the duties of her particular job and the best ways of doing it, some one person must have the responsibility. The personnel division, in consultation with the buyer, selects a person qualified in the following respects:

1. Has high standards for work and conduct for herself.

2. Has a friendly manner and is interested in training new salespeople.

3. Knows what the new staff member should be taught and how to teach.

Whether this person be the assistant buyer or a sponsor, the buyer and the sponsor must understand what their responsibilities are to the new salesperson and the sponsor given time from her regular duties to do them. If a salesperson has this assignment, she is usually compensated in some extra way for the time which it takes away from her opportunity to sell.

After a week or two of employment, a training representative finds out from the new salesperson whether she has been taught department procedures and job responsibilities, and if she has been given help in carrying them out. It is important to learn from the buyer and the sponsor the aptitude and interest the salesperson is showing in her performance. If she is not fitted for the job, she can be taken from the department. If the sponsor has given her too little attention, a plan can be developed for correcting the situation.

Important Factors in Staff Morale. According to morale surveys, a study of the comparative results of selling departments on any one selling floor has shown clearly that, within the same physical environment and under the centralized administration of identical management policies, staff morale varies greatly in the several departments due to the one variable—department leadership.

There are several factors which influence considerably the salesperson's enthusiasm for good work. The most important ones are:

1. Sound personnel policies which insure a good place to work.

2. Fair pay for all work done. While wage payment plans are administered by the personnel division, the buyer shares the responsibility through recommendation of merit increases.

3. Interesting work. It is the responsibility of the employment office to place the salesperson in a selling department in which she is interested. However, interest can be sustained and increased through the opportunities which the department offers for learning and development.

4. Opportunity for advancement. When management consistently fills positions above the beginner's level by members of the organization who have demonstrated their ability, ambitious staff members are given the incentive to work hard for advancement. The buyer can support this policy by recommending the advancement of a stock clerk to salesperson, salesperson to assistant buyer, and in some cases assistant buyer to buyer.

5. Opportunity to learn more. This is the buyer's responsibility. He is the expert on the department's merchandise, he knows through daily contacts with his staff the particular needs for instruction, and his position of authority gives the greatest acceptance to all that he teaches.

6. Having superiors who are courteous, considerate, understanding and appreciative. The buyer is the manager in the selling department, and often there is joint responsibility with the floor service manager. How the manager handles the new salesperson can make the working life of that person a worthwhile and satisfactory experience. The pleasant relationship which is developed be-between the salesperson and the manager helps to

compensate for the trying situations and periods of high tension inseparable from selling.

7. Getting credit for all work. Since the salesperson is aware that her pay is largely determined by her sales figures, she is apt to approach the less interesting duties of care of stock, displays, stock counts, etc., with little enthusiasm. Praise for the good performance of her various non-selling duties is particularly heartwarming and makes the task more attractive.

The Buyer as a Teacher. While the discussion of selling techniques and the presentation of demonstration sales and films showing selling procedures which are conducted outside the selling department provide background knowledge for better selling, it is the belief of many buyers who have been successful salespeople that selling skills must also be learned from experience on the job.

In answer to the question, "How do people learn to sell?" several buyers have emphasized that the less experienced can also learn from observing their more skilled associates. A merchandise manager who had been an outstandingly able buyer believes that the buyer needs to observe continuously the selling activities of his salespeople, discuss with them better ways of handling observed situations and encourage them to bring to him their problems and questions; that through this day-to-day contact he not only gives them more knowledge of selling techniques, but he also develops self-confidence and enthusiasm.

Department Meetings. The department meetings which the buyer holds with his staff serve as the source of the information about new merchandise, plans for sales events, reports on successful department activities in which the salespeople have shared, problems which the ideas and efforts of the group may help to solve. The buyer endeavors not only to give information, but to arouse group spirit so that the staff will work together as a team in turning plans into successful results.

The group meeting is not an occasion for criticism. Group criticism at best is disheartening to everyone, and at worst can result in group antagonism. There usually are a few people who are the most blameworthy. When the buyer talks privately with each of these, showing her specifically how her work should be improved and its relation to the successful operation of the department, the desired results are more apt to be obtained.

To give the buyer assistance in doing a good teaching job, the training department can provide information, recommend good methods for individual and group instruction, and help develop plans for meetings. When the buyer has learned how to organize information and present it so that it is interesting and clearly understood, he is rewarded by a better informed and more enthusiastic selling staff.

The Buyer as a Leader. The buyer who has insight into human nature is aware that his salespeople are individuals, that they are responsive to the kindly use of authority and that they fear the harsh voice and the abrupt command. It is essential to their well-being that their leader show respect for their human dignity by treating them courteously and with consideration.

There are many problems, business and personal, which arise in the life of every salesperson. If she is to be free to focus her attention on the business of selling, she must get some relief from the burden of her worry. It is natural to seek help from someone in whose judgment and integrity she has confidence.

When the buyer can be the understanding listener, he renders a great service. If the problem lies within his own department, he will be active in its solution. Again he may refer the person to another executive whom he believes better qualified to give the counsel needed.

Often, just by listening he may have assisted the salesperson to get a better perspective of the problem so that she can solve it herself. In any event, the buyer has been a friend in need, and the salesperson's appreciative response manifests itself in the effort to do a better job and in deeper personal loyalty.

Salespeople Need Recognition. It is an economic necessity that people be paid for their services, but the dollars and cents in the pay envelope are not enough. The salesperson needs the praise that she has earned to give her self-confidence and to encourage her initiative. The salesperson accepts well-deserved praise as an evidence of the buyer's goodwill and is more kindly disposed toward the inevitable corrections which are a necessary guide to her improvement. Praise and constructive criticism are inseparable tools which the good leader uses in teaching, directing and developing his staff.

Discussing with salespeople plans for the new season, consulting them about customers' wants before the trips to market, and talking with them from day-to-day about the customers' acceptance of merchandise are procedures which many successful buyers use. Salespeople have suggestions which are valuable to the conduct of the business. Salespeople, like all human beings, also have the urge to express their ideas and want to be listened to.

The wise buyer brings up definite problems for discussion at his meetings. A general request for suggestions may bring a demand for an air-conditioning system or something else equally beyond his jurisdiction.

When a salesperson's suggestion is adopted in part or whole, she is apt to accept considerable responsibility for making her "brain child" successful in operation. The recognition which the buyer gives her in the presence of her associates stimulates the entire department to think of further ways for improvement.

Helping the Buyer. The buyer who is eager to grow will welcome all the help his store's personnel division can give him in developing an understanding of human relations and leadership. He will make available to the training department his specialized knowledge of his department's merchandise and its selling problems, so that by cooperative effort they can work out effective selling techniques for his people. He will realize that some of the most potent factors for creating good morale lie within himself and within his sphere of responsibility.

CHAPTER 34

SALES PROMOTION AND PLANNING

BY

PHILIP J. TROY

Department store organization charts generally show the sales promotion division as a separate "pyramid" responsible for advertising, display, and public relations. The bald listings on such charts, however, cannot convey the full function of the division adequately, nor can they define the extent to which its work touches virtually every phase of store operation.

If we conceive of sales promotion as the coordination or utilization of every activity that helps to promote sales, we see that it includes not only direct conrol over all forms of advertising, display, and publicity, but also close liaison with all merchandise divisions, mail and telephone orders, advertising research, credit promotion, sales training, and any operating departments likely to have direct customer contact.

Modern Philosophy of Sales Promotion. Today, many stores are coming to believe that the buying and promotion of merchandise are so closely related that the merchandising staff should seek and accept leadership from the sales promotion division. These stores believe they can buy with more confidence because they have coordinated their sales and promotional planning with their buying plans. Through research, the sales promotion division becomes a positive force in helping buyer and merchandise manager decide which classifications and price lines should be most energetically promoted.

In such stores, instead of just buying and selling merchandise, the story becomes one of "buying to sell" based on extensive research. This approach makes it of utmost importance that the sales promotion manager possess a broad merchandising background.

The Importance of Proper Planning. Sales plans should be developed with a clear concept of the job they are to accomplish. Each month's plan should be a clear picture of what the store, division, or department wants to achieve, based on the best facts available.

The advantages of proper sales planning are many. First such sales planning allows the promotional course to be set well in advance. Next, of great importance, it allows sufficient time for adequate promotional preparation. Finally, it enables sales planners to control promotional expenditures since they know exactly where they stand in relation to the over-all picture.

Types of Promotions. The objective of all sales promotion effort is to sell more merchandise, keeping the profit element in mind. This may be accomplished either by institutional promotion (which builds store prestige and store acceptance over a long period of time) or by merchandise promotion, aimed to draw immediate traffic and volume. Very few stores spend appreciable parts of their advertising budget on institutional advertising, but there are stores who do little or no insitutional advertising in the belief that their budgets should be devoted exclusively, or almost so, to the promotion of merchandise. Most stores, however, attempt to strike a happy medium, depending on store character, between institutional and direct merchandise promotion.

Institutional Promotion. Institutional promotion builds confidence in the store over a continuing period of time by promoting the significant advantages of the store in relation to its competitors. Such promotion may stress the quality of the store's merchandise in general. It may stress the extent of its assortments, its leadership in fashion, its convenient customer services, or its extremely active participation in civic affairs.

No matter where the emphasis may fall, this type of promotion builds goodwill and attracts steady customers rather than the one-time shopper. Its disadvantage is that it is almost impossible to measure its results, except over a long period of time.

Merchandise Promotion. The opposite of institutional promotion is merchandise promotion, which has immediate sales as an objective. It attempts to create traffic by bringing more people to the store than would have come had there been no promotion. Such promotions may feature either merchandise at regular price lines or, more often, merchandise which has been purchased for special selling, or reduced for clearance. The objective is greater sales volume, both in the merchandise promoted, and in the rest of the store as a result of the increased traffic generated.

Regular price-line promotion insures fairly steady daily business at the regular markon. It often fails, however, to create unusual customer traffic because people know they can buy the merchandise at any time. On the other hand, special value sellings or clearance promotions draw more immediate traffic, but too often this traffic is composed of one-time or "bargain" shoppers.

Policies of individual stores vary regarding types of merchandise promotions. In addition to regular price-line selling, most stores feature store-wide events—anniversary sales, birthday sales, dollar days, etc. Some confine their special sales activities to departmental or divisional events—January White Sale, August Furniture Sale, August Fur Sale, etc. Although a very few stores allow special sellings only on a limited number of carefully selected items or classifications, almost every store depends on periodic clearance sales to make room for new, fresh stock.

Length of Special Sellings. Many store executives frown upon one-day sellings, feeling that it may inconvenience some customers to shop on the appointed day. The chances of inconvenience are lessened, considerably, when the merchandise is on sale for several days, or even longer.

One-day sellings are inconvenient for customers also because they frequently cause poor service. When customers focus their attention on a single item or group in a single department, the regular flow of traffic is increased manyfold and the regular salespeople cannot adequately service the crowd. This is disturbing to regular shoppers, who may choose to disregard special events of such nature. Some higher quality stores, therefore, do not favor one-day sellings, despite their more immediate and certain sales response.

Many stores find that a three-day selling combines the advantages of (1) focusing considerable attention over a short period on certain items, and (2) extending the selling over a longer period so that customers can buy the merchandise without encountering traffic disturbances.

The disadvantage of a week-long selling is that it is difficult to maintain both customer and clerk enthusiasm over so long a period of time. Moreover, unless there is a continuous infiltration into the department of fresh merchandise in the proper size and color range, the assortment becomes broken.

Some stores feel that special-value selling should be taking place somewhere in the store every day for immediate traffic building purposes. With the increased traffic, it is hoped that there will be a corresponding increase in total store volume.

The Six Months' Promotion Plan. Almost without exception, every store makes up a six months' promotion plan. In some stores this is handled entirely by the sales promotion department. The facts and figures are taken from the store records. The merchandiser and buyer are consulted only in a general way although each is given a copy of the completed six months' plan as it relates to his division or department.

Very often, the buyer and merchandise manager are helpful in digging out and providing the information which goes into this plan. In the final analysis, however, the sales promotion

director must insure that the plan he submits to management
includes at least the following information:

1. A list of feature events used, by department, division and storewide for previous year.

2. Tabulation of sales results achieved by the above events.

3. Proposal of corresponding events and their dates for the upcoming season.

4. List of other special promotion efforts of last year such as radio or TV programs, feature windows or interior displays, direct mail pieces, style shows, festivals, "weeks", etc.

5. Recommended list of those to be repeated and/or improved with suggested dates for the same.

6. Sales for each month plus advertising dollars spent and advertising percentage to sales resulting.

7. List of important events of major competitors each month.

It is the usual practice that this plan be submitted to management by the sales promotion manager at least 90 days in advance of the upcoming season. After meeting with the merchandise managers and other store major executives, the sales promotion director completes the preliminary plan and issues copies to all executives involved.

Quarterly Planning. As previously indicated, the six months' plan is a skeleton plan wherein management has committeed itself to definite dates, events, budgets, etc. The next logical step dictated by modern retailing thinking is to prepare and present a quarterly research plan which offers top management, merchandisers, and buyers, a much more complete and informative picture of what took place last year, and what is contemplated as strategy for the upcoming quarter of this year.

Quarterly planning is prepared almost exclusively by sales promotion, and presented to the merchandise divisions approximately 60 days in advance of a given quarter, in order to allow them ample time to digest the data submitted and still have lead-time to work the markets for the promotional objectives outlined.

Briefly, the quarterly plan offers the following:

a. A one-page summary of the quarter in question for the previous year, plus a few observations on highlights for the same quarter of this year.

b. A separate analysis for each month within the quarter pointing out the following:

— sales attained last year by store versus this year's plan.
— number of selling days last year versus this year.
— days gained or lost versus last year.
— storewide events, this year versus last year.
— specific holidays, this year versus last year.

c. Outstanding departmental performances last year versus previous year.

d. Outstanding departmental promotions last year.

e. Relatively poor departmental performances for the months of last year.

f. Least productive ads from last year.

g. Weatherwise, the picture last year.

h. Federal Reserve figures compared with performance of the individual stores last year.

i. Promotional strategy for each month this year *and* important dates and events to remember.

j. A chronological listing of all own advertising run this month last year—good or bad.

k. A listing of all "important-looking" ads run by selected major competitors, submitted in "cluster" form (by natural departmental breakdown, e.g., all major competitors' furniture ads, appliance ads, etc.).

l. A listing of the "top twenty" volume-producing departments for the month last year.

Finally, in collaboration with the merchandise managers, the sales promotion head submits a list of "promotional objectives" as specific proposals for each month in question. These "objectives" are established after much research and discussion and pretty generally include: (a) a list of a store's own successes from the previous year; (b) a list of the "best" promotions that competition had to offer; (c) a list of what, based on current observations, seems most timely and value-right if "objectives" can be met as to timing, quantity and price in today's markets.

The benefits of such quarterly information can and should be of incalculable value to merchandisers and buyers. Last-minute planning and market work is then largely relegated to the dark ages. A buyer or a merchandiser can now take a complete look at a natural "season" and, with a minimum of effort on his part, become informed and alerted to prepare *in time* a professional job of sales planning.

Monthly Promotion Plans. Approximately 7 weeks in advance of the specific month under consideration, fortified with the data furnished them in the six months' plan and the quarterly plan, merchandise managers submit their detailed requests for advertising to the sales promotion office.

One week later, the sales promotion division has fitted the various requests into a preliminary plan which closely adheres to the advertising budget for that month. Very shortly thereafter, a meeting is held among the store head, the various merchandise managers, and sales promotion, at which time the preliminary plan is presented, reviewed, and revised to the point of producing the final plan. Many times this session will require a full day of discussion. This plan is then issued to all concerned, not later than one month in advance of the month in question. Each buyer receives only that part of the total store plan which pertains directly to his department(s).

Flexibility of the Monthly Plan. Recognizing the fact that no monthly plan can remain static, leading stores allow for regularly scheduled weekly advertising meetings, attended by all major executives involved. The purpose is to receive and review ad copy for the entire week beginning Sunday three weeks hence, to review results from the previous week's advertising, to discuss and apprise all concerned of any known or contemplated changes in schedules and plans brought about by current market conditions, delayed delivery, local situations, budget adjustments, etc.

Any schedule or plan must be flexible as changes are bound to be made. So long as stores operate under conditions subject to change, no advance plan can be 100 per cent perfect. Every step must be checked carefully, and far enough in advance, to reduce errors to a minimum. This avoids time-wasting, money-wasting discussion, and consequent last-minute alteration, not only of advertisements but of entire promotions as well. A common weakness is for altogether too much emphasis to be placed on the importance of an advertisement itself, and, inversely, too little upon the foundation of merchandise, timing, and service, on which the success of the advertising rests. Here again, proper advance planning reduces waste and the element of change insofar as is possible.

Cooperative Advertising. Cooperation from resources in the store's advertising is so important that it has been given a chapter of its own in this book. It should be pointed out here, however, that there are often occasions on which the sales promotion staff can help the buyer in his negotiations with resources. Some manufacturers want to see a plan of how the allowances will be used, others want something more substantial than just a tear sheet of the ad to convince them that their money was wisely applied.

In such cases, a well thought out presentation, prepared by the sales promotion staff for the resource, can generate good will and smooth the buyer's future path with the maker concerned. The sales promotion division may not have the time to perform this service every time cooperation is offered and accepted, but it will rarely refuse the buyer who asks for it in behalf of an important resource that has been either particularly helpful or particularly difficult.

Furthermore, and of great importance, from its broad knowledge of what leading manufacturers in numerous other industries are presently offering in the way of cooperation with departments throughout the entire store, sales promotion can be most helpful in guiding individual buyers and merchandisers to obtain more complete cooperative programs than may have been originally proffered by a specific resource.

Programmed Merchandising. Where merchandising and sales promotion activities mesh smoothly, a store, division, or department can carry its plans a step farther and program its promotion with key resources. In such cases, the store analyzes its performance with a resource's line, decides how large an increase it can hope to achieve with strong cooperation from the resource plus creative promotion at the store level, and then discusses possibilities with the resource. Knowing that the store is planning a well-rounded program for a sizable increase, the resource may offer substantial help in promotional allowances, in sales training, in preparing itself to give fast fill-in service, and in other ways. With all-around teamwork, dramatic increases in sales of the specific line can be achieved, and benefit accrues to the resource, the department, and the store.

Pre-Planned Objectives. A sound basis for planning events is to research past experience in the store or department and determine what timing, what appeals, what types of merchandise, and what price ranges, have the strongest pulling power among the store's customers. When the sales promotion division does research of this type, it provides the merchandising division with the framework for a special value event that has more than average chances of success. In such cases, the buyers go into their markets with specific objectives to seek out suitable items or promotion groups, for the event proposed by the sales promotion division.

This is exactly the reverse of what happens when a department suddenly finds a "hot" item. In one case, the buyer discovers the promotable merchandise and the sales promotion staff devises advertising to support it. In the other, the sales promotion division's research points up the opportunity and the buyer seeks appropriate merchandise offerings for the preplanned event.

The Trend to Tie-Ins. Buyers for department and specialty stores in recent years have been offered an increasing number of opportunities to link their advertising and displays to those of resources, or fiber and fabric producers, or consumer magazines, or even travel services, automobile manufacturers or dealers, and other goods and services not part of the department store pattern.

Although some of these tie-ins may be excellent in themselves, the sales promotion division may refuse them. One reason may be that too many similar tie-ins have already been accepted by other departments of the store, with the result that the store's own name seems to be somewhat unduly submerged. Another reason may be that the suggested tie-in, although new to the buyer, is not new to the store or community. Still another reason may be that the display materials or advertising requirements present too many problems or for other reasons may be undesirable.

The sensible buyer will not commit himself to a tie-in offer, no matter how attractive, until he has had an opportunity first to discuss it with his merchandise manager and the sales promotion division, to get the considered store-wide viewpoint.

This procedure offers a far better chance of achieving maximum benefits if, indeed, the proposal is to be accepted at all.

The Use of Direct Mail. Almost every department has some merchandise that is eminently suitable for direct mail advertising. Mailing costs run quite high, however, and unless costs are wisely balanced against possible yield, a department can lose money on some of its mail offerings.

The advice of the sales promotion division, which has studied and checked results on direct mail offerings throughout the store, should be solicited. Often the experience of other departments (and other companies) provides indications of the elements most likely to produce successes or failures in this area. Much valuable information is readily available on direct mail, its use and results, and the buyer can learn much from a study of it. At the same time, he should realize that direct mail is rapidly becoming a very expensive medium and should be used only for departments and types of merchandise particularly responsive to it.

Warehouse Sales. Departments mainly in the home furnishings division of some stores have found warehouse sales an effective way to attract bargain-conscious customers and move large quantities of hard goods. This is not for every store or department, however. What is needed is, first, a large pool of potential customers who will respond to an offer of this kind. Next, the location must be the warehouse itself or a selling place remote from the store. (It is important that the carnival atmosphere does not interfere with other departments.) Also, a substantial inventory of off-price merchandise and special purchases so that the promotion can be big enough to warrant strong promotion. Usually, in discount store style, service is minimal and there is an extra charge for delivery. Advertising may or may not be in the same media that the store uses regularly—depending on whether or not the offering is aimed at the store's regular clientele. The most successful promotion formula has been the use of newspaper space backed by selected radio and TV spots.

In staging a warehouse sale, the buyer foregets many of the lessons he has learned in his ordinary promotions. He will probably have no windows to be concerned with, and his display facilities will be primitive. Essential, however, are good signing and proper ticketing of items, so that shoppers can sell themselves with little or no help from clerks.

Advice to Buyers. At this point, it would be well to enumerate what every buyer should consider in planning his advertising.

1. Promotion should be concentrated largely in the major classifications in his department and then usually at best-selling price points.

2. Regular price advertising should be largely restricted to proven best-sellers—whether your own or some other store's successes.

3. Successes, not mistakes, should be repeated.

4. Profitable items (not low markon) should be promoted in the majority of cases.

5. All advertising, whether newspaper, radio, TV or feature display should have a specific purpose—news value, high fashion story, legitimate savings, repeat success, etc.—or it should never come into being.

6. All advertising should be backed by aggressive, intensive inside-the-store promotion—especially dramatic point-of-sale display and signing.

7. All advertising should be backed by informed, interested salespeople, whether on the floor, on the phone order board, or in mail order. Good buyers make sure of this.

8. Advertising copy should be written with great care and complete information. Wherever possible, the buyer should discuss both copy and sample with the layout specialist, copywriter, and

artist involved—not to instruct, but to get across the features that will result in a more potent ad. Transmit your own enthusiasm!

9. Sign copy should be as carefully written as advertising copy—and as complete, within the space limitations of a sign card. Good, informative signing is a strong and continuing selling force working for you during the life of the sign.

10. Remember to get ad copy and samples to the advertising department on time—and to remove samples promptly thereafter. Cooperation with advertising department personnel will pay you big dividends.

11. Keep yourself informed as to "other store activities" such as radio and TV programs, style shows, special events, storewide promotions—each or any of these, may give you an opportunity for an "extra" tie-in to the advantage of your department(s).

12. Above all, know the promotion plan for your own department(s) thoroughly. In most stores, dates are set well in advance so that every person and every department will have adequate time to prepare for promotions. Know your store's timetable and adhere to it.

13. If yours is a store with branches, make sure you do everything for the branch that you do for the main store. Touch all the bases. See they have adequate stocks, signs, informed people, dramatic display, advertising identification in your ad— "the whole bit."

14. Make it a firm rule never to buy merchandise merely to get cooperative advertising monies.

Branch Store Advertising. There are cases where the branch store is located in another city having its own newspapers, and where the circulation of the metropolitan newspapers does not provide sufficient coverage. Under these circumstances, the advertising in the metropolitan newspapers is placed also in newspapers in the branch store city.

Trained advertising personnel, particularly layout artists and illustrators, may not be available in these branch cities. Also, it is rather expensive to create entirely new advertising for the comparatively small circulation of the newspapers in the branch store cities.

Because of these factors, one or two persons may sometimes be added to the staff of the main store advertising department to adapt the layouts, copy and art of main store advertising, for the use of the branches. In the branches themselves, another person or two may receive this material, deal with the newspapers, and in general conduct bona fide advertising departments.

Budgeting for branch store advertising can be done in several ways. One method is to follow the main store budgeting procedure on a scaled-down plan. That is, a separate store budget, broken down by divisions and by months. Another, is to permit the divisional merchandise men, with top management approval, to decide how much of their multiple-store budget they want to spend on the branch stores.

The buyer's responsibility, however, remains unchanged, no matter what the procedure may be for handling branch advertising in the store. It is his responsibility to see that the sales promotion division at the main store and the personnel in his department at the branches are kept informed about the merchandise to be advertised and its presence or absence at each individual branch.

Radio and Television. Radio and television still appear to remain somewhat of an enigma to the retail industry. With newspaper and direct mail costs continuing a steady upward trend, especially in recent years, it is not through lack of desire on the part of most major retailers that this is so.

Sizable retailers in many large cities have attempted to use radio and television yet have either utterly failed or have allowed their total advertising budget in these media to drop down to less than five per cent. A limited few have demonstrated the rare ability to handle these media and have persevered, apparently at least to their own satisfaction. Be this as it may, the vast majority of retailers today spend a very nominal part of their total advertising budget in radio and television, often settling for a limited regular schedule of "spots", plus a "flurry" of the same to fortify a particularly large storewide effort in the newspapers.

The truth is that there are no easy solutions or magic formulae to the proper and economic use of these media in retailing today—certainly not in the sense that newspaper lineage is bought and exploited in almost every store in the country. There are signs, however, that progress is being made—and progress will not be denied. Nevertheless, it still remains the number one challenge to the country's sales promotion experts, and to the television and radio industries, if you will, to come up with the answers, definite, provable techniques, that will deliver to the retailing industry as a whole the sales advantage and economic growth which must be there for the taking. The wise buyer will watch developments in this area and keep alert to opportunities for his own department's merchandise in these media.

Credit Promotion. Volumes have been written by experts on the subject of credit promotion. It would be presumptuous to assume that one could adequately cover the subject in a few paragraphs, or even pages, in this chapter on sales promotion.

As a buyer, it is essential to your success that you fully recognize and appreciate the power of credit as an aid to getting additional business. Next, take the time to inform yourself of the various customer credit plans offered by your store. Seek out the ones which best serve the particular needs of your customers, then plan to get the maximum in sales from their use.

CHAPTER 35

DISPLAY CAN INCREASE YOUR SALES

BY

ALAN A. WELLS

Do you, as a buyer, obtain all the sales that are available to you through planned display? In all stores and departments, there are always unexploited possibilities. The buyer who is alert to what display can do for him can improve his own departmental performance and his competitive position in the community by utilizing display to the full.

Consider, briefly, the advantages of display:

1. Display involves little merchandise risk.

2. Display is a *daily* sales stimulant for your department, if handled with consistency and imagination.

3. Display operates at *point-of-sale.* If it arouses the interest of the customer, she can immediately satisfy it.

4. Nothing presents your merchandise more perfectly: it is "live," in color, frequently in assortments.

5. Window displays can at times attract as many viewers as an ad would, at a fraction of its cost.

6. Interior displays in your department or elsewhere in the store, appeal to your most eligible prospects, the people who are already in the store.

7. Display involves only modest charges, often none.

In the light of these advantages, it seems reasonable to suggest that every buyer give at least as much time to display as to advertising. A buyer who seeks to harness the power of display will buy a few pieces of merchandise expressly for window or departmental set-up. He will devise unit or assortment displays, and arrange his merchandise in ways to stimulate impulse buying. He will give real attention to the signs that go into his displays, making sure that they incorporate information and salesmanship. He will give his department a fresh and inviting air by changing his displays every few days.

Working with Display Director. In a store where a sales promotion manager (or equivalent) and a display director are functioning, there is certainly a display program that schedules windows, interior tie-ups with major events, seasonal store dress-up, special events of various types, and periodic freshening of departments. All of these move on schedule—except the departmental dress-up. Even in stores where a member of the display department is assigned to a floor or group of related floors, it will still be impossible for a display staffer to work in each department often enough to maintain the desired standards. A portion of the responsibility, then, remains with the buyer.

In smaller stores with smaller staffs, or in shops that employ free lances or rely upon the best efforts of their managers, the situation is the same: departmental display does not receive sufficiently frequent attention.

In such a case some expedient should be devised by the buyer, with his management's approval, to correct this situation as far as possible. A common solution is to assign responsibility for departmental displays to an assistant buyer or head of stock or salesperson who shows aptitude.

Duties of Display Aides. For those persons assigned to work on a department's own displays, the buyer should lay down guidelines, letting them know exactly what is expected of them, and why. For example:

1. Dust or polish every morning without fail. Nothing is so disenchanting to the customer as the lack of cleanliness.

2. Straighten and "perk up" display merchandise, especial-

ly when overnight covers have been removed. Replace anything wrinkled or soiled.

3. Several times a day, check merchandise displays that are open for customer selection. The more interested people are in the merchandise, the more likely they are to handle it and disarrange the display. Restore everything to good order as often as customer traffic permits.

4. When merchandise has been sold from a display, replace the exact style and color, if possible. It is important to preserve the fashion or color theme that may have been established by the original arrangement. If a duplicate is not available, consult Mr. X (name of person or persons qualified to decide.)

5. Within the limits of Point 4, change displayed merchandise at least once a week.

6. Report at once any fixtures that are broken, chipped, scratched, discolored, or dirty.

7. Do not clutter a display area, like a ledge, with boxes, books, odd pieces of merchandise.

8. Do not use manufacturers' displays or fixtures without approval.

Getting Maximum Results. The buyer or merchandiser who realizes what good display can do to increase sales will actively cooperate with the store's display department. This is what he should do:

1. Notify the display director every time he buys something new or striking. *Show it to him.* Creative people are alert to ideas, are actively looking for them. Your merchandise may fit into some current project, or it may be sufficiently exciting in itself to inspire the display manager to build a window around it.

2. When you intend to feature a number, particularly in a window, be sure to buy enough pieces to make a strong display—to show that, for example, the style comes in three colors, or the color in three styles.

3. Buy a few pieces occasionally for their display interest alone: a novelty in your field, a color you would not stock in

depth, a lush item above your regular top price line. You may end up selling them without profit but, to your department and to your store, their attention value will be worth many times their cost in markdowns.

4. Make lists (and keep them in a designated place!) of merchandise from your department that is shown in windows. Put down price, size of displayed items, other sizes and colors available, whether orderable. When a display develops a prospect, let your department be ready!

5. Give the sign writer enough information to prepare an informative or provocative sign that lends point to your display. Try especially to provide the specification most often requested by customers, or an "idea" line that tells the benefit of owning the merchandise.

6. When an ad breaks or a window is opened for your department, have a prominent showing of the same merchandise within the department itself.

7. Make a record of display results, just as you do of advertising response, and for the same reason; for future guidance in selecting items to be featured.

Store Policy in Display. Any suggestions offered to the buyer must be considered in the light of his own store's policies and regulations. In display, as in every other function, one store's objectives may be quite unlike those of another.

Some stores, for example, expect their windows to be primarily a "front" to proclaim the character of the business. Sales of the displayed pieces are a secondary consideration in such cases. A typical window of this type may show only one or two pieces of merchandise, generally as they would appear in use, and in a contemporary, or historical, or fanciful setting. Prices may be omitted.

Other stores aim to obtain direct sales from window displays. Therefore, they generally show more units of merchandise per window, indicate the prices of each article, and possibly feature price.

Store policy directs which extreme, or which point between

the two extremes, is to be adopted. Since windows should con-scientiously and consistently project the ideas that manage-ment wishes to convey, the buyer's plans for window merchan-dise must be within that framework.

Other Window Policies. Some stores are quick to take into account in their windows the current weather—heat, cold, rain, snow. This usually attracts favorable attention to the store, as do tie-ins with city-wide events. The buyer's window plans should be attuned to store policy in these respects, too. If his store is quick-moving, he should be so, too, and ready with appropriate merchandise at short notice.

The question of whether or not to use windows for tie-up with advertising is also one for store policy, rather than the buyer, to settle. Many managements ban sale merchandise from the windows, aside from storewide and traditional pro-motions. Their decision is based on the logical argument that each selling medium should do its own job, and that duplica-tion of media is wasteful. Other managements have a different view. They claim, especially in promotional stores, that *plus* sales can be achieved by *concurrent* use of media. Experiment-ing in individual instances indicates which is better.

Store Policy and Interior Display. Store policy and practice naturally affect interior display, and this has become more ap-parent with the prevalence of self-service of one sort or an-other. In the self-selection area, display is regarded as the Number One selling influence. It provides the merchandise with identity, selling information, persuasion to buy; it can suggest the purchase of second items or encourage a switch in brands. Some merchandise resources, alive to this advantage, spend as much for interior display props and packaging as they do for advertising.

A buyer who wishes his department to move noticeably fast-er or more slowly than others in the store toward self-selection and other forms of interior display must, of course, discuss his plans with his management, so that his department does not differ sharply from its neighbors in its display approach.

Branch Stores. In many cases, only interior display is available in the branch stores, and thus it must carry a double responsibility. The first is that of creating a store impression and arousing a desire to come inside, as in case of "open window" architecture. Second, it must offer frequently changed selling messages because its audience visits the store frequently.

To achieve these aims requires better than average display personnel and props—and better than average effort on the part of the buyer.

Branch or main store, however, interior or department display is *selling at the point of sale*—at the spot where a department stands to profit by all the promotional efforts the store has provided in its behalf. A buyer should not content himself with less than the best for his department.

CHAPTER 36

MAIL AND PHONE SELLING

BY

H. H. BENNETT

Not all of a department's sales are made on the selling floor. Some of them will be made by telephone; others, by mail. Both of these avenues of communication have long been important to the department store, in reaching out for business as well as in serving customers who, for one good reason or another, either prefer to or are not able to shop in person.

Today, when the typical department store finds its customers widely scattered and with their time well taken up during business hours, the wise use of mail and telephone facilities becomes an important means of building maximum volume. Although this is true of almost any store or department, it is particularly applicable to stores in congested downtown areas. Even with suburban branches, many such stores find that they are not within easy reach of all of their present and potential customers, and that it behooves them to make shopping at home attractive to customers.

There is also the matter of items of merchandise that, by their very nature, lend themselves to mail and phone ordering. Many customers prefer to order such items in these ways, and expect from the department store the convenience of being able to do just that.

Serving the Customer. Our purpose in this chapter, then, is to show the buyer how he can reach his customer and serve her better by mail and telephone. We are not concerned here with going into the home, literally, to sell her. That subject, in-the-home selling, has a chapter of its own elsewhere in this book.

The emphasis given to mail and telephone, both for receiving orders and for soliciting business, varies from store to store. Some managements invite only minimum use of the mails and telephone, preferring to bend their efforts toward building customer traffic within the store. Others believe that, if people want to shop by mail and telephone, the thing to do is to reach out for that business and learn to handle it profitably and effectively. Mothers of young children, for instance, find it difficult to shop in person even at conveniently located centers, as it is hard to handle a family of little ones during a shopping expedition, or even to get outdoors at all when the weather is inclement.

Store policy will determine the extent to which the buyer applies the suggestions offered in this chapter. If the management finds it too costly to handle mail and telephone orders, selling through these channels should not be pushed beyond limits by any one department.

In the matter of telephone solicitation, management may limit the number of departments that may use this device during a given period, because no customer will welcome a dozen calls a week, each from a different department of the same store, particularly if some of them come at inopportune moments. Also, if telephone solicitation in general is being overdone locally, a department store may decide to cut down its own activity of this type, to avoid reaping the accumulated irritation of customers who have been plagued with phone offers to teach them dancing, shampoo their rugs, slip cover their furniture, and so on.

Personal Following. One of the most familiar forms of mail and telephone selling is the personal following. Notably in departments selling wearing apparel, each salesperson is encouraged to give her name to the customer as well as to maintain a file of information on each customer she has served. Her notes indicate size, style and color preferences, items bought, quantities, etc. From time to time, the salesperson calls or writes her customers, in her own name, to tell them of merchandise that should interest them.

The most successful salespeople make a point of learning the customer's needs and preferences so thoroughly that they can actually select garments for her from the new stock as it comes in. Then they tell her what they think she will like, and invite her in to see the new things—a technique very flattering to the customer and, when it is well done, highly productive of sales and customer loyalty.

When such an operation is applicable, the buyer's responsibility is to keep his salespeople interested in maintaining their lists; to provide them with facilities for keeping orderly records; to point out merchandise suitable for such personal selling; and to make sure that salespeople allot time for making telephone calls or mailing out their personal notices.

Special Solicitation. Many buyers develop lists of special customers whom they advise by mail or phone that they are going into the market. They suggest that they will be happy to look for anything special the customer may have in mind. This technique, too, flatters the customer and shows her that the store is interested in her.

A variation of the personal following idea is adopted in some stores that maintain specially trained telephone solicitors. These salespeople call customers "cold" to tell them about a merchandise offering, an item which sometimes is not even available on the selling floor but is reserved for this one purpose. In the case of personal following, the customer and the salesperson concerned already know one another by name; in "cold selling" they do not. In both cases, however, the store is using the telephone to tell an individual customer about a particular offering in which it hopes she will be interested. Neither type should be overdone, particularly the cold call from a solicitor who is a stranger to the customer.

Departmental Mailings. A department's contacts with its customers through the mails are not always on the person-to-person basis. There may be occasions for mailings on a large scale—for example, from the piece goods department to women who attended a dressmaking school at the store and who are therefore presumed to be interested in sewing. Or there may be lists of people who attended a do-it-yourself show, or a lecture on baby care, or who bought a featured brand of shoes, shirts, hosiery, or bed sheets.

People on such lists may be expected to respond eagerly to notices of special sales in the appropriate departments, or to announcements of new merchandise about to go on sale.

Mailings on such a scale are usually handled by the store's sales promotion department, particularly if they come up year after year—like seasonal clearances, for instance, or back-to-school sales. In the case of well established events of this kind, the buyer's obligation is to contribute a strong merchandise offering and the facts about it.

If there seems to be a niche for a departmental mail event that the established mail events do not take care of, the buyer may originate the suggestion himself.

Branches and Mailings. If a store has branches, the buyer must remember to specify in his mailings whether or not the merchandise is available at the branches, as well as at the downtown store. Even though a mail order form is enclosed, there are always some customers who want to see the goods before they buy, and they should be told where to find it.

Some stores maintain their mailing lists in such a way that a buyer can direct his offer to those areas most likely to contain responsive customers. A garden furniture offering, for instance, would probaly pull more replies from suburban communities than from apartment house developments in the downtown area. A friendly visit to the mailing room will acquaint the buyer with what that department can or cannot do for him by way of selecting his best prospects for each offering.

Store Mailings. Aside from what the department does on its own, there is also the opportunity to participate in store-initiated mailings. In this category, the most familiar example is the statement "stuffer"—the promotional enclosure, often in the form of several offerings, each from a different department —that goes out with the charge account customer's monthly bill.

Whatever may be said for or against the statement enclosure as an advertising medium, the buyer will generally find many of his resources ready to cooperate in such advertising. Often their cooperation will take the form of providing the actual enclosures at nominal cost or at no cost but that of mailing out the material. A maker of stationery may print up an enclosure on one of his newest papers; a sportswear house may provide full-color leaflets on its new line; a shirt house may do an expensive swatching job.

The buyer will also find, however, that many of the other departments of store are eager to have material sent out for them, too. In short, he will meet plenty of competition for a place in the statement envelope, and there may be times when he will count on an enclosure only to be asked at the last minute to step aside for something more urgent from another department.

To avoid disappointment, the buyer's first step is to make sure he has a good item to promote and a clear story to tell about the results that may be expected from it. If he has merchandise, displays, and newspaper advertising all lined up to back the mailing, his chances and his sales results will be better than if he simply asks for a statement enclosure on the grounds that it has been a long time since he last had one.

Catalogues. Stores usually mail special catalogues to customers at Christmas and on such occasions as back-to-school or the opening of a new fashion season. Many of these catalogues are store-wide or division-wide projects, cutting across department lines. Others, however, are one-department affairs— housewares, baby wear, toys, for example.

In store-wide or division-wide catalogues, the buyer has somewhat the same situation with respect to competition from other departments that he has with statement enclosures. The space is usually in big demand and he needs to put in his bid early. He needs to "sell" his item to management for inclusion in the mailing by pointing out its possibilities and his program for coordinating his other selling efforts with the catalogue.

Vendor Participation. Some stores encourage or even insist upon vendor cooperation in these catalogues. The vendor in effect buys advertising space for his product in the store's mailing piece. In such cases, the buyer has the task of selecting the vendors to whom catalogue opportunities will be offered, and of showing them why the catalogue is a worthwhile medium for them. For the vendor, the catalogue represents inexpensive advertising with a virtual guarantee of strong retail cooperation in stocking and displaying his product. For the retailer, such vendor cooperation means better produced, more frequent catalogues than would otherwise be possible.

Other stores discourage vendor participation firmly; they want their buyers to select catalogue items without the possibility of being influenced by a vendor's willingness or unwillingness to pay a share of the costs.

It is up to the buyer to operate within the framework of the policy laid down by his store on this subject, and to understand that policy well enough to make it clear in the market when he has either to request or refuse vendor cooperation in the catalogue.

The importance of the copy itself in selling merchandise by catalogue should not be underestimated. It is worth the buyer's while to study the catalogues of the major mail order companies, to see how much detail they give in a minimum of space. With these examples in mind, he should set down for his own sales promotion department every fact and selling point about his merchandise, so that his store's copy writers can do right by his item.

Mail and Telephone Orders. In addition to what the store or department may do by way of direct mail, the department will receive mail and telephone orders from other sources. Customers take it for granted that anything advertised by a department store in their local papers can be ordered by mail or phone—so much so that, in the case of clearances and odd lots, stores find it necessary to specify in their advertisements that they will not accept mail and telephone orders on items where this is the case. This also avoids disappointing customers who come in personally to buy, only to find that the merchandise has been sold out to telephone and mail customers.

When a box or other device in a newspaper ad, or an order blank in a catalogue, invites the customer to mail in her order, care should be taken that the order form provides space for complete information. Not only should there be space for style, size, color, etc., but there should be provision for a second or even third choice in case the customer's Number One choice is sold out.

The precautions that are taken to insure accuracy and completeness on customer orders, together with proper care in the filling of those orders, will go far to keep returns to a minimum. A large percentage of returns usually means an unprofitable operation.

To facilitate telephone ordering, all merchandise advertisements, whether newspaper or direct mail, should show the store's telephone order number, so that the customer can pick up the phone and place her order without searching through the directory.

Buyer's Responsibility. On any advertised item, the buyer has a special responsibility to see that his stock is adequate and can be filled in quickly. This responsibility is particularly serious when the customer is invited to buy by mail or telephone. If the buyer has grossly underestimated his needs and the customer must wait weeks for her order, the store's prestige is certain to suffer. Besides, the longer it takes to fill orders, the the greater the chance of "don't wants", "changed mind", etc.

Customers who come into the store for one item often walk out with an entirely different one instead, even if the one they originally planned to buy is actually in stock. Customers who order from their homes, however, know only about the advertised item. That is the one they order, and that is the one the store has to supply. Rather than risk being sold out of an item before the mail and telephone orders come in, the buyer should set aside a reserve stock just for this purpose.

Serving the Telephone Customer. Many stores go a long way to encourage the customer to place her order by telephone. Some have their order boards open on Sundays, so that the customer, leafing through the newspaper and having the impulse to respond, can place an order.

Another aid to the telephone customer is featured by some stores that reach out for business from areas beyond the range of local calls. These stores establish suburban telephone numbers, and in their advertising invite customers to place their orders through the suburban number at the cost of a local call, instead of using the store's regular number and paying a toll charge.

Not every store reaches out in these ways for telephone business, but the fact that some do this has the effect of making the customer increasingly conscious of the telephone as a means of placing her order with any and all department stores. It also means that, whether or not the buyer's own advertising specifically solicits telephone orders, he must be prepared for them. They are likely to come in any case.

Briefing the Telephone Operators. The buyer may at times find that his advertisement cannot answer all the questions that may come up in the customer's mind. For example, if a garment is advertised as available in small, medium, and large sizes, some customers may ask if it also comes in extra-large.

If there is room for such questions in the customer's mind, the telephone operator should be briefed with whatever additional facts may be needed. This is particularly important if the board is open on Sundays or at other times when the store itself is closed and there is no one in the department to answer a question.

Selling Additional Items. The incoming telephone call, whether or not it is in response to an advertisement, is *an excellent opportunity for suggesting additional items.* Some stores have achieved splendid results by training their order board girls to suggest any item that is on special sale, regardless of what item prompted the customer originally to make the call. Thus, if the hosiery department is having its semi-annual promotion, the operators will mention hosiery to everyone who calls; if a particular blanket is being featured, they will mention the blanket.

The buyer, then, will seek this help from the telephone staff when he has a major event involving an item susceptible to this treatment. And, when an item from his department is to be featured in this way, he will make sure that the girls on the order board know all about it and share his enthusiasm for it. Just as the departmental salespeople need to be enthused with the facts on the eve of an important promotion, and need to know what is advertised, so do the telephone sellers.

Telephone Technique. In many stores, some or all of the telephone orders go directly to the department for handling. In such cases, the salespeople need briefing not only on what to say about the merchandise, but also on how to handle telephone calls generally. A part of the buyer's job is to coach his own selling staff in suggesting second items to telephone customers—not only how to make the suggestion, but what to suggest.

If something new has just come into the department, or if a staple item is on sale at a special price, it can be made a matter of routine to mention that item to each telephone customer.

A type of call to which the department must be particularly alert is the one that comes as a result of having seen a magazine or other advertisement of a manufacturer's new product "at all good stores." The customer who is prompted to buy it may call first her favorite department store. If it has the item, she credits the store with being wide awake. (The buyer will of course have been tipped off to this by the manufacturer, and the department alerted accordingly.)

But what if the item isn't in stock? The wise buyer makes

sure that his people know about it and coaches them in what to say to customers who ask in person or by telephone for it. If the item is on order, they should know when it is expected and whether or not to accept orders for delivery when the stock arrives. If the buyer does not intend to carry the item, or if by chance it is carried as an exclusive in a competing store, they should be told of any similar item that can be suggested in its place.

What Items to Offer. In discussions of mail and telephone selling, one often hears questions as to what items are suitable for featuring in this way. From one store that has been highly successful in this special field comes the suggestion that housedresses and inexpensive daytime dresses have proved good. So have sheets, cases and other household linens; cosmetics and toiletries; soaps, housewares, lingerie, notions, men's and boys' items; curtains, stationery.

It is not always possible, by any set rule, to predict results of mail and phone order solicitations. The buyer, merchandise manager, and sales promotion manager discuss each item that is suggested and decide jointly on its suitability. In one store, the executive who supervises the handling of mail and telephone orders sits in on these conferences, and his advice has helped to increase volume and decrease returns.

Customer returns or refusals (if conspicuously high compared with those for mail and telephone orders generally at that store) are an index of the unsuitability of an item for mail or telephone featuring.

Some stores place a minimum limit on the unit price of any items offered for sale by mail or phone. This is generally done to avoid having the cost of delivery out of proportion to the item's retail.

Limitations are also placed on lowest or highest retail prices for mail order in terms of actual store or departmental experience with customer response to advertised offers. Sometimes certain prices produce better response than others; sometimes those above or below certain points are poor producers. In large cities where several papers are published, the prices that bring good response may be different from one newspaper to another. Experience teaches the buyer and his superiors what to expect.

Study Results. The buyer should carefully study his records of mail and telephone orders, item by item. The information will help him gauge his needs for this special field of selling, and it will sharpen his perceptions in selecting or rejecting items for this purpose.

Above all, the study of his own records and those of other departments will help him to understand a very important customer—the one who has demonstrated her confidence in the store by mailing or telephoning her orders to it. She is a customer well worth cultivating, and it is up to the buyer to analyze her needs and to see that she gets helpful service from his department at all times.

CHAPTER 37

WHAT THE BUYER SHOULD KNOW ABOUT CREDIT

BY

R. M. GRINAGER

Credit in today's consumer society, in one way or another, touches practically every person over 21 years of age. It is one of the main cogs in the machinery of our consumer economy because it makes it possible for a person to buy needed goods and services when wanted—all at once, and to use them while paying for them out of income.

We, as merchants, are naturally interested in credit as a help, or aid, to selling. It is well for the merchant to understand mercantile credit also, but our purpose here is simply to acquaint the buyer with how consumer credit is used in department stores and specialty shops today.

People use credit to get what they want—when they want it. They could use it, for instance, to buy what you offer for sale. Therefore you should understand what prompts a customer to use credit, or to decide not to do so. Without that understanding, your sales and profits will be less than they could be.

Brief History of Credit. Although many think of credit, especially in retail stores, as a modern merchandising innovation, records have been found of credit transactions entered on clay tablets in the Biblical city of Ur, which dates back to 2000 B.C. Colonial shops in America used credit to tide farmers over until they harvested their fall crops. Daniel Webster recognized the importance of credit. He said, "Credit has done a thousand times more to enrich mankind than all the gold mines of the world. It has exalted labor, stimulated manufacturing, and pushed commerce over every sea."

As far back as credit may date, it took modern methods to make possible the role it plays in American life today. A person need only go into a modern credit office to realize that old-fashioned methods could never begin to handle the immense volume that retailers now consider everyday routine business.

Credit and the Economy. Credit is a way of putting the good and useful things of life within the reach of the average person. It has given him what kings and dictators have promised for centuries but have never been able to deliver. By contrasting the American standard of living with that of any other country in the world, we can see clearly what credit—as a tool for buying and selling—can accomplish.

It is difficult to realize just how much credit has enabled us to add in terms of extra retail volume. The growth of sales on credit by department stores since World War II has been fantastic, and has reached the point where stores make from 60 to 75 per cent of all sales on some form of credit. This ratio continues to increase.

Credit has become essential to the merchant as a tool for selling, and to the consumer as a tool for buying. To our customers, it is a way of getting things when needed and paying for them when convenient.

Why People Use Credit. It is significant for you, as a buyer, to realize that people will in many cases buy needed items before they actually have the money to pay for them. Thus we compete with other sellers not only for the money the customer has in his hand, but also for his future earnings—the dollars that he will pay out of his income in future weeks and months. In a very real sense, this puts the department store in competition with the auto dealer, the home improvement contractor, and others for the dollars the consumer will earn.

As a buyer, you seek to understand what prompts a customer to buy a refrigerator, or a mink stole, or any other item in your inventory. You should also understand what motivates people to make purchases on credit. Here are some of the reasons that customers have given for using credit:

1. Charge accounts make shopping easier and more convenient.

2. Charge accounts enable one to establish a credit rating.

3. A charge account allows one to buy without readily available funds.

4. A charge account eliminates the need to carry cash and the fear of losing it.

5. A charge account makes it easier to exchange items and return purchases.

6. A charge account enables an easier and better budget and provides a record of purchases and payments.

7. A charge account makes telephone and mail order shopping more convenient.

8. Credit plates are good identification for cashing checks and in emergency business transactions.

9. A charge account is a mark of prestige, a status symbol.

10. A charge account identifies one as a regular customer, thus assuring better service.

11. Charge account customers receive advance notices of special sales.

Customers also tell us that they like charge accounts because, with them, they can avoid layaway deposits, avoid the writing of numerous checks, avoid C.O.D. fees and staying home to wait for deliveries, and avoid "Asking my husband for the money."

Other customers like charge accounts for such advantages as ease in cashing checks, a close feeling of relationship with the store and the ability to take advantage of bargains. People also open charge accounts because the store is close, parking is free, the personnel is competent, delivery is free, or even, "I can pay my gas bill there."

Why People Do Not Use Credit. In spite of the popular acceptance of credit in general, there are still those who do not like to use it. As a merchant or buyer, you should recognize that there are customers who believe:

1. A charge account makes buying too convenient, too easy.
2. Charge accounts are only for those who have full time work or substantial incomes.
3. It is better to wait and pay cash.
4. It is improper to go into debt.
5. Service charges are an expense.
6. There is danger of losing one's credit identification and the possibility of having others use it.
7. Customers tend to shop only the stores where they have charge accounts, and often miss bargains at others.
8. Some stores ask too many personal questions on credit application.
9. "I don't want too many charge accounts. One or two is all right."
10. "I object to carrying a whole bag of credit plates."
11. "My husband objects, even though he likes to charge himself."

Understanding the Customer. Perhaps some of these reasons for or against charge accounts are not logical. But who can say your customer makes a logical decision in buying a pink dress instead of a red one, or two chairs instead of a sofa?

Certainly your experience has already told you that customer logic is often fallacious, inconsistent, irrelevant, capricious, transparent—but absolutely irrefutable. And the customer is always right—misinformed, perhaps, inexact, bull-headed, fickle, and ignorant—but never wrong.

In other words, you may not agree with the logic the customer uses to reach a decision as to whether or not to open an account or buy your merchandise, *but you had better understand it in order to cope with the problems of retailing.*

Why Credit Is Extended. In general, credit is used in the retail field to increase the sale of merchandise and to render customer service. Regardless of how you may define credit sales promotion or use credit in your particular business, the successful efforts in that area boil down to *using credit to sell more.*

You should not lose sight of your goal: profitable sales. The charge customer can and usually does buy more. There is a bond of relationship between the charge customer and the store from which she gets a regular monthly bill. Tests have shown that shoppers tend to read the advertising of stores with which they have accounts, and to think of these stores first when a need occurs.

Two out of three people your store or department sells *now buy on some form of credit.* The number of credit customers and the percentage of credit sales are constantly increasing.

Credit And the Salespeople. The most capable and the most experienced salespeople suggest credit often, because they find it a good tool for making a sale or closing a transaction. You, as a merchant, will be working with salespeople and should direct them in using credit in their everyday selling—in addition to your own use of it when planning promotions, displays, advertising, etc.

Salespeople should be reminded that it is to their advantage to suggest charging or opening a charge account because:

1. Customers like shopping with credit plates. It is convenient and pleasant.

2. Customers like to pay for purchases out of earnings without disturbing their savings.

3. Many customers are on budgets or allowances; they plan carefully and like to keep records.

4. Customers want to take advantage of bargains, buy what they want, when they need it, at the most advantageous price.

5. Customers do not like to stay home and wait for deliveries or pay C.O.D. fees.

Salespeople should also be made to understand that credit helps them sell more and faster, makes their jobs easier, because:

1. Customers shop in stores where they have accounts and read the ads of these stores first.

2. Credit makes closing easy when the salesman has determined what the customer wants and should have, and the salesperson suggests a practical payment plan.

3. Credit makes it easier to achieve higher unit sales: two, a set, a dozen, a higher priced item.

4. Credit makes possible the impulse sale to the customer who came unprepared to buy.

Good salespeople listen for clues and suggest credit when it helps close or increase a sale. Typical openings are: "I like this, but frankly I am not prepared to buy it today." "A pair would look so nice . . ." "I would rather have this but, if I buy these I will need a bag to match." "It is difficult to decide between these. I would like to have them both." "This is what I like, but it is more than I can spend."

Most stores lose hundreds of sales daily for lack of a timely credit suggestion. This can be avoided if you train and encourage your salespeople to suggest credit.

Knowing Your Credit Department. There is nothing complicated or mysterious about the operation of the credit department. A visit to the one in your store will undoubtedly be enlightening. Get acquainted with your credit manager. Ask him to take you through his office and show you how accounts are opened, approved, and how purchases are authorized.

You will soon realize that the credit department is an integral part of the store's selling program. Its goal, like that of your own department, is profitable sales with minimum expenses and losses. And more than anyone else, it wants good customer relationships. Anything else comes back in the form of complaints and adjustments.

Your credit department is not fighting for the biggest list of credit customers in town, or the widest distribution of credit plates, or the greatest percentage of credit sales to total volume. The end goal of credit efforts is *sales—and a profit*—and nothing else.

Knowing Credit Policies And Plans. Every buyer or merchant should know what credit plans are available at his store and should be able to suggest how easily an account can be opened, or to suggest the exactly right credit plan for a particular customer. It is not necessary to know all the details of the credit operation, but one should know enough to answer questions intelligently and to see that salespeople are making the most advantageous use of the store's facilities. It is important to know *terms,* and what types of merchandise are sold on credit in stores which do not make it available for all.

Most stores today have formalized credit policies, just as they have merchandise and adjustment policies. Familiarize yourself with these, because this will benefit you when making decisions involving your advertising, promotions, sales, etc.

It will also help you to understand the store's requirements for credit, why and how credit transactions are authorized, and why certain safeguards are necessary to prevent losses, bad debts, fraud, delinquencies, etc. For, after all, no sale is ever completed until the total cost has been paid in full.

Get to understand, too, why approvals are sometimes delayed. By so doing, you will probably be able to help in speeding up authorizations for transactions that might otherwise be held up.

Conclusion. As a merchant, it is your job to sell. The majority of sales in department and specialty stores today are made on some form of credit. The credit customer can and does buy more and cherishes a bond of relationship with the store that does not exist between the store and its cash customers. Your store's list of charge customers is your best list of prospects for additional business. These are customers you know well. You are familiar with their ability to purchase and their paying habits. These are the people you should be glad to have simply say, "Charge it, please." So long as our factories can produce goods that people want to buy, and so long as people can be motivated to buy these goods, credit is your most useful tool for selling. Use it wisely!

CHAPTER 38

TRAFFIC, RECEIVING, AND MARKING

BY

E. H. WABLER

The larger department or specialty store provides its merchandising staff with centralized facilities for traffic, receiving, and marking. It is the purpose of this chapter to explain how buyers can use these expert facilities wisely and for the greatest benefit of both the individual selling department and the store as a whole.

Traffic. Transportation has become so intricate and its cost has become so formidable that the possibilities for speed and savings challenge even the expert retail traffic manager. No buyer can, in addition to his other duties, be familiar with the ever-changing transportation field, nor can the average vendor know or employ a traffic expert who knows the best routes and schedules to the hundreds of points to which the company's product is shipped. (NRMA provides a shipping instruction service for smaller stores unable to employ a traffic manager. This service is provided at a nominal cost to members and brings about real economy and savings in transportation costs.)

From his day to day experience, however, the retail traffic manager is familiar with the desirable routes and existing schedules between the great majority of shipping points and the store. Constant use of the traffic department's advice on shipping becomes an important part of the buyer's duties if the departmental charges for transportation are not to impair the final profit materially.

Transportation levels rose rapidly after the end of World

War II; so did the prices of many kinds of merchandise. But whereas merchandise prices may rise and fall with economic adjustment, higher transportation rate levels, once established, are generally regarded as reasonably permanent. The lower the cost and retail selling price of a department's merchandise, the greater the percentagewise effect of transportation costs.

Transportation Rates and Profits. The effect of transportation rates upon profit is readily demonstrated by a simple example. Assume an article weighing six ounces, plus two ounces of packing material; it then weighs one-half pound for shipping purposes. It is traveling in a shipment of more than 100 pounds and is coming to the store from a distance of about 650 miles. It will retail at $2.50—a selling price based on a 40 per cent markon.

The freight rate for our hypothetical shipment will be $6.33 (per 100 pounds) or 3.165 cents for each article. This will represent 1.266 per cent of the retail selling price and will reduce the 40 per cent markon to 38.72 per cent. By express, the same shipment will be subject to a rate of $9.35 per 100 pounds, or 4.675 cents for each article. This will represent 1.87 per cent of the retail selling price, and will bring the 40 per cent markon down to 38.1 per cent.

Rates that prevailed years before might have been perhaps half as high and their effect on a $2.50 retailer would have been correspondingly smaller. Even then management was interested in seeing that its transportation dollars were not spent unwisely. Buyers were urged then, as they are now, to safeguard the profits of their departments by *working closely with their traffic managers on routings*. Rate increases make it more important today than it was then.

Point of Origin. To obtain best results from the store's traffic department, it is necessary to know the point or points from which each vendor ships. Although he maintains offices or even a factory in New York City, a vendor may also ship from distant points off the main transportation arteries located in New England, the Carolinas, Texas, or the deep South.

It is of extreme importance that the buyer ask for the "shipping point" and show this on the store copy of the order form. Increasing vendor use of factories located away from central market areas and main line points of supply makes this information important—especially so if delay in transit or some other emergency should require the store's traffic department to trace the shipment.

When a new shipping point is named by a vendor, the buyer should take the order to the traffic manager as soon as he returns from the market and have a routing designated by the traffic department and sent to the vendor. Two different freight routings from the same shipping point may vary as much as ten days in time in transit; two ways of air shipping may differ widely in cost, yet both may use the same planes.

For best possible service, the store's own traffic manager should be consulted about each new point of origin.

On some occasions, the buyer may find that the vendor ships from a far distant point. As transportation rates are largely based on distance, the buyer may discover, through discussion with the traffic department, that a *retail price higher than originally planned* will be necessary for the profitable sale of merchandise bearing such an unusual transportation expense.

Knowing that, the buyer may try to locate a resource for similar merchandise that can be shipped from a nearer origin point, with a correspondingly lower transportation cost.

Special Shipping Problems. There are many other situations that can arise, either at the market or in the store, that are best handled by consulting the traffic manager promptly.

A common one, for example, is that of the special promotion for which large purchases are made. Just as the advertising schedule is made out to dovetail with the buying plans, it is important to plan the transportation well in advance of the shipping time, too. To wait for the very last minute before consulting the traffic department sometimes means risking that appalling situation in which advertisement appears but the merchandise to support it is still in transit.

Perhaps there is some emergency that calls for special speed, or perhaps there are floods or other causes of delay along the store's usual shipping route. Particularly in such cases, neither the buyer nor the vendor should route the shipment. The traffic manager is familiar with current transportation blocks and with ways to handle them. By a simple telephone call, he may protect an express shipment so that no delay occurs at transfer points along the way. Or he may route a shipment by air rather than overland.

On the other hand, if a shipment would normally go by air, the traffic manager at the store may know that either the originating or terminal airport is closed by foul weather, and he may find other shipping channels to get the goods quickly to the store.

Even though the buyer is in the market when urgent shipping questions arise, he should nevertheless refer these problems to his traffic department. He will usually find it much cheaper to telephone or telegraph his store than to risk needless shipping costs and delays.

The Packing House. Packing houses, or package consolidating agencies, have long been important in the New York shipping scene. Their existence and profitable use by the department stores are due to the fact that the carriers have minimum weights per shipment; shipments below that minimum weight travel at no reduction in cost because of their small size. If several light shipments from the same city can be consolidated into a single shipment there is a distinct saving.

For example: Minimum freight charges are sometimes based on 100 pounds. If such is the case, *a 33-pound shipment would cost as much as one of 100 pounds.* Three such shipments, however, combined into one lot, would weigh 99 pounds and the charge would still be the same as for one of them.

Another example: The Railway Express minimum on a five-pound package forwarded about 650 miles is $3.00. Twenty packages of the same weight, if separately shipped, would cost $60.00. If delivered to a packing house and combined in a single shipment of 100 pounds, *they would be carried at the 100-pound rate, or $9.35.* The packing house charges 18 cents a package for its service, or $3.60 on this shipment. That would make the total $12.95, or a saving of $47.05 over the cost of transporting 20 separate five-pound shipments.

Non-Monetary Considerations. The packing house has another advantage, aside from the money it saves. Its output is large enough to justify direct delivery of its shipments to the rail terminal. Separate small shipments clear through Railway Express Agency's sorting terminals which, though remarkable operations, cannot possibly compete in speed with the packing house's direct haul to the carrying railroad.

The packing house also has its disadvantages. Its closing deadline is usually five or six o'clock, and the vendor's truckman must deliver shipments to it before that time. On the other hand, the pickup wagons of the Railway Express Company accept shipments long after the packing house deadlines and, of course, much later than the time when the vendor's truck must start out for the packing house.

The over-all packing house advantages, however, far outweigh this later Railway Express Agency pickup, and the buyer should insist on the vendor's compliance with the store's shipping instructions.

If he has any doubt about the value of consolidating packages, or if he has trouble making it clear to vendors why they should comply with the store's request, it will be worth his while to visit the store's traffic manager and to make a brief study of the express arrival records. They will provide him with ample data to make his point in the market.

Receiving. Experience has shown that the widely varying receiving loads of the store departments (which make up the store) are most economically handled by a centrally supervised group of checkers. The central receiving department makes sure that the exact quantities and style numbers shown on the invoice have been received at the store.

The receiving process assures that loss and damage to merchandise in transit will be discovered and claimed from the carrying agency for credit to the selling department. It also protects the selling department from loss because of a vendor's poor packing, omission or style substitution, and maintains a system to charge such losses or substitutions to the vendor instead of letting them contribute to inventory shortages.

The average receiving room operates most smoothly when it has a backlog of merchandise not needed on the exact day of its arrival. In his daily receiving room contacts, therefore, the buyer or assistant should indicate not only those shipments wanted for immediate selling, but also any that are not immediately needed and can be held aside until the more urgent ones have been checked.

In their dealings with the receiving department, it is well for the buying staff to consider that a good portion of the pressure in the receiving room is due to the fact that fast receiving service is expected to compensate, if possible, for late placement of orders, vendor delays in delivery, and delays in transit.

Buyers and merchandise managers, endeavoring to hold down the month-end stock total, often require vendor delivery of merchandise just after the month's closing. Such peak loads are frequently a source of added payroll expense in the receiving department, and they do not always result in favorable store personnel relationships. Whenever it can be done, buying plans should so be made as to level the receiving room's peaks rather than to emphasize them.

It is also a good idea to discuss with the receiving manager and with the checkers who serve the department any exceptionally large volume of purchases. This will let the receiving department gauge the unusual service requirements that are coming up and plan in advance to cover the heavier than ordinary load of work. It will also make them partners in the adventure and as anxious as the buyer for its success.

For some departments, the receiving room may handle order control or other recording functions. In such cases, the buyer or assistant should attend the requirements of these services promptly in his daily visits to the receiving room. Courteous, friendly, businesslike conduct pays dividends in the service departments just as it does on the selling floor or in the market.

Marking. In the light of present day recording and stock control, price marking has become an important field in its own right. Simply attaching a price ticket to an article no longer constitutes good marking. The type of ticket selected should fit the article, should carry a standard arrangement of the necessary information, and should be so located on the merchandise as to promote the sale by making it easy for sales-people and customers to find the facts quickly.

In apparel departments, the use of different ticket colors for each size has been found to simplify selling, stock keeping, and stock control recording. In other departments, like stationery or notions, where the unit price may be only a few pennies, marking may be eliminated altogether.

If there is no definite, published marking plan for his department's merchandise, the buyer and marking supervisor should study each article sold in the department and decide upon the ideal price marking for each. The plan should cover the marking spot on each article, the most desirable price ticket for it, and the minimum data necessary. Later, if changes seem advisable, the buyer should again take up the problem with the marking supervisor.

Planned arrivals of unusual volume should be discussed with the marking supervisor, just as with the receiving manager, so that plans can be made in advance for handling the merchandise expeditiously. Within a large store's marking room are several specialized groups, some of whom are adept at machine marking; others, at hand marking. Some are trained to handle bulk wares; others, to handle lines like jewelry, hosiery, or fine underwear.

Since those skilled at one kind of marking are not necessarily efficient at other types, the supervisor has to have enough markers with the needed skills ready to handle the shipments when they arrive.

If the buyer expects merchandise that he must personally see in order to assign retail prices to it, he should visit the marking room more than once each day. This practice will give his department faster service by avoiding delays in putting his goods into work, and it will also help the marking supervisor arrange to have a smooth flow of work for each of the specialized skills among his markers.

When remarking is to be done, either on the selling floor or in the marking room, the buyer or assistant should have the marker verify the quantities and prices on the price-change memorandum. This practice will help diminish inventory shortages and is just as important in that respect as the rejection of longhand price marking by the wrapping and inspection service.

The more conscientious the buyer is about his marking room duties and about the proper retailing of his invoices, the more likely he is both to get his merchandise to the selling floor quickly and to keep avoidable types of inventory shortage from creeping in.

Unit Packing. Many articles sold in department stores are most easily and profitably handled when unit-packed by the vendor in cardboard or corrugated containers that provide protection from soiling and breakage during stockroom handling and delivery.

Being designed especially for the article, the vendor's pack usually opens up in the customer's home much more attractively than if the article had been boxed or wrapped in the store. Furthermore, unit packages are more easily handled through receiving and stock rooms than bulk packed items.

Some buyers avoid purchasing unit-packed merchandise,

for which the vendor usually makes an additional charge, if the cost of such packing is charged to the cost of merchandise in the selling department. Yet if factory unit packing saves labor costs and breakage at the store, it is only reasonable that the packing be charged to the department that benefits directly.

Items like soft wares may sometimes be satisfactorily unit-packed in heavy glazed cardboard boxes. In fact, some mills use these boxes for standard packing without making an additional charge. The cost, however, is obviously included in the billed price even when it is not shown on the invoice as a separate item.

Buyers whose merchandise lends itself to unit packing should make a thorough study of its possibilities. They will probably find, as many departments have already found, that unit packing promotes salescheck filling and dispatch in the stockroom or warehouse, that it frequently helps solve stockroom and receiving room space problems, and that its savings and advantages far exceed the cost.

Invoice Routine. Among the methods and systems used in department store practice, perhaps the widest variations are those connected with invoice routine.

Common to all these varieties, however, is the constant demand that the buyer sign, pass, or clear the invoice to the office for entry. The repetition of this request may become very tiresome to the busy buyer, but it is important beyond the mere clearance of the invoice file.

The prompt and proper recording of all purchases is highly important to top management. The figures compiled on the various departments are needed to formulate financial budgets, make promotional plans, and guide merchandising. Prompt and accurate reports are possible only when all purchase invoices are cleared without delay.

Purchases withheld from the record render this year's figures misleading and next year's efforts toward minimum stocks just that much more difficult to achieve.

Vendor Relations. Should differences arise between the traffic department and a vendor, the buyer would be wise to remain in the background while the traffic department and the vendor straighten things out.

In the case of merchandise returns, on the other hand, the buyer will want to put himself prominently into the picture. He may rely on the traffic department to remove retail price tickets from the merchandise, and to pack it neatly and ship it wisely. But he himself has the responsibility of sending a pleasant letter ahead of the shipment, letting the vendor know the reason for the return.

If a return is made because the vendor is at fault in some way, it is customary for return transportation to be charged to him. The store usually bears the cost, however, in the return of memorandum goods, returns accepted as an accommodation to the store, and in transactions where the situation is delicate—as, for example, if the buyer has overestimated his needs of a particular item, or size, or color, and the vendor has agreed to help him out by accepting a return.

The traffic department cannot hope to know the background of every return or claim upon a vendor that it handles for the various selling departments. To make sure that the transportation charges are handled in fairness to both store and vendor, the buyer's best course is to tell the traffic department about any unusual situations, so that it can lend its assistance in protecting the store's and the buyer's standing in the market.

CHAPTER 39

THE FUNCTION OF RETAIL RESEARCH

BY

ALFRED H. GUTTMAN

Retail research in a department store is probably the least known, the least definite, and the least established function to be described in this manual.

The term *retail research* itself is somewhat misleading because the word *research* has too theoretical, too distant, too impractical a sound for this fast moving, empirical business. The word *research* fails to imply the function of *solving* in addition to that of *investigating*.

In addition, the term *retail* is also misleading because the areas to be investigated and solved range from retailing questions to questions of production and expense and physical handling of merchandise. Other terms such as *planning, methods, systems* have been used to designate this staff work but since none of the alternatives supplies a more accurate or more complete description, many stores use the term, research.

The Need for Research. To appreciate the need for retail research, one must understand that retailing is a highly competitive, intricate, and ever changing business. New forms of distributing merchandise to the consumer are continually arising. New forms of service are continually being offered. The buying population is constantly shifting. New methods of promoting, operating, financing, controlling, buying, and servicing are being developed. More efficient methods of operating must continually offset increasing pay rates and increasing costs of materials and services. The value of traditional practices must continually be reconsidered. Wise long range goals to fit community changes and competitive conditions must be determined. All these require constant critical examination and investigation, and thoughtful and penetrating consideration.

This activity, this attitude of mind *is* research and it is a continuous need if a business is to live and prosper.

Who Does Research? To meet the above needs, a progressive retail business is constantly "researching". Such research is being performed by all its major executives and proportionately by all of its operating executives.

In this sense, research is performed by merchandise managers. Profitable merchandising is the result of delicate manipulation of the elements which contribute to sales volume, to good will, to satisfactory gross margin, and to minimum expense under always changing conditions of market, fashion, season, competition, etc.

Critical examination and investigation is a continual process performed by the merchandise manager as he guides, assists, directs and trains his buyers. Similarly, each buyer should be researching in his area, exploring ways of increasing his sales, improving his gross margin, and reducing his expense.

Obviously, research is not limited and should not be limited to a small separate staff group. Nevertheless, there are research areas which these divisional executives cannot accomplish and which a competent research department can.

The Research Department. The function of a research department is not to supplant but to supplement storewide critical appraisal and action for improvement. It does this where special training, special skills, special experience, a special staff, or independence of action can provide help or can accomplish objectives that operating people have not been able to accomplish.

The research functions contributed by the research department can be grouped into three areas as follows:

1. Improving, coordinating, recording, and modi-

fying (as needed) the basic routines by which the store carries out its day to day operations.

2. Providing factual information, and when justified, drawing deductions from that information in order to help others solve problems or reach policy decisions.

3. Solving difficult problems and developing and introducing new operations, to do which special skills, broad store experience, new approaches, and freedom from operating responsibilities are required.

Influence of Top Management. The extent to which a research department works in each of these areas and the kind of work it does depend upon the background, the experience, the interests of the top management individuals in the company.

In some companies, one or more top management individuals prefer to explore and weigh the large amount of statistical data received from all sources, while in other stores, major executives call upon research department personnel to condense, arrange, highlight, and do "exception" reporting of the statistical data available.

In some stores, top management calls on the research department to solve practical, down-to-earth operating and merchandising problems. In others, top management asks a research department to provide more theoretical examination of general problems or to provide figures of past results and current trends for many purposes, including the spurring of less successful sectors of the business.

A major factor which determines the kind of work a research department will do is the kind of person that top management chooses to direct its research department because what the department will do depends upon the background, experience, and special skills of its director. If, for example, this person is statistically minded and trained, the emphasis will differ from what it would be if his training were in operations, and methods, and technology.

In what follows, examples will be given of work being done by research departments in large stores today.

I. The Basic Routines. One of the fundamental functions best assigned to a staff group like a research department is the synthesis and recording of store procedures; particularly those procedures which involve personnel of more than one major division. Most stores have *systems* in writing for several hundred such procedures.

Each one of these must initially have been studied to determine the best possible method to accomplish the necessary objectives. In the course of this study, the views of each operating person concerned are obtained; alternate suggestions are proposed; conflicting desires or opinions are resolved to arrive at a "best method"; agreement of all concerned is obtained; and the agreed procedure is committed to writing in some standardized form.

It is worth noting that there is a great difference between a verbal understanding and a written statement. Writing requires preciseness and therefore in the process of committing to writing what was previously considered a completed agreement, one always discovers many loose ends not provided for. The resultant precise record prevents many later difficulties in the operating process.

These written procedures when distributed to all concerned become the basis for the major part of a store's routine operation.

The function also includes the necessary revision of these procedures each time a change in policy or practice in any area requires a modification of existing routines.

Design of Printed Forms. Another directly related function is the designing and controlling of all printed forms. This follows, since *forms,* which are really *work guides,* are in all cases related to the procedures themselves and frequently involve many areas of the store's operation.

To provide for and synthesize the procedure requirements of many different store areas and the further need to provide satisfactory forms at the lowest purchase cost and lowest in-use cost calls for a staff department and the application of a research attitude.

The above functions are the most basic of those properly assigned to research or similar staff departments. However, if this were the limit of the functions assigned, it would be better to refer to such a staff group as a *systems department* or as a *procedures department* rather than a *research department*.

II. Providing Factual Information. This area of activity of the research department is to help others solve a problem or determine policy.

Dependable and truly applicable facts are often elusive things—and the importance of being able to obtain facts that are reliable and that are applicable cannot be overestimated.

One of the functions of research is to provide, where obtainable, the correct facts so that those with adequate technical knowledge and experience can make better judgments.

In some cases, this may only be a matter of collecting and organizing specified information. In other cases, it may include deductions and presentation of the implications of the facts collected. Or in some cases, suggestions or recommendations for action resulting from such information may be made.

Following are typical cases of this area of research department activity.

Example: Advertising. A store spends a large sum of money for advertising itself and its goods. It wants to get the most possible for its money. It has to decide the best combination of media to use. It has to decide how to present its story.

In one store, the research department makes annual surveys to know the newspaper reading habits of its customers and to find where they live. The store wants to know the relative readership and the relationship of their customers' residence to area of newspaper circulation with the object of finding the most effective means of reaching its market.

In another store, it studies the results of a catalog promotion —for timing, for areas to which it is sent, for personal vs. mail and telephone response, for relative effectiveness of different items—all to determine the value of the catalog or to improve the next catalog, if any.

Some managements have asked the research department to study the results of radio and television advertising to determine the desirability of using these to supplement newspaper advertising.

Sooner or later, most research departments are called upon to provide some factual information or evaluation in this field.

Example: Selling Management. Many research departments conduct studies of customer traffic by days of the week and hours of the day. This information helps to determine the relationship of full-time to part-time people, the scheduling of lunch hours and relief periods, part-timers' hours of work schedules, the need for per diem extras, night hour coverage, etc. With such data, the selling management can more satisfactorily staff the store to meet the customer load and do it at least possible cost.

Example: Unsatisfactory Performance of Selling Departments. A selling department's volume or profit or both may be declining or may be poor compared with other similar departments. Such a department needs study to find the difficulty and to remedy the situation. There are many possible contributing factors.

In most stores, this analysis is made in the merchandise area since it is the most basic work of the merchandise division. In some stores, however, the research department is called upon to study a selling department's operation in such a situation. Sometimes, as an overall study. Sometimes, to locate some facts not indicated in the available detailed statistics. In some cases, to compare merchandise assortments, promotional methods, department layout, merchandise presentation, selling technics, etc. with other stores. Factual material from such analysis may lead to the solution of the problem.

Example: Statistical Guides. Research departments in some stores take various internal and external statistical information available to the business and organize it and correlate it so that top management can appraise trends more easily, or can notice and correct unfavorable situations, or can plan ahead more accurately.

Example: Mail and Phone Business. An area of a store's business that is frequently subject to policy scrutiny is the business done by mail and phone. In most stores, there are no separate audited figures for this business. It becomes lost in the totals of each selling department's business.

Stores at intervals become concerned either about this business being underdeveloped or being overdeveloped. The profitability of part or all of this business is frequently in question. Also the nature of the customer (as compared to the in-person shopper) response to various forms of publicity, service problems, the technical equipment and procedures—all of these questions have been subjected to management scrutiny. The research department in such cases collects the facts necessary to decide on some action or policy under consideration.

In all of the above examples, the research department has been called upon to provide information for others to use. This is a most common function and a valuable one. Its purpose is to enable a better decision to be made or to expedite some plan or activity in which any member of the management may be engaged.

III. Difficult Problems; New Operations. In this area, the research assignment is to tackle a difficult problem, one that has stubbornly resisted solution, find an answer, and after acceptance, make the actual installation, adjusting and modifying for new obstacles as they arise—to the point where the operation can be taken over by the regular operating people.

The same kind of approach will apply where top management has determined a solution or a new policy or new theory concerning a major area and needs an implementer with the imagination and skills necessary to put it into practice.

Research Department as Catalyst. In the examples which follow, it should be understood that other skilled groups work on these changes at the same time. Among these might be the store design department, outside architect designers, the store construction department, outside contractors, the operating executives directly concerned.

The research department works with all of these specialists, each helping the other. To a great extent, the research department, knowing the ultimate working mechanism it is trying to create, can act as a catalyst, meshing the activities of these separate groups, each of whom is concerned with one technical part of the whole edifice.

Cooperation is also needed from carpenters, electricians, draftsmen, sign shop, display department, personnel department (personnel shifts must be fairly and diplomatically handled as the work progresses), the training department, etc.

The research department uses its good relationship with the managers, supervisors, and staff of every working division in the store to achieve the end result desired.

Example: Reorganization of a Selling Department. A major selling department with complicated physical problems involving large and varied assortment (like drugs, housewares, notions, stationery, china, glass, sporting goods, etc.) may have a problem of high expense, or bad service, or poor profit, or staples out of stock, or high complaints, or any combination of these.

Assume the stage has been reached where, after study to which the research department may have contributed, top management has arrived at a set of basic merchandising and service principles by which it wishes to operate the department and clearly knows what general objectives it wishes to achieve. The assignment is then given to convert these objectives into a practical reality.

In one such case, the department tackled was a housewares department where most of these problems existed. Here the procedure followed included proposing and setting up a basic ordering policy concerning amounts and frequency, a control system, a shift of much merchandise from warehouse to store, creation of periphery reserves, reviewing with buyers many items and lines carried, condensing selling space, more effective presentation of merchandise, better clerk and customer information, cooperating in the design of new selling floor fixtures for specific merchandise needs, improved buying and clerical and receiving facilities, design of special equipment for some operations, complete reorganization of warehouse receiving, stock location, and order filling methods for this department, and the introduction and follow-up of the entire process, including the instruction and training of all key people.

The research department in such a situation is not only involved in determining what, and how, and in designing all physical equipment required, but also in selling its proposals, step by step, to all the operating people involved—from the merchandise manager to buyer and his staff, as well as to the clerical and stock personnel.

Example: Business Machine Study. New specialized, highly technical equipment is continually being developed to take over the elaborate clerical functions involved in all business. Some equipment is specialized for our business. Where the use for this equipment falls completely within the controller's office area, its desirability usually would be appraised easily by members of the controller's office itself.

However, if the equipment represents a complete change in routines, and if it involves specialized technical knowledge, or if the use or purpose involves operating areas outside the controller's division itself, then it is properly assigned to the research department. Most cases involving the consideration of punch card tabulating equipment, the adoption of prepunched marking tickets for machine tabulation of unit sales, or the newer, electronic data processing equipment would fall into this category.

In such cases, not only does the desirability (cost, etc.) need to be determined, but also a high degree of specialized skill is necessary to overcome the normal and always underestimated obstacles which arise in the course of introducing such a procedure.

Example: Reorganization of a Non-selling Department. An area that has been a difficult one in many stores is the receiving of incoming merchandise. The major difficulties are the delay in processing papers and merchandise, the excessive amount of time which buyers and their assistants have to spend in the receiving process, the discounts lost, and the excessive physical handling of merchandise.

For years, all stores have made slight improvements by modifications of the existing process but hardly enough to overcome the new problems created as the stores grew in volume and increasing quantities of merchandise had to be handled in space not easily enlarged. In addition, stores are aware of the fact that industry is using mechanical equipment effectively for handling goods and that they may benefit in that area also. The problem calls for an entirely new approach.

Some stores assign such a problem to outside consultants. But in this situation, where the research department has in its staff the special technical skills required and the imagination and talent needed, the use of the research department is much more desirable because there is hardly any operating process in the store that is more entwined with a myriad other operations than this one. All of these enmeshed processes and the department managers and other supervisory people to be consulted for each part of the process are known to the research department staff.

In one solution to this problem, the research department achieved the following: movement of physical merchandise not restricted by delayed "papers"; paper movement speeded up with alternate processes to take care of a reasonable percentage of unavoidable delay; mechanical equipment that meets all hourly, daily, weekly and seasonal needs and yet allows the flexibility required by this business; goods processed quickly and accurately; no further need for the buyer or his assistants to spend an unreasonable amount of time in the receiving area.

A major additional result expected, and accomplished, was a substantial reduction in cost.

Other non-selling areas, in which a great deal of similar work has been undertaken have been in service building layout, mechanization, and operation; in wrapping and packing and the movement of send goods to and from the wrapping and packing stations; in workrooms; in adjustment operations; in delivery operations; in furniture processing, warehousing, and delivery; in special mechanical problems such as carpet handling, palletizing of bulk merchandise, and developing improved rolling equipment.

Developing of Physical Aids. In connection with this third category of research department activity, it is worth noting that the complications of this business may be divided broadly into two kinds.

The first set of complications grows out of merchandising: the decisions of merchandise selection and assortment and presentation; the intricate and delicate manipulation of figures; and questions of special purchases—promotions—seasonal shifts—etc. In this area, we presume the selling department managers and their superiors are experts because this is "retailing".

The second set of complications revolves around the repeated physical handling of goods, the processing of papers and the maintenance of the records upon which day to day actions are taken. These enter in many ways into the expense of a department and therefore into its eventual profit or loss.

The goods-handling effectiveness can be greatly increased by proper physical equipment—equipment that usually must be especially designed for the purposes at hand. This equipment, which may be elaborate or may be as simple as shelf heights and widths exactly suited to the merchandise, can contribute much to simplify the continuous in-and-out physical handling of merchandise.

Consider that a department store receives approximately 50 pounds of merchandise for each $100 of sales. This bulk of merchandise must be moved or handled ten to fifteen times. This means that for every $100 in sales we eventually handle 500 to 1000 pounds of merchandise!

Another category of equipment is that integrated with the clerical procedures—equipment so designed that it facilitates memory and establishes routines. Very often it is such equipment more than instruction which sustains routines necessary to the smooth running of a department.

This is an area which can be a special contribution of a research department and which if not contributed from such a source is not likely to be attained at all. In general, it is this whole third area of research department functions that presents the greatest possibilities of unique and valuable help to the business.

Store Associations. Over and above the three general areas mentioned above, where a store is part of an association of stores, like the Associated Merchandising Corporation, the research department also acts as a coordinating center—receiving and distributing materials coming from the association and generally assisting in collecting special information from other stores as desired.

Future of Research. As can be seen, a research department has important contributions to make in the department store business. The extent of its contribution depends on the wisdom of top management in creating it and in staffing it and on the assignments they give to it. Its value to the buyer lies in his awareness of how it can help him and in his willingness to accept its findings, when they apply to his department, as being the result of unbiased fact-finding and analysis.

CHAPTER 40

THE CONTRIBUTION OF THE RESIDENT BUYING OFFICE

BY

ADELE C. ELGART

Nearly every department store and departmentized specialty shop today makes available to its buyers the services of a resident buying office. The buyer who familiarizes himself with the functions of his store's office and learns to use its facilities intelligently can make his market trips more productive and his entire operation more successful.

Evolution of Resident Buying Offices. The buying office began, early in this century, as an organization devoted solely to the placing of orders. Since then its services have expanded steadily, and today it affords vital advisory services to management, market analysis, and advice and assistance on every phase of merchandising, publicity, and store-keeping. Nevertheless, the buying office's primary specialization and responsibility is *coverage of the markets.*

The buying office's expansion has come about because it provided information and services that stores individually could not possibly afford.

The resident buying office, independent or store owned, is the eyes and ears of the store in the market. *It is the market representative of the store* and headquarters for store personnel on their buying trips.

A resident office is set up to serve a group of non-competing stores, each of which is usually in a different city from the others. It gives its clients certain specific advantages they could not otherwise enjoy; it plays an important part in retail merchandising and in the distribution of merchandise. Its service is not always thoroughly understood by the buyers whose managements have placed it at their disposal. The purpose of this chapter, therefore, is to explain what such offices do, and how the buyer can get maximum benefit from them.

Types of Resident Office. There are several types of resident office. One of these is the cooperatively owned type, completely controlled by the stores that own it and that it serves. In such offices, there is usually a board of directors, whose members are executives of the owning stores, to set policy and determine the type and scope of services. Outstanding examples are the Associated Merchandising Corporation, Specialty Stores Association, and Frederick Atkins, Inc.

A second general classification is the resident office that is a division of a corporation that owns a chain of department stores. Such offices serve only the domestic member stores of the corporation. Examples would be Allied Purchasing Corp., Associated Dry Goods Corp., Gimbel's Central Buying Office, Macy's Corporate Buying Division, May Department Stores.

A third classification, the largest, is the independent resident office whose relationship to the stores is that of a private professional service to a client. Resident office and stores are completely independent of one another and enjoy mutual freedom in setting their own policies. Examples are Arkwright, Independent Retailers Syndicate, Kirby Block & Co., Felix Lilienthal & Co., McGreevey, Werring & Howell, and Mutual Buying Syndicate. These are "across-the-board" offices, meaning that they serve clients who handle both soft and hard goods.

Among the independently owned buying offices there is also a type referred to as the specialty office. This type concentrates on women's or men's apparel, or both, women's fashion accessories, and, frequently, infants' and children's wear. Examples are Jack Braunstein, Inc., S. Irene Johns, Inc., The Mary Sherwell Office, and William Van Buren, Inc.

A fourth type, not very common nowadays, is the office owned by and run for a single store. Marshall Field & Co., Meier and Frank, and Neiman-Marcus operate such offices.

Mention should be made here of still another type of office. That is the one set up by the millinery syndicates—lessees of millinery departments in department and specialty stores. These operate like the wholly-owned offices, except that they concentrate in this one field.

There is finally the merchandise broker, who receives no remuneration from the store but is paid a percentage by the manufacturer with whom he places his client's business. Such firms are not considered to be resident offices and are not permitted to use the name.

Location of Resident Buying Offices. The majority of resident buying offices are in New York City, since it is the primary market as well as the most diversified and comprehensive.

Some of the other market centers throughout the country also require continuing coverage. Consequently, wherever client demands indicate, some of the larger resident buying offices maintain well-staffed branches. Chicago and California are examples of such market centers.

Selection of a Resident Buying Office. A store's own needs are the determining factor in selecting a resident office for affiliation. Elements to consider in making such a selection include:

- The extent of the office's market coverage, its fashion judgment, and its merchandising knowledge.

- The size and ability of its staff.

- The scope of its services, such as cooperative buying, development of private brands, economic forecasts, market analyses, fashion information; availability of assistance to help cure sick departments, etc.

Large offices usually have separate divisional staffs for basement, budget, and better merchandise to insure their clients the widest possible coverage of the market.

Organization of the Resident Office. The resident buying office is generally organized along lines that correspond closely to that of the merchandising division within a store.

Like the store, the office usually has one or more buyers for each classification of merchandise. Because of the vastness of the market, large offices may have as many as 15 buyers, for example, for dresses, each covering certain size ranges and price lines intensively.

It is the job of each buyer to cover thoroughly the entire market or segment of it that has been assigned to her. This means constantly checking and evaluating resources, alerting stores to changes, and keeping on tap information about changes and new resources for the benefit of store personnel concerned. To a resident buyer, knowing the market means knowing individual styles and rack conditions, to be able to meet the specific needs of all their visiting store buyers. The resident staff constantly keeps its stores informed of current market conditions, using bulletins, flash reports, and other forms of rapid communication.

Divisional Heads. Divisional department heads in a resident office correspond to, and work closely with, the divisional merchandise managers of stores. They maintain constant contact with the merchandise heads in stores, alerting them to market plans and trends.

As in a store, the primary function of a divisional head is to direct and supervise the activities of the resident buyers who report to them. They are also responsible for organizing and directing divisional meetings. Another function of theirs is to work with store steering committees in developing group purchases and private brand promotions.

A part of the responsibility of both the divisional heads and the buyer is the establishment and maintenance of good vendor relationships. Most resident offices maintain sample rooms where at scheduled hours or by special appointment salesmen can show merchandise or confer with resident and/or store buyers.

Cooperation Between Stores and Resident Offices. The full benefit of the services of a resident office cannot be realized unless there is complete cooperation between the resident buyer and the store buyer. It is to the advantage of the store buyer to take the resident buyer into his confidence on all store plans.

If the resident buyer is notified in advance of the buyer's plans for a market trip, the New York buyer will scout the market beforehand for the store's particular needs, thus saving market time for the buyer. Most stores require their buyers to register in the New York office in any case, and encourage them to make appointments ahead with the New York buyer to discuss conditions affecting their departments.

Ordering For Stores. Frequently the resident buyer is called upon to handle "open-to-buy" for the stores. That is, the store sends in what is called an open order, which specifies price lines and the amount of money to be spent, but leaves the choice of the resource and the type of merchandise to the judgment of the resident buyer. To do this, a resident buyer must be thoroughly acquainted with the individual store, the type of merchandise it sells, its peculiar climate problems and all the other factors involved in the selection of merchandise.

In addition, the resident buyer places reorders on successful numbers and special orders. Included in the office buyer's service to the store are follow-ups and checks on delivery upon request of the store.

The resident buyer also keeps the store buyer constantly informed about new fashions, best sellers, new items and market changes by means of constant bulletins.

Facilities Provided. Most of the larger offices provide private offices to be assigned to store heads and merchandise managers. In addition, there are private office facilities for buyers, with telephone service, and, of course, a service to care for the store buyer's mail and to receive telephone messages for him while he is in the market.

Secretarial help, facilities, and railroad reservations, and provisions for seeing salesmen may also be provided.

Follow-Up. Most store buyers find it to their interest to clear copies of all orders and reorders through the resident buyer, since this enables the market representative to keep a careful check and to follow up if necessary to insure prompt delivery of the merchandise.

The typical resident buying office will have a follow-up system for its client's orders, and will report to the store the new delivery dates promised by the manufacturers.

Important Advisory Services. The advisory service of top resident office management to store owners and the general management of the store sometimes includes economic research and advice, a study of economic and merchandising trends, and timely and accurate analysis of the effect new legislation, new market problems and other such items of interest to management. Usually there is at least one executive meeting a year, attended by top management and store owners, where a program of mutual interest is arranged.

Fashion Service. In most large offices, there is a fashion director and a staff of fashion market reporters. Two fashion clinics are held each year, in advance of the market. At these, stores are briefed as to new fashion trends and their importance. This fashion service often includes brochures which provide fashion information in written and often illustrated form to be used in fashion training programs in the store, as well as to refresh the memories of buyers and merchandisers.

Fashion offices usually issue some special form of bulletin devoted to fashion themes and backed up with merchandise the stores may order. Fashion information is sent regularly to the stores as it develops in the market.

The fashion division also works with individual stores in mapping out fashion promotion plans, suggests themes for windows and interior displays, and offers advice on fashion shows, their planning and production. The fashion division also plans color and fabric promotions for cooperating member stores.

Divisional Meetings. Very important to the store buyers and merchandisers are the advisory services at the merchandising and buying level. Most large offices schedule seasonal divisional merchandise meetings, and at these meetings the market is reviewed, special merchandise shown, and problems peculiar to the particular market are discussed. A large office may have as many as 50 of these meetings a year and they embrace practically every phase of store keeping.

Another important advisory service is in promotion and display. Actually, this is more than an advisory service, although annual sales promotion meetings provide for an exchange of information and the spotlighting of new developments in sales promotion techniques.

Very important among the services in this field is the development of mailing catalogues of a quality very few stores could possibly afford on their own. In addition, special promotional tools are made available to stores, such as mats and advertising layouts for special office-sponsored promotions and basic item promotions. A service involving the purchase of supplies and display material may also be offered.

Bulletin and Information Service. All resident offices use some form of bulletin service for sending stores information on new fashion items, promotional items, and best sellers. This is one of the most important functions of a resident office and most of this information stems from the office buyer. In addition to reporting items that develop in the market, best sellers are regularly reported.

Some offices have regularly scheduled executive letters from top management, designed expressly for store management and dealing with economic trends and general market conditions. Other executive letters go from divisional heads to their opposite numbers in stores. Usually these letters cover background facts, market information, and recommendations.

Information For The Buyer. In advance of any general movement to the market, such as takes place when buyers converge on a market center to see a new season's lines, the resident buying office staff scouts the market and prepares a report that will give the store buyer a background on the situation. This may cover such points as fashion trends, supply and demand, the growth or falling off in importance of particular items, price trends, and so on.

The report may be given orally at meetings held by the resident office for groups such as piece goods buyers, infants' wear buyers, buyers of fashion accessories, etc. Or, as is common practice for some staple departments, the report may be in the form of an attractive booklet that is sent out to the store in advance of the normal time for the store buyer to leave for the market.

Thus, orally, or in writing, or both, the store buyer is given a briefing on the general situation in the market. Against this background, he will find it easier to ask questions, seek information, and make decisions concerning his department in particular.

Central Buying Programs. Several resident buying offices have set up some form of central buying for certain lines of popular priced merchandise—dresses, for instance. This has often proved invaluable in enabling independent stores to be competitive with the chains in these popular price lines. It permits them to operate on lower stocks, yet at the same time to have a constant flow of new merchandise.

This is how such a program works. Purchases are made entirely in New York, but the individual stores report sales and returns from day to day. When the resident buying office sends a few pieces of a new number into each of the stores it serves, its own unit control department soon has the combined figures of all the stores to guide the buyer. With a nationwide picture developing virtually before his eyes, the buyer at the resident office can quickly spot trends, send in reorders of running numbers, and cut off those that have little acceptance.

Since the operation depends entirely on figures, it is essential that there be no delay at the store in sending to New York the information required by the central buying operation. Efficient cooperation between department heads in the stores and the New York office is the foundation for success.

Group Buys. Through the resident buying office, it is usually possible to arrange for some or all of the member stores to participate in a group buy. This is a purchase in which a number of stores participate, so that, by underwriting a large order, they can have merchandise confined to them in their individual communities, or can secure a lower price reflecting the economies made possible to the manufacturer by such large quantities.

The resident buyer may alert the member stores to an opportunity for such a buy at a meeting of buyers, or through special bulletins. It is up to the individual store to decide in each case whether or not it wishes to go along with the group; usually, it is definitely advantageous to do so.

A Private Brand Program. More and more stores have found it necessary to develop private brands to meet price competition or to enhance store individuality. Most resident offices therefore have a program to develop items that will bear private brand labels.

As a rule, the resident office works closely with a steering committee of store buyers, and together they write specifications for the item considered. It is then the duty of the resident buyer to take these specifications to top resources and have samples made up for the approval of the steering committee. Once an item is approved, it is placed in the private brands program and usually some form of promotion and publicity is suggested.

The store then has the responsibility for building customer acceptance for these private brand names. Almost every department in the store that deals in any way with basic staple items participates in such a program.

Purchasing Program. Because there are often special opportunities to buy in the market, and especially to buy in large quantities, many resident offices have established a merchandising service to take advantage of these opportunities. Under such a program, a resident buyer is able to make an advantageous purchase of desirable merchandise at off-season prices or to secure for the stores special price concessions on such things as discontinued lines or overstocks. The success of any such program, of course, depends wholly on the skill and knowledge of the buyer and the merchandising staff of the resident office *and the cooperation of the store buyer.*

Jobbing Service. In some cases, the resident buying office functions as a jobber. It makes purchases in its own name, warehouses the merchandise, and ships to its client stores on demand. It also arranges to have some items drop-shipped from the mill or manufacturer.

Where the resident office does jobbing, there is usually a jobbing subsidiary that operates exactly as other jobbers or wholesalers do, and is entitled to any special discounts or privileges the manufacturers make available to the jobbing trade. It is also able to purchase from mills that do not sell directly to retailers.

Under this arrangement, the jobbing subsidiary resells to member stores at a nominal profit. Sometimes outside stores are permitted to use the service at a stipulated fee.

The jobbing activity usually concentrates on staple items, like piece goods, blankets, towels, sheets, etc. For many of the items, the office may work up its own specifications and arrange for the factory or mill to produce the goods during its dull period. The savings made through quantity purchases, off-season orders, and so on, are passed along to the stores.

Foreign Office. Some resident buying offices maintain offices in key cities abroad for the purpose of having on-the-ground contacts with foreign merchandise sources. Others have good connections with commissionaires abroad, who act for the office and its member stores in the foreign country concerned.

Whether or not the resident office has its own buyers abroad, it usually has a specialist on import problems on its headquarters staff, to whom the buyer and his management may go for advice and information on the complexities of buying abroad. This specialist may have in his office a display of items available from foreign sources, so that the buyer can see the actual merchandise just as he would in the showroom of a domestic resource.

Some of the offices also have export departments, and serve stores abroad. For these, they may select, buy, crate and ship American merchandise, pay for the merchandise, handle all the "papers" necessary.

Figure Exchange—Research and Analysis. Close cooperation by member stores makes possible the exchange of merchandising statistics, operational expense items, payroll, advertising costs, and best selling items. Research and analysis can then determine the major contributing factors to successful store operation.

Material thus gathered by the buying office has this advantage: Unlike figures collected on a broad, national scale, the buying office figures are gathered from stores catering to approximately the same class of trade and not in competition with one another. Thus the buyer can supplement what he learns from general yardsticks, applicable to the entire retail trade, with facts gathered from departments of his own type and with whose individual operations he can be reasonably familiar.

Through its many and varied services, then, the resident buying office has broadened its work from simple buying help to information on fashion trends, economic trends, and changes in the market, and has come to serve also as a clearing house for information on retail operations.

CHAPTER 41

OPERATING STATEMENTS

BY

HARRY L. MARGULES

The typical department store draws up statements periodically that break the operation of a department into its component parts. If the department is below par, a careful analysis of the statistics presented in the statement may indicate where the trouble lies. Having that information, the buyer is able to concentrate on the possible cure.

Obviously, then, it is to the buyer's advantage to know how to read and analyze the departmental operating statement, and how to use it to guide his efforts toward improving performance.

Monthly Operating Statement (M.O.S.). The buyer receives, or should receive, a least once a month a report on the profit position of his department compared to the previous year and to the budget. The first factor in the profit of a department is the amount of gross margin—a figure for which the buyer is almost entirely responsible.

Periodically, therefore, and usually once a month, the controller's office prepares an operating statement showing the gross margin position of the department. Several other related facts, such as selling salaries and advertising costs, may be shown, but the monthly report is designed primarily to furnish the gross margin information.

The form of the statement will vary in different stores, as will the amount of information presented, but it generally contains as a minimum the elements shown in Figure 28. The figures shown in our illustration are very nearly the actual figures of a real department, and the reasons for the condition of the department, as developed in the discussion, are also actual.

MONTHLY OPERATING STATEMENT
X DEPARTMENT

For Period Ending_____ 19____

	This Year	Budget	Last Year
Sales:			
Net Sales—Month	$ 84,000	$ 90,000	$ 90,000
Percent of Increase or Decrease		(d) 6.7	(d) 6.7
Net Sales to Date	$670,000	$730,000	$640,000
Percent of Increase or Decrease		(d) 8.0	4.7
Transactions to Date	210,000	245,000	240,000
Percent of Increase or Decrease		(d)14.3	(d)12.5
Average Gross Sale to Date	$3.40	$3.00	$2.80
Customer Returns Percent to Date	6.8	6.5	6.2
Turnover to Date (Number of Turns)	2.2	2.5	2.7
Stock on Hand at Retail	$300,000	$260,000	$350,000
Gross Margin:			
Initial Markon			
Month	38.9%	40.0%	39.9%
Year-to-Date	39.7	40.4	39.9
Markdowns (Percent to Sales)			
Month	12.0	6.0	2.0
Year-to-Date	7.5	5.0	3.0
Workroom Cost to Date (Percent to Sales)	2.0	1.0	2.5
Shortage Reserve to Date (Percent to Sales)	1.5	1.5	1.8
Discount Earned to Date (Percent to Sales)	2.0	2.3	2.2
Discount Earned to Date (Percent to Purchases)	3.2	3.5	3.4
Gross Margin (Percent to Sales)			
Month	30.8	36.9	37.1
Year-to-Date	34.3	37.4	36.7
Gross Margin (Dollars)			
Month	$ 25,872	$ 33,210	$ 33,030
Year-to-Date	$229,810	$273,020	$234,880
Selling Salaries to Date (Percent to Sales)	4.9	5.0	4.7
Advertising to Date (Percent to Sales)	3.9	4.0	3.4

Figure 28

The purpose of citing a case history here, rather than merely showing a form, is to illustrate how the Monthly Operating Statement discloses the statistical results which are a surface reflection of the operation, and how it is necessary to analyze these results in order to understand the true character of the operation.

Analysis of M.O.S. The net sales figures given in the Monthly Operating Statement are below both the budgeted figure and that of last year, while the net sales for the year to date are below the budget, but slightly ahead of last year. The department is not servicing the same number of customers, as is indicated by the decrease in the number of transactions. The dollar sales position would be very poor except for the substantial increase in average sale over both the budgeted figure and that of last year.

In this particular case, the increase in average sale is due to general conditions affecting all items in this department and is not due to a change in policy. Since the increase came fortuitously, a downtrend may set in in just the same way. The buyer must be watchful to anticipate any such downtrend.

Obviously, if the average sale should decrease as the transactions have decreased, the resultant drop in sales volume will present serious problems.

Had the increase in average sale been due to a deliberate attempt on the part of the store to trade up, the store management would have had to decide whether to continue, discontinue or modify that policy.

Actual vs. Budgeted Sales. In many cases the comparison of the actual sales with the budgeted sales in the monthly Operating Statement is better than a comparison with the previous year. Market conditions and other factors may vary greatly from year to year, and the showing of the department against the previous year alone may seem unduly good or poor. Budgeting, if carefully done, sets a goal to be achieved under conditions as they actually exist.

A very effective measure of the sales position of a department is to be found in the departmental sales figures for the larger cities, released monthly by the Federal Reserve banks. At times the department's increase looks very good or very poor until the city figure is available, and one sees the general trend for the community. Because Federal Reserve figures are not available as quickly as those of the store, no attempt is made to show them in the Monthly Operating Statement. The objective should be at least to maintain one's sales position in the community and, in fact, to increase one's share of the market.

Returns from customers are stated as a percent of gross sales. They measure the ability to retain sales originally made. Figure 28 shows no unusual situation, although there is an indication of an increasing trend. The trend should be carefully watched and if it continues to increase, a study of causes should be made. To reduce returns is equivalent to getting additional sales.

Turnover or Stock Turn. Turnover figures show a slower turn for "this year" than "last year" even though the stock is lower and sales are higher. At first glance one would question the correctness of the turnover figure and no doubt the buyer would challenge the figure. However, in the situation on which these figures are based, an investigation would reveal that they are correct.

Turnover is the resultant figure of sales divided by average stock, and the reason for the seeming discrepancy is that the *average* stock for this year is higher for the period than that of last year. The department started the year with an inventory which was too high and, of course, the turnover figure, being based on average stock, reflects that condition. It is another illustration of the fact that an unhealthy overbought condition requires time for liquidation.

Each turn of stock produces sales and the profit from such sales. Therefore, the higher the turnover the greater the profit return on the dollars invested in average inventory.

Inventory or Stock on Hand. Stock on hand is shown on this statement at retail prices. Some stores show it at cost prices. Either way is permissible and the decision as to which shall be used depends upon the thinking of management. Under the retail inventory method, the stock at retail prices can easily be converted to a cost figure.

In analyzing the actual figures, we find that this department shows a stock which is larger than the budget but less than last year. As indicated in the discussion of turnover, the stock reduction job of the period is better than indicated on this report alone because the opening inventory of the department was very high. Naturally, a buyer and the store management receiving these reports every month should be fully aware of the various charges, and therefore be able to appraise the results of the merchandising operation.

In view of the rather large reduction of stock during the period, the fact that it ended up higher than the budget would not be considered as very serious because the trend is in the right direction.

Gross Margin. Gross margin is the result of several elements. The principal ones are initial markon, markdowns and discounts. Other elements such as workroom cost and shortage have, as a rule, a lesser effect. Sometimes, however, workroom cost gets too far out of line and the shortage turns out to be unexpectedly large. Each element will be discussed separately.

Markon. The initial markon is the difference between the initial or first retail price and the cost of merchandise. It is shown as a percentage of the retail price. The figure shown on the M.O.S. is the result or accumulation of all the markons for the month or the period to date, both high and low. It means, however, that to achieve a desired (budgeted) result, low markon goods bought must be offset by the purchase of high markon goods. The markon indicates and records the cumulative result of the thinking and judgment of the buyer with regard to the initial retail selling price of the items received during the period.

An important element in the cost of merchandise is the cost of inbound freight. This is added to the cost of purchases and thus reduces the markon.

The initial markon is the starting point of the final gross margin. Unless the "initial" is right, the final "gross" will not be right.

Markdowns. Markdowns comprise the reductions in the retail price which become necessary for a number of different reasons. The effect of the markdowns is, of course, to reduce the final gross margin.

In the illustration, the markdowns for the month are 12 per cent, as against a budgeted figure of 6 per cent and a last year figure of two per cent. Obviously, such a difference calls for an investigation to determine the reason or reasons. The cumulative markdown of 7.5 per cent for the period is also out of line with the budget and with last year and calls for an explanation. The fundamental cause for the high markdowns, in this instance, goes back to the overbought stock condition at the opening of this period and the necessity of reducing that stock.

A large inventory is a danger signal. It does not automatically reflect an unhealthy stock condition. It demands an analysis of the composition of the stock. Does it contain sizable "lumps", broken assortments, "old stock" or does its size reflect quantities of goods for later promotional effort? As always, by getting the facts, the proper course of action can be taken.

Some stores budget markdowns very carefully and expect the buyer to operate within the budgeted figure; others budget it as an advance estimate and do not expect close conformance, while still others do not budget markdowns at all. Hence, one finds a difference among stores as to the content of the Monthly Operating Statement and also as to the manner of interpretation.

In the illustration, markdowns are shown in terms of percent to sales. Some stores also show dollars because they feel that that is a more accurate measurement than percent to sales.

Workroom. Workroom cost consists of the cost of the work which is necessary to put the article in condition for use. In ready-to-wear it covers alterations; in furniture it consists of polishing, finishing and checking; in appliances it means initial servicing, plus service during and after the installation; in draperies and carpets it means the cutting, sewing and installing of the merchandise, and so on. Some workrooms make a charge for the work and others do not.

The final net loss or net cost of the workroom operation, which is its cost reduced by any income received from customers, is charged against the parent selling department. This charge reduces the gross margin just as do the markdowns.

The workroom operation in many instances is very large and is an important factor in the success of the parent department. The buyer, inasmuch as his department is charged with the loss or net cost, is entitled to a statement of the operations of the workroom.

At this time, in examining the charge for workroom on the M.O.S., we see that it is less than last year, but double the budgeted amount. Here again, if one knows that last year's operation because of scarcity of help or inefficient help is not a good basis for comparison, one should base his conclusion instead on the comparison with the budget. When one does that, it is immediately apparent that some further analysis should be done; an increase of 100 per cent is too much.

Shortage. Shortage reserve is an amount which is accumulated month by month by taking a certain percentage of sales to offset the difference between the book inventory and the actual (physical) inventory. These figures are usually stated at retail but may also be stated at cost.

If the actual difference is less than the reserve which has been accumulated, it is an increase to the gross margin; but if the actual difference is greater than the reserve, it is a reduction of the gross.

The percentage to be used in the monthly calculation is determined at the beginning of the year and is not changed from month to month. In many stores it does not appear at all on the M.O.S., but it is, of course, included in the calculation of the final gross margin percentage.

The adjustment between book inventory and physical inventory is made after the year-end physical inventory but may be made whenever a physical inventory is taken. When the adjustment is made, the shortage figures reported are actual rather than reserve.

Discounts Earned. These figures show the discounts received from or allowed by vendors for prompt payment of invoices. They increase the final gross margin. The percentage on the M.O.S. is based on sales since it is an element of gross margin. However, the percentage based on purchases is usually shown too, since that is the way discounts are obtained from vendors.

In many lines, discounts are firmly fixed and the buyer cannot obtain better terms. However, it is the responsibility of the buyer to see that the discount which he does receive is not lower than the accepted trade figure. Efforts by vendors to reduce discounts should be resisted.

Gross Margin. The gross margin percentage for the month in our illustration is only 30.8 per cent compared to the budgeted figure of 36.9 per cent and last year's of 37.1 per cent. This is due primarily to the lower initial markon and the higher markdowns. The year-to-date percentage of 34.3 per cent is also substantially below the budget and last year, and again it is because of the initial markon and the markdowns.

Management must decide if these discrepancies are normal in view of the stock reduction program and the experience of other stores, or if the fault lies entirely in the selective and operating ability of the buyer. If the latter is the case, something should be done to enable him to correct his mistakes and to avoid them in the future.

As a rule, gross margin must be large enough to cover the costs of doing business. As expenses rise, so should gross margin dollars.

Expenses. Selling salaries and advertising percentages are shown as a matter of information and as a summary of the month's operations or of the period to date.

The Monthly Operating Statement therefore gives the buyer and the store management a complete monthly picture of the gross margin position and the trend of a department. Summary M.O.S.'s are prepared for each merchandise division and for the store as a whole.

Dollars versus Percentages. The actions of a department in buying and retailing merchandise, in taking markdowns or in making sales are entered in the accounting records in dollars and cents. Figures issued to buyers are also stated in dollars. However, dollar figures are also converted to percentages for purposes of comparing and evaluating one period with another, one department with another, one store with another.

Percentages are the common language for measuring results, for budgeting and controlling operations. The percentage technique has become a scientific element in retailing.

Through experience we learn how large a markon percent on all goods purchased it takes to cover the usual markdowns, shortages and workroom cost and produce a satisfactory gross margin sufficient to cover expenses of the business and leave a satisfactory net profit. Working toward a markon percent goal gives a buyer control over his merchandising operations. The use of percentages all the way down to net profit is designed to guide and control operations toward a satisfactory bottom line—the net profit line.

There are those who maintain that the emphasis on percentages is too great. They say reduce expense; buy better and so reduce markdowns; go after volume; go after dollars, not percentages.

There is much to be said for this point of view. Actually, percentages are only a means to an end. They are a guide. Bills are paid in dollars, not percentages. Thus, there are times when markon percent should be sacrificed to produce more sales dollars, and in turn more gross margin dollars. But there is a limit to this sacrifice. If costs of doing business keep rising, and a store is operating efficiently merchandise-wise and expense-wise, it takes more markon on the average—more markon per cent, not less—to produce a satisfactory and just net profit.

Departmental Net Profit Statement. Another financial statement of a merchandise department is one which shows the net profit of a department after charging it with the expenses of operation. This is usually an extension of the Monthly Operating Statement carried down to net profit. It is customarily issued semi-annually or just annually. (See Figure 29.)

In determining the net profit of a merchandise department, we find two kinds of expense, direct and indirect.

Direct expenses are those that belong to the department; they come into being with the department and cease if it is

DEPARTMENTAL NET PROFIT STATEMENT
X DEPARTMENT

For Period Ending_____ 19____

	This Year	*Last Year*
Net Sales	$670,000	$640,000
Gross Margin	230,000	235,000
Percent to Sales	34.3%	36.7%
Direct Departmental Expenses:		
Selling Salaries	33,000	30,000
Advertising	26,000	22,000
Buying	20,000	17,000
Receiving & Marking	5,000	4,000
Wrapping & Packing	8,000	7,000
Delivery	13,000	11,000
All Other Direct	20,000	18,000
Total Direct Expense	$125,000	$109,000
Contribution to Overhead	105,000	126,000
Overhead	60,000	52,000
Net Profit or Loss	$ 45,000	$ 74,000

Figure 29

discontinued. Such expenses as the buyer's salary, salaries of the assistant buyers and salespeople, and advertising fall in the category of direct expenses.

In many stores detailed statistical records are maintained in order to obtain an accurate record of the cost for each merchandise department of such items as receiving, marking, delivery, auditing sales checks, handling orders and invoices, wrapping and packing supplies, etc.

Obviously, the greater the number of expense items which are charged to each department on a definite statistical basis, the more accurate the final result will be. However, the task of gathering the necessary data creates additional expense for the store.

The indirect expenses include rent, maintenance, the salaries of general store executives, and such other items which will continue to exist even if the department is discontinued. The money spent for these purposes pertains to the operation of the store as a whole, but if a net profit or loss figure for each merchandise department is to be determined, these general or overhead expenses must be taken into consideration.

Charging for Overhead. It is difficult, and perhaps impossible, to determine accurately how much of the overhead expense to charge to each individual department. For example, we have no way of measuring the cost of the time and thought that the present manager, the merchandise manager, the controller, and other executives may give to one department as compared with the time and thought they give another. It is difficult, too, to determine the relative value of each part of a store's floor space, in order to decide how much a department shall be charged for rent.

Stores deal with this situation by prorating or apportioning most of their indirect expenses to the various departments. Sales is a common basis of proration, but for certain expenses, other bases may be used. Rent may be apportioned on the basis of floor area. In this way, all the expenses of operating the store are in one way or another portioned out among the various departments, and the value of each department to the store can be expressed in terms of net profit or loss.

The net profit figure for a department, however, may vary considerably depending upon the amount of expense which is prorated to it. Because departmental net profit figures cannot be scientifically accurate, due to the large amount of cost which is prorated, the value of a department to the store is often judged by its contribution to the store's overhead or indirect expense bill.

Contribution Method. To determine its contribution, a department is charged with its direct expenses. Some stores charge only selling salaries, advertising, and buyer's salary and expense; others include additional items such as receiving, marking and delivery expense, as we indicated previously.

Some stores end their department statement with a "contribution" figure and do not prorate the general overhead at all. Others feel that while the "contribution" figure may be the most valuable, they also want to see the net profit or loss, even though they realize it is not a scientifically accurate figure and may be difficult to defend.

Contribution figures may be part of the Monthly Operating Statement but are usually shown semi-annually or just annually.

A form of statement which combines both the contribution figure and the final net profit or loss is shown in Figure 29.

This statement also is comparative with last year and therefore shows the trend. An examination of the statement shows that the trend is in the wrong direction. With increased volume, the percentage of gross margin is down; the direct expense shows a disproportionately large increase; and, of course, the final net profit is lower. If one chooses to judge the department only on contribution, one finds that this too is lower than last year.

Again, in order to apply intelligent corrective measures and policies, the buyer, the merchandise manager, the controller and others must have more detailed information. A study must be made of the merchandise lines which are carried, the vendors from whom the goods are purchased, the price lines, the promotional activities of the department and the many other factors which have a bearing on gross margin.

Obviously, in the departmental results illustrated, expenses have increased too much, particularly selling salaries, advertising, and buying.

The high selling cost may be the result, first of all, of too much effort to get additional volume—effort which sometimes achieves only unprofitable volume. Perhaps the buyer is not quick enough to take markdowns on odds and ends, and less desirable items, and is thus slowing up the movement of his stock.

It may be that his average sale is low, and that a drive toward raising it is needed. It may be that his stock assortments are poorly balanced, or incomplete, and that his department is missing sales on that account.

The trouble may be that his department is over-staffed, or that his salespeople are indifferent or poorly trained. It may be that, although his salespeople are excellent, he has not been promoting the kind of merchandise that brings people into the store.

It may be that his stock is badly arranged, and his salespeople are spending more time running back and forth than waiting on customers. It may be any one of a number of things, and someone should make it his business to trace down the cause of the trouble as soon as the operating statement discloses its existence.

Executive Use of Departmental Net Profit Statement. There is considerable difference of opinion among stores as to which executives should receive departmental net profit statements. Some stores, on the theory that buyers have no control over overhead items, do not give them a departmental net profit statement. Other stores do furnish buyers with this information. Basically, the extent of the responsibility of the buyer determines the information he should receive.

If a buyer is held accountable for final net profit of his department, or if his bonus is based upon it, he should periodically receive a statement which tells him his results to date. Such statements may be issued monthly, quarterly, semi-annually or annually, depending upon the thinking of the management.

In some stores the buyer's salary is directly related to the profit showing of the department. In general terms there is always a relationship between salary and profits. Many stores have contracts or agreements providing for a base salary plus additional compensation related to profits. The latter is usually a percentage arrangement. Some arrangements provide additional compensation figured as a percent of sales in excess of a certain sales base, provided a required gross margin percent is achieved; still others base additional compensation on contribution after deducting certain specified direct expenses such as advertising, selling salaries, etc.; and some stores base additional compensation on net profit after deducting all expenses, direct and indirect.

CHAPTER 42

MERCHANDISING ARITHMETIC

BY

E. R. AUS, C.P.A.

The buyer in the typical retail organization finds it necessary to use arithmetic often in the course of his daily work. Plans and reports which he must prepare and reports issued by the store which he must analyze require him to have a firm grasp of the principles and application of basic arithmetic. Merchandising arithmetic is simply an extension of ordinary arithmetic into the specialized area of retailing.

Many new buyers find that they have forgotten much of the knowledge about arithmetic acquired during their formal education. Therefore, it is strongly recommended that all buyers have in their personal reference materials a fundamental text on business mathematics to provide assistance in their daily struggles with fractions, decimals and percentages. This should also help to conserve the amount of time spent in these endeavors, since these texts present short cut methods for solving arithmetic problems of a repetitive nature which are easily applied to many of the situations found in retailing.

Retail Inventory Method. In order to understand the record-keeping systems which apply to the department under his supervision, the buyer should be familiar with the Retail Inventory Method, the method of accounting used today by most department stores.

The system gets its name from the fact that *stores can take physical inventory of their stocks at the marked retail prices and then determine the cost valuation of the inventory on the basis of a percentage relationship between cost and retail.*

The procedure entails recording the inventory at the beginning of a period at both cost and retail for each department, or classification, or section. Then purchases are entered throughout the period at both cost and retail. Adjustments in the retail price are recorded as they occur. Thus total cost and total retail figures are available for all merchandise handled during the period.

The difference between cost and retail represents the amount of markon on that merchandise. Expressed as a percentage of *retail,* it becomes the markon percentage for the period.

Book Inventory. This system of accounting requires the buyer to "retail" each invoice for his department—that is, to indicate the retail prices at which the merchandise will go into stock. Each invoice is charged to the department at both cost and retail. The retail figure is modified from time to time by any upward or downward adjustments (markups or markdowns) in selling price. Sales are recorded currently.

To obtain the book inventory, or *the amount that should be in stock at a given time,* we add to the starting inventory, at retail, all purchases and markups. We subtract any cancellations of markups. We subtract sales and markdowns (less any cancellations of markdowns) and arrive at the inventory figure.

Here is an example, with all figures at retail:

Opening inventory (beginning of period)		$20,000
Purchases during period		40,000
Markups		100
Total inventory and additions		$60,100
Sales	$30,500	
Markdowns—net	3,600	
Total deductions		34,100
Book inventory (Inventory which should be on hand)		$26,000

Physical Inventory. In order to check the book inventory figure, a physical inventory or actual count of merchandise is taken ordinarily at least twice a year. It is calculated from the *retail* prices on the merchandise. Any difference between the physical inventory and book inventory is a stock shortage, or overage, as the case may be.

To calculate the stock shortage percentage, the amount of shortage, at retail, is divided by net sales for the period. Thus, if net sales have been $30,500 and the stock shortage is $305 at retail, the stock shortage percentage is $305 divided by $30,500, or 1%.

Cost Inventory. It is necessary, of course, to know the value of the inventory at cost at the end as well as at the beginning of the period, in order to determine the profit or loss for that period. The retail figure is therefore reduced by the amount of the markon, or multiplied by 100% minus the percentage of markon (the complement of the markon percentage) to obtain the cost valuation. If the markon is 35%, the cost value of the stock on hand is 65% (100% minus 35%). If the retail inventory is $26,000, the cost is 65% of that amount or $16,900.

Figure 30 shows in detail how the inventory is calculated at cost and retail under the retail method.

Markon. The difference between the billed cost price (before deducting cash discount) and the original retail price of merchandise is known as the *markon*. In referring to the difference between the delivered cost of merchandise and the retail price placed on it when it is originally put into stock, the term initial markon is used.

Cumulative markon, or markon to date, is the difference between the total cost and the total retail of merchandise handled to date, including the inventory at the beginning of the period.

Maintained markon is the difference between the delivered cost of merchandise and the price at which it is actually sold. This gives effect to price adjustments made on the merchandise

COMPUTING INVENTORY, RETAIL METHOD

	Cost	Retail	Markon
1. Opening inventory (lines 9 and 11 of preceding period)	$20,000	$30,000	$10,000
2. Purchases, less returns to vendors....	40,000	74,000	34,000
3. Freight, express and cartage, inward.	2,460		−2,460
4. Markups less markup cancellations..		100	100
5. Total of inventory plus additions (Markon percentage, 40.00%)	62,460	104,100	41,640
6. Net Sales		80,000	
7. Markdowns, less markdown cancellations (5.625%)		4,500	
8. Total retail deduction (sum of items 6 and 7)		84,500	
9. Resultant retail inventory (retail inventory on line 5, column 2, minus item 8)		19,600	
10. Calculation of cost percentage: (a) Total percentage 100.00% (b) Percentage of markon (line 5) 40.00% (c) Percentage of cost 60.00%			
11. Cost inventory (item 10-c applied to item 9)	11,760		

Figure 30.

during the period, but not allowing for workroom costs and income from cash discounts.

To illustrate, suppose that the following example (Figure 31) represents our transactions, excluding Sales, with respect to merchandise during a given period:

The markon percentage of item 1 is the relationship developed in the preceding period which was used to reduce the ending retail inventory of that period to cost. It was computed in the same manner as the relationship in item 3. The percentage shown in item 2 (c) represents invoice markon, the relationship of the difference between delivered cost and retail to the retail of purchases to date in the current period.

The cumulative markon percentage, item 3, includes beginning inventory and all additions in the computation of the

	Cost	Retail	Markon	Markon Percentage
1. Opening inventory	$12,000	$20,000	$ 8,000	40.0%
2. Additions:				
(a) Purchases, less returns to vendors	58,000	99,000	41,000	
(b) Freight, express and cartage, inward ...	2,000		−2,000	
(c) Total purchases and invoice markon ...	60,000	99,000	39,000	39.4%
(d) Markups, less markup cancellations		1,000	1,000	
(e) Total additions	60,000	100,000	40,000	
3. Total inventory plus additions and cumulative markon	72,000	120,000	48,000	40.0%
4. Markdowns, less markdown cancellations ...		−6,000	−6,000	
5. Maintained markon performance	72,000	114,000	42,000	36.8%

Figure 31. Maintained Markon.

relationship. The process is carried a step farther by including the reduction of retail caused by markdowns, and we have, in item 5, the maintained markon.

Note that the maintained markon percentage of 36.8% is significantly lower than either the invoice markon of 39.4% or the cumulative markon of 40.0%.

The percentage of markon in all cases is computed *on the selling price.* This base is used because most relationships in retail accounting which are computed for comparative analysis, expenses, profits, etc., are expressed in terms of *percentage of sales.*

Calculating Markon Percentage. To calculate the markon percentage on an individual invoice, divide the amount of the markon in dollars by the total retail of the merchandise. For example, 10 dresses are invoiced at $6.75 and retailed at $10.50

each. Transportation costs on the shipment are $2. To calcu-
late the markon percentage on the invoice:

Total retail (10 × $10.50)	$105.00
Less delivered cost (10 × $6.75, plus a $2 transportation charge)	69.50
Markon	$ 35.50

$$\frac{\text{Markon}}{\text{Retail}} = \frac{\$35.50}{105.00} = .338, \text{ or } 33.8\%$$

To calculate the markon percentage on merchandise bought
throughout a given period, the accumulated amount of markon (the difference between the total accumulated cost and retail figures) is divided by the total of the inventory at the beginning of the period at retail, plus the purchases at retail during the period. For example:

	Cost	Retail
Stock on hand, February 1	$20,000	$30,000
Purchases, month of February	4,000	6,000
Purchases, month of March	3,000	5,000
Purchases, month of April	5,000	9,000
Total stock handled	$32,000	$50,000

To find the markon percentage at the close of the period,
first subtract the total cost, $32,000, from the total retail,
$50,000. The difference, $18,000, is the amount of markon.
Divided by $50,000 (the accumulated retail figure), it equals
.36, or 36% markon.

Merchandise Gross Profit, Gross Margin, Net Profit. *Merchandise gross profit* is the difference between net sales and the
cost of merchandise sold. Cost of sales includes the invoice cost
of merchandise sold before deducting cash discounts, incoming
transportation costs, alteration and workroom costs, and the
cost value of markdowns taken during the period. The calculation of merchandise gross profit is made on a season-to-date
basis, and the current month's cost of sales obtained by subtracting previous to-date costs.

Gross margin is merchandise gross profit plus cash discounts earned during the period.

Net operating profit is gross margin less operating expenses.

The entire computation is illustrated as follows:

	Cost	Retail	
1. Inventory—beginning of period ...	$ 85,900	$143,600	
2. Additions:			
a. Purchases season to date	101,600	165,900	
b. Markups season to date		1,500	
3. Total merchandise handled season to date	187,500	311,000	
4. Cumulative markon percent			39.71%
5. Removals from stock:			
a. Net sales season to date		174,000	
b. Markdowns season to date		12,800	
c. Total removals		186,800	
6. Remaining inventory at retail		124,200	
7. Remaining inventory reduced to cost (Cost percentage 100.00% minus 39.71%)	74,880		60.29%
8. Cost of stock removed season to date	112,620		
9. Cost of stock removed previous period to date	71,600		
10. Cost of stock removed in the current month	41,020		
11. Other merchandise costs in the current month:			
a. Workroom costs	200		
b. Other Cost of Sales	150		
c. Inventory shrinkage provision..	330		
12. Total cost of sales for the month...	41,700		
13. Sales for the month	61,770		
14. Merchandise gross profit and percentage to sales	20,070		32.49%
15. Cash discount on purchases	1,400		
16. Gross margin and percentage to sales	21,470		34.76%
17. Operating expenses	18,500		
18. Net operating profit and percentage to sales	2,970		4.81%

Item 1 is the closing inventory for the preceding period.

Item 2a represents the amount of gross purchases, less returns to vendors and allowances made, and includes inward freight, express and cartage charges.

Item 15, cash discounts earned, includes interest for anticipation in the payment of invoices, but does not include those discounts (trade discounts) which are a reduction in the cost of purchases.

Item 11a is the net cost of alterations or workroom operation, after giving consideration to income and credits for work performed.

Item 17 is the total of all operating expenses, such as salaries and wages, advertising, rentals, taxes, interest, delivery, traveling, communication, insurance, repairs, depreciation, professional services such as legal and accounting, and miscellaneous items.

Gross Margin, Net Profit Percentages. The gross margin percentage is calculated on the basis of net sales by dividing the amount of gross margin by the net sales. In the example just given, the gross margin percentage is $21,470 divided by $61,770 (sales), or 34.76%.

The net operating profit percentage is calculated in the same way, on the basis of net sales: $2,970 divided by $61,770 or 4.81%.

Markups. It sometimes happens that upward revisions are made in the original retail price. A change of this kind is called a *markup* and is added to the initial markon. If subsequently some of the merchandise is repriced at a lower level, the downward revision in price is recorded as a *markup cancellation*. If the reduction is greater than the entire amount of the markup, the excess amount is taken as an ordinary markdown.

Markdowns. When the marked price of an article is reduced from the price at which it was expected to sell, the change is known as a *markdown*. The amount of markdowns for the period, when expressed as a percentage of sales for the period, is the markdown percentage.

Whenever a retail price is raised after merchandise has been marked down, it is considered a cancellation of markdown, and is known *as a markdown cancellation.*

For example: If 10 jackets with a retail price of $18 each are reduced to $12, the markdown is $6 ($18 minus $12) on each, or a total of $60 on the 10. Suppose the price had been reduced for a special sale. When the sale is over, the buyer marks the five remaining coats to retail at $16. The cancellation of markdown will amount to $20 on the five ($16 minus $12, or $4 per coat).

To calculate the net markdowns for a period, the markdown cancellations are deducted from the gross markdown amount. To illustrate:

Markdown (original, 10 coats, $6 each)	$60.00
Markdown cancellation (5 coats, $4 each)	20.00
Net markdown	$40.00

Planned Markon. The following problem illustrates how to find the planned markon on purchases, at retail, when the planned operations are:

Expenses	29% of sales
Markdowns	8 " "
Stock shortages	2 " "
Alteration charges	2 " "
Profit desired	5 " "
Cash discounts (credit)	4 " "
Planned net sales	$1,000

To bring about the planned net sales on which these percentages are based, the purchases made, at retail, must include the markdowns (8%) and stock shortages (2%). That is, the retail value of the purchases must equal 110% of the planned sales.

The markon must cover expenses (29%), markdowns (8%), shortages (2%), alteration charges (2%), and the desired profit (5%), less the cash discount (4%)—or a total of 42% of sales. Dividing 42 percent by the retail value of the purchases (110%), the required initial markon percentage is found to be 38.2%.

Or, stated in dollars, it is necessary to provide:

$290 for expenses
  80 " markdowns
  20 " stock shortages
  20 " alteration charges
  50 " net operating profit
$460
Less 40 for discounts earned
$420

Since the planned markdowns and inventory shortages are $100, the initial retail amount must be $1,100. Dividing $420 by $1,100, the result is a required initial markon of 38.2%.

Calculating the Retail Price. To find the retail price of an article that will produce a 35% markon, all computations will be made on the retail basis, with the retail price represented by 100%. Therefore, if we know the markon percentage, its complement is the percentage of retail represented by the cost, in this case 65%. We find the retail by dividing the cost in dollars by the 65%.

For example, the cost price is $130, and the desired markon is 35%. Cost percentage is 100 minus 35, or 65%. Divide $130 by .65, and the result is $200, the retail price.

Terms and Discounts. The terms of an invoice define the concession in price, known as the cash discount, that is made by the vendor as an inducement to prompt payment. Terms are stated as the percentage of such discount and the length of time during which this concession will be available. Concessions that are based on quantity purchased, *and not upon the manner of payment,* are known as quantity discounts.

Trade Discount. A trade discount is usually given as a certain percentage off the list price without regard to the time in which the purchase is paid. In practice, it is usually recorded and deducted at the foot of the invoice rather than under the caption of "terms." It may be given as one figure or as a chain of successive discounts. If a chain of successive discounts is given, each discount is calculated on the net price remaining after deducting the preceding discount.

Cash Discount. A cash discount is a percentage off billed price granted as a concession for paying bills within a stipulated time. A cash discount of 2/10 means, for example, that 2% may be deducted from the bill if it is paid within 10 days of its date.

E.O.M. (End of Month) Terms. E.O.M. terms mean that the days for allowing discount are counted *from the end of the month in which the shipment is made* and not from the date of the invoice.

As a general rule, merchandise shipped on E.O.M. terms on or after the twenty-fifth of one month is considered as if it had been shipped on the first of the following month. If the terms are 3/10 E.O.M. on an invoice dated May 27, the three per-cent discount is deductible if the invoice is paid by July 10.

R.O.G. (Receipt of Goods) Terms. Some stores located at a distance from the source of purchase get R.O.G. terms, which means that the period for discounting does not start *until the goods are received.* The purpose of this arrangement is to permit the stores to check their merchandise before payment falls due for discount.

Anticipation. With the vendor's consent, a store sometimes pays a bill before it falls due and deducts anticipation at the rate of 6% a year. This is taken because the vendor has the use of the store's money ahead of time and the store, therefore, charges him interest for it. Anticipation is taken in addition to whatever other discounts may apply.

Turnover. *Turnover* expresses the relationship of stock to sales during a given period, usually a year. It is stated in terms of the number of times a stock is turned into sales. In this respect it is an index of merchandising efficiency.

In computing the rate of stock turn, average stock at retail is divided into net sales at retail for the period. Average stock is the sum of the retail inventories at the beginning of each year, season, month or week, added to the ending inventory and divided by the number of inventories used.

This example illustrates the computation of turnover:

Inventory, February 1	$12,000 retail
Inventory, March 1	14,000 "
Inventory, April 1	16,000 "
Inventory, April 30	18,000 "
Sales, February-April	27,000 "

To find the rate of turnover for the three-month period, first obtain the average stock. We divided by four because we are averaging four figures, even though the figures represent three months' stock, inasmuch as we are considering both *beginning inventory* for the first month and *ending inventory* of the last month.

$$\frac{12,000 + 14,000 + 16,000 + 18,000}{4} = \$15,000$$

Then divide the sales by the average stock for the three months to obtain the stock turnover rate for the period:

$$\$27,000 \div \$15,000 = 1.8 \text{ turns}$$

Inasmuch as three months represents one-fourth of the year, the number of stock turns a year at this rate would be four times 1.8, or 7.2 turns.

Stock-Sales Ratio. *The stock-sales ratio,* while also expressing a relationship between sales and stock, differs from turnover in that the stock is divided by sales, rather than sales by the stock. The ratio is generally for one month, and is secured by dividing the inventory at the beginning of a month by the net sales of that month. It shows the number of months that would be required to dispose of the first-of-the-month inventory at the rate of sales for the current month. It is used in planning the amount of stock required at the beginning of a month to produce the sales planned for that month.

For example, if the stock on June 1 is $18,000 at retail, and sales for the month of June are $6,000, the stock-sales ratio is:

$$\$18,000 \div \$6,000 = 3$$

If the planned sales for another department for the month of July are $20,000, and the planned stock-sales ratio is 3.5, multiply these two figures to estimate the stock that is needed on July 1:

$$\$20,000 \times 3.5 = \$70,000 \text{ stock}$$

Capital Turnover. The *capital turnover* figure is a means of comparing the money invested in stock with the sales for the period. Thus, to find the capital turnover, divide net sales by stock *at cost*. If the average sales for the period at retail are $12,500, and the average stock at cost is $10,000, the capital turnover would be:

$$\$12,500 \div \$10,000 = 1.25 \text{ turns}$$

Open-to-Buy. *Open-to-buy* is the term used to denote the amount of money available for merchandise purchases, stated in terms of retail dollars. At the beginning of a period, usually a month, it would be the amount of planned purchases for that period.

Since it is very important for the buyer to know at frequent intervals the balance of his open-to-buy for the remainder of the period, interim open-to-buy is calculated by deducting from the planned purchases for the period the amount of merchandise already received and in transit, and the retail amount of orders placed for delivery within the month.

This may be illustrated by the following example. All figures are at retail.

Planned purchases for May	$10,000
Unfilled orders—May 15	1,000
Merchandise in transit on May 15	600
Merchandise received, May 1-15	6,500

OPEN-TO-BUY REPORT MAY 15

Merchandise received	$ 6,500
Merchandise in transit	600
Unfilled orders for May delivery	1,000
Total commitments	8,100
Planned purchases for May	10,000
Open-to-buy balance, May 15	$ 1,900

Planned figures being but expectations, actual results will vary from what was planned, necessitating either plus or minus adjustments in planned purchases at frequent intervals, usually at the end of each week. This means that the original planned purchases figure is revised to compensate for variations in sales or stocks from the plan. An increase in sales over the plan acts to increase the planned purchases. However, if sales are under the plan or if purchases for the previous period have exceeded the plan, the planned amount of purchases for this period is reduced.

To illustrate, suppose the following data represents the condition of a department on May 15 (all amounts at retail):

Initial markon percentage	40%
Planned purchases for May	$7,000
Planned stock, May 1	9,000
Planned sales, May	8,000
Actual stock, May 15	10,500
Actual sales, May 1-15	4,500
Merchandise in transit at cost	1,100
Unfilled orders for May delivery	2,000

Note that the sales are $500 ahead of planned figures, as $4,500 has been sold during the first half of the month, while the plan was for only $8,000 for the entire month. This means that the purchase allotment may be increased $500 at retail. Also note that the actual stock is $1,500, at retail, above the planned amount ($10,500 minus $9,000) and the purchase allotment must be decreased by this amount.

The calculation at retail of the open-to-buy adjustment is:

Planned purchases for May		$7,000
Add variation of sales from plan		500
		7,500
Deduct variation of stock from plan		1,500
Adjusted planned purchases		6,000
Less: Merchandise in transit	1,100	
Unfilled orders	2,000	3,100
Open-to-buy, May 15		$2,900

CHAPTER 43

YOU'RE THE NEW BUYER—NOW WHAT?

BY

THOMAS W. JOHNSTON

Stepping into one's first job as a full-fledged buyer has points of resemblance to driving a car or flying a plane solo for the first time. You have had plenty of training and advice, and people who should know have confidence in your ability to perform. But now you are on your own, eager to do the right thing, yet with no one at your shoulder to supervise, to guide, to correct you, to anticipate your problems, to lead you to the right decisions. Your future is in your hands to make.

In the way a new buyer takes over his first department he can make things easier or more difficult for himself—succeed or perhaps fail. This chapter is concerned with what to do when the great day comes. It is designed to help the new buyer be a credit to himself, to the people who prepared him for the job, and to the store whose management now reposes sufficient confidence in him to entrust capital and its good name to his management.

Approach the Job with Humility. Nothing quite matches actual experience as a teacher. Experience is the one thing that you as a brand new buyer lack—and it is the one advantage your predecessor had over you, if he had nothing else at all. Therefore, approach the job prepared to learn from the previous buyer's work. The trail he has left behind him may be studded with strokes of genius or cluttered with mistakes. Or both! Whatever the situation, there is much to be learned by studying what he has done.

As a first step, discuss the department's present condition with your own merchandise manager. He can point out to you where your predecessor excelled and where he may have been weak. With that background, you are in a position to give priority to those phases of the job that most urgently need improvement.

If your predecessor is available, listen to what he has to say. There was undoubtedly a reason for everything he did or did not do in the department. Ask for the thinking behind his decisions, so that you will know why things are as you find them. You may find, for example, that the stock arrangement you inherit was the fruit of much trial and error experimentation. If you know about each of the various earlier plans and why it was discarded, you will avoid going back unknowingly over ground that has already been covered.

Throughout your first year, if your predecessor remains available, as he will be if he has another assignment in the same store, continue to check with him, particularly as you approach each new season. In that way, you take advantage of what has been learned before you entered the picture, and, with that background, you can develop your own variations as you gather experience and confidence.

Know Your Objectives. Your management has certain objectives for your department and certain ideas about how it wants that department to develop. Make sure you understand these thoroughly, so that you will operate within the framework of the goals and policies your management has established for the entire store. Yours is one department among many; it obviously can't go off on a tangent of its own; it must keep in step with all the others in its merchandising, promotion, and general atmosphere.

Background and history are important in understanding the present situation and future possibilities. Your first source for this background, of course, is your merchandise manager. You will find yourself turning to him repeatedly for information and guidance during your first year. Such requests for facts and advice will not be interpreted as indicating any lack of initiative on your part; on the contrary, they will be expected, and you will probably find your merchandise manager prepared to invest a good deal of his time in orienting you into your new job. Once you are firmly on your feet, you will need less briefing.

If you have the opportunity, or can make one, for talks with your store's controller, merchandise control supervisor, personnel director, and operations director, by all means take it. These are people who can fill you in on the history and development of the store and on the facilities that are available to you in the management of your department. The more you know about the organization in which you serve, the more effectively can you function.

One Step at a Time. No one can be expected to learn everything at once. This may be your first buying job, but the chances are that you are not the first new buyer with whom the people around you have worked. They will quite understand if you need time to master each situation or operation as it comes to your attention. Take the time! It is wiser to proceed slowly, if you must, than to rush ahead unprepared.

A good first step in the learning process is to make sure that you put it in several hours a day on the selling floor. Only in that way can you get a first-hand knowledge of your customers and their needs. Make sure, however, that your time on the floor is used for study and observation. Serve some customers yourself, if possible, so that you get to know what they like. But even when you are on the floor for purposes other than waiting upon customers, let your eyes and ears work for you constantly. You need a clear picture of your customer in order to buy for her.

Your customer's preferences are reflected, of course, in unit control records, in want slips, in remarks by salespeople, in the questions salespeople put to you. Nothing, however, quite takes the place of actual contact and observation. Don't short-change yourself on this score.

"New Buyer" Markdowns. A serious error made by many buyers is to look through the stock in a department at the time they take over and to mark down much of it—partly because it has been bought by someone else, and partly to release funds immediately for new purchases.

The error is particularly serious when a brand new buyer commits it, because he does not yet have the buying skills his predecessor probably had. The previous buyer, after all, had worked both at buying and at operating this particular department. The chances are, therefore, that if stock dollars are released by unloading some of the goods on hand, the new buyer, in his very newness, will invest them less skillfully, and thus risk greater markdowns in order to move what he has bought.

A wiser approach, when you take over your first department, is to accept the stock that you find, exactly as if you had bought it yourself. After you have studied its rate of sale, decided how many weeks' supply you should have on hand, and have planned accordingly, you may even decide that the merchandise you found is pretty nearly what you yourself would have put there if you had done the buying. If, however, you find that in some areas it is not what you think it should be, then marshall your figures and your reasons, talk things over with your merchandise manager, and take steps to unload.

Learn About Resources. Learn from your merchandise manager, and from your predecessor, if he is available, about your department's resources. How dependable are they? How much follow-up do they need? What helps will they give you without being asked and what helps must you ask for or even insist upon? The more know about the characteristics and service of your principal resources, the more efficiently can you operate.

Ask your merchandise manager to review with you the regular resources of your department, and draw up a list of them. Then draw up, with his help, a secondary list of other resources with which your department may not now deal, but that you should visit when you are in the market. In this way, you will use the past experience of your store and your department to make sure that your market time, even on your first few trips, is invested where it is likely to do your department the most good.

Advice from Vendors. A department's key vendors usually make themselves familiar with its operation. They compare its performance with that of other accounts and are often in a position to point out missed opportunities, to give valuable advice on timing and trends, or in other ways to put practical suggestions before the buyer. The new buyer, however, cannot expect to know how sound this advice is until he has developed a background of his own on both the department and its resources.

Sensible procedure is to listen to all, but to defer action until you have weighed their advice carefully. Some manufacturers really understand retailing and study each individual account's operation. Others may be superficial or may have hobbies of their own that they ride whenever they get an interested audience. It takes time to know one from another, and to know which of the sound suggestions offered are in fact applicable to the buyer's own department.

It is wise to discuss decisions on resource suggestions with your merchandise manager. With his deeper knowledge of the store and his wider experience, he is in an excellent position to decide which advice is right and worth acting upon.

Shopping the Competition. Every new buyer, as well as every experienced one, has a school in which he can learn practical lessons any day of the week—his department's competition. It is sound practice to shop the competition conscientiously, studying their assortments, watching shopper reaction to their offerings, seeing what ideas they have that can be adapted to one's own department, and seeing what errors they make that should be guarded against.

A certain amount of information about the competition may come to you through other sources in the store—reports on what they are promoting, checks on their assortments and prices, etc. This is good and useful information to have, but it does not quite take the place of a personal visit, in the course of which you can train your eye to spot strong and weak points. If these visits do nothing more for you than sharpen your awareness of the strengths and weaknesses of your own operation, each such visit is accomplishing a great deal for you.

Analyze Your Operating Figures. As a buyer, you are responsible not merely for the sales of your department, but for making its operation profitable. Study the operating figures for previous years, if they are available to you, and see if any of the elements that you can control are significantly out of line. Your merchandise manager will probably show you where your department has been doing better or more poorly than others in the store, or than comparable departments elsewhere.

A study of this kind will help you locate the spots that most urgently need corrective work. For example, customer returns may be unduly high. To correct this drain on your department's profits, you will look into the causes of returns. Perhaps poor selling prevails; perhaps workmanship in the merchandise has been poor; perhaps values have been poor. Whatever the causes, you will give top priority to finding ways to counteract them before you get down to the minor flaws in operation.

Analyze Past Advertising. In your merchandise manager's office, or in the office you took over from the outgoing buyer, or in the advertising department, you will probably find a file of past advertising done by your department, with notations of the results achieved. Study those for your department—the failures as well as the successes—in order to gain insight into what merchandise and what appeals bring the best response from your department's customers.

The value of the past advertising record is to know what you'll be up against and what successful promotions to repeat or replace.

If there is a similar file available on the promotions of your principal competitors (if there isn't, begin one immediately), by all means include that in your course of study. The value of this record is to know what your competitor has done and may repeat, so that you may meet or anticipate him.

Reports will probably reach you, too, from your store's buying offices, and through trade publications, of promotions run by stores in other cities. They are all grist for your mill—all textbooks for your course in what sort of promotions ring the bell for departments like your own.

Make sure to consult your advertising manager for what help he can give you. His advice may help avoid mistakes.

Analyze Your Classifications. The more information you have on sales and stocks for each individual classification within your department, the better. You may get such data through your store's merchandise controls, or you may have to develop it yourself, but you should have it to guide your planning.

Measure each classification's importance to the department in terms of what percentage of your total sales it represents. Compare this figure with similar figures from other stores, if such figures are available to you. Compare the figures for your own department from year to year. See which classifications appear to be doing well, and which ones seem to be lagging.

In some classifications, you may already be in the lead, so far as local competition is concerned; in others, the competition may have outdistanced your department. Consider competitive position as well as past history and future possibilities, and then decide which classifications most need, or will best repay, your most strenuous efforts to build them up. It may be that your best bet is to "play from strength" and to continue building an already strong classification. Or it may be that you should concentrate your attention on correcting the weaker areas.

When you have gathered all the facts, considered them, mapped out a tentative plan of campaign, talk it over with your merchandise manager.

Write Out Your Plan. Your store undoubtedly has a written statement of policy for the guidance of all its executives. You need a written statement of departmental policy *for yourself.* You have studied your department, its background, and management's aims for it. You have seen where things have been going well and where correction is needed. The written plan becomes your blueprint. List on it the things you mean to do first, those which can wait a bit, and those which can be left to go along on their own momentum for the time being.

You'll change your plan as you go along, undoubtedly. But form the habit of planning on paper. It's a very good way to come down out of the clouds and to transform hopes and wishes into procedures and priority lists of things to do.

Prepare for Market Trip. Preparation for any market trip is serious business, as other chapters of this book have explained. But for one's first market trip the preparation must be thorough indeed. Long before you are ready to look at any line, you should:

a. Conduct merchandise reviews of each classification and sub-classification to be purchased. This includes deciding how broad an assortment you want to have in each price line that is to be carried, and how much you plan to purchase in each price. This is in terms of *units.*

b. Next, develop your *dollar classification* open-to-buy.

c. Add up the dollar outlay you plan, to get the total amount you expect to spend on the trip.

d. Make up a selling plan by week and by month in advance of your trip. The purpose behind this is to make sure that you arrange for deliveries to support your sales plan.

e. Submit these plans to your merchandise manager. If he agrees to your selling plan, perhaps with revisions, he will arrange to support your plan with appropriate sales promotion.

Now you have the basic minimum of facts to guide your market work: what you need, when you need it, and how you plan to promote it. You may also have a great deal more detail, of course, to remind you about colors, or sizes, or resources that warrant special attention. It is better to prepare more facts than you need, even if some of them never come out of your briefcase, than to plunge into your first market tour without adequate data. For that matter, your watchword on any market trip should be: "Be prepared!"

Aim High. A final bit of advice: Don't be afraid to make decisions. Everyone makes some wrong decisions, and you will make some, too. But if you use all the help available to you, you won't make quite so many as you would otherwise.

Some mistakes are due to carelessness or unwillingness to listen. For these, there is little excuse. Other mistakes are the result of aiming high, and are the natural price one pays for experience. Let yours, if you are to make any, be of this latter variety, a part of the learning process. Aim high!

Good luck!

INDEX

INDEX